AF371921

Studio of the South
(L'Atelier du sud)

Arles

ndiana Sadie Laska Eric Palgon Alicia Vaïsse Adee Roberson Clément Rodzielski Alake Shilling Mona Varichon Jacob Eisenmann Andy Robert Alexander Zevin Blake Rayne Candida Alvarez Nova Bryan

aura Owens Julie Beaufils Miriam Laura Leonardi Gabriele Garavaglia Charlotte Houette François Lancien-Guilberteau Parker Ito Julien Ceccaldi Alvaro Barrington Naoki Sutter-Shudo Asha Sche

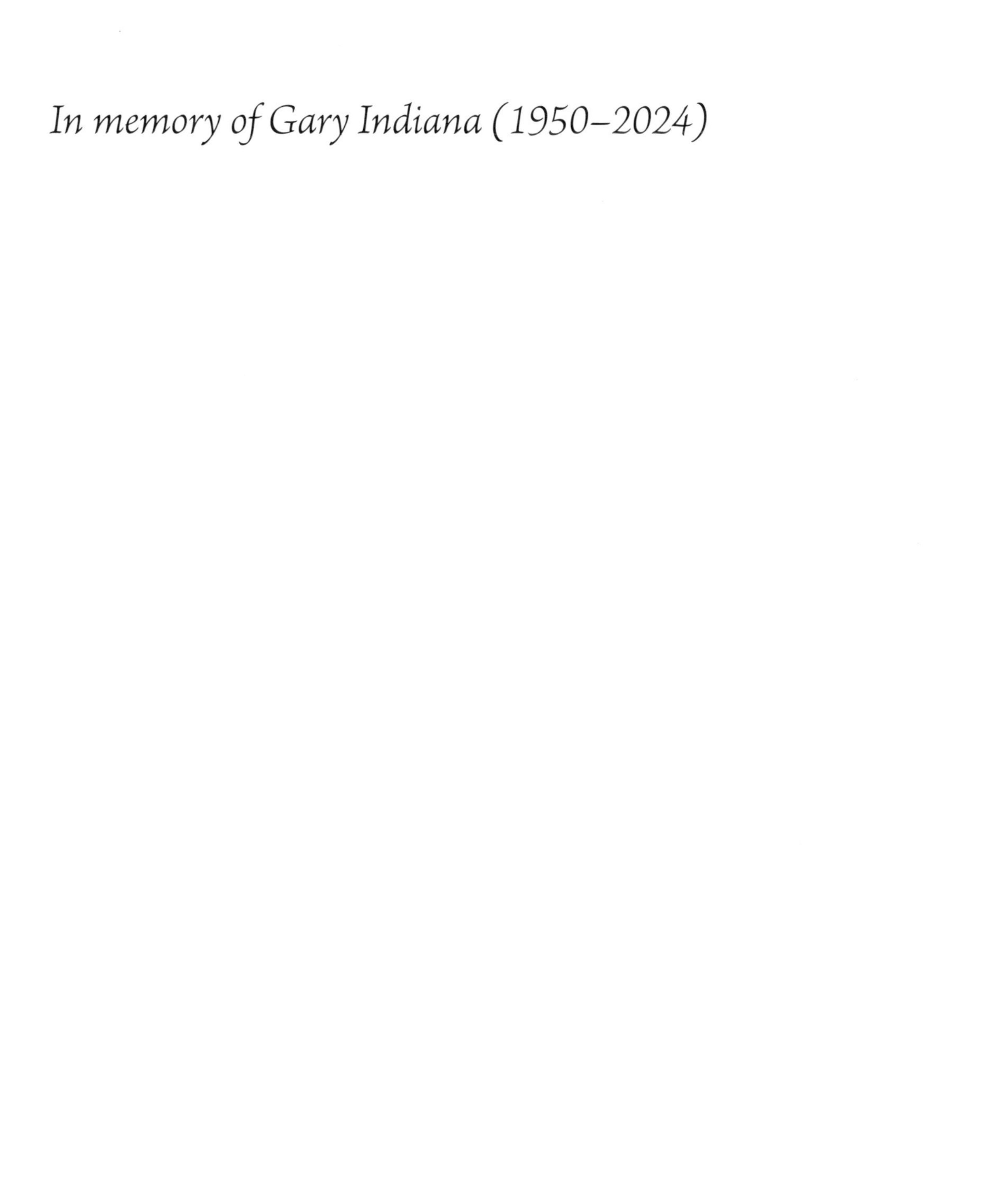

In memory of Gary Indiana (1950–2024)

LUMA   jrp|editions

...aura Owens Julie Beaufils Miriam Laura Leonardi Gabriele Garavaglia Charlotte Houette François Lancien-Guilberteau Parker Ito Julien Ceccaldi Alvaro Barrington Naoki Sutter-Shudo Asha Sche...

FOREWORD
Maja Hoffmann

The Studio of the South residency program in Arles, initiated by the artist Laura Owens and realized by LUMA, was a continuation of the immensely successful exhibition of Laura Owens's work at the Fondation Vincent van Gogh Arles in 2021. The residency initiative represents a remarkable convergence of place, history, and contemporary creative dialogue. Taking its name from Vincent van Gogh's idealistic vision for a collaborative artists' atelier in the South of France, the residency invokes a legacy of artistic community while reimagining its relevance in the twenty-first century. Laura managed to create a unique space—equal parts studio, salon, and incubator—which unfolded within the landscape of Arles, a city synonymous with artistic fervor and aesthetic transformation. It is here that Laura and LUMA, together with the Fondation Vincent van Gogh Arles, built a dynamic platform where emerging and established artists and thinkers could work, converse, and imagine freely within a space shaped by mutual curiosity and collective engagement.

More than offering simply a geographical relocation or a change of scenery, the Studio of the South residency invited a recontextualization of artistic process. It asked what it means to share space as artists in a world increasingly shaped by fragmentation, digitization, and solitude. In response, the residency brought together a vivid and varied group of practitioners whose work spans new and traditional media and conceptual frameworks. Each artist was chosen not only for the strength of their individual voice but for the possibility of resonance—with Vincent van Gogh, with Laura Owens, with Arles, and with each other.

Among the artists who contributed to this unique moment in time were Julie Beaufils, who drew inspiration from the lunar and solar cycles, allowing their rhythms to guide her paintings; and Miriam Laura Leonardi, whose painterly investigations navigated the intersections of language, media, and identity. Together with Gabriele Garavaglia, Miriam also created during her residency an experimental fantasy film set in Arles. Following them in the residency, Charlotte Houette brought her vital explorations of abstraction and color that distort visibility and pattern. Charlotte and François Lancien-Guilberteau together hosted film screenings in the space, under the title of *Ciné-club Totale Dérive*. Parker Ito added his distinct sense of humor to the residence, employing a range of techniques to explore the effects of the internet in the aesthetics of authorship. Julien Ceccaldi blended manga aesthetics with themes of desire, exploring the lines between cuteness and morbidity. Alvaro Barrington mixed together personal history and cultural memory, drawing from his Caribbean heritage and Brooklyn upbringing. Naoki Sutter-Shudo fused meticulous craftmanship with irrationality to create enigmatic compositions, while Asha Schechter explored the life cycle of images within our networked culture, challenging traditional perceptions of photographic representation.

The late Gary Indiana was also part of the Studio of the South. He will always be remembered as a most charismatic, multifaceted artist, writer, and cultural critic, whose work incisively dissected the undercurrents of American society and contemporary realities. His presence in Arles was pivotal and very important for the program.

Furthermore, Sadie Laska contributed to the residency with her vibrant, collage-driven practice, while Eric Palgon brought poetry and art together with materials from nature. Alicia Vaïsse expanded on relationships between human and animal worlds during her residency, and Adee Roberson contributed a multicolored mural painting in the residence's main bedroom. Clément Rodzielski offered his distinct way of questioning the circulation of images, using printed material to comment on the nature of production and reproduction. Alake Shilling brought playful fantasy and boundless imagination, while Mona Varichon introduced personal narratives alongside the chronicling of contemporary life from marginalized perspectives. At the same time, Jacob Eisenmann did a number of wall murals, including a portrait of Laura Owens. Andy Robert worked on his painterly practice and explored the poetic side of his work during his residency, while economist Alexander Zevin added a layer of critical thinking, examining the evolution of political systems. Blake Rayne mysteriously inserted two coins into the structure of the building in a witty gesture toward institutional critique, while Candida Alvarez experimented with materials, colors, and Pop influences to create multilayered works that fuse stylistic influences. Last but not least, Nova Bryan contributed witty and inventive paintings on parts of the staircase walls of the Studio of the South.

Together, these artists helped to realize Owens's vision of an evolving atelier—a Studio of the South that is not fixed in time but responsive, open, and experimental. This publication serves as both documentation and extension of that experiment. It captures moments of making and dialogue, solitude and exchange, and ultimately testifies to the enduring power of shared creative inquiry. In the spirit of Van Gogh, but on terms entirely their own, these artists have helped to shape a new kind of collaborative future, rooted in history and alive to the now.

VINCENT & THE VAN À GOGO CLUB
Bice Curiger

Don't feel uncomfortable about hanging them in a corridor, in the kitchen, on the stairs. My painting is made to be seen above all against a simple background. I try to paint in such a way that it looks good in a kitchen, then sometimes I notice that it looks well in a drawing room too, but I never bother myself about that. Here in the south we have bare walls, white or yellow, or decorated with wallpaper with big coloured flowers. So it seems to me that it's a matter of proceeding by means of oppositions of bright colours. It's the same with the frames—the frames I use cost me 5 francs at the most, while the less solid gilded frames would cost 30 or more. And if the painting looks good in a simple frame, why put gilding around it?[1]

Arles: We have no idea why Vincent van Gogh got off the train here on his way from Paris to Marseille.[2] Was it because of Adolphe Monticelli's absence from Marseille? Van Gogh greatly admired Monticelli, who placed indistinct images of small people at sunrise or sunset in marvelously pastose layers of paint. The South held an irresistible pull on Van Gogh's imagination. And it was there that Monticelli could be seen moving about in his white suit and straw hat.[3]

Perhaps Van Gogh was put off by the idea of being in a big city again. Perhaps he was satiated by city life in London and Paris, satiated by the industrial revolution, by its gloomy and bleak consequences that collided with the otherwise shiny elegance and opulent extravagance of urban life. He wanted to be closer to nature, to the people who cultivated it, and, in a sense, to his vision of Japan.[4]

He seems to have made the right decision. Assuming that "right" adequately describes what he both praised and bemoaned during the fifteen months that he lived in Arles, which would prove to be the most important, most productive period of his creative life.

Touching and telling is not only his admiration of Monticelli and of Paul Gauguin but also his enthusiasm for what others were doing, as is recorded in his impassioned comments on what he was reading, indicative of his great modesty as an artist. Time and again, he told his brother Theo that he was not yet ready, not yet mature enough as an artist to show his work. But he did dream of being able to present his paintings in a café someday.

When reading Van Gogh's letters, there is no mistaking how discriminating and impassioned he was in his appreciation of the cultural achievements of others. He took nourishment from the work of his creative colleagues, from those practitioners who contributed to, corrected, and counteracted the movements of his time. This also shaped his own position within the collective, though without deliberate intent.

Is it this aspect that exerts such an enduring appeal among a younger generation of artists? We must not forget that Van Gogh had the idea of founding a collective studio in Arles. In 1888, he dreamed of sharing his house with locals and other artists from Paris, of turning it into a full-fledged, vibrant studio. The Yellow House on the place Lamartine—destroyed by bombs during World War II—had a guest room and was "decorated," a word that Van Gogh used in reference to mounting his paintings and Japanese prints on the whitewashed walls. He wanted to convert the house into a place for work and relaxation, a place that would foster an artistic community and define the future of art.

ura Owens Julie Beaufils Miriam Laura Leonardi Gabriele Garavaglia Charlotte Houette François Lancien-Guilberteau Parker Ito Julien Ceccaldi Alvaro Barrington Naoki Sutter-Shudo Asha Schec

The present publication introduces the building on rue du Cloître in Arles, which LUMA converted into temporary housing for an extremely attractive group of artists (from the United States, Great Britain, France, and Switzerland). They left traces of their stay in the form of creative interventions, such as wall paintings, hanging sculptures, cups, curtains, and cushions.

A visit to the building reveals Van Gogh's continuing relevance and impact on contemporary artists. It is living proof of what a familial atmosphere can bring about, of what can be created and "concocted in the kitchen" of art and society! This present-day Studio of the South demonstrates what can happen when a loosely formed "collective" takes action.

Equally relevant today is Van Gogh's boundless, undiminished popularity, fascinating for embodying the extremes of cliché and authenticity with respect to the role of the artist and the concept of art. The juxtaposition with creations by contemporary artists underscores how much the Van Gogh clichés have been propagated not just by mass culture but by art history itself, through fixation on the history of style, formal innovation, and the myth of the artist as heroic loner.

After World War II, a schism in art became increasingly polarized: art critic Clement Greenberg's belief in the absolute autonomy of art beyond any reference to external reality was diametrically opposed to the burgeoning movement of Pop Art with its emphasis on the everyday. In the title of a small collage made in London in 1956, Richard Hamilton asks, *Just what is it that makes today's homes so different, so appealing?* The work instantly became a Pop Art icon. It not only invited the daily reality of postwar life to take a seat—or rather a stand—in art; it also included the socially modernized private sphere, symbolized by the latest kitchen appliances, the refrigerator, and sexy bodies. The resulting whirlwind has not died down; it continues to whip up society and culture through the broad appeal of genres and disciplines that have effectively undone the distinction between high and low.

In 1956, the same year that Hamilton's title-cum-manifesto went "viral," Vincente Minnelli came out with his best-selling film *Lust for Life*, in which Kirk Douglas plays Van Gogh. The fact that high culture also took to examining the artist as a social role model is demonstrated by Antonin Artaud's polemical treatise of 1947, "Van Gogh: The Man Suicided by Society," which was held to exalt the moral purity of the artist.

It is this cultural territory that is staked out in the twenty-first century by the *VAN À GOGO CLUB*,[5] which awaits artists arriving in Arles today with all of its affirmative, familial artistic energy.

[1] Vincent van Gogh to his sister Wilhelmina, Arles, October 21, 1889, letter 812, https://vangoghletters.org/vg/letters/let812/letter.html.
[2] On February 21, 1888.
[3] Monticelli is mentioned in fifty of Van Gogh's letters.
[4] In a letter to his brother Theo, Vincent van Gogh describes the extremely rare snowfall, the colors of the cliffs, and the white-capped mountains, which make him think of a Japanese landscape. February 21, 1888, letter 577, https://vangoghletters.org/vg/letters/let577/letter.html.
[5] See Miriam Laura Leonardi's framing of the door in the stairwell of the rue du Cloître residence, p. 39 in this volume.

ndiana Sadie Laska Eric Palgon Alicia Vaïsse Adee Roberson Clément Rodzielski Alake Shilling Mona Varichon Jacob Eisenmann Andy Robert Alexander Zevin Blake Rayne Candida Alvarez Nova Brya

STUDIO OF THE SOUTH: EVERY DAY I WRITE A ROOM
Julie Boukobza

Some of our key words are Brunelleschi, burgundy, persimmon, dahlias, and tonka bean.[1]

A forty-five-year-old American woman writer, the narrator, hires an interior decorator called Claire. The decorator is the wife of Davey, the narrator's young, would-be lover. Claire's mission is to refurbish the narrator's motel room in the outskirts of Los Angeles, where the narrator has escaped from her family for a short, secret trip. This room, of course, does not belong to the narrator; she pays to stay there like any other customer, yet she insists on this twenty-thousand-dollar renovation. This shabby, all-American motel becomes the dreamy backdrop of an "elegant" midlife crisis, draped in silk, satin, velvet, and chintz. The color palette is powder pink, creamy nude, and flushed apricot. The scent of immortal roses mixed with unfinished business dominates.

This narrative comes from *All Fours*, the most recent novel by American writer and artist Miranda July. It might befit the definition of what an unconventional artists' residency program could or should be: it arrives at the perfect moment, when one finds the need to change the scenery of his or her life—minus the midlife crisis—in order to work, think, and inhabit life in new ways. Residencies are deeply emotional affairs, with the artist leaving their country, house, studio, and loved ones for the sake of reinventing their work. Or sometimes, they may not have all these other elements in their life, and the residency can become their home. For example, the solitary late writer Gary Indiana tells us in this book that his time in Arles was one of the happiest of his life. Sometimes you also bring your family along. Is a residency meant to mend hearts? Of course not. It does not have to be as emotionally draining as Rachel Cusk's novel *Second Place* (2021). It doesn't have to be about creating a total work of art, such as Jean Cocteau's fabled Santo Sospir villa (ca. 1950–1960) on the French Riviera. A residency does not have to be a political statement, like Judy Chicago's *Womanhouse* (1972) in Los Angeles. A residency is something as open-ended as a "blank canvas," as artist Miriam Laura Leonardi says. American painter Laura Owens did, in some ways, envision this residency program in Arles, called Studio of the South, as one of her own paintings—the final touches to which are known to nobody but Owens. At the beginning of the COVID-19 pandemic in 2020, in a three-story yellow house (aptly matching Van Gogh's) lent by LUMA founder Maja Hoffmann, Owens began inviting her friends, peers, and friends of friends to "restore, make art, write, or maybe learn about the region as I have."

As a strong first gesture, she laid the foundations of the residency by adorning both bathrooms of the house with colorful tiles, leftovers from her public commission at LaGuardia Airport Terminal B in 2020. She created a whimsical blue landscape that instantly set the tone for the project. It almost evokes the ancient mosaic traditions imbedded in the Roman past of Arles, and nods to the Mexican-style frenzy of tiles done by her peer and close friend, the artist Jorge Pardo, at l'Arlatan hotel, a few streets away, completed in 2018. Then, Owens discreetly hung two of her own paintings in the house. On a table in the living room, she placed a matching guest book, and created delicate, colorful silk curtains and embroidered cushions. She freely painted the kitchen backsplash, initiating an unspoken dialogue with the artists residing there. "There's a candle to light the stairs / Where my dreams await someone to share."[2]

The dream of an artists' community, reminiscent of Van Gogh's failed attempt at the same with Paul Gauguin in the fall of 1888, found success here, albeit in an unexpected and unconventional manner, more than a century later. The artists mostly moved in one after another, staying for two weeks to two months. Occasionally, due to long-standing friendships, their stays would overlap, but they rarely worked side by side. They primarily "decorated" the house on their own terms, or contributed independently to this "social sculpture," to quote Blake Rayne (another former resident). The house transformed into a more socially active space, like a nineteenth-century-style salon, through *Totale Dérive*, a ciné-club organized by Charlotte Houette and François Lancien-Guilberteau. This event took place every other week and featured films selected by various artists from the circle of residents, including Mélanie Matranga, Julie Beaufils, Gary Indiana, and Laura Owens herself, welcoming in the local Arles scene. The artists never treated the house like a museum; they moved works from previous residents around, covered them, or hid them under the bed. The painting above the bed in the main bedroom changed countless times. This could have been a source of tension, yet surprisingly, it never was—this was perhaps one of the tacit rules of this newly invented game. There was no precious care taken; the house became the artists' home, if only for a limited time. This is why Studio of the South became more than a beautiful house or a stunning exhibition. It was a trial by fire, an experiment. It was an unusual attempt to blur the boundaries between life and art, to expand the possibilities of what an institution can offer, and to deepen the relationships between artists and their peers, patrons, and audiences. Three years later, when the residency concluded, Laura Owens took over the house for a few weeks. She framed Alake Shilling's work by painting around it and added to (or "dressed") two characters from Parker Ito's ink drawings. With the help of her talented child, Nova Bryan, Owens expanded the murals on the staircases as if it were all part of her artistic vision. To quote Gaston Bachelard in *The Poetics of Space* (1958), "We write a room, read a room or read a house." If one could read this house a century from now—contemplating this total artwork made of 171 artifacts, admiring this constellation of bold and unassuming gestures that mixes completely different approaches to art and our times—what thoughts would emerge, and what remnants of its spirit would endure in Arles, in contemporary art history, and in our minds?

[1] Excerpt from Miranda July, *All Fours* (Riverhead Books, 2024).
[2] Lyrics from the song "It's My House," sung by Diana Ross, 1979.

FEBRUARY–SEPTEMBER 2020
Laura Owens

One of these days you'll see a painting of the little house itself, in full sunshine or else with the window lit and the starry sky.[1]

The first time I traveled alone, I took an overnight train to Arles. The pace and scale of this small town, with its agricultural fields just outside the perimeter, felt much more familiar than Paris. Growing up in rural Ohio, I had seen the French landscape in paintings like Vincent van Gogh's *Two Poplars in the Alpilles near Saint-Rémy* at the Cleveland Museum of Art, but now my real-life encounter revealed that the commonplace scenes had some similarities to my childhood home. I was living in France with friends, doing an internship in Paris as part of my undergraduate studies. Hoping to see the art and architecture of my art history classes, I was inspired to make this excursion to the South alone. I had to see the place where Van Gogh wanted to paint outside and gather a community of artists to share resources and discourse relevant to the new ideas in art at the time. Reading his letters, I imagined him arriving in Arles in 1888, thoroughly isolated in his interior world. This image intertwined with my depressed and lonesome twenty-one-year-old self. Staying in a hostel with my guidebook, I hoped to glimpse what he saw: "Nature here is extraordinarily beautiful. Everything and everywhere. The dome of the sky is a wonderful blue, the sun has a pale sulphur radiance."[2]

I walked through the Roman amphitheater with my sketchbook and found a payphone where I could call a friend. I took a bike ride to see the sunflowers. It was very quiet for summer. I did see some of the annual photography festival, the Rencontres d'Arles. This citywide, international photo exhibition was just as easily absorbed by Arles's citizens as the county fair would be in my hometown. This would never happen in the States, and this receptive audience expanded the contours of what I knew to be possible in a small town. There were not many international vacationers in Arles in 1991, and so my foreignness felt a bit hidden, disguised by all the French tourists who had traveled to look at new photography. Arles felt very sleepy, very windy, very hot, and very Roman.

Between this first encounter with Arles and my move to the city almost thirty years later—just weeks before the COVID-19 lockdown—I visited every few years. It was always a little changed, and every year there seemed to be more people. I felt familiar to this place; it had witnessed me in my embryonic state when I was first trying to call myself an artist. Like the previous foreign painter, I was a visitor; he had pointed out the sky, rolling hills, rivers, weather, graves, and people, turning sharply toward the smells, sounds, light, and color. I was magnetically drawn to this land of painting and continued to make return visits. A place tangled in the origin stories of painting itself: cave walls, Simone Martini, ex-votos, Paul Cézanne—all giving me some permission to keep moving forward when the rest of the world was so vehemently opposed to the idea that painting was still relevant. Back when I first visited Arles in the early 1990s, contemporary art in the United States was dominated by Relational Aesthetics. Many of my teachers, including Michael Asher, made painting and the history of painting out to be suspicious and anti-Marxist. But in France, I found the Supports/Surfaces movement, BMPT art group, and Van Gogh's own writing on proto-socialist ideas, which all led me to question the consensus view at school.

In 2014, I was invited by Bice Curiger—and encouraged by Maja Hoffmann—to create a show at the Fondation Vincent van Gogh Arles. Through a series of events that, in hindsight, seem just as cosmic as Arles's magnetic pull, my show continued to be postponed for one reason or another until the spring of 2020. Bice had invited Mark Godfrey to co-curate the show, so for many years, we would meet up to see Van Gogh paintings and ask museums to loan work. Our discussions centered on how to make an interesting Van Gogh show within a contemporary art context given his ubiquity. The conversation always returned to the problem of finding a way to see the paintings as free from their author's legacy. I was continually impressed by Van Gogh's every minor work, especially his still lifes, which ended up having a great impact on my developing relationship to his art.

It was a given that you couldn't hang Van Gogh on contemporary white gallery walls and that special low lighting would be necessary to meet the terms of strict loan agreements. Covering the walls with paintings to act like wallpaper and adding two anonymous artists' works alongside my own and Van Gogh's allowed for a layered context where identity shuffled around itself.

All of this helped us in our goal to create a context that would allow the exhibition audience to actually see Van Gogh's paintings again, simply as paintings, at least for a few minutes. Carefully dodging the narrative structure, the torrential myth, we hoped to avoid the drama that fuels this singular artist. When simultaneously representing the pinnacles of both tortured artist and market

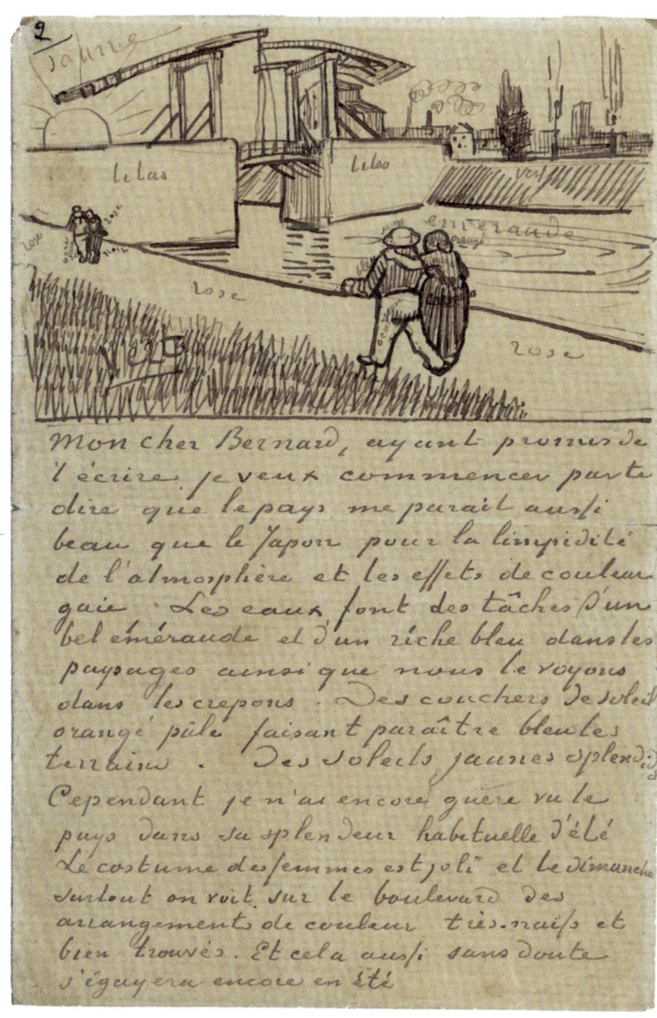

Mon cher Bernard, ayant promis de t'écrire, je veux commencer par te dire que le pays me paraît aussi beau que le Japon pour la limpidité de l'atmosphère et les effets de couleur gaie. Les eaux font des taches d'un bel émeraude et d'un riche bleu dans les paysages ainsi que nous le voyons dans les crepons. Des couchers de soleil orangé pâle faisant paraître bleu les terrains. Des soleils jaunes splendi[des]. Cependant je n'ai encore guère vu le pays dans sa splendeur habituelle d'été. Le costume des femmes est joli et le dimanche surtout on voit sur le boulevard des arrangements de couleur très-naïfs et bien trouvés. Et cela aussi sans doute s'égayera encore en été

A letter from Vincent van Gogh to Émile Bernard, March 18, 1888

value, Van Gogh's work often becomes just an image of itself—his name now exists simply as a stand-in for the ideal romantic artist. I told Mark and Bice I wanted to instead foreground his unfazed idealism and highlight the lesser-known narratives: he was an art dealer, a collector, and a great writer and reader. Most of all, I wanted to continue with his aborted plans for a Studio of the South.

After moving to Arles, Van Gogh's idealism around the South and the landscape grew, much like my own. Our shared objective was to establish an artists' community in Arles; after moving to the small town in 1888, Van Gogh invited fellow artists, including Paul Gauguin and others, to join him. We could revive the project in the present day and fulfill some of the utopianism of his original intention for artists to work together. Knowing that "we surely have the right to wish for a state of affairs in which money wouldn't be needed in order to live. However, since everything's done with money now, we must think hard about making some while we spend it,"[3] he opted at first "quite simply to take a mat and a mattress and make a bed in the studio on the floor,"[4] with the intention of promoting ideas of communal property, shared resources, and resilience in numbers. He said, "In principle, in theory, I'm for an association of artists protecting their livelihood and their work."[5] He was reading about Edmond de Goncourt's "Maison d'un artiste" and there was palpable enthusiasm in anticipation of "living in a studio of our own with Gauguin.…I'd like to do a decoration for the studio. *Nothing but large Sunflowers*."[6] Later he wrote, "It's not the least little bit urgent, but I have my idea. I really want to make of it—an artist's house but not precious, on the contrary, *nothing precious*, but everything from the chair to the painting having character."[7]

Our current ideas of Van Gogh's biography reinforce mythologies of survival through pain and poverty in order to valorize the value form. Vindicating his dreams for the Studio of the South was an important part of exhibiting his art once more and recuperating his legacy; I wanted to foreground these aspects of Van Gogh that are often completely ignored and yet worth remembering.

In January 2019, Laura Lord and I traveled to Arles in order to find a house or apartment to host this residency that would ultimately grow into an exhibition. Maja was enthusiastic about the project, and LUMA's invitation followed. The generous offer to host the Studio of the South provided resources—as Theo van Gogh had to Vincent—and on-the-ground support needed to fulfill the vision of working with many artists over a long period of time in Arles. Questioning the idea of the vernissage by transforming a domestic space into an exhibition space over months or years was something I had wanted to do in my own work since my early attempts in 2001. From 2013 to 2018, I had worked with dozens of artists, collaborating and curating with Wendy Yao of Ooga Booga at 356 Mission, a large exhibition and events space in Los Angeles, where I first showed my own work. I used the space as a studio for a year and then opened the studio to the public, removing my tools and paint materials and inviting Ooga Booga's bookstore to use part of the space and Asha Schechter's project the Vanity to use an unassuming closet as a gallery within the exhibition. We hosted events and had an apartment to house artists that came to make shows. After this experience of making work in situ, where studio visits were synonymous with exhibition viewing, I became aware that a show can begin before you even realize it is happening. The unfinished and finished oscillate. A domestic space—where kitchens, toilets, and bedrooms can all be part of an exhibition terrain—offered more opportunity to blur exhibition, studio, life, and functionality. A residency where artists lived in the exhibition space and added to the exhibition during their stay was a continuation of this line of questioning.

aura Owens Julie Beaufils Miriam Laura Leonardi Gabriele Garavaglia Charlotte Houette François Lancien-Guilberteau Parker Ito Julien Ceccaldi Alvaro Barrington Naoki Sutter-Shudo Asha Sch

Van Gogh wrote to Theo about this shared studio: "My idea would be that in the end we'd have set up and would leave to posterity a studio in which a successor could live. I don't know if I'm expressing myself clearly enough, but in other words: we're working at an art, at matters that won't be of our times only but which may also be continued by others after us."[8]

My then twelve-year-old child Nova and I arrived in Arles in February 2020, where my show at the Fondation Vincent van Gogh was scheduled to open in the spring. We settled into a rented house, and Nova enrolled in a local school while I continued the work for the show. Within weeks, France entered lockdown and we decided to remain; a decision that would forever change my life. Mona Varichon and Jacob Eisenmann had come to join us in Arles to help with the show, but we only saw them a few times before we were suddenly instructed to remain indoors. A physical paper *attestation de déplacement dérogatoire* was required in order to leave the house, so we Zoomed from two blocks away from each other and tried to figure out these fast-changing rules. Somehow we had bikes, and once the initial April lockdown ended, we took rides around the countryside, just as I had done when I had visited in the 1990s, looking at sunflowers and the Langlois Bridge made famous by Van Gogh's painting. I had rented a house in Mouriès from Alicia Vaïsse for my family in preparation for the Fondation exhibition opening scheduled for May, but now that wasn't going to happen. As soon as we felt there was little risk in sharing a space, we moved there to live as a group.

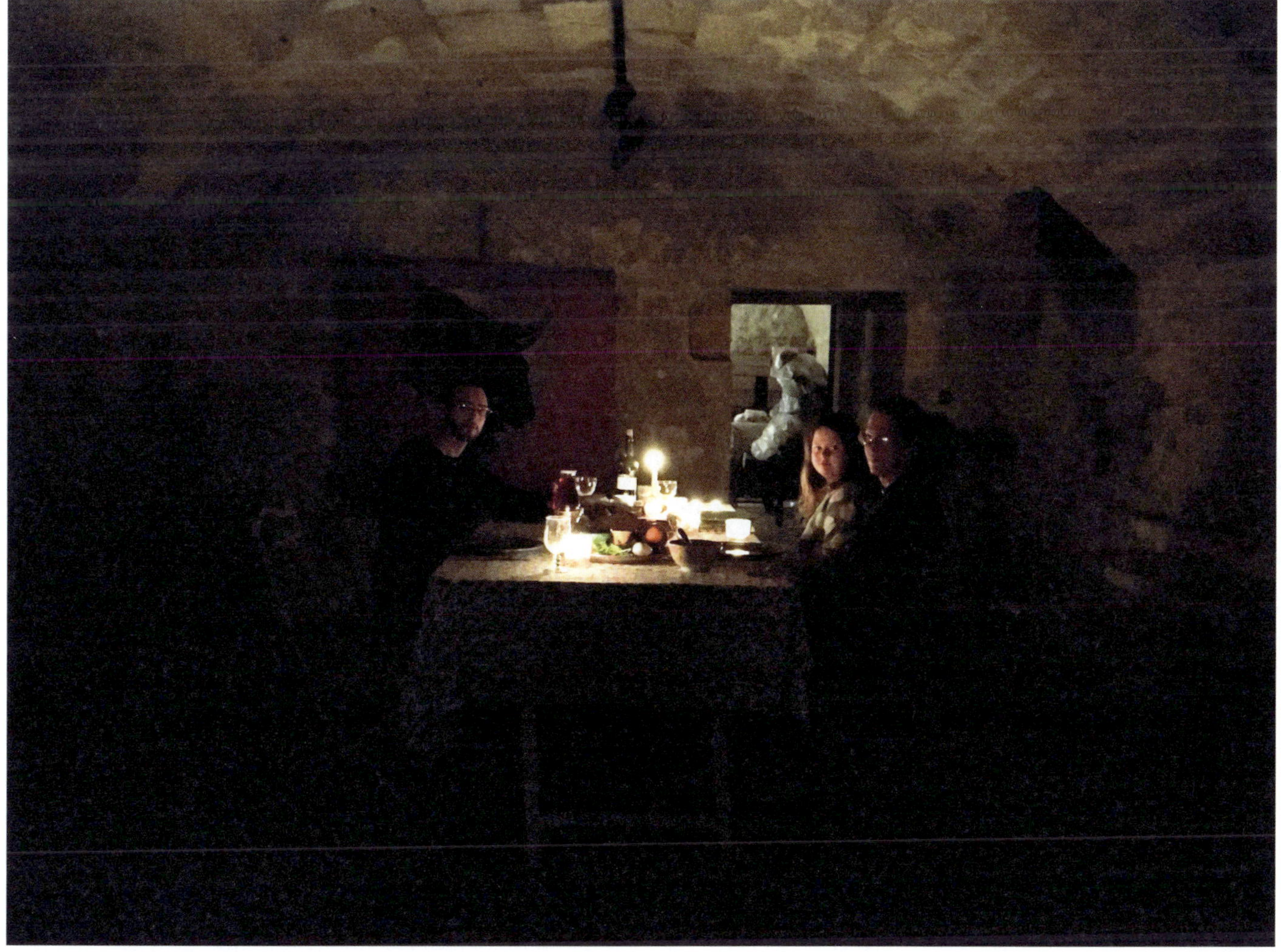

Jacob Eisenmann, Nova Bryan, and Laura Owens at their Passover Seder in Arles

My favorite memory before we left Arles for Mouriès is of the four of us breaking the rules and holding a Passover Seder in the cave-like cellar of our rented house in the center of Arles. We worried we would be caught by the police as the basement window grates were open to the street, and we thought they could hear us reciting the Haggadah that Jake had written especially for the occasion. Looking back, this night was the true beginning of the Studio of the South—when we joined together after our long isolation, pooled resources from our diminishing pantries, shared a meaningful dinner, and connected through friendship, gratitude, and grief.

Mona and Jake continued to make art throughout the lockdown. For Jake's birthday, together we made him handcrafted games: a deck of cards, backgammon, Scrabble, and a chess set. Nova opened a coffee shop in the kitchen. Jake and Nova collaborated on songs to be released on forthcoming albums. Plein air painting happened by the canal de Craponne across the road from our house, and we felt even more connected to Van Gogh and his time in the Alpilles. Once COVID-19 subsided, we continued having outdoor painting sessions in Mouriès with other artists. And on a visit to Domaine du Possible, where Nova was attending school, Jake and I led a workshop in plein air painting for a group of art students.

When my show finally opened at the Fondation the following year, my investment in Arles was greater than I could have ever imagined. My year in Arles expanded; time slowed down. I went to the Médiathèque to research the history of Van Gogh, the past plagues, and Voltaire's musings

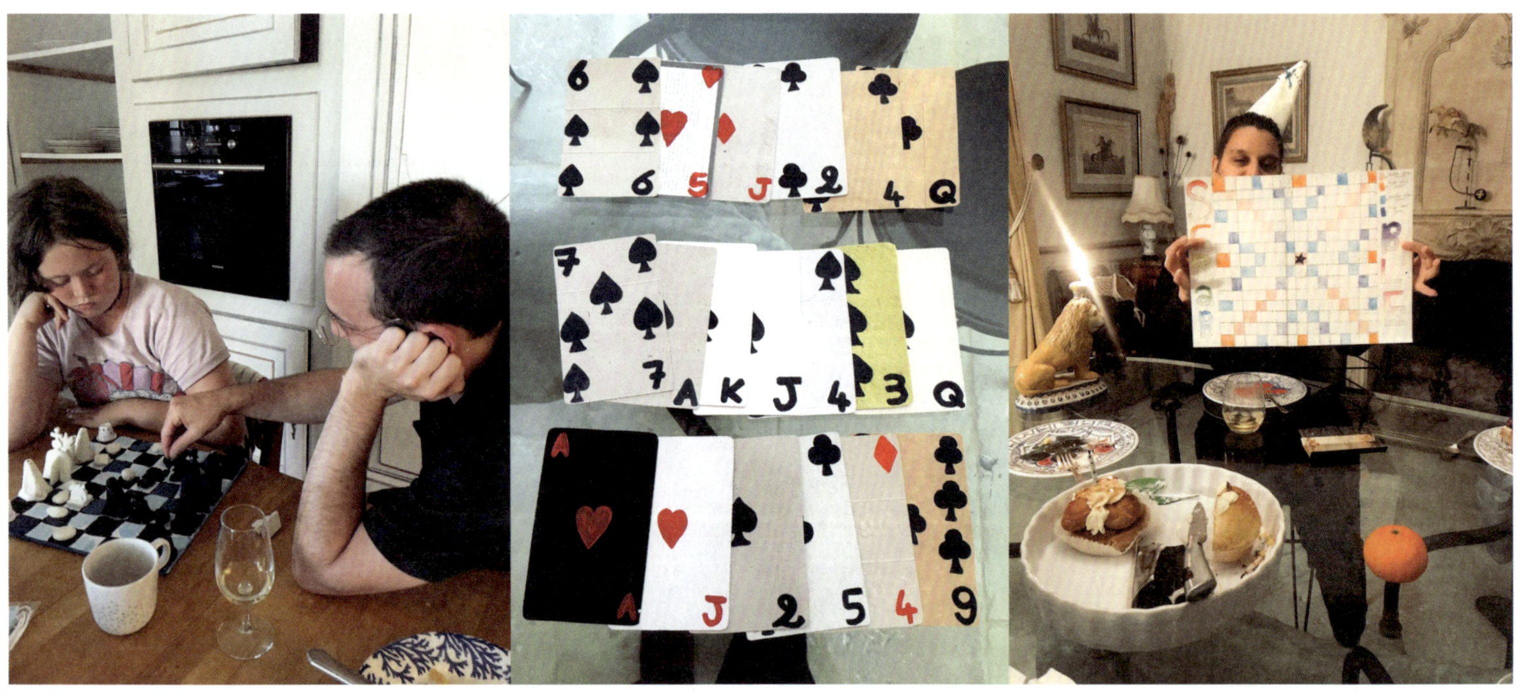

Nova and Jacob playing chess on a homemade board; homemade cards; Mona Varichon with homemade Scrabble

Laura Owens Julie Beaufils Miriam Laura Leonardi Gabriele Garavaglia Charlotte Houette François Lancien-Guilberteau Parker Ito Julien Ceccaldi Alvaro Barrington Naoki Sutter-Shudo Asha Sche

on Mauraco, a horse legendarily burned at the stake in Arles around 1606. I fondly remember scrolling through microfiche with Julia Marchand. Later, when I realized the street upon which the Fondation Vincent van Gogh is located was named after Dr. Fanton, a heroic doctor who died while treating his patients during the cholera outbreak of 1884, the historical past and the present appeared to have no distance from one another. Apogee Graphics (Asha and I) made a poster in Dr. Fanton's honor to celebrate the show.

Similar to the Fondation's floor-to-ceiling installation that referenced domestic spaces and avoided white walls, I imagined that Studio of the South resident artists would live within and add to the "exhibition in situ" of the house, eventually covering the walls, furniture, and floors of the building. Their experiences could accumulate and the art would sit alongside their clothes, the assembled ephemera of their time living in the house, and abandoned objects. I hoped that, over time, one artist might respond to another or inspire them to make work, paint, move, or make furniture; and by the end, a twenty- or thirty-person exhibition would emerge that had not been curated (was this an anti-curatorial impulse?) but instead *accumulated*. The palimpsest would be the sight line.

The dilapidated office building that Laura and I had first seen had been transformed into an intimidatingly blank, extremely vertical domestic space. Mona's practical "let's get it done" attitude motivated Jake, Nova, and me to christen the walls of this very white, empty house, starting at

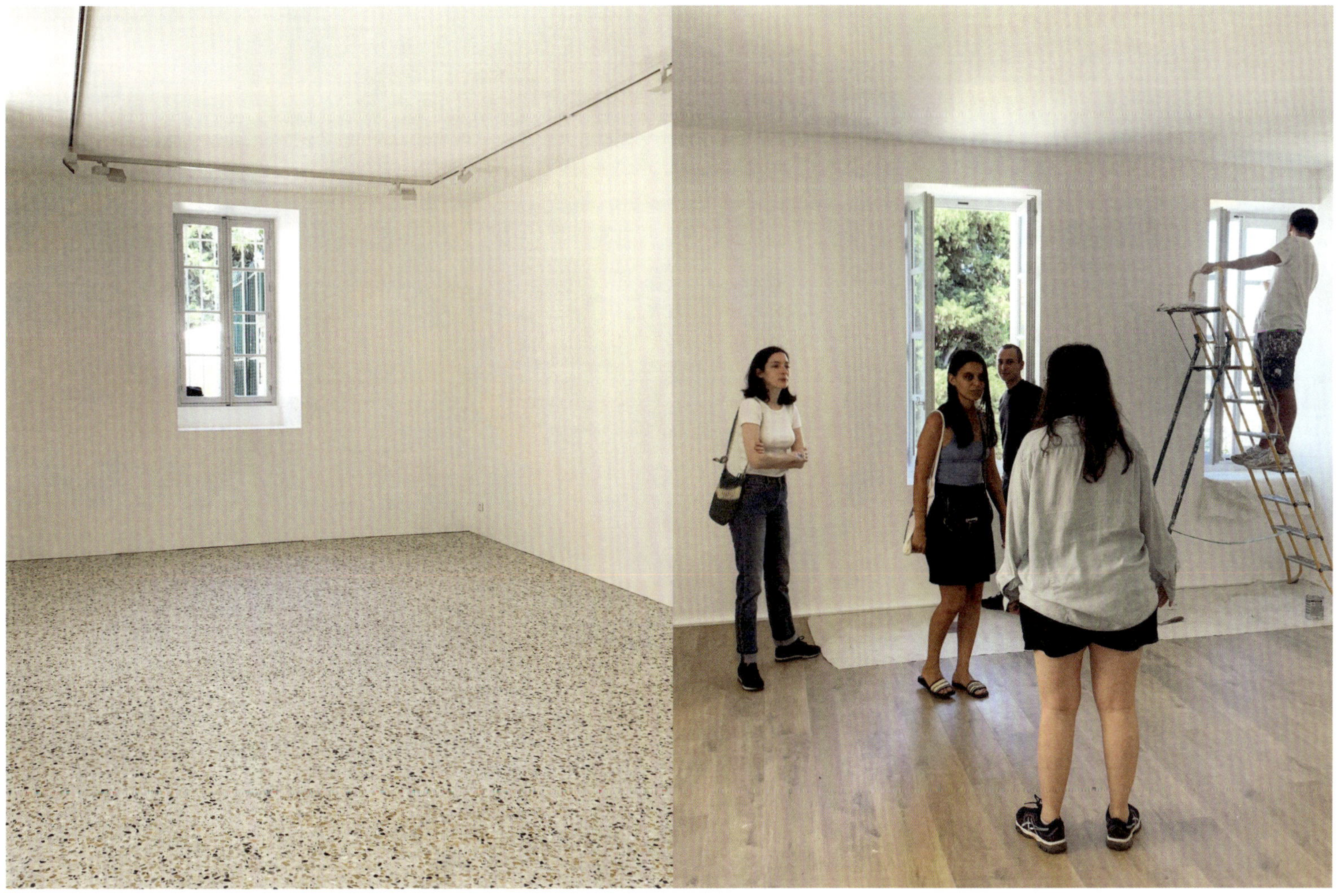

Julie Beaufils, Mona, Jacob, and Laura visiting the residence

first in an unplanned fashion by painting the hallway at the top of the stairs, all of us squeezing into the stairwell clutching little jars of Flashe paint. I painted a four-inch yellow border around the edges of all the walls while Nova and Jake painted portraits and vignettes. I used remaining tiles from the large mural I had just completed in New York and ordered a few more tiles to reference images from Van Gogh's work as well as my own. Elliot Kaufman arrived in June 2021 to install the tile mosaics in the bathrooms with Fabrice Auffret. Back in the studio in Los Angeles, we researched how to print fabric dyes and resists on silk to create CMYK imagery that could be seen from both sides when printed on sheer curtains, reusing imagery from the wall paintings of the Fondation show. Similar motifs appeared on several hand-dyed linen pillows with crewel embroidery, hand-stitched with flowers, seashells, and stickers, thereby linking the two exhibitions.

Malak El Zanaty Varichon, Mona's mother, visited us from Paris the first summer. Malak was also an artist with a long-standing connection to Van Gogh. Mona found a local ceramicist named Tina Tourneur, and together with Nova and Jake, we made dinner plates, bowls, and decorative dishes for the kitchen.

It was important to me to make a private blog only for the residents. In some ways a total failure, I hoped it would be a catalogue of stays and a place to leave notes and tips for other resident artists. To initiate the blog, we fabricated posts penned by Van Gogh and Gauguin. There was an openness and unspoken ambiguity to any rules around how to navigate painting on top of

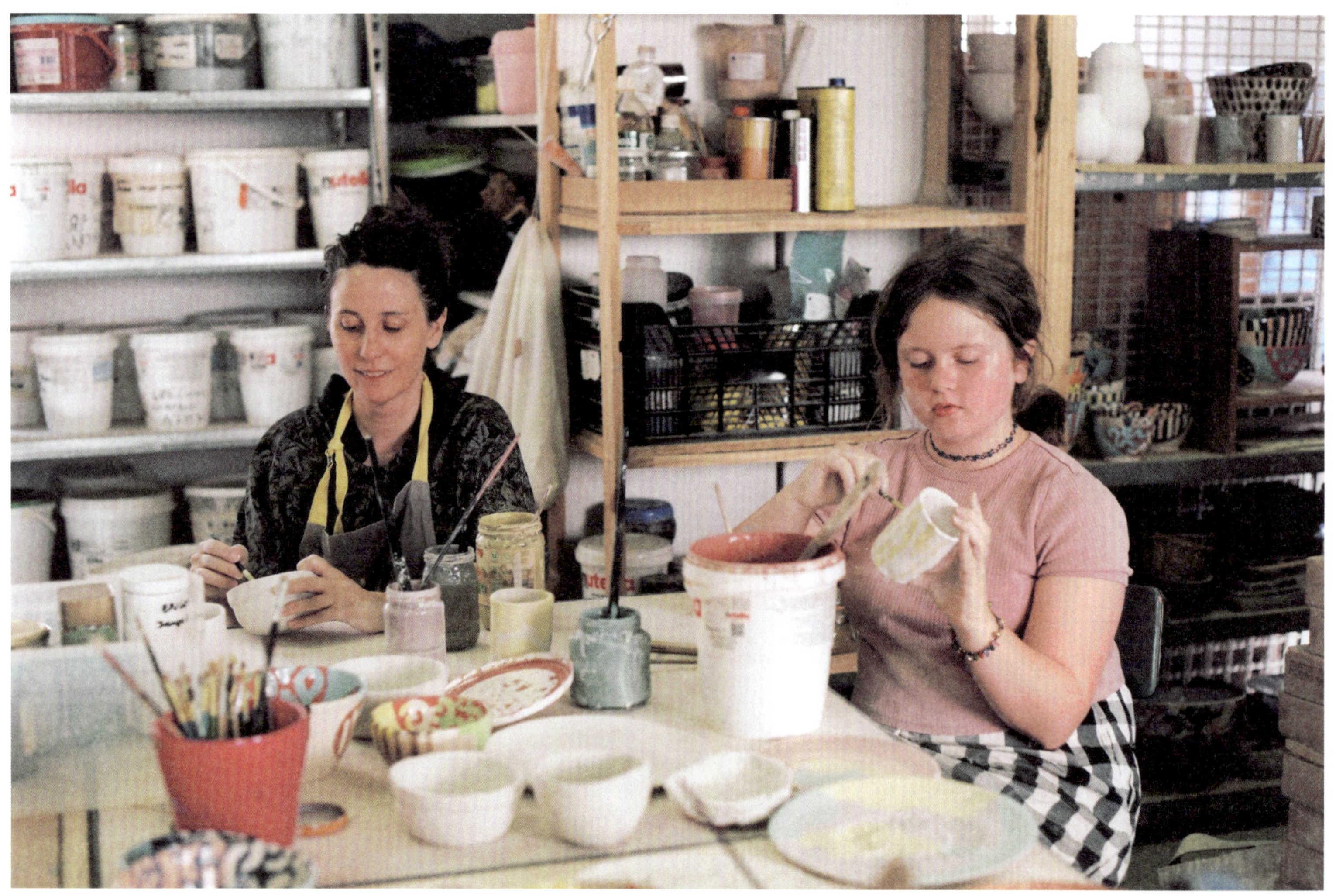

Laura and Nova making ceramics

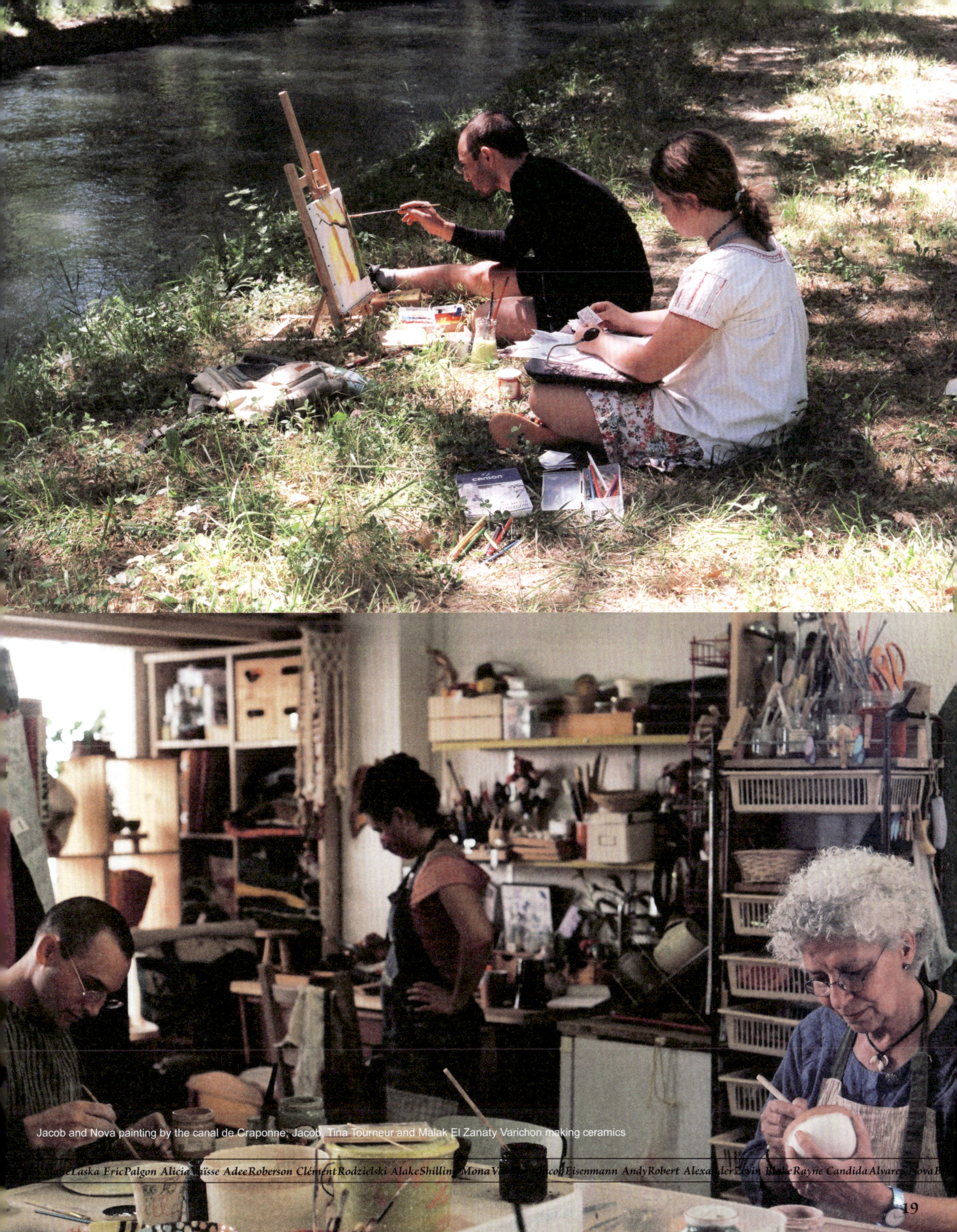

Jacob and Nova painting by the canal de Craponne; Jacob, Tina Tourneur and Malak El Zanaty Varichon making ceramics

each other's work, moving each other's work, and the essential questions of "where" and "when" is the art. Was this art? Or material, or ephemera? I hoped an answer would evolve through the process and emerge out of consensus; at the time, I didn't have one.

I had wanted to invite a wide variety of artists from around the world, both those I knew and some I had never met. But the pandemic, with its never-ending rule changes and travel restrictions, upended that idea. To avoid the project languishing indefinitely, I had to invite only French or European artists who were flexible with their time. Mona recommended a list of artists and writers, many of whom eventually came to the Studio of the South. I had been a fan of Miriam Laura Leonardi's since I saw her work at Bel Ami in Los Angeles, and I also thought of Naoki Sutter-Shudo, who I suspected might have a French passport. By painting the windowsills and using an IKEA chair as a canvas, Julie Beaufils, significantly the first official resident, made an important impact and path for the artists who were to follow.

Miriam's *Concerto Improvviso* was the first performance event, subversively charming and unassuming. I remember feeling we were finally coming together indoors after an epidemic nightmare.

I met Alicia in 2019 through Julia. We spent many long days and late evenings over the three years painting the hallways of the residency side by side and struggling to find a ladder that could get us up ever higher on the stairs. I saw Alicia the most, and we discussed what more should happen; she lived in nearby Mouriès, and we would meet up routinely when I was back in town.

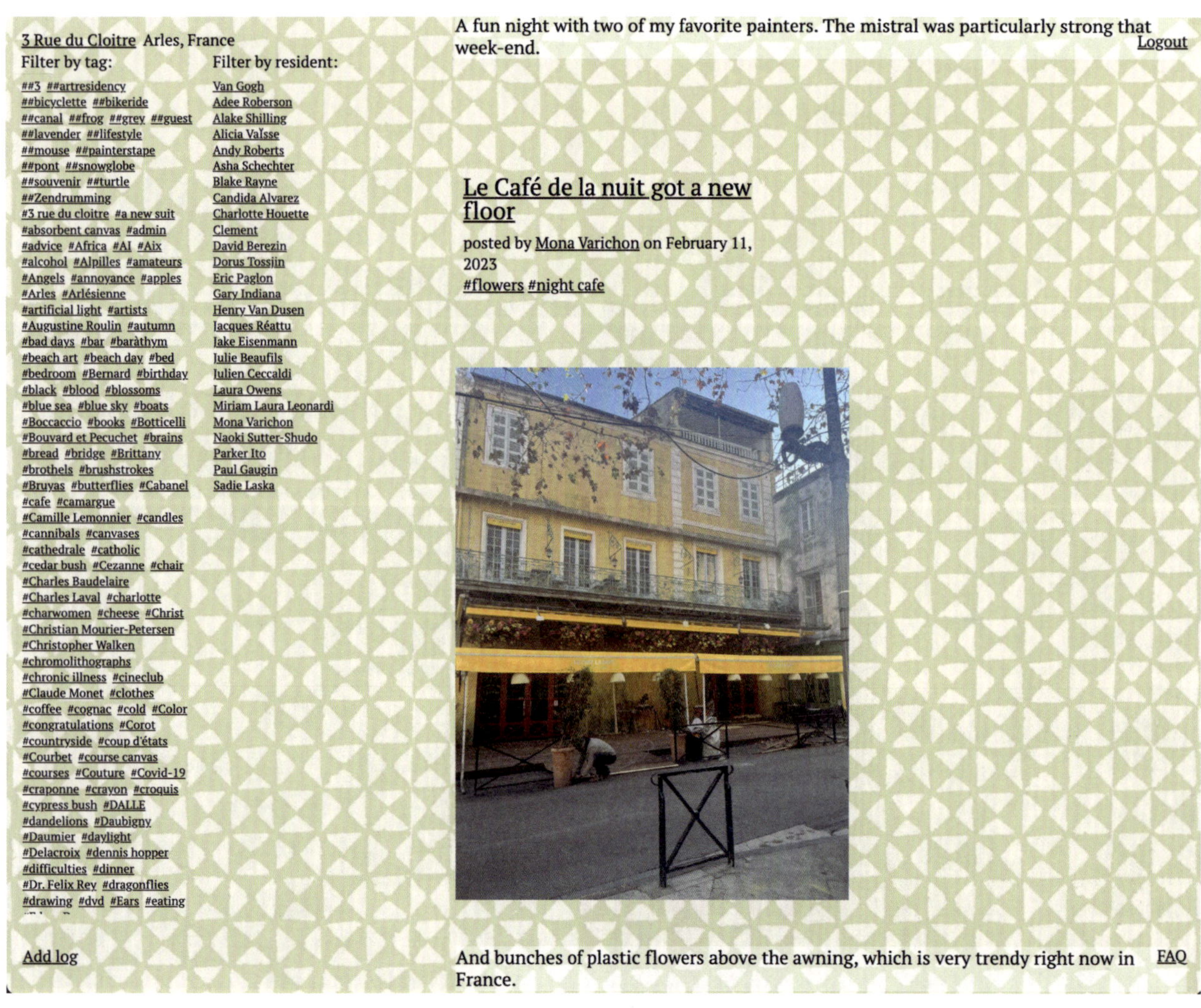

The residents' blog

After my show at the Fondation Vincent van Gogh closed in 2021, and with my kids back in high school, I had to spend significant time in Los Angeles. I texted with Andy Robert a lot when he was in Arles, and got cryptic pictures of delicious-looking food. I felt some anxiety about inviting people and wondered whether or not they were having a good time, so it was always a relief to hear that they had made it and were with friends or enjoying themselves. There was no expectation to make any work. I was hoping they would all just get something out of it and perhaps meet each other and local artists. I saw Candida Alvarez for dinner one night at the place Voltaire. She encouraged me to let go of some work obligations—permission I needed. I was so exhausted, trying to parent two teenagers and make large-scale exhibitions. Van Gogh's enthusiasm for making art grew when Gauguin confirmed he was coming to Arles; similarly, the residency supported me and gave me energy I needed. For their ciné-club, Charlotte Houette and François Lancien-Guilberteau transformed the studio into a makeshift living room open to the public, creating a residency within the residency through which they invited more artists to present films and invited more Arlésien•nes to join our miniature scene.

Although the house could be viewed as an exhibition throughout the duration of the residency whenever a new artist arrived or invited guests over, the Studio of the South officially opened to the public at-large in November 2023, when a concurrent group show of the resident artists' work was staged at the Fondation Vincent van Gogh. This real-world deadline of "the opening" produced a flurry of activity.

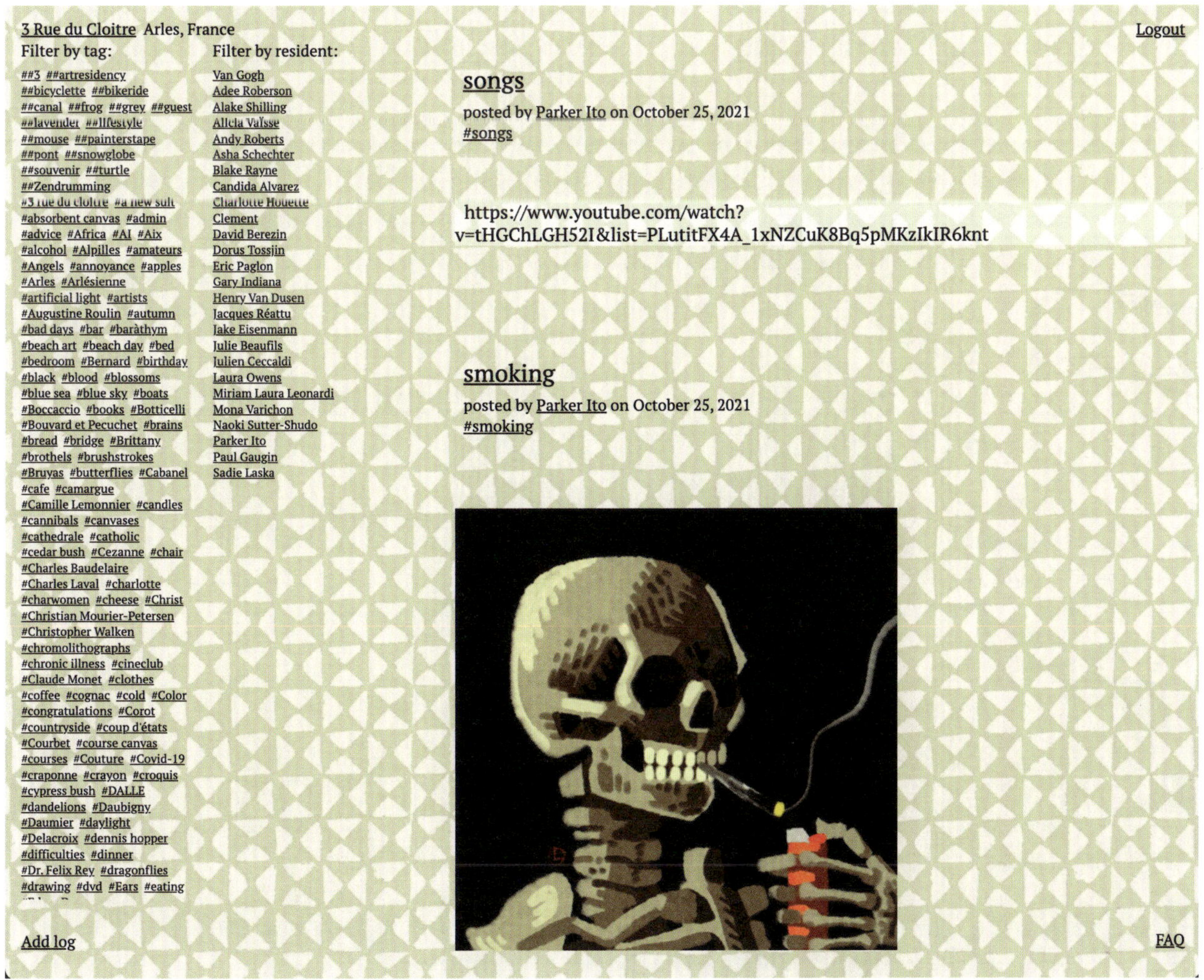

Luckily, Blake Rayne had curated a wall of paintings and drawings, a mix of art and non-art hung in a grid that pulled many works together, salon-style. I started pinning up random drawings, ephemera, and collages in the bathrooms and odd corners—all that I found left in the house, not knowing what it was or who had left it. And Alicia and I kept painting more walls with Nova, sometimes with new baby Lou nearby.

Nova declared either they or Parker Ito must have contributed the most work to the house; this was a funny competition for Nova and, naturally, it provoked one or two more wall paintings from them. Parker's enthusiasm was unmatched and paved the road for more responses than any other artist. I placed a paper doll's dress over the anime figure that Parker had painted in the kids' bedroom. Naoki responded to Parker's CAPTCHA painting, and in the kitchen, Elliot decided to paint the *Les Misérables* head on Parker's *Some Days Things Don't Go Your Way!* and changed the words to "moi non plus." I think these call-and-response collaborations were some of the better moments in the house.

The opening of the Studio of the South in November 2023 culminated with many of the artists who had returned to Arles gathering for dinner at the house. It was incredible to see and hear everyone together, and rewarding to have many of their very best pieces and new installations included in the exhibition at the Fondation.

Still, when the house opened to the public, I felt like more could have accumulated in the space. Good things tend to feel cut short; they just end. About a year later, Gary Indiana died. I miss

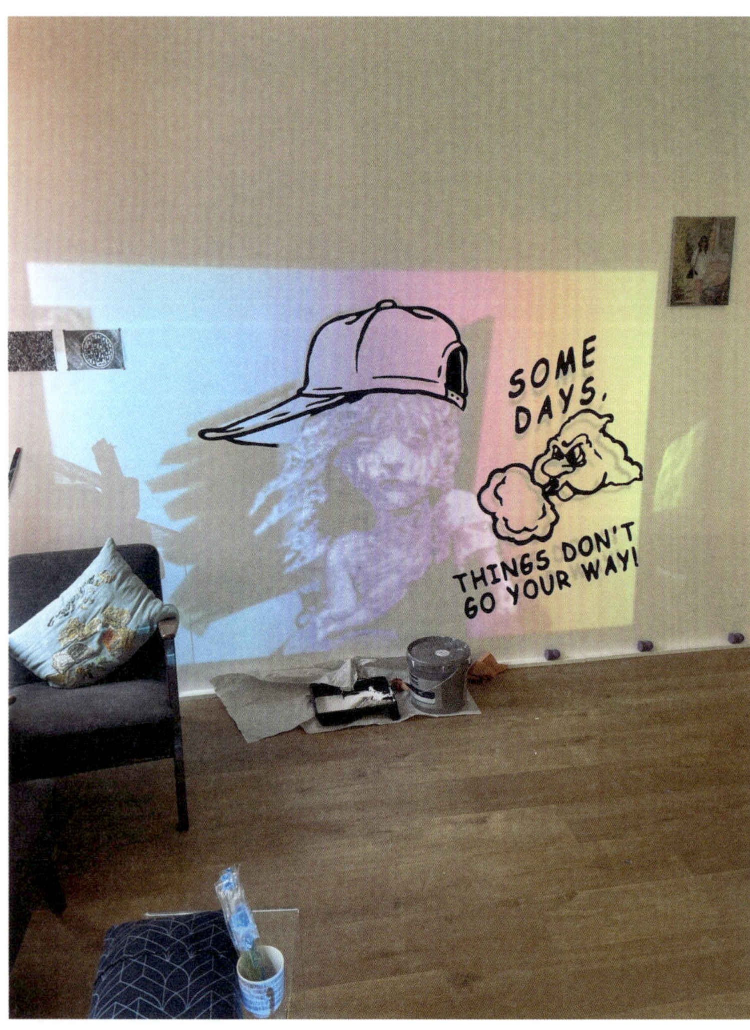

Elliot Kaufman projecting an image from *Les Misérables* to paint on top of Parker Ito's work

him every day. He was in love with Alicia, bonded with Charlotte and François, and Asha grew to be one of his closest friends, perhaps because of the forced proximity while they were both in Arles. And, like all of us, Gary had some kind of elastic bondage to Alex Zevin's charmed ways.

Artists tend to embody contradiction, craving time and space alone to make their work while also needing a community in order to feel that what they are doing is worthwhile. I am so grateful to remember Gary roaring with laughter in this house among his new friends.

The more I think about it the more I feel that there's nothing more genuinely artistic than to love people.[9]

1 Vincent van Gogh to Theo van Gogh, September 9, 1888, letter 677, https://vangoghletters.org/vg/letters/let677/letter.html.
2 Vincent van Gogh to Theo van Gogh, September 18, 1888, letter 683, https://vangoghletters.org/vg/letters/let683/letter.html.
3 Vincent van Gogh to Theo van Gogh, September 23/24, 1888, letter 686, https://vangoghletters.org/vg/letters/let686/letter.html.
4 Vincent van Gogh to Theo van Gogh, May 4, 1888, https://vangoghletters.org/vg/letters/let604/letter.html.
5 Vincent van Gogh to Theo van Gogh, September 18, 1888, letter 682, https://vangoghletters.org/vg/letters/let682/letter.html.
6 Vincent van Gogh to Theo van Gogh, August 21/22, 1888, letter 666, https://vangoghletters.org/vg/letters/let666/letter.html.
7 Vincent van Gogh to Theo van Gogh, letter 677.
8 Vincent van Gogh to Theo van Gogh, letter 682.
9 Vincent van Gogh to Theo van Gogh, letter 682.

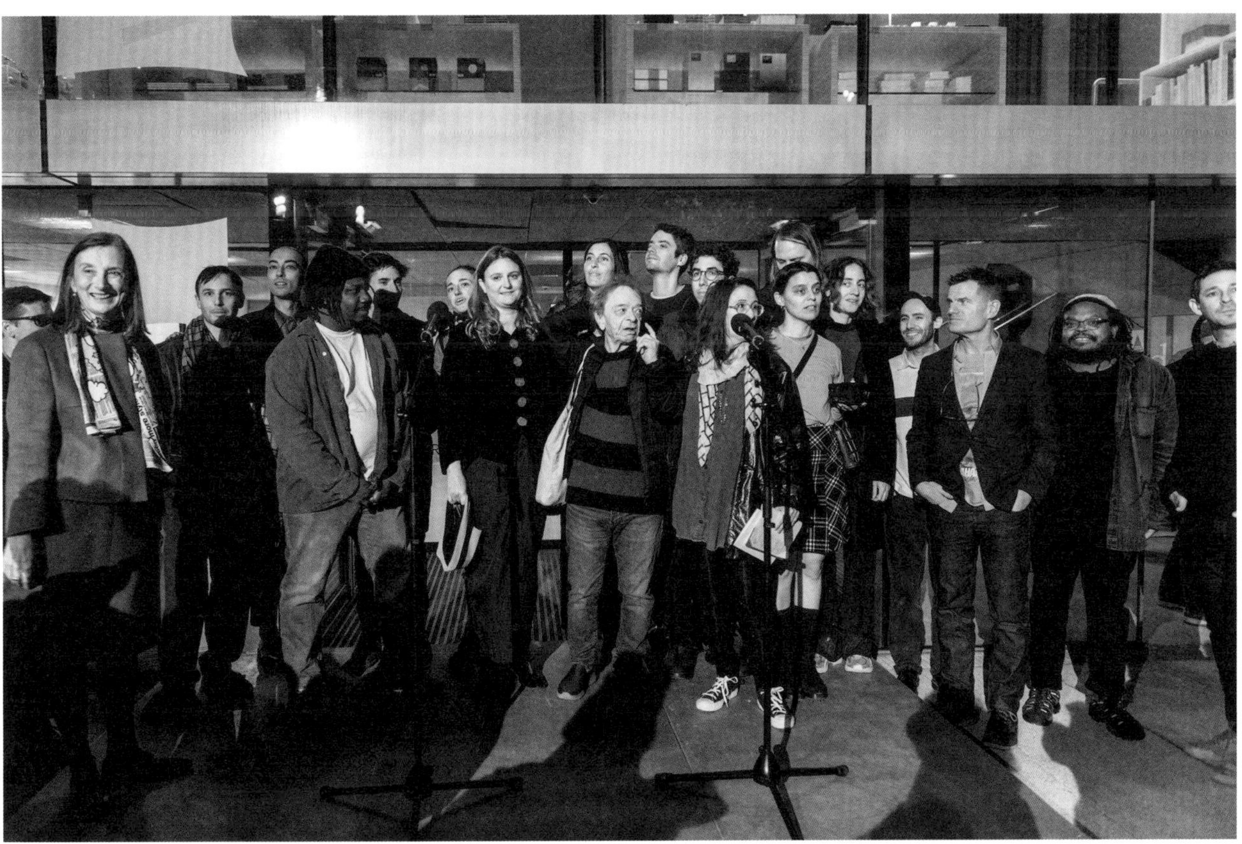

The opening of the exhibition *Studio of the South* at Fondation Vincent van Gogh Arles, November 17, 2023

SEPTEMBER–NOVEMBER 2020
Julie Beaufils

Vincent van Gogh was not one of one of the artists who had a big influence on me, probably because I'd seen a lot of his work when I was a child with my parents at museums, and he was used as a public example to show that artists are freaks. And that's kind of voyeurism. My family would also use him to dissuade me from pursuing a career in the arts. People would insist on the dramatic aspects of his life instead of focusing on the true sensibility of his work, and that seemed unfair. Probably because I grew up in France, his life story over-shadowed his work. I think that coming to Arles and listening to Laura Owens and Mona Varichon talking about him changed my mind, as I really started to be able to actually look at his paintings.

I knew of Laura when I was living in Los Angeles, but I had never met her. I would go to 356 Mission often, and I knew she was running the place. Later, I met her through Mona in Mouriès. We were spending the holidays together with Mona and Jacob Eisenmann. It was casual. Then she told me about the house and took me there to see the renovations that were taking place. She asked, "Do you wanna come next month?" I had never been to Arles before, and it was a

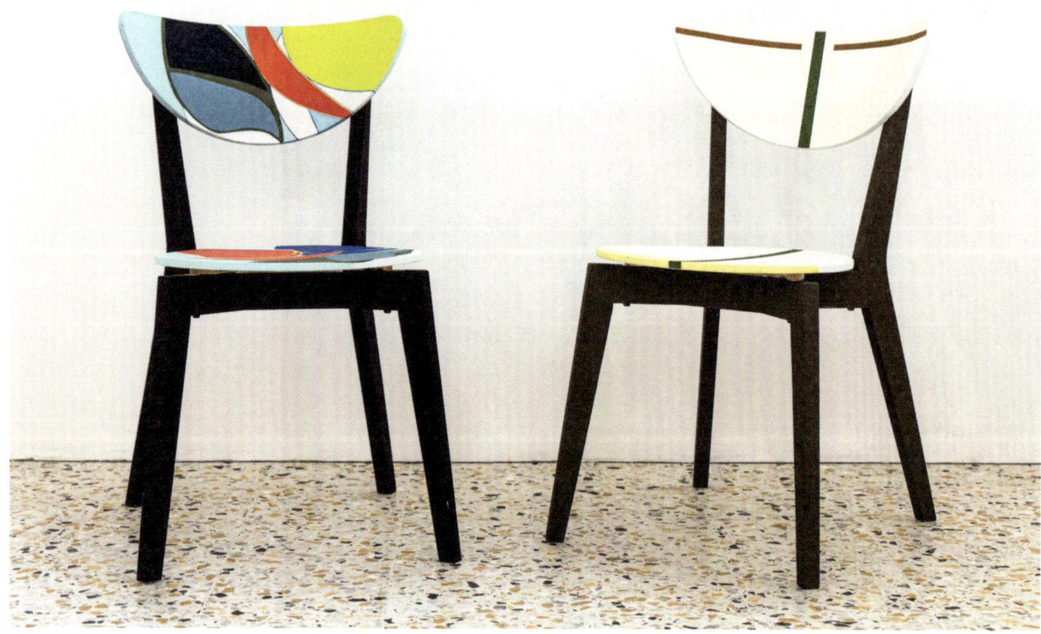

Julie Beaufils, *Chaises*, paint on chairs

reconnection to Provence. Being in Arles with friends was a new way of connecting Provence to art—and to contemporary art, actually—and it made sense to me.

I thought the house was really beautiful. When I visited it, there was no furniture, and to me it was kind of a blank canvas. I immediately felt the tranquility of the place. The emptiness was inspiring.

I moved to Arles at the end of September 2020. At first it was a fresh start, and I took it as a gift to have such a big space where I could experiment with new things. Then Laura, Mona, and Jacob came to set me up in the house, which was nice, but they had to leave one week later. So I started to feel the solitude. I considered leaving earlier, but after one week, it seemed a pity to go back to Paris while having such a big space available, even if it meant being alone. When I first got to the house, there was no furniture. There was no art. Laura had asked for certain second-hand furniture she had picked to be moved in. But then, I think, the LUMA residency team brought brand-new furniture to make the house more comfortable: a table to eat at, a washing machine, things like that. It then felt like a brand-new seasonal vacation house, which I appreciated.

The COVID-19 lockdown happened a few weeks after I had moved in. I thought about going back to Paris. Then Julie Boukobza advised me to stay. She stayed, as well, with the LUMA residents, so I was not completely alone. For two months, written justifications were mandatory to go outside, but we found ways to meet. During lockdown, I would mainly work in the studio and go for bicycle rides in nature. I would go to the bridge over the Petit-Rhône; even during winter,

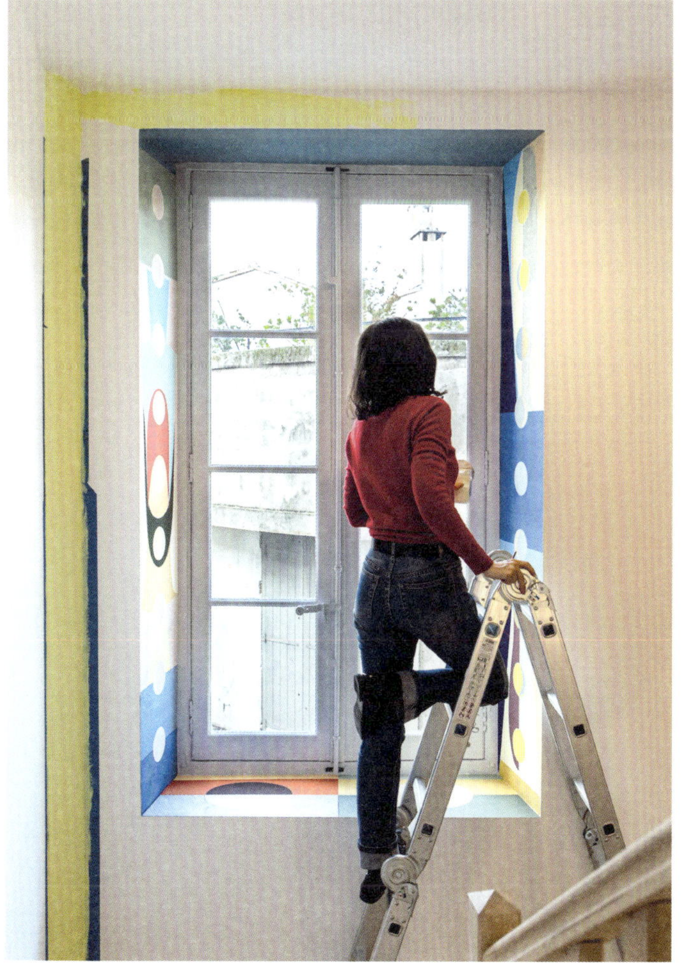

Julie painting *Voyeur*

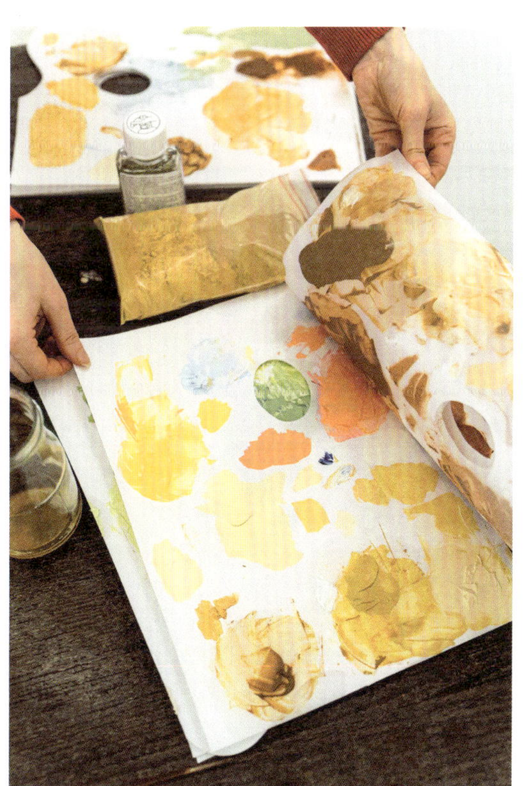

Pigment tests

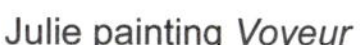
adiana Sadie Laska Eric Palgon Alicia Vaïsse Adee Roberson Clément Rodzielski Alake Shilling Mona Varichon Jacob Eisenmann Andy Robert Alexander Zevin Blake Rayne Candida Alvarez Nova Brya

it was sunny and beautiful. One night, I had dinner at the house of François Halard, who has this amazing house with so much art inside. I had dinner with them, and it was just an incredible evening. Arles was completely closed and dark. Once I stepped inside the house, there were paintings by Cy Twombly, among other artists, on the walls; a fountain inside the courtyard; it felt like an oasis of warmth. At the end of lockdown, the High Art gallery team arrived in Arles and threw a dinner party for Lucy Bull's show at their new space. After such a strict lockdown, I remember it was fun to hang out with such a big group of people.

The instructions for making works inside the house were not very specific. It was not formally explained. I talked to Laura a little bit, and to Mona, and that's how I understood that the concept was to actually produce something as part of the house. I chose the windows because it was the lockdown and I wanted to be looking outside while working. I thought it would be beautiful to be next to the window. Also, I had visited the Château d'Angers before coming to Arles, and I had seen these subtle frescos around the windows there. There were seats near the windows for the ladies of the castle while they were waiting for men to come back from war. I was waiting for the lockdown to be over, so it made sense to me. I chose to illustrate that feeling by drawing a kind of lunar calendar and outdoor landscapes. While I was painting, I was actively listening to NPR to keep up with the American election. This political race was also a kind of a wait before a final outcome. The house felt American because of Laura, Mona, and Jacob being in the

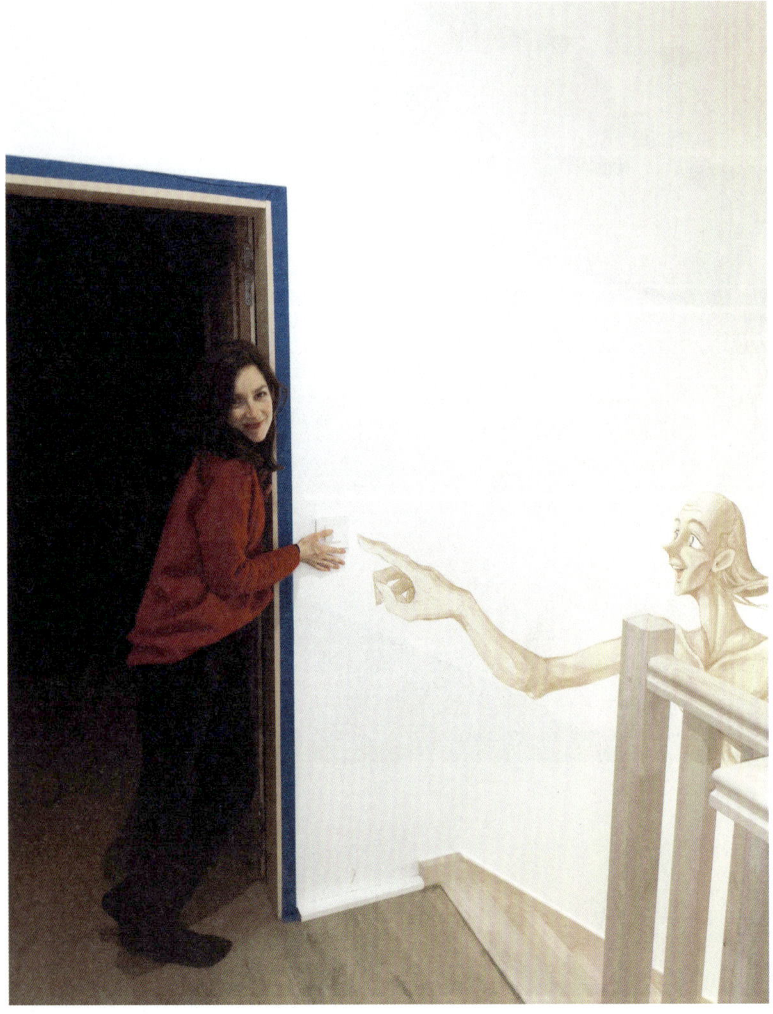

Julie with Julien Ceccaldi's *Soaring Francis*

United States. For some reason, I felt closer to the States than Provence. Also because I started watching *Seinfeld*, which was comfort food for the brain because of its normality when everything was not normal.

We had a visit to the Atelier LUMA with Julie and the LUMA residents. There I saw they were making all these sustainable materials for architecture and buildings. I thought the colors were beautiful. So I asked, "Can you actually make some pigments that I could use to paint with?" So they made two little bags of pigments, and I started painting with them. The light coming from the pigments was really bright. LUMA arranged a trip to Roussillon so I could shop for pigments. There's a furniture-paint shop where they sell pigments coming from the surrounding mines. There's a kind of clay there that is red, and I could find all sorts of red ochers. That's how I started to paint with pigments. It was a completely new way of working; the paint can be quite liquid and transparent. The owner of the shop dissuaded me from using titanium white pigments because it would cover the softness of the color. I couldn't use it on the walls of the house, though. So I used acrylic paint. I also painted two kitchen chairs. I knew Laura thought that they looked too "new." I had never done something site-specific before, but seeing Laura being so easygoing about it encouraged me to try, even just for fun. I felt a little bit intimidated being the first person and making the first marks in the house. I felt freedom but also expectations. I felt like I had to have something to show at some point. That's why I put a little bit of pressure on myself to finish the murals in time.

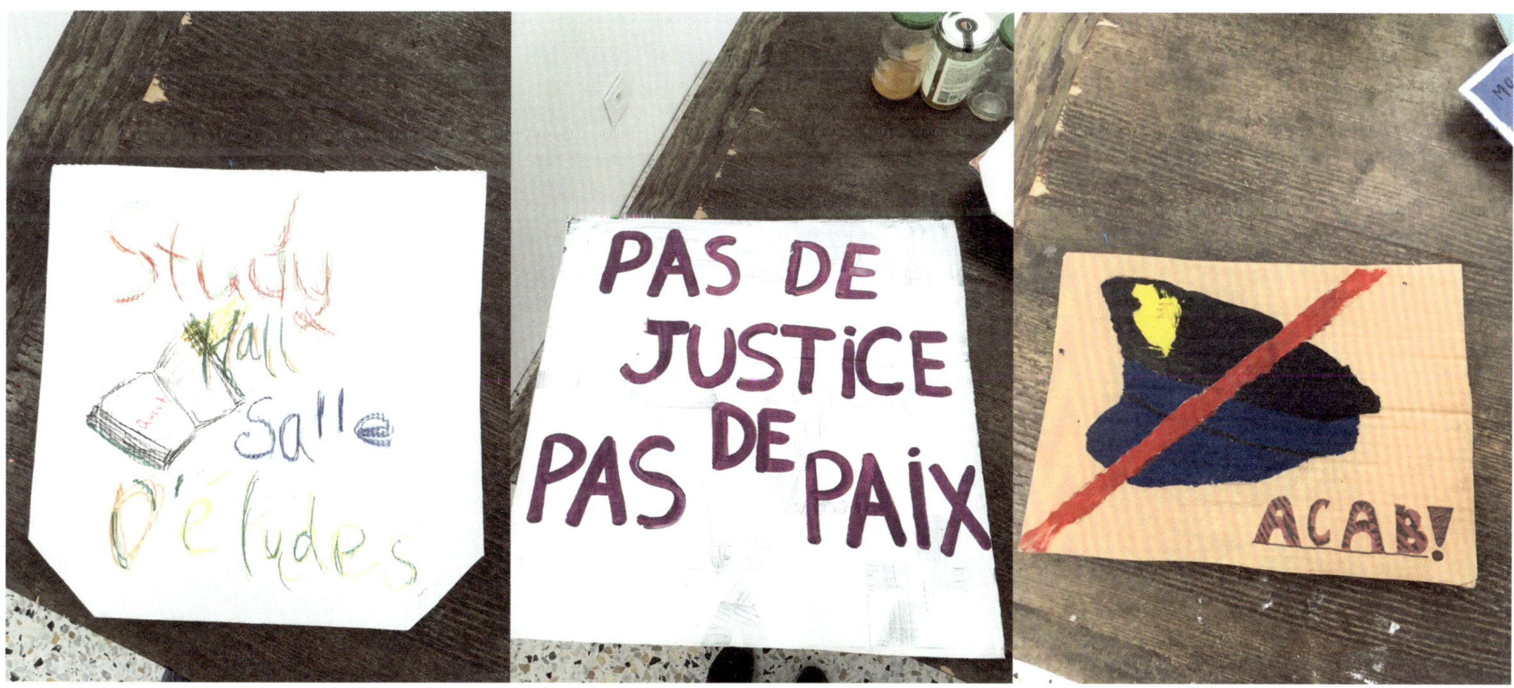

Signs made with Nova Bryan and Laura Owens for Black Lives Matter protests in Marseille

When Parker Ito was there, he left two vases with orchids on top of one of my window paintings. It was completely OK to put stuff around while living in the house, but leaving things permanently would hurt the paint, unfortunately. With the sun coming in, the colors would change. If there's an object, it would leave a mark and make the color different. So I sent him an email asking him to remove them. He apologized and said he didn't realize they were on someone's artwork. He had randomly put flower pots there and agreed to take them out. I don't think it was an essential part of his work, and he didn't seem to care. Later, I had a conversation with another resident about it. She was saying, "This is the game of the house: putting stuff on other people's stuff." She's right, but I think it depends. Personally, if I had arrived after everyone, I would have chosen a place that doesn't hurt or overshadow anyone's work. I didn't know it was going to go that goofy, though. I think it became a chain reaction, and in the end, it's better that we didn't take ourselves too seriously.

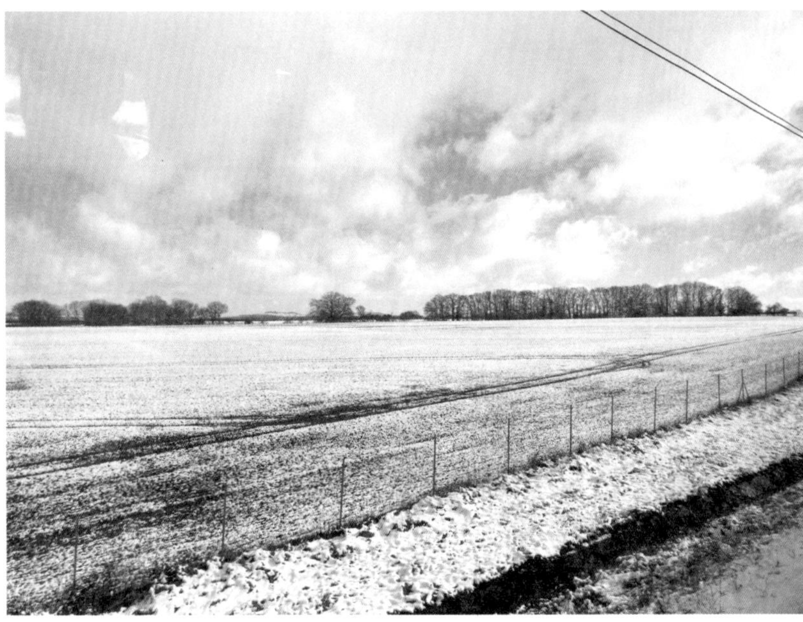
View from the train to Arles

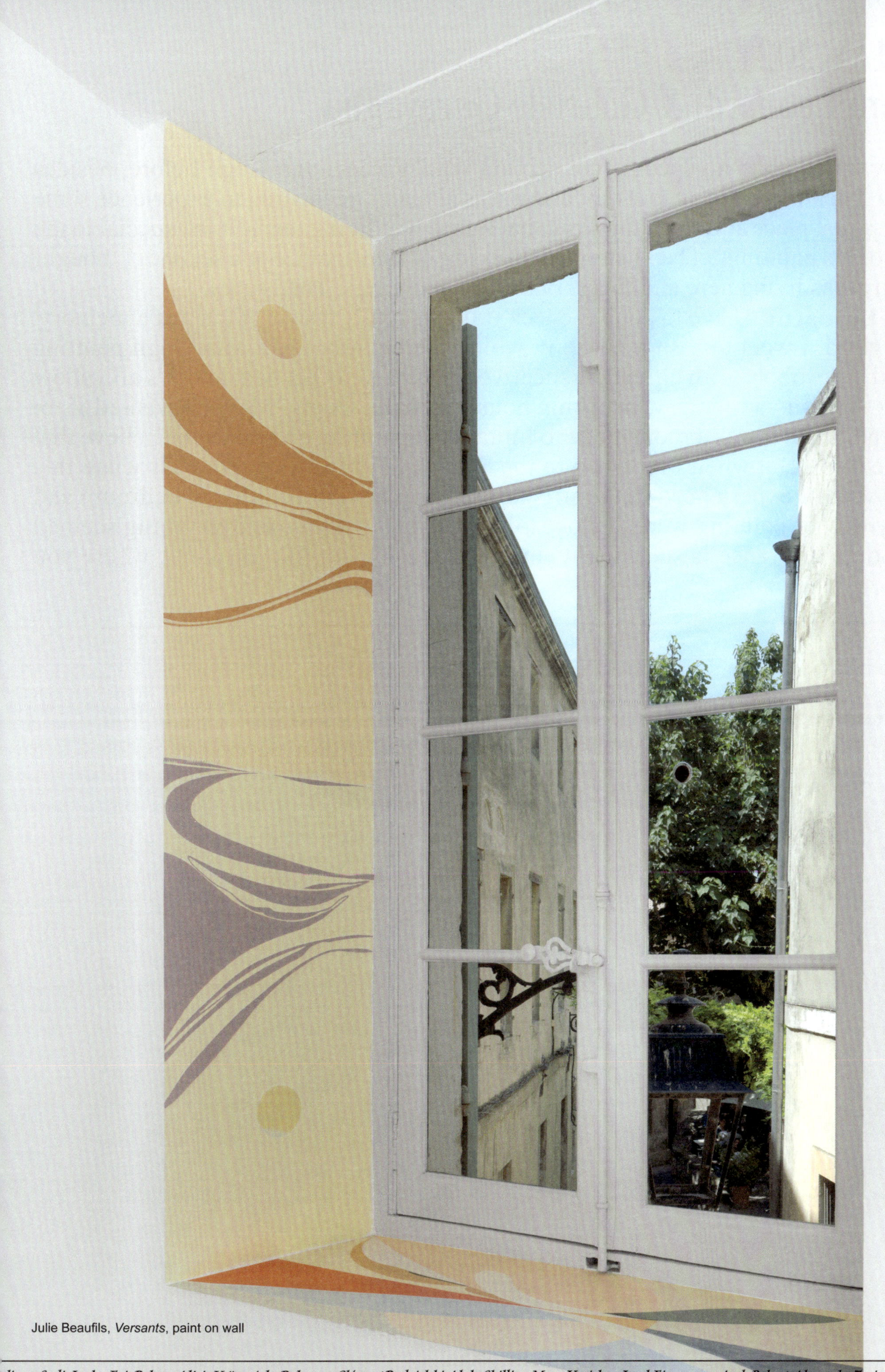

Julie Beaufils, *Versants*, paint on wall

diana SadieLaska EricPalgon AliciaVaïsse AdeeRoberson ClémentRodzielski AlakeShilling MonaVarichon JacobEisenmann AndyRobert AlexanderZevin BlakeRayne CandidaAlvarez NovaBrya

Miriam Laura Leonardi & Gabriele Garavaglia

Gabriele Garavaglia: I had no specific connection with Vincent van Gogh before, besides knowing his story. Then when I went to Arles, and it was actually interesting to experience some of his paintings in a real place and time, thinking that figure was living there. It felt special to me to live inside one of his paintings. Then I stopped thinking of him again. For a second, I thought, Oh, wow! This guy was living here and this is one of his paintings. That's cool.

Miriam Laura Leonardi: I have to double-check if this is really true or if it's just a memory: I think that, as a child, I went to visit a house in which the bedroom of a Van Gogh painting was reconstructed, all wobbly with unreal perspectives, and there is his bed, and it's all yellow. But I don't know if this is a memory, or if this house actually exists. Maybe I visited it, or I visited in my mind. Like, it was a room made to imitate the painting and made me believe that this was where he slept. But when I returned to the South of France, I couldn't associate this memory with anything I experienced in the streets; the trippiness of the yellow bedroom and this hallucinatory way of painting weren't close to what I saw in Arles, as everything seemed quite soft—the South of France is such a soft environment. It's not like Brussels, where you

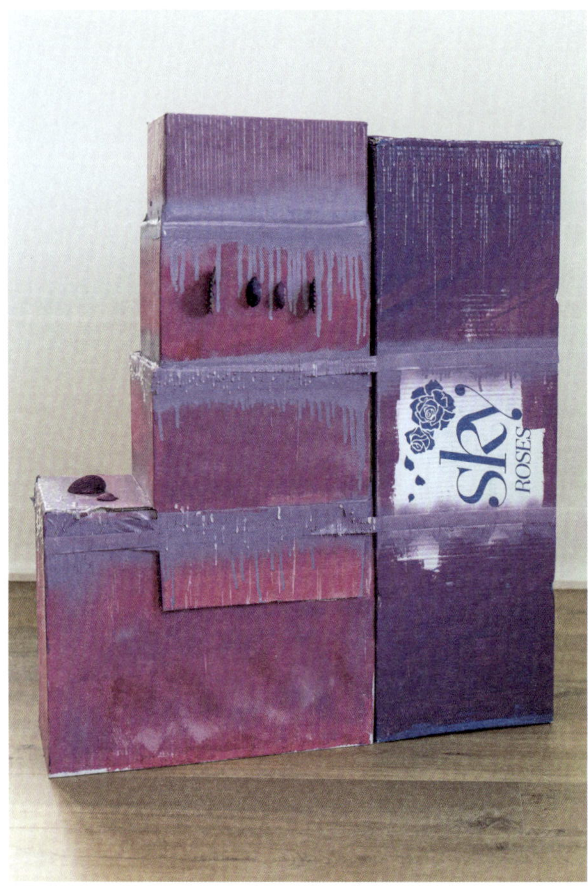

Miriam Laura Leonardi, *All-In-One RAL Bar (Skylounge)*, cardboard and paint

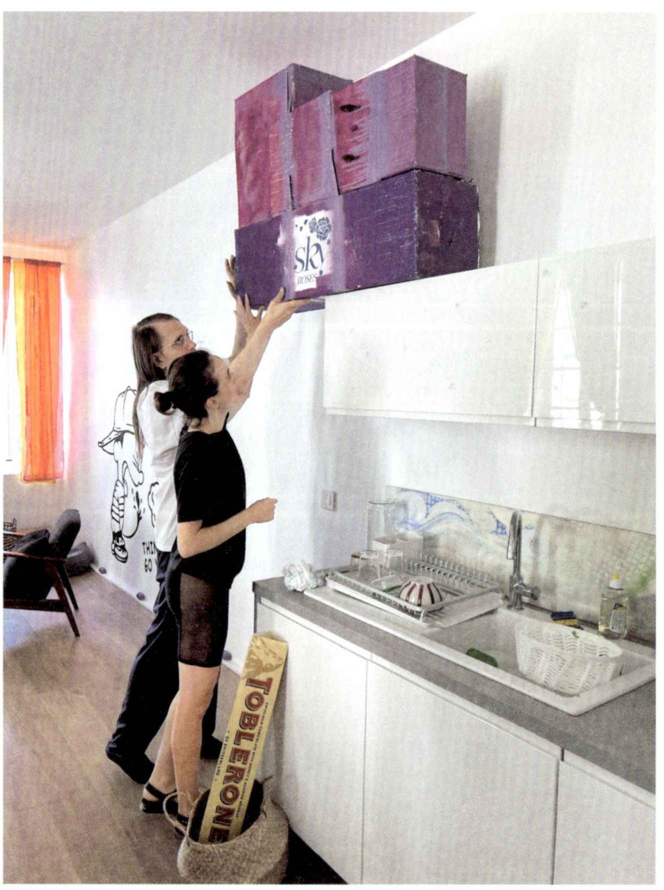

Miriam and Gabriele Garavaglia installing *All-In-One RAL Bar (Skylounge)*

feel like you're in a René Magritte painting. Somehow, I felt in the South of France that I'm not in a Van Gogh.

GG: I felt the opposite. Before the residency, I knew the work of Laura Owens in broad strokes; then I discovered the human-being Laura. When I went there, through Miriam I got to know her better. I bought the "blue book" catalogue of her work (published by the Whitney Museum of American Art) and read all the email between her and the galleries and the extracts from David Foster Wallace's texts. I wonder if some of those messages were love messages or only business messages. I discovered her in Arles, and it was a fantastic discovery. I like to go to painting shows, but I do not dig into the work of painters much. When I do research, I research something else. It was beautiful to discover simultaneously the work of Laura and her kindness.

MLL: I hadn't meet met her before in person, but I had been at her place in 2018 when Mona Varichon was taking care of Nova and living in Los Angeles, and I was in town for an exhibition at Bel Ami. That winter, I screened this unreleased documentary film, *Casey in Wonderland*, about Casey Johnson and her adopted daughter. Mona told Laura about it and Laura said she would be curious to see it. So I sent the film to Laura, and only years later, I found out that she had subsequently watched it with Nova and found it extremely sad. Another year, I participated in Frieze with Bel Ami, and Laura bought a little work of mine. I remember

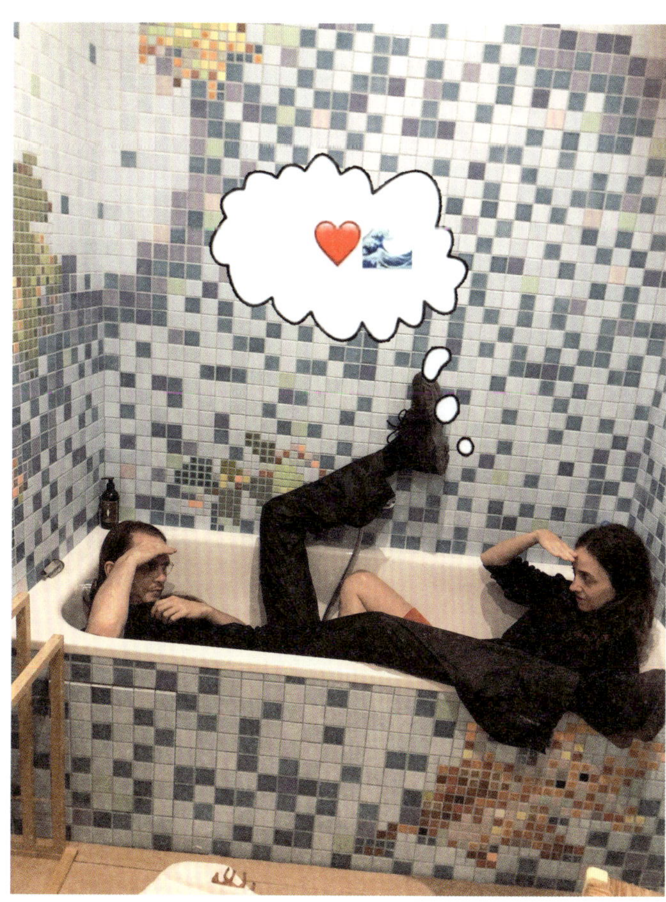

Miriam and Gabriele in the bathtub in a video they texted to Laura

diana Sadie Laska Eric Palgon Alicia Vaïsse Adee Roberson Clément Rodzielski Alake Shilling Mona Varichon Jacob Eisenmann Andy Robert Alexander Zevin Blake Rayne Candida Alvarez Nova Brya

that she might have asked Asha Schechter if I was a decent human being before she decided to acquire something. And then I met her for the first time in Arles. I invited her for dinner at the residency. But it went quite wrong because I was not prepared to cook for a vegetarian, and had thought I could just buy the local ravioli with *taureau* (bull) inside. So I wanted to impress her with some Swiss cuisine by making *rösti* (pan-fried potatoes) with an untested recipe for an autumn sauce, like a vegan creamy sauce. I thought it was horrible, but she was kind enough to say that she really liked it. So that was our first meeting.

GG: I had a residency in Arles before, in 2017, for a different project. It was organized by The New Museum, and it was called *Ideas City*. But also, my hometown in Italy is a very small, remote village. It's the twin town of Arles, so I always knew about Arles when I was a child growing up. They really look like each other—or a little bit. Anyhow, my longest experience was the one at the Laura residency, because the previous one was just two weeks in the construction site of the LUMA tower. We were sleeping there…

MLL: Yeah, I don't think I'd ever been to Arles before. Or at least I don't remember. My first impression was, it creates a sensation like the film *The Cabinet of Dr. Caligari*—like, all the streets end up in the same place. It's a bit of a labyrinth, and you think the city is big, but it turns out to narrow itself down very fast because you stop crossing the bridge leading to the other side of the river. It became a small place with a lot of rumors carried by the mistral. It was still under

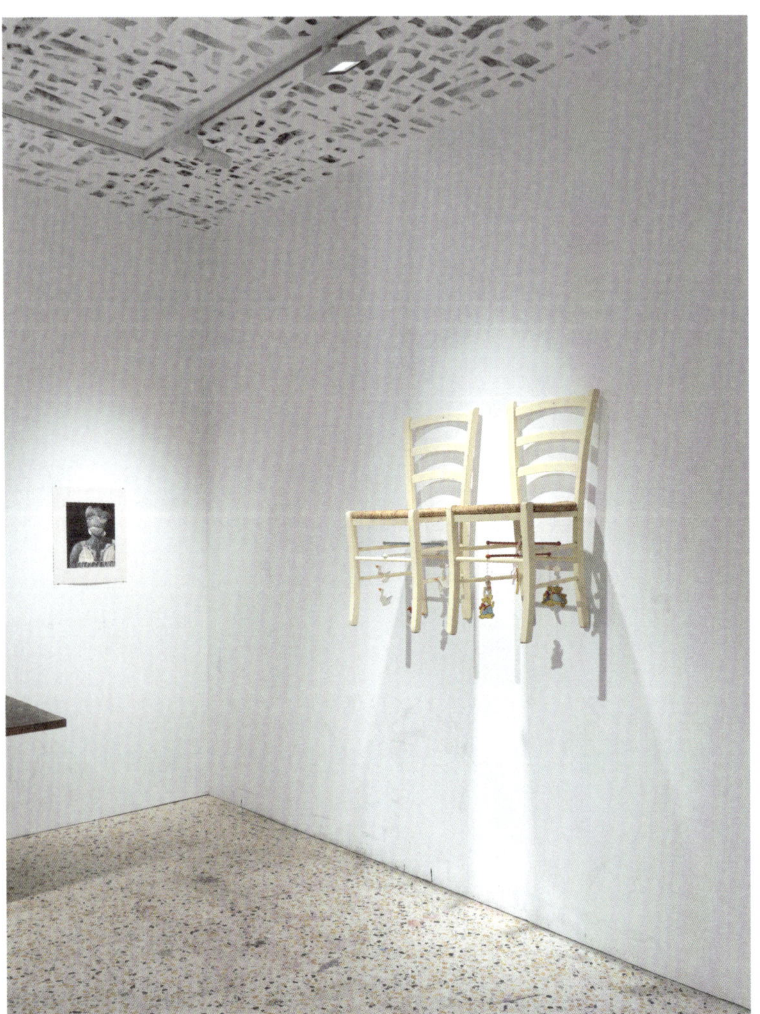

Gabriele Garavaglia, *Cursed Childhood*, mixed media

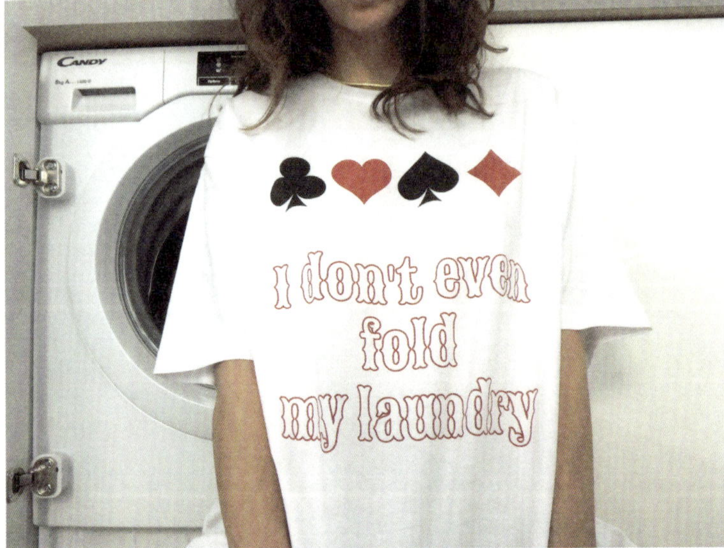

Miriam wearing a shirt of her own design

the COVID-19 lockdown, so there was a curfew at seven o'clock, even though Julie Boukobza organized for us a permit that would allow us to go out after the curfew. During that time, we discovered the only good place in France for cappuccino. And it was because, somehow, an Italian ended up getting locked into this town and decided to make some cappuccinos meanwhile.

GG: It was more that this guy was somehow stopped in Arles because of the lockdown, and he started working for this existing bar. So all of a sudden, the cappuccino was good, and everyone went there. When the lockdown ended and this guy left the city, the cappuccino was bad again. In the house, for me, it was particularly unclear due the fact that it was at the very first stage and was pristine, and so it was really difficult. I had the impression that it's difficult to add anything and that every gesture would become super important, and as I was somehow there because of Miriam and not because of direct contact with Laura, I felt intimidated by doing something really present. When I came back later, it felt pretty clear that everyone was welcome to contribute, but at the beginning, it was difficult.

MLL: Yeah. For me, I remember that Julie Beaufils had painted the window frames, but Laura's curtains were not there yet, so there was literally nothing besides some wooden furniture, and it had a bit of an Airbnb look. It didn't feel cozy, and I was a bit shy to—for example—paint on a wall; which, at the end of the residency, I did. So it took me quite a while to take the house as a canvas. I'm not a painter so I should not even say "to take the house as a canvas," but

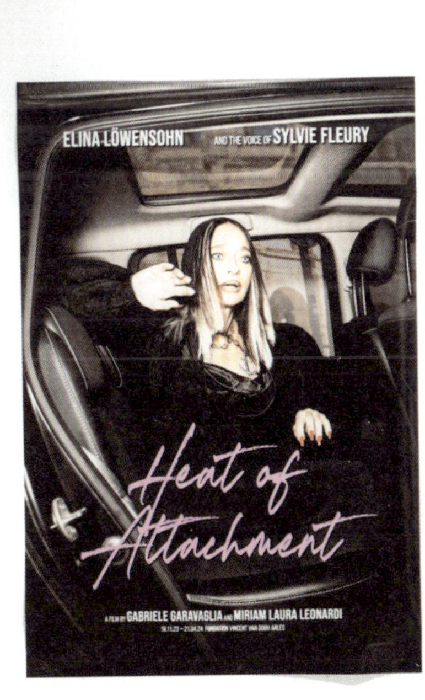

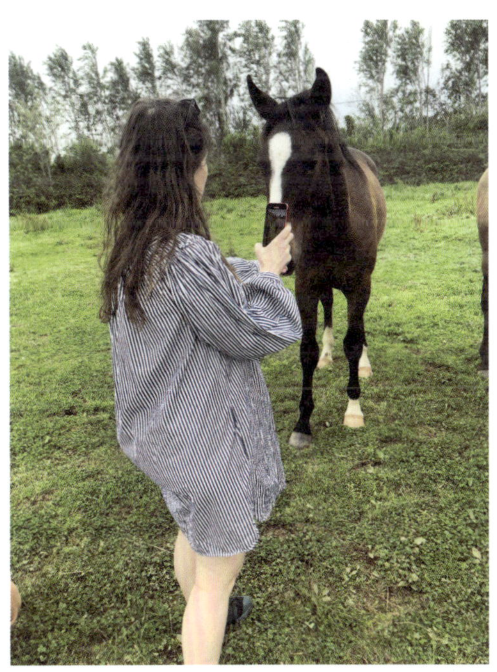
Laura Owens in Mouriès

Poster for *Heat of Attachment*, a film by Gabriele Garavaglia and Miriam Laura Leonardi

metaphorically. It seemed more functional than an art project in the beginning. And then, it's the house of a stranger, but the stranger is not there. The big change actually happened when Laura's curtains arrived. It got cozy all of a sudden. And I felt more free and protected to do whatever I would do in my own house. I started with a doorframe, which is just paper taped around the doorframe of the sleeping room. It says, "VAN À GOGO CLUB," which obviously came from being in Arles, although during the lockdown, there were no places offering *à gogo*. An *à gogo* deal is when a restaurant offers, for example, *moules à gogo*: as many mussels as you can eat. It's an abundance of something that you usually don't overconsume. Which became contradictory because it was lockdown and there was no abundance at all. And also, in the town itself, there is no abundance of Van Gogh paintings since the museum doesn't own any; it has to get them on loan.

GG: So when I was there, I only left one trace, which is an instruction-like piece on top of the stove. It's the dimensions of an A4 paper; basically, it's instructions for a Xerox copy machine implanted in a kitchen. I used the space too as a studio to actually design an exhibition I had somewhere else at the time. And then I did something again for the space when I came back at the end of the residency because it felt like everyone was more than welcome to add stuff. So I just found a series of objects around and I installed them on the wall. "An assemblage," like Laura said. And it's a sort of representation of a cursed childhood in the Camargue.

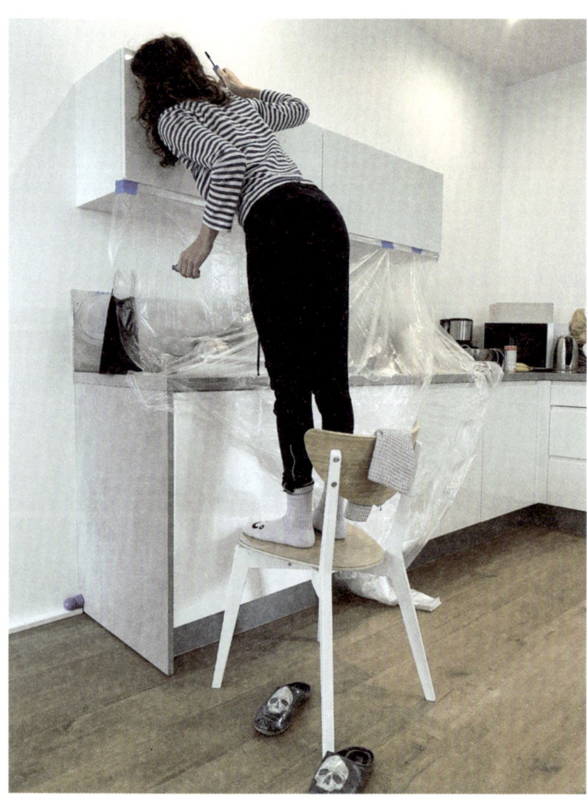

Miriam making *Butterfly Kiss* on the cabinet

Miriam Laura Leonardi, *Butterfly Kiss*, mascara

I always wanted to write Laura, but somehow I never did; I didn't thank her enough for this experience. I really think that what she initiated had an impact on the lives of some of us, just in the sense that we encountered each other in a place and got to know each other, and even if it's a spread-out community, I still met people I would not have met before. They are inspiring, and I can always somehow go back to them or refer to them. So I just thought, like, what a pragmatic, real impact this project had. Sometimes it's just, like, a visualization of something. In this case, it was really changing the course of some social existence. So thank you, Laura.

MLL: I knew some of the other artists before, like Asha, Mona, and Naoki Sutter-Shudo, but many I didn't, and I feel anyhow that now I could call all of them and talk about something personal without a problem—in a way, even the artists who I didn't meet during the residency but just at the end, briefly, at the opening. Somehow there was a ground of trust. This trust seemed to establish itself between the artists, probably coming from the fact that Laura trusted all the artists.

GG: It's interesting that Laura is a sort of a space herself because, by going and meeting Laura, it's like you go to a place where you meet other people. It's not always the same, but I know that if I go to meet Laura somewhere, I might meet some of you. Not everyone, but it doesn't matter if it's New York, Los Angeles, or Basel. She's the aggregator, somehow.

MLL: The days there were quite empty, in a way.

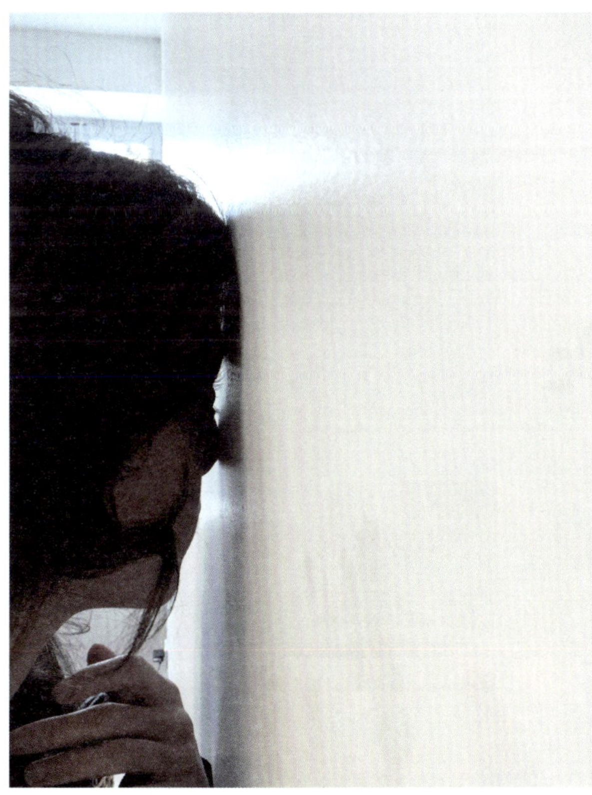

Miriam making *Butterfly Kiss* on the cabinet

GG: I think it was very specific, also, of this COVID-19 moment. So it was not ordinary, but ordinary for that specific moment. I guess we both were teaching also, at that moment, from a distance. So I do remember having classes at the computer at the window, looking at the good-looking priests next door to the residence. We would go on walks.

MLL: Yeah—eat a *fougasse*, try to cook stuff that we found in the city. We did some bike explorations. It's, like, a bit of a vacuum in my memory; I just have a memory of a big space because the sleeping room is so high. You have this big space around you physically and mentally, and you just fill it up with one or two little things a day. I would look at the neighboring Roman amphitheater ruins and just repeat the same thought: How could this big rock still be on top of these two pillars for twenty centuries? And that was my day. There was a bit of a social life on the weekends; I remember some *apéros* and dinners, for which we all used our permits to stay out. It was slow, but actually I quite enjoyed not having to socialize too much during the residency. I sometimes went to drink pastis on the main square with the obelisk at six o'clock, and at seven o'clock I went home, drunk, to sleep.

My impression of the house at the very end was that it motivated everyone to keep going. I remember that, in the last few days, everyone came with another brush in hand and added something more. There was this weird rush of doing more; it felt like there was a deadline, which I really liked. There were no rules. There was no criteria. There was just a group energy

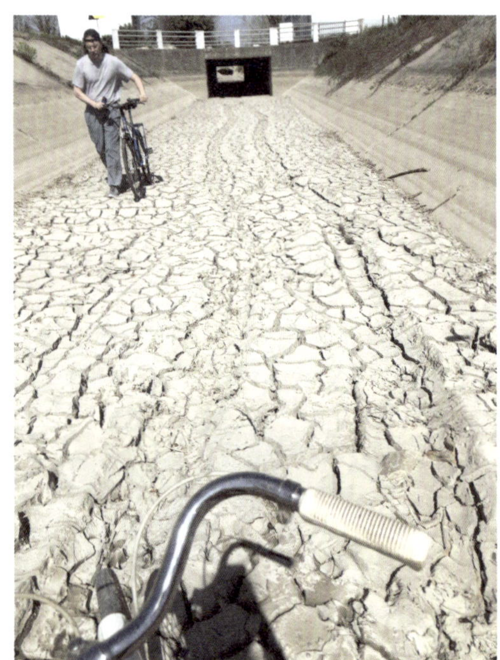

Riding bikes in the outskirts of Arles

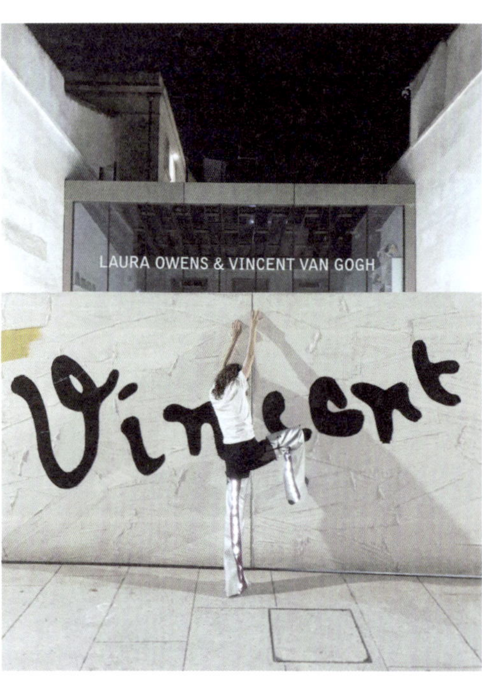

Miriam at the gates of the Fondation Vincent van Gogh Arles

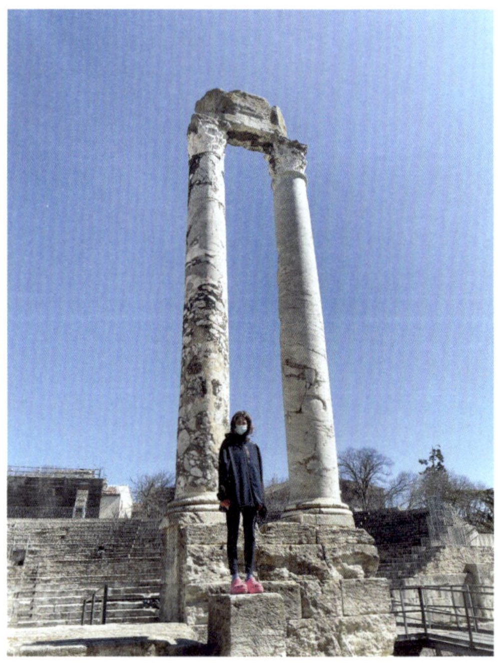

Miriam in the Roman Theater, Arles

driving it. I have more memory of this than of the actual look of the house. I don't even know who did what, exactly, but it also didn't matter since everything was just connected to an experience. So I thought it looked quite fantastic.

GG: But also, at the end, you lose a little bit—this authorship here and there—because people just interacted with other artworks, overwrote, added elements, so it was also a collective gesture. I felt it was a mega-mess in a positive way, somehow. This collective work made me feel, like, an easiness to do art, you know? Like, it felt less of a heavy gesture and more that it can be playful and simple and easier and closer to your heart.

MLL: At the end, it was more about the house and the people than about the art itself. Right? Like, you felt all these people there. I don't know how it was for everybody else, but I also thought that there was an interesting observation in the fact that, for example, I just left everything there, which was also obliged by the fact that I did work that could not be removed, and I used very cheap material. I don't know how it was for everybody who took the work back, but I didn't feel attached at all to what I did or where it would go. I kind of liked just to leave it there.

GG: It's interesting because, even if they want to refresh the house and have another residency, for example—or even not a residency—they can't simultaneously not demolish the artworks, somehow. So it's really, like—what do you do with that?

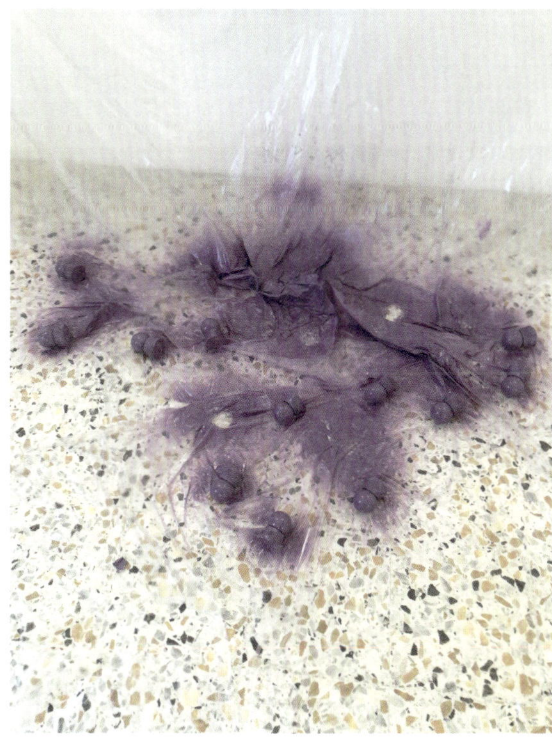

Miriam painting *Bullied*

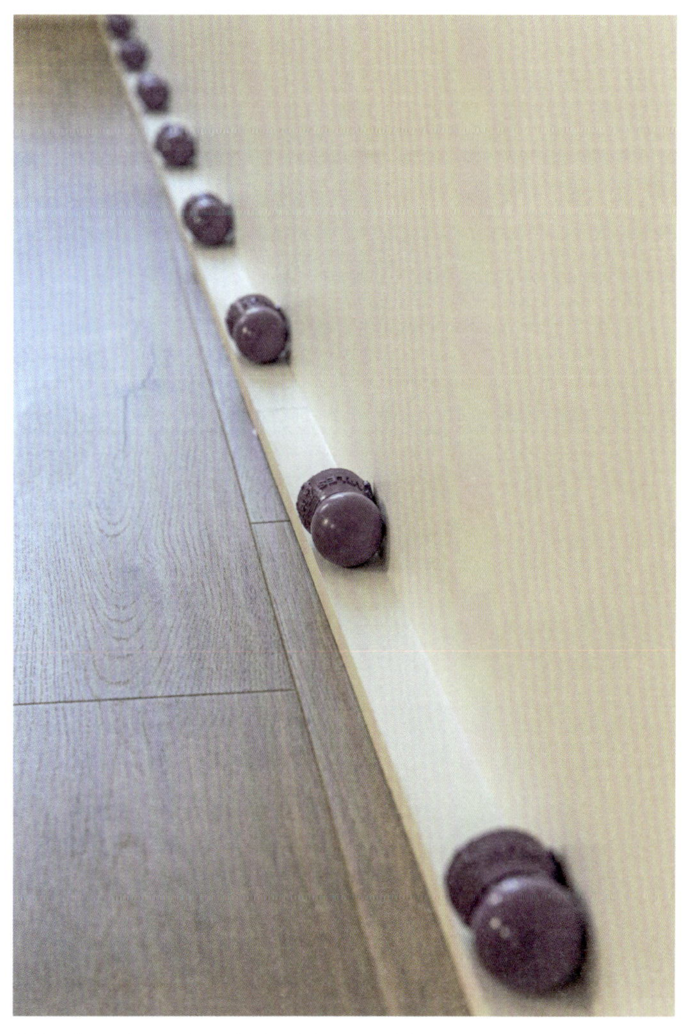

Miriam Laura Leonardi, *Bullied*, painted snowglobes

MLL: I think they can unless you told them to give them back. But I didn't.

GG: It's such a strong gesture to destroy artworks. I mean, I can do it with my artwork, but I don't know if someone else can, you know? An institution cannot just decide to burn down the art of twenty-five artists without permission. Can they?

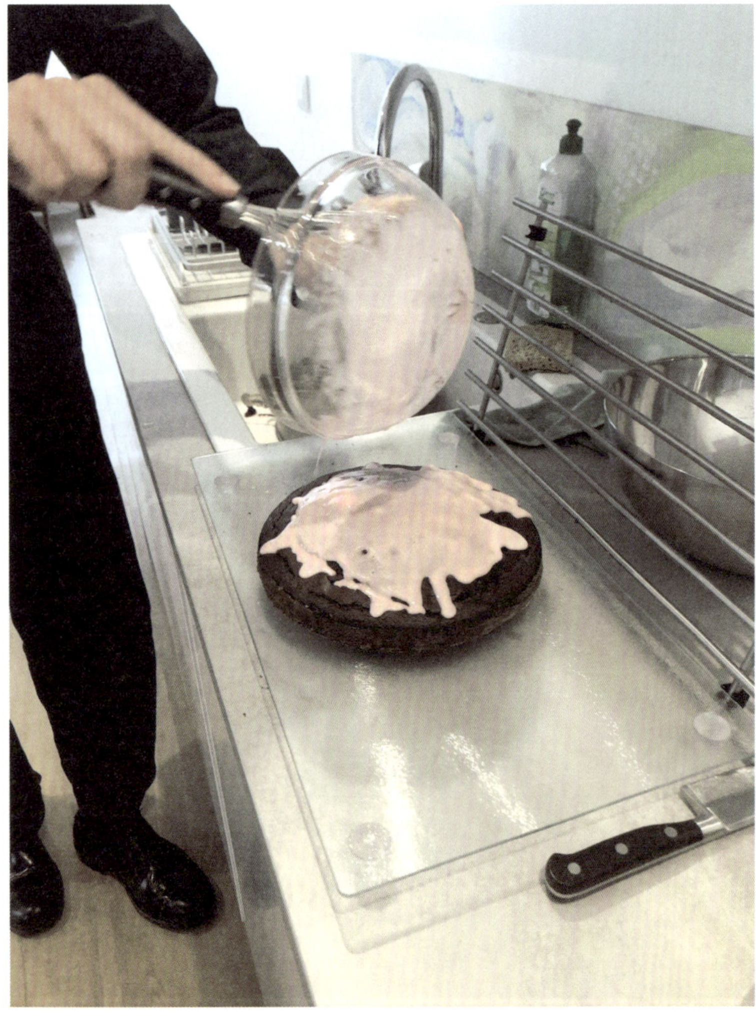

Alexandre Khondji making a cake for Miriam's piano concert

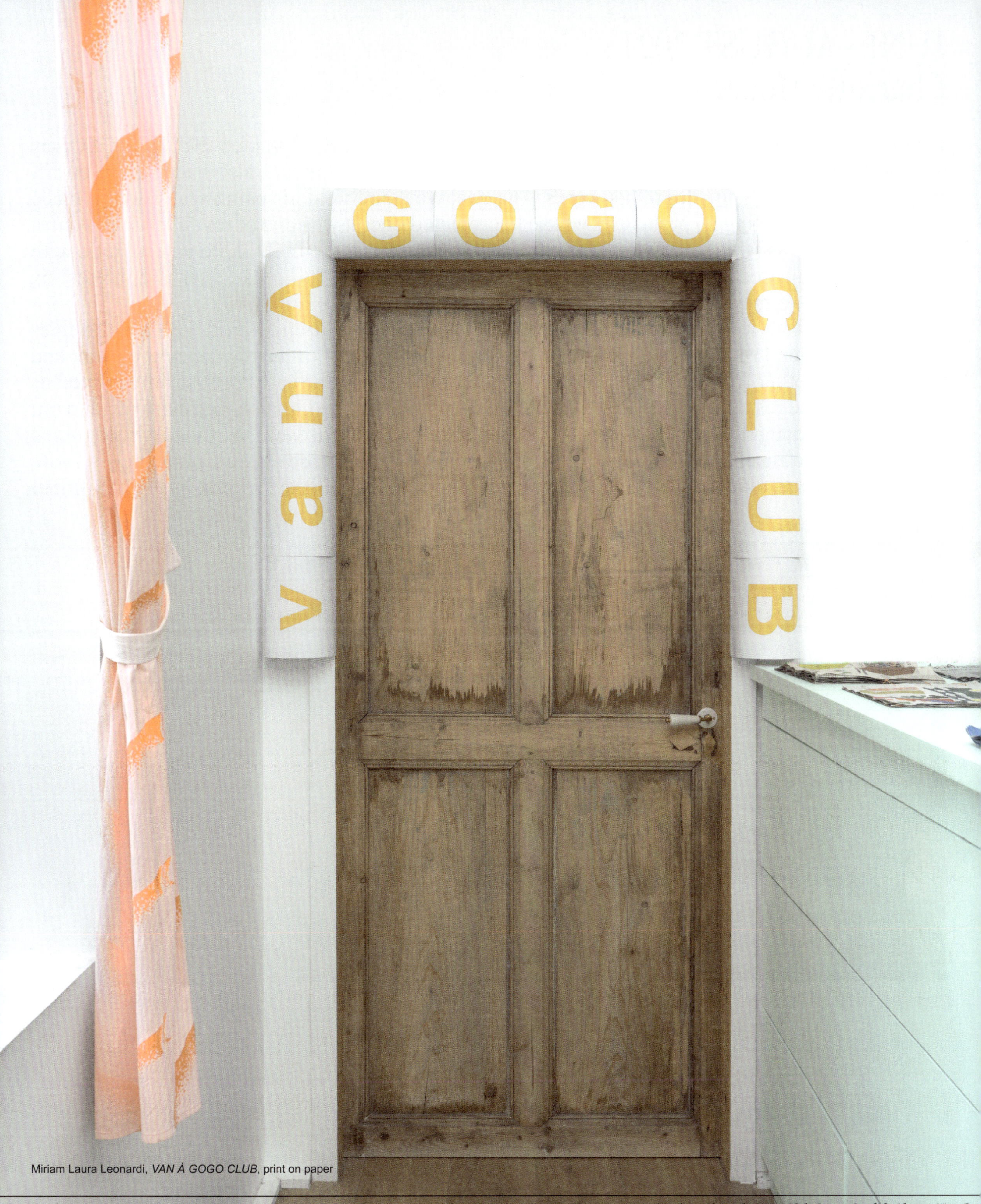

Miriam Laura Leonardi, *VAN À GOGO CLUB*, print on paper

JUNE–AUGUST 2021
Charlotte Houette

I grew up in Paris and have always been drawn to art. As a child, I visited the Musée d'Orsay several times and was mesmerized by Vincent van Gogh's paintings. I also had a game on my PC, a CD-ROM with puzzles of his works. The goal was to rebuild his paintings, piece by piece, and I remember feeling so proud every time I completed one. It was one of my favorite pastimes.

I first met Laura Owens about ten years ago, through Eric Palgon. In 2012, he visited Paris with Laura, and we shared a lively dinner together. The evening was full of laughter and interesting conversations—a memorable night.

Fast-forward to a few years later—I was traveling to visit my friend Alicia Vaïsse, who lives in Mouriès, when I reconnected with Julie Beaufils. She was part of the residency program, and we knew each other from our time at the Beaux-Arts de Paris in the early 2000s. Julie invited us for a drink at the residency house. I was with my partner, François Lancien-Guilberteau, and our three-year-old daughter, Hilma. To my surprise, Laura was there as well. We quickly recognized each other, reminiscing about our dinner years before. What made this encounter even more serendipitous was that, not long before, my friends and I had published a book by Amy Sillman,

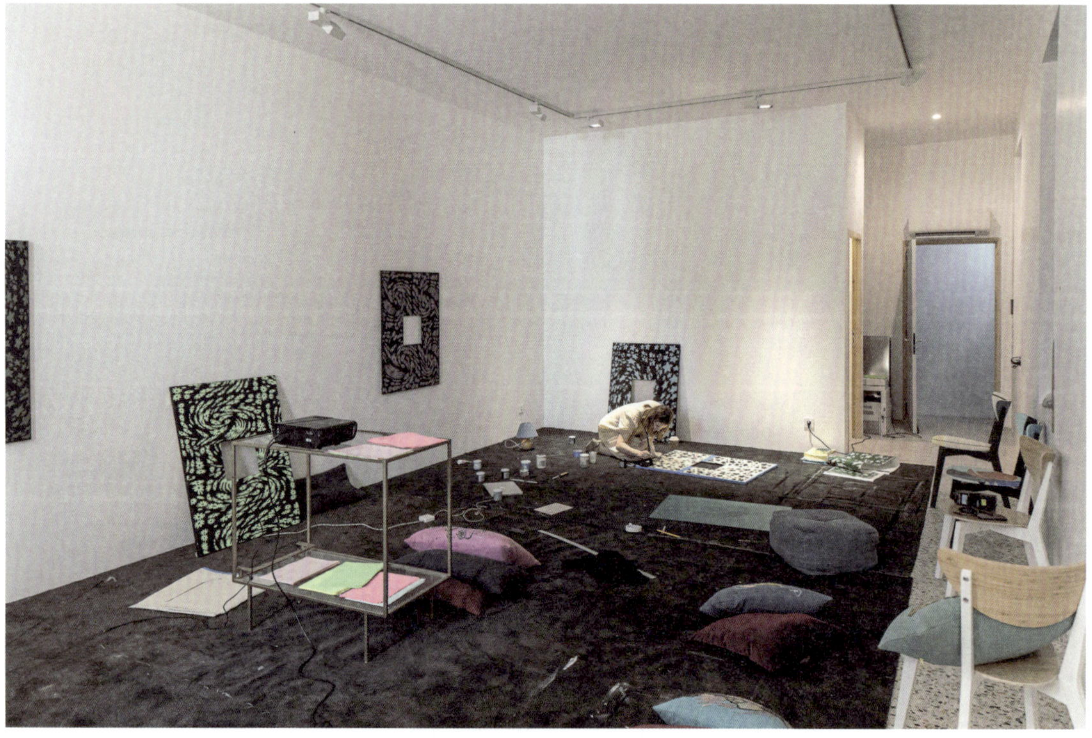

The studio during Charlotte Houette and François Lancien-Guilberteau's residency

which included an essay about Laura's work. I brought her a copy. That evening rekindled our connection, and Laura eventually invited me to join the residency program.

Although I had been to Marseille and nearby areas before, I wasn't very familiar with Arles. I had visited the Rencontres d'Arles only once, so this residency felt like a new adventure. It was also my first time doing a residency with my family, which made it even more special. Our first challenge in Arles was finding a school for Hilma. Luckily, we discovered one just across the street from the house: École maternelle le Cloître. The school's director and the other parents were so welcoming, and it was heartwarming to be part of this community, even for just two months.

This residency was more than an artistic experience; it was a chance to connect deeply with a new city, revisit old friendships, and create lasting memories with my family. The first thing we did was try to organize the ciné-club. There was a community café on the same street called Odysette. The people there were politically engaged and had strong opinions about LUMA. They were the first people I met in Arles, as mutual friends had suggested I reach out to them. They were very involved and active, and I found it inspiring to hear their perspective and have thoughtful conversations with them.

When we arrived at the house, we were struck by how beautiful it was. It felt like a privilege to be there, and we were excited to make the most of it. The house was still fairly empty as we were only the third residents to stay there. Miriam Laura Leonardi had previously used the studio

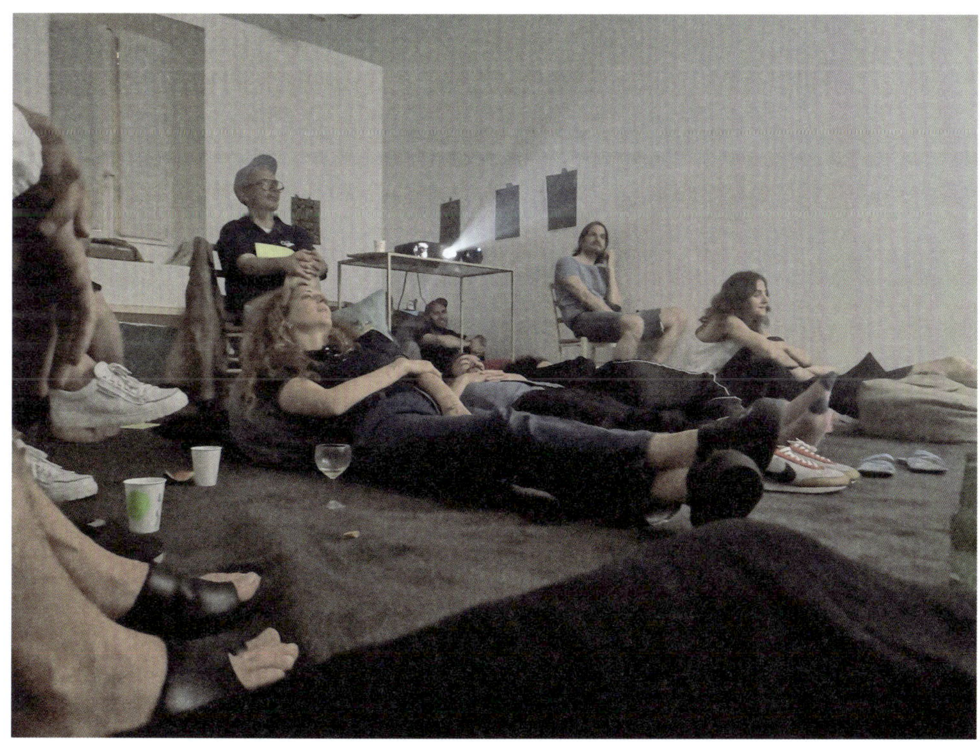

Mélanie Matranga and Antoine Trapp's *Ciné-club Totale Dérive* screening

diana Sadie Laska Eric Palgon Alicia Vaïsse Adee Roberson Clément Rodzielski Alake Shilling Mona Varichon Jacob Eisenmann Andy Robert Alexander Zevin Blake Rayne Candida Alvarez Nova Bry

and left a few works in the kitchen, which were beautiful and gave the space a certain charm. However, she hadn't filled the walls, so I had plenty of room to imagine and create freely. Julie had worked on the windows, which were stunning and added a special atmosphere to the house.

One thing that was a bit unclear when we arrived was how the space could be used—the "rules of the game" weren't entirely defined. We had a stipend to support us, which helped cover some needs, and we worked with what we had to make the residency as productive and inspiring as possible. At first, I started thinking about how to approach production and explore the possibilities within the residency. I imagined how much more could be done with additional resources, but ultimately, I decided to focus on making the most of what was available. For instance, I had envisioned creating a neon sign for the ciné-club. I loved the idea, but instead, I ended up having to work with what I had on-site. There was Flashe paint in the house, so I thought, Why not use that? We organized the ciné-club and screened films, and I painted directly on the walls to transform the space.

What stayed with me most was navigating the creative possibilities within the house. How much freedom did we have to reshape the space? What would remain after we left? And how much energy should I invest in something so tied to the residency itself? There was a certain openness to the experience that encouraged exploration. At the same time, I tried to balance this freedom with a sense of purpose, creating something that felt meaningful within the residency's unique context.

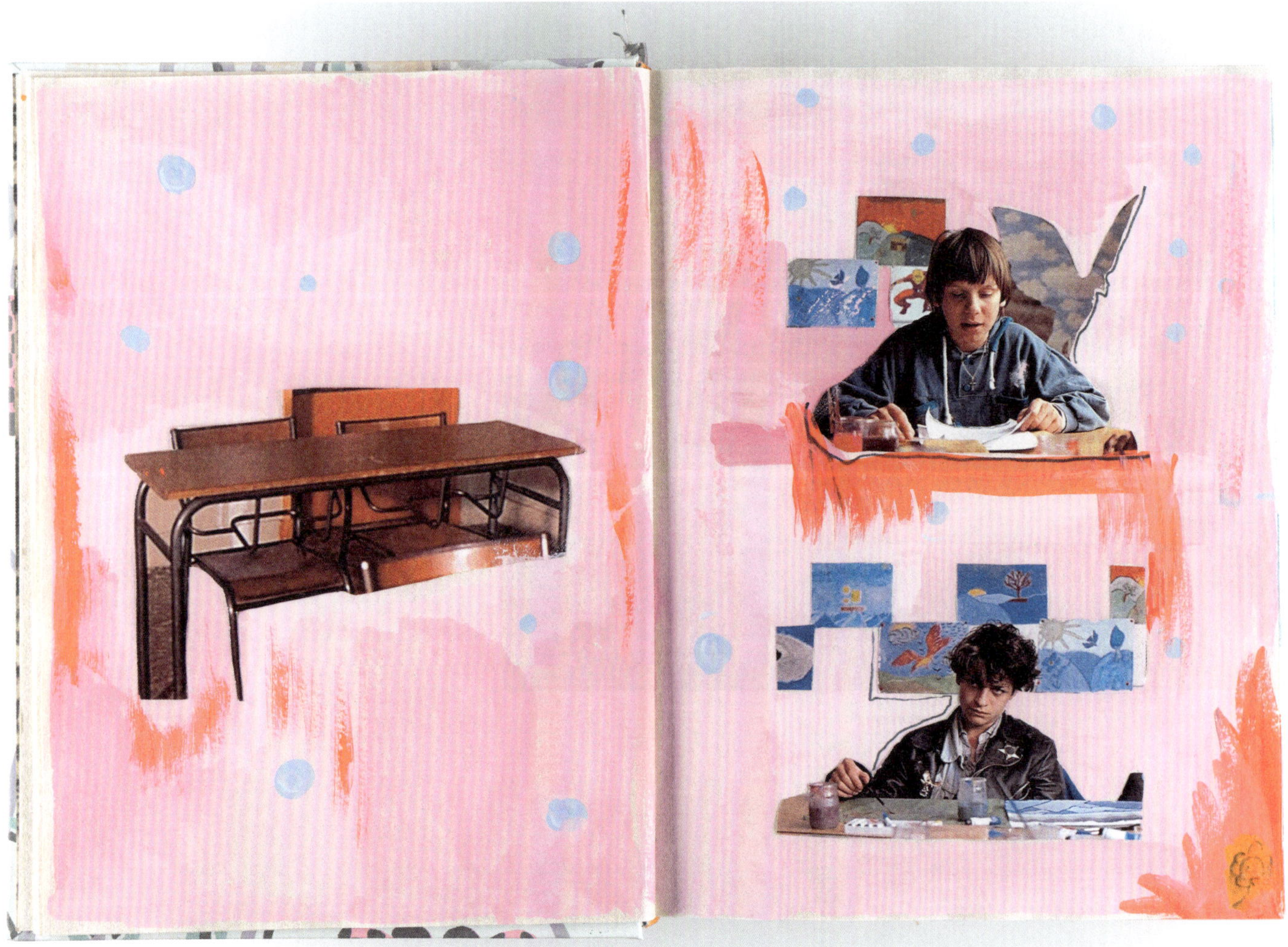

Paint and collage in the guest book

Painting the house felt like reconnecting with my teenage self. Back then, I used to scribble song lyrics on my bedroom walls and fill every inch with whatever came to mind. It reminded me of that freedom—the joy of painting just for the fun of it, without any rules or expectations.

Laura had already started painting, and Nova Bryan, Mona Varichon, and Alicia had added their touches too. It felt natural to keep the momentum going and turn it into a collective project—a big, shared piece of art we could all contribute to. The small bathroom seemed like the perfect place to start. Nobody had worked on it yet, and it felt like a hidden corner waiting to come alive. The bathroom tiles weren't finished at the time, so I'd paint while watching Elliot Kaufman work on them—it gave the whole process this spontaneous, in-the-moment energy. Using Laura's color palette made it even more meaningful, like I was building on what was already there and adding my own layer. The house was always open to others, and that openness naturally inspired collaboration.

Organizing something like the ciné-club felt like the perfect way to connect with people in Arles—bringing art and community together in a way that felt natural and genuine. The project was called *Ciné-club Totale Dérive*, and I organized it with François. The idea was simple: each week, we invited someone to screen a film of their choice. Participants could pick any movie they wanted and write a short text about why they chose it, and we'd create a small zine featuring their text and an image. To spread the word, we used Instagram and put up flyers around the city. It wasn't always easy to attract locals who weren't familiar with LUMA, but some did come, and when they did, we had really great discussions. This project was particularly meaningful to me because I had done similar collective projects in the past, like The Cheapest University. Sometimes, people walking by the house would stop and ask about it, and we'd invite them to the screenings. One evening, my friend Olga Rozenblum, who was visiting, decided to screen a film. She chose *Live Nude Girls Unite!*, a documentary about the efforts in the 1990s of dancers and staff at The Lusty Lady, a San Francisco peep show, to unionize. Olga was initially hesitant about showing the film in the house. She was concerned it might be controversial, especially given the house's history. She spoke with the community café, Odyssette, who were open to hosting the screening but didn't want it directly associated with LUMA. It was a tricky situation—this kind of discussion would have been so engaging inside the house, but I didn't want to push too hard. Instead, we decided to screen the film by the banks of the Rhône. The outdoor screening turned out to be an incredible experience. Many people showed up, sitting together on the riverbank as the Rhône flowed quietly nearby. The warm evening was lit by the stars, the same stars Van Gogh once painted. It felt magical, almost surreal. It reminded me that, while the residency created space for projects like this, some of the most meaningful moments happened outside the house, in connecting with the local community. Creating an alternative ciné-club in a house is always a leap of faith. You set the stage, but the magic only happens when people choose to join in. It's challenging—you can't force people to come or convince them to watch a film. Sometimes

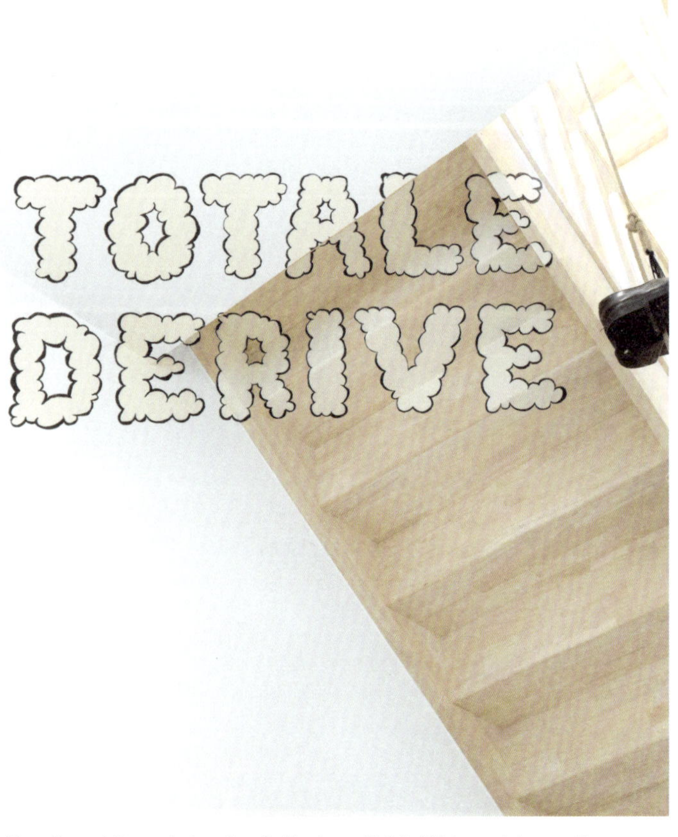

Charlotte Houette and François Lancien-Guilberteau, *Totale Dérive*, paint on wall

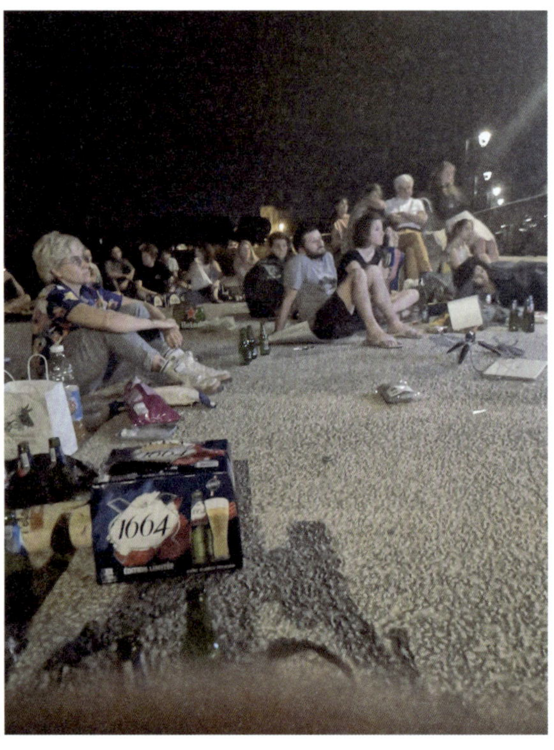

Screening of *Live Nude Girls Unite!* (directed by Vicky Funari and Julia Query, 2000) on the Rhône

they'd think, Why watch a movie here when I can just stay in bed and stream it? But every time someone walked in, curious or excited, it made the effort feel worth it.

During my time at the residency, I made five paintings for a show in Treignac. The idea for these paintings initially came from a request: Some friends had asked me to create an album cover for their band. I began exploring the concept of "moving parts" in my work, which eventually became the foundation of the series. The first week I arrived in Arles, I visited Alicia's horse farm. That night, a baby horse was born. I was on psychedelics when I witnessed its birth, and it was a truly magical moment—watching this newborn foal under the stars, while immersed in the effects of mushrooms, felt surreal. That experience left a deep impression on me, and this series of paintings was directly tied to that moment. I completed all five paintings during the residency. They went on to have a life of their own, appearing in three different shows. Some were exhibited in Treignac, while the rest came back with me to Paris.

I returned to the residency a few times after my initial stay. Julie Beaufils and I revisited the house during the winter, in February 2022. Being among the first residents was an exciting but slightly frustrating experience—we didn't get the chance to interact with the layers of work left by others. I've always thought it would be amazing to return and continue building on the project, adding more layers to the house. The rules were never entirely clear—who knows, maybe we could have even destroyed the place and it would have been fine!

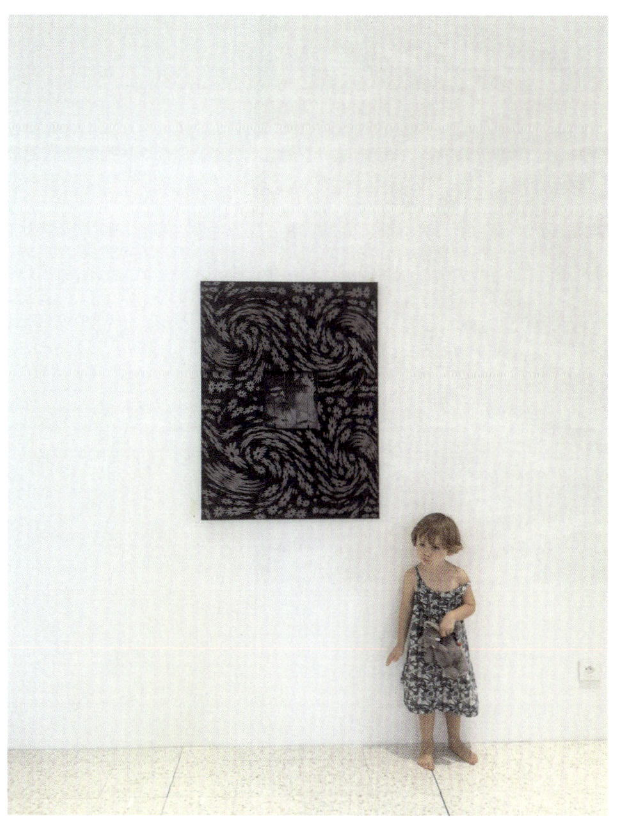
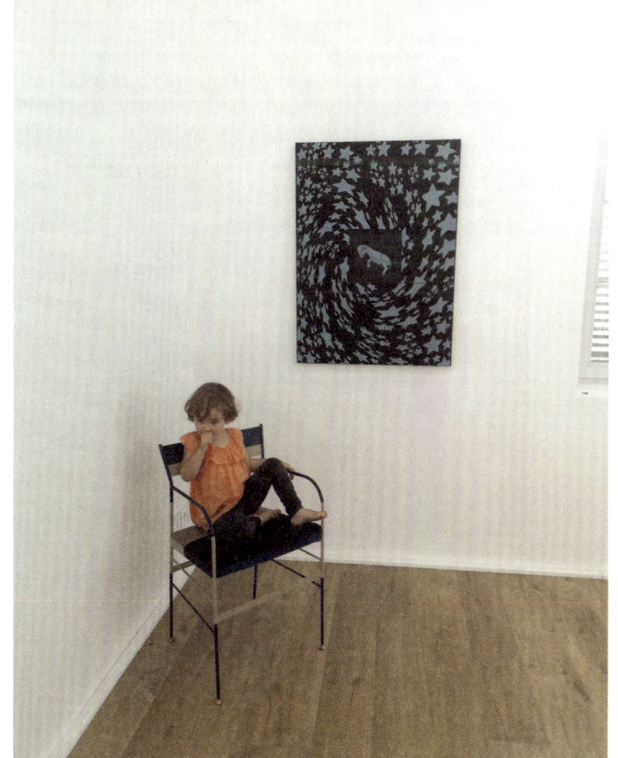

Charlotte and François's daughter Hilma with Charlotte's paintings

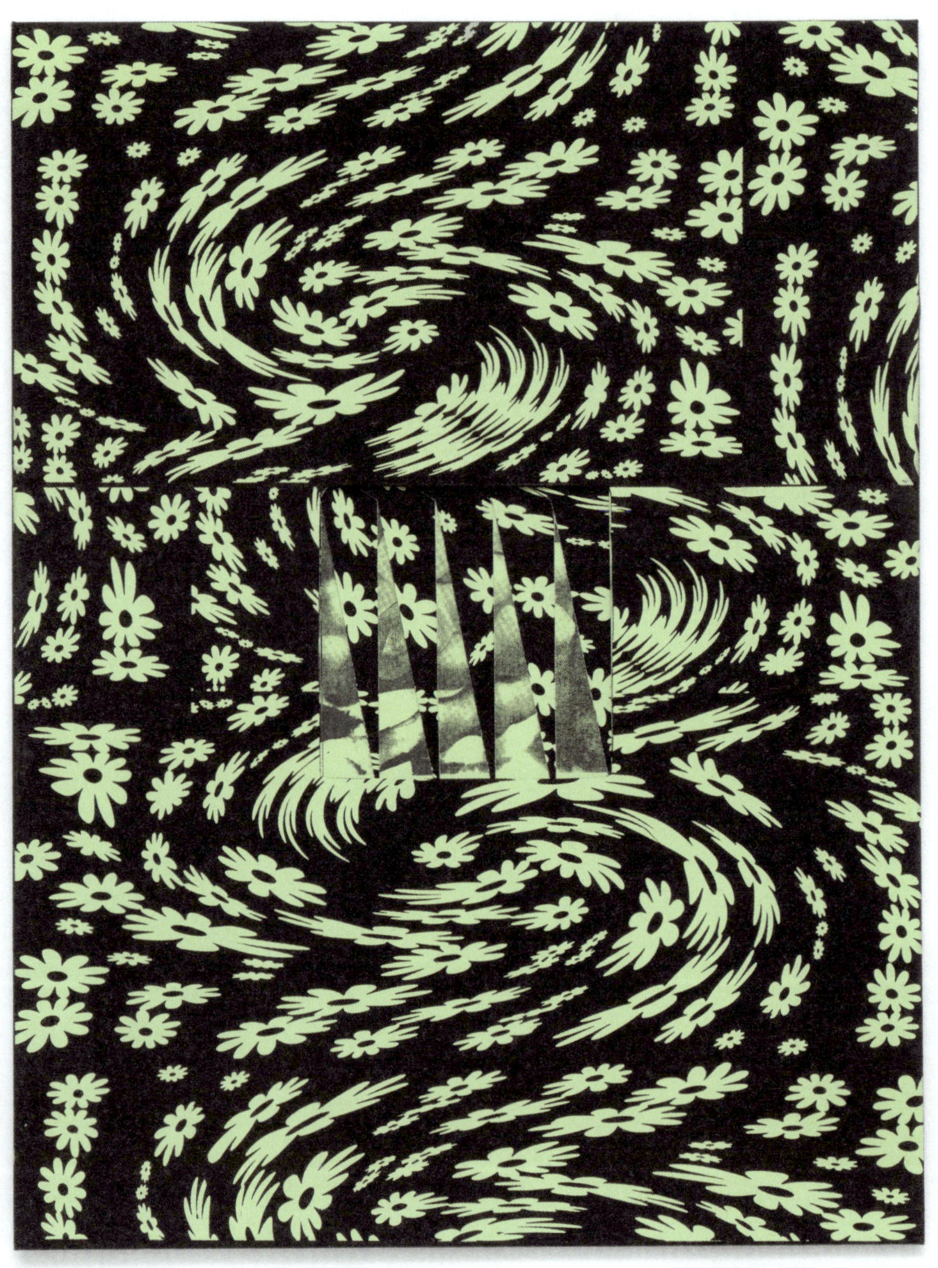

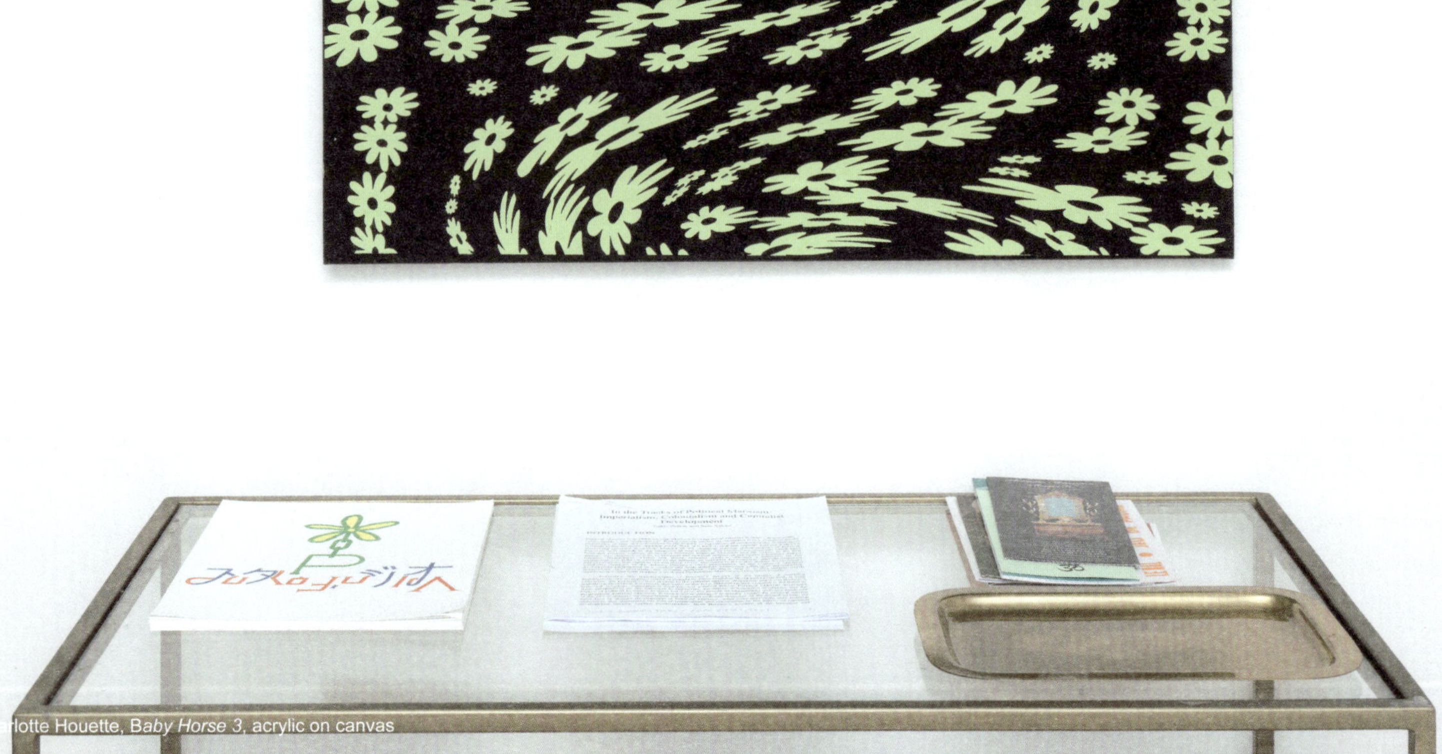

Charlotte Houette, *Baby Horse 3*, acrylic on canvas

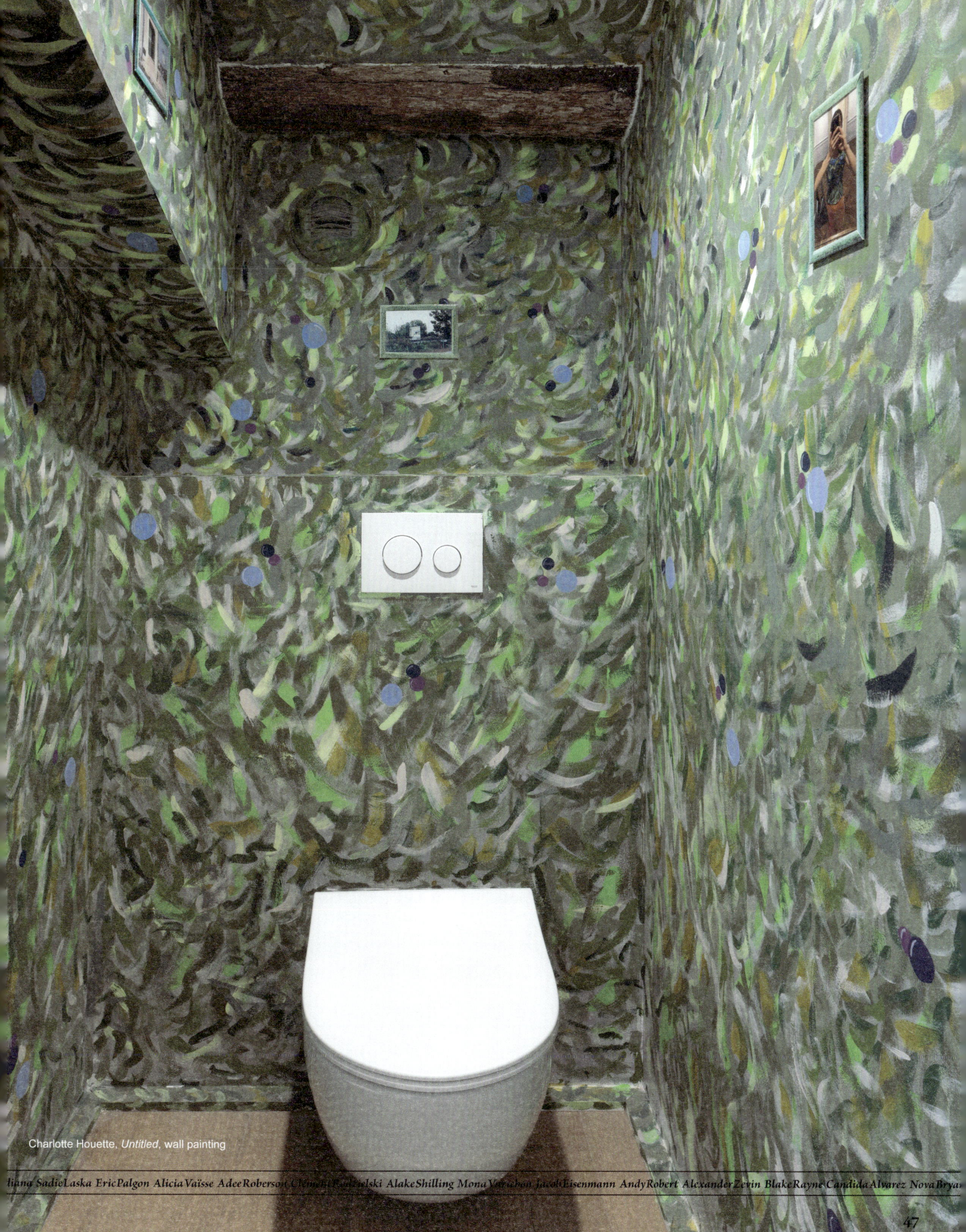

Charlotte Houette, *Untitled*, wall painting

Adding layers on top of others' work felt like such an exciting idea. The house itself seemed unfinished, like it was meant to keep evolving. Naoki Sutter-Shudo had already covered one of Parker Ito's works with a slightly transparent fabric, blending the two and creating something new. It made me wonder: Was this the real purpose of the house? To be a place where no work is static, where everything can be transformed? I never asked Laura directly, but I kept thinking: Could we build on what's already there? Could we reshape it, or even disrupt it entirely?

Laura had a painting in the living room, and it made me think about how we could start "the game" there. At the Fondation Vincent van Gogh Arles, I'd seen an exhibition in which stickers were printed on top of everything. It was irreverent and playful, as though the art itself invited participation. Some pieces felt untouchable, but others seemed to ask for interaction. That idea stayed with me—it was a reminder of how art can constantly shift depending on what we bring to it. In the bathroom, there was a painting by Sadie Laska in this beautifully tiled space. It felt like a sacred corner, almost impossible to touch. But then I wondered, What if we added something small, like a poster, just to change the dynamic? Sadie's painting of the Eiffel Tower on fire felt bold, maybe even provocative. Was it a hint to start tearing things down, to rebuild? It captured that balance between respecting what exists and wanting to take risks.

I still think we should return and continue the game. During the LUMA opening, I met other

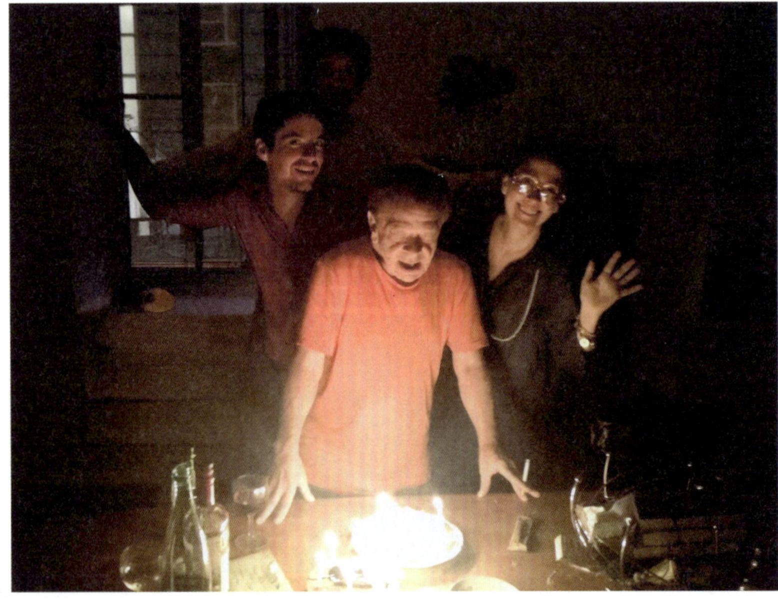

François, Alexandre Khondji, Gary Indiana, and Laura Owens celebrating Gary's birthday

artists, and we talked about collective projects. I imagined a small group of us going back to the house and turning it into a living, collaborative piece of art, adding layer after layer.

The opening itself was surreal. There were so many fascinating people there, like Liam Gillick, whom François and I ended up talking with at length. We joked about staging a performance in the house. I suggested he could fake a fall down the stairs, like something out of *Jackass*. It was absurd, but the idea of creating something playful in the space felt so right.

Making a film with everyone would be amazing—whether it's a comedy, a love story, or something completely unexpected. The house has this energy that invites experimentation and collaboration. It's the kind of place that makes you want to come back, to keep adding to its story, and to see what new layers could emerge.

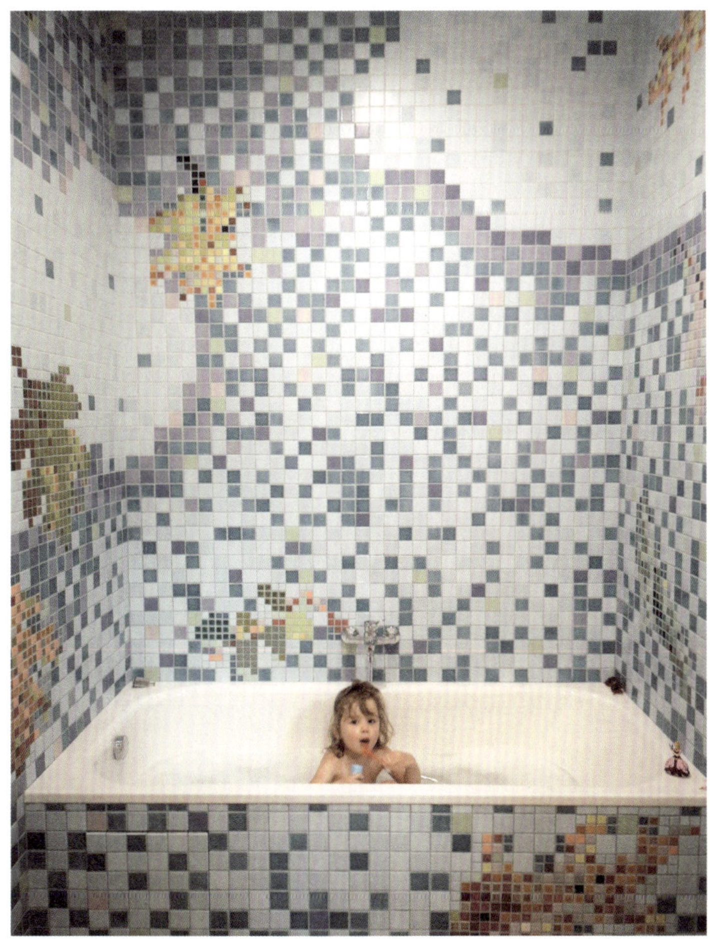

Hilma in the bathtub

JUNE–AUGUST 2021
François Lancien-Guilberteau

Regarding Vincent van Gogh, I had read the correspondence between him and his brother Theo. I tried to get into the work, but maybe also because I studied for a while in Amsterdam, there was too much being said about Van Gogh, too many fucking tote bags. I'm not saying that the residency did anything to change that. But I can just say that I went to the Van Gogh show at the Musée d'Orsay a few months ago, and I was really deeply moved. Really. Rarely I've been moved by this body of work. So maybe there was actually an effect, a Van Gogh effect, from spending time in Arles. That actual body of work was not done in Arles, but at the end of his life, in Northern France. They had one of his last series, which is done on panels that are 50 × 150 cm. So a bit like a movie-screen format. Those really spoke to me.

I had just met Laura Owens once, at dinner in Arles during Julie Beaufils's stay. That's when we were invited for dinner, and that's when I met Laura.

I had been to Arles as a kid. I have very slight memories of the arena. I also used to spend time in Nîmes when I was a kid, at my parents' friends' house. So we probably also spent time in Arles. But it was a very different experience—because I was a kid, of course, but also the city

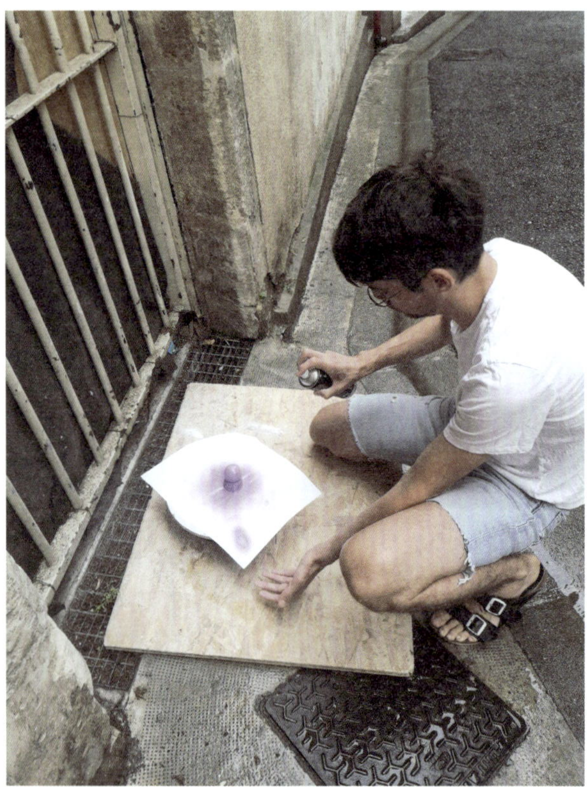

François Lancien-Guilberteau respraying Miriam Laura Leonardi's sculpture

was very different and much more working class back then.

I had just opened a solo show in Treignac, and I was kind of hoping the residency would be a break. I was also not the main guest. I was with my partner, Charlotte, rather than actually invited, and I was hoping it would be a moment when things settled, and that was definitely not what I should have expected. When we arrived, LUMA was about to open. There were a lot of parties. And we were with our daughter, so it was not at all the peaceful interlude I'd expected. Arles is a city where you can really see a certain power structure. What seems more diluted in a big city becomes really visible all the time in a city like Arles. It was interesting to see, when you were having a drink, that people sometimes were talking about the art world but were lowering their voices.

When we got to the house, there were things in the staircase, and there were Julie's works around the windows, and there were some paintings by Jacob Eisenmann and Mona Varichon, an installation by Miriam Laura Leonardi. And they were installing the bathroom mosaics by Laura. It was not clear what the boundaries were between what we could do and what we could not do. It took a while before we felt free to do whatever we wanted, or what was the deal. And I think it had to do with basic contract and money things that were settled while we were there and made things much easier. I think this sort of shyness—if we compare to things we saw developing after us—it seemed, for the people after us, much more obvious. Or maybe it's just us,

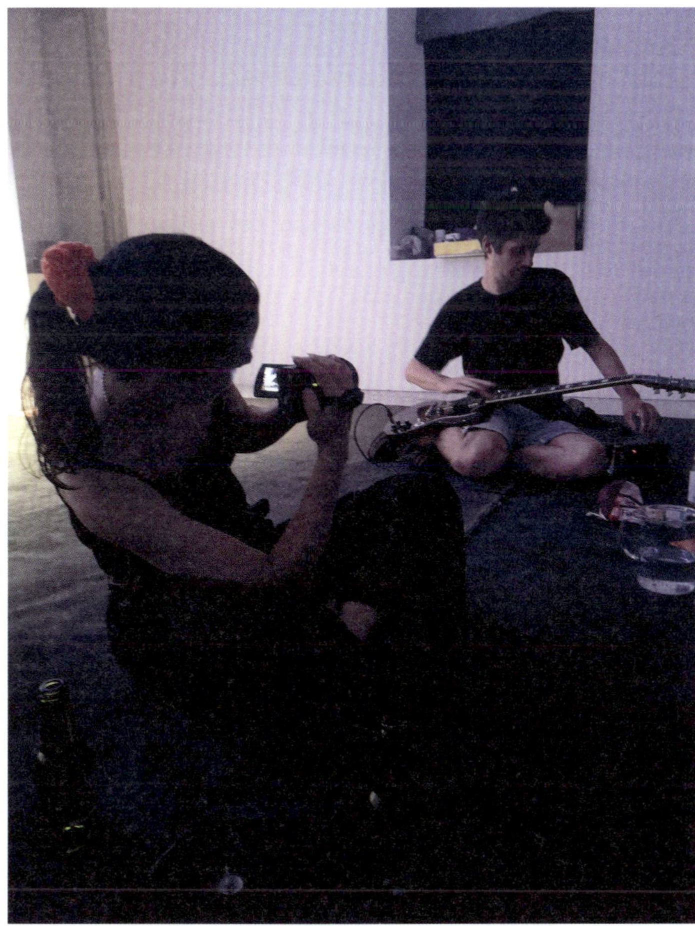

Mona Varichon filming François performing

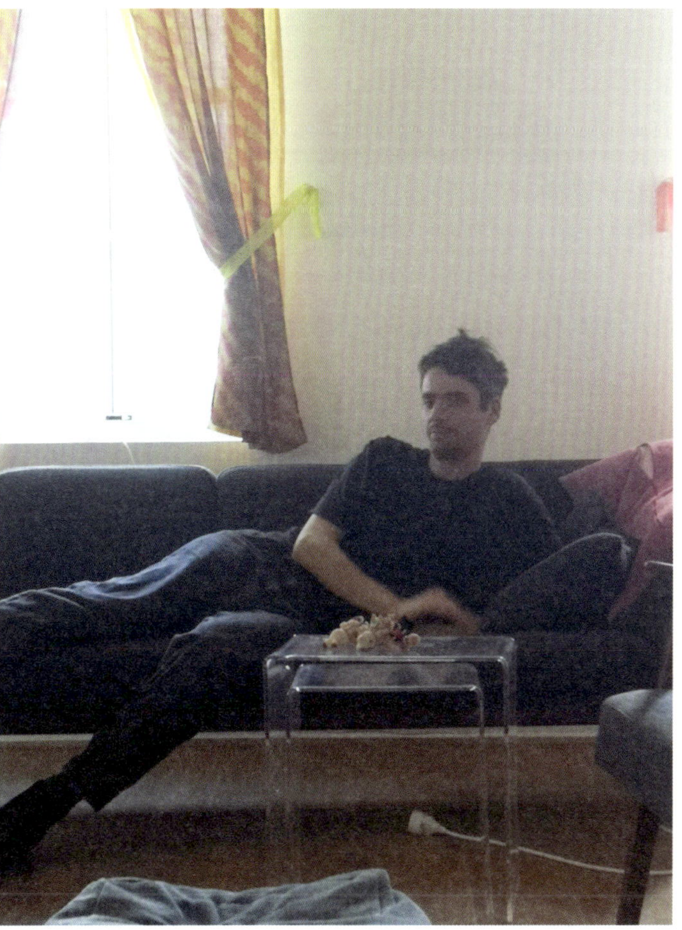

François on the couch

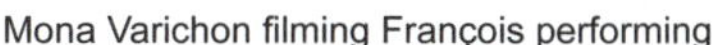
ndiana Sadie Laska Eric Palgon Alicia Vaïsse Adee Roberson Clément Rodzielski Alake Shilling Mona Varichon Jacob Eisenmann Andy Robert Alexander Zevin Blake Rayne Candida Alvarez Nova Bry

but this fact that we were not sure what was the limit of what was doable had also led us to do this film club, to make a thing that was a more social thing than a painting.

We opened the studio several times a week. I don't remember how many film nights we did. But the first idea was just to open the studio, make it public, and invite people. We were meeting a lot of people in Arles through the openings and through the art world, but also through the school, because our daughter was finishing the first year of kindergarten in Arles. So we met some parents there. So that was the first idea: trying to find a way to open the space, to invite someone to choose a film, and to have this person write an introduction to the film that we would print. We did a little zine and we organized drinks and food for the people who would come. And then there was a bunch of zines and kind of a little community, I think, even if it was short. It was not, like, a huge group of people. But there're some people who definitely showed up every time. It was called *Ciné-club Totale Dérive*.

When I was there, I had planned to make music but could not really get the right focus. *Totale Dérive* took a lot of time and energy, and basically what I did was help organize that project. Also, I did some field trips in the area to visit isolated chapels that have these ex-votos, which are basically little gifts you make for the church in order to get a wish fulfilled, or to thank whatever saint is related to your church for fixing your leg, or whatever. And usually it takes the form of a painting or small object. So I was really interested in that.

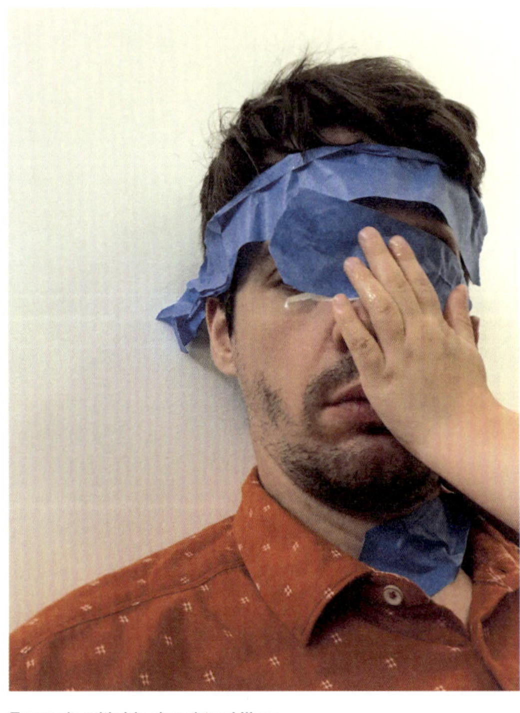

François with his daughter Hilma

The Big Bird was supposed to present the amphitheater. It was painted next to the window where you have a great view of the ruins, and the Big Bird comes with a text piece made of breadcrumbs. And so the bird is pointing his hand toward the theater ruins, and the text piece says "ars gratia artis," which is the Metro-Goldwyn-Mayer motto. It means "the art honors the artists." The bird was kind of a reference to the first film we screened, *De bruit et de fureur* by Jean-Claude Brisseau. There's a yellow bird appearing in this film, but not this Muppet bird.

The residency did create some links between some of the people who spent time there, definitely. But that was also a moment when the COVID-19 restrictions were lifted. So it was also a time of exultation. I think our film project really helped also to connect people, really helped to shape the project in that direction. It just simply created friendships, I think. Like, for example, when we organized Gary Indiana's birthday. It was just super nice.

The title *Totale Dérive* came from my time in Amsterdam when I was studying there from 2010 to 2012. There was this guy Jeffrey who was organizing a film club in squats. Three or four times a week, he was presenting an underground film in one of the many squats of Amsterdam. One of his film nights was called *Cinema Dérive*, a reference to the Situationists. For me, and for a lot of expats, it was really a kind of meeting point. I became obsessed with movies at this specific moment in my life because it was a way for me to speak about my feelings and to connect with other people through film. I think film clubs are a way to connect. And that was crucial for me

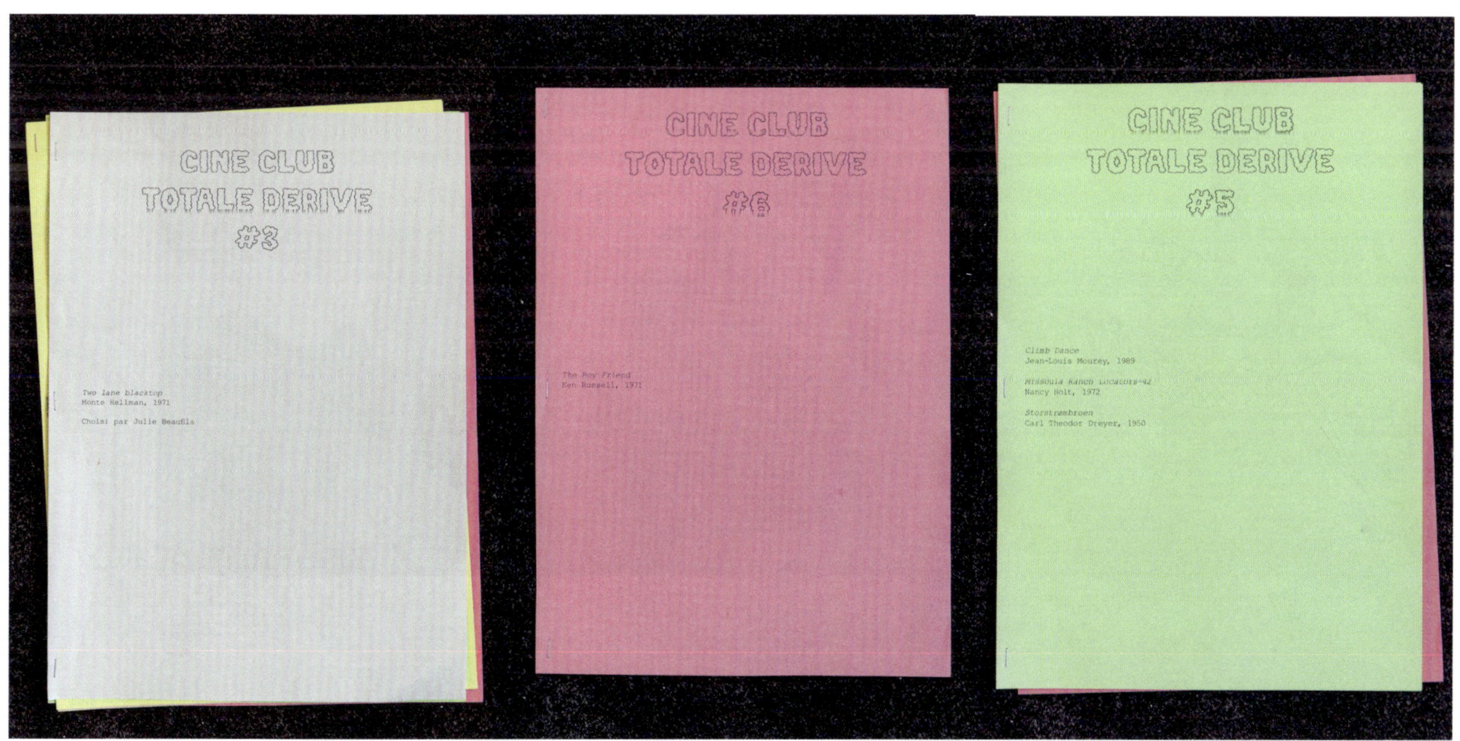

Zines for various *Ciné-club Totale Dérive* screenings

at this time because, sometimes, being an expat can be very lonely. And it worked the same way in Arles. That was a great way to make friends!

Seeing the final form of the house was nice, of course. My experience in this short moment of time when we were in the house—there was definitely a lot going on. But most of it did not leave physical traces. And about what's left in the building—hard to say. I still don't really know what it is. It also depends on what they want to do with it. It really depends on how they want to present it. You know, a suggestion would be, keep the house open for the people who've been there. Don't close the thing. If you start framing it by closing it, you start to define it. Then it's just a bunch of artworks in a building, and if I put myself in the shoes of a random spectator, I'm like, "Cool, a bunch of lucky artists lived there."

If it's a project that keeps going on, and if the people who spent time there and made something can keep on doing it, that's where the meaning is: in using it and living inside with the artworks. And that's what's interesting. I think it should keep changing and growing, and stay alive somehow.

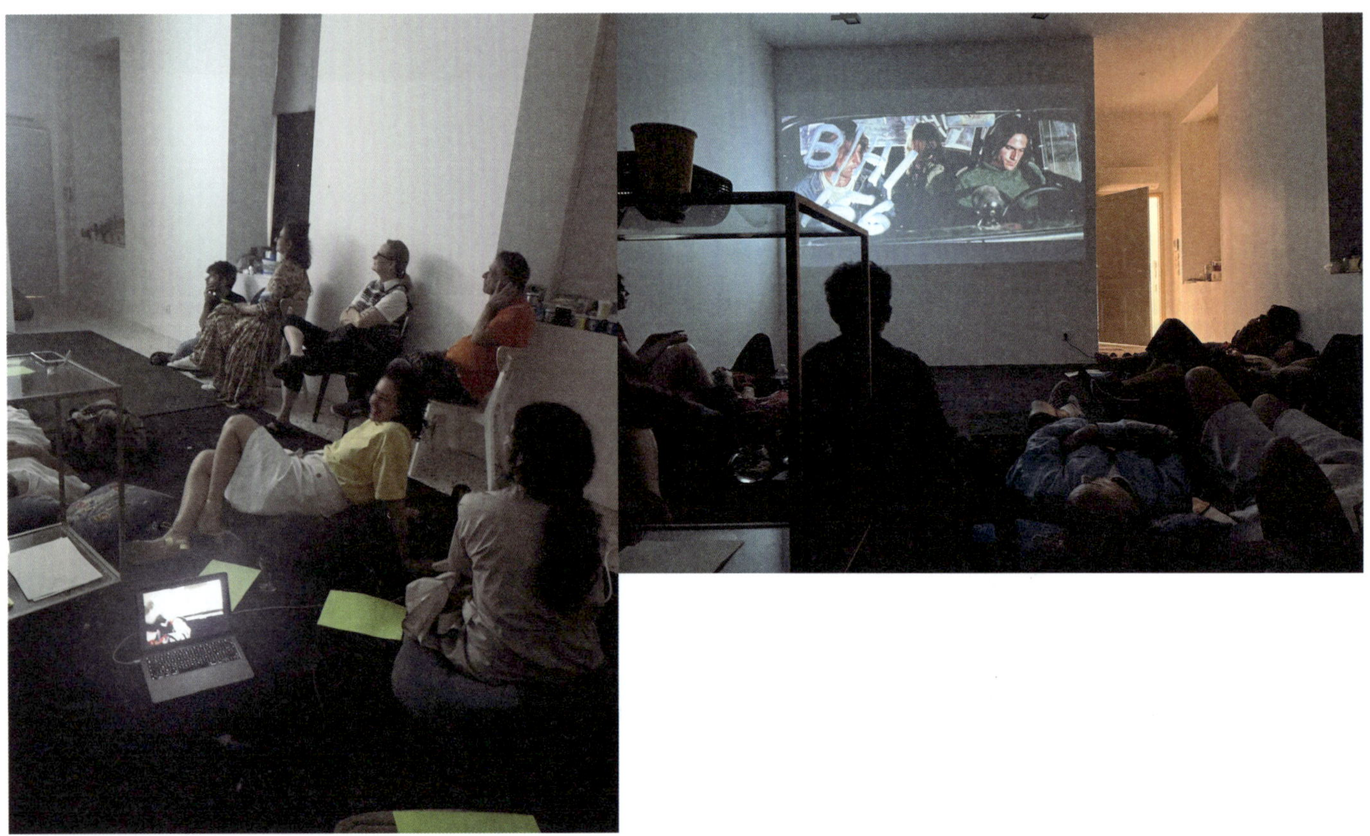

The audiences at *Ciné-club Totale Dérive* screenings

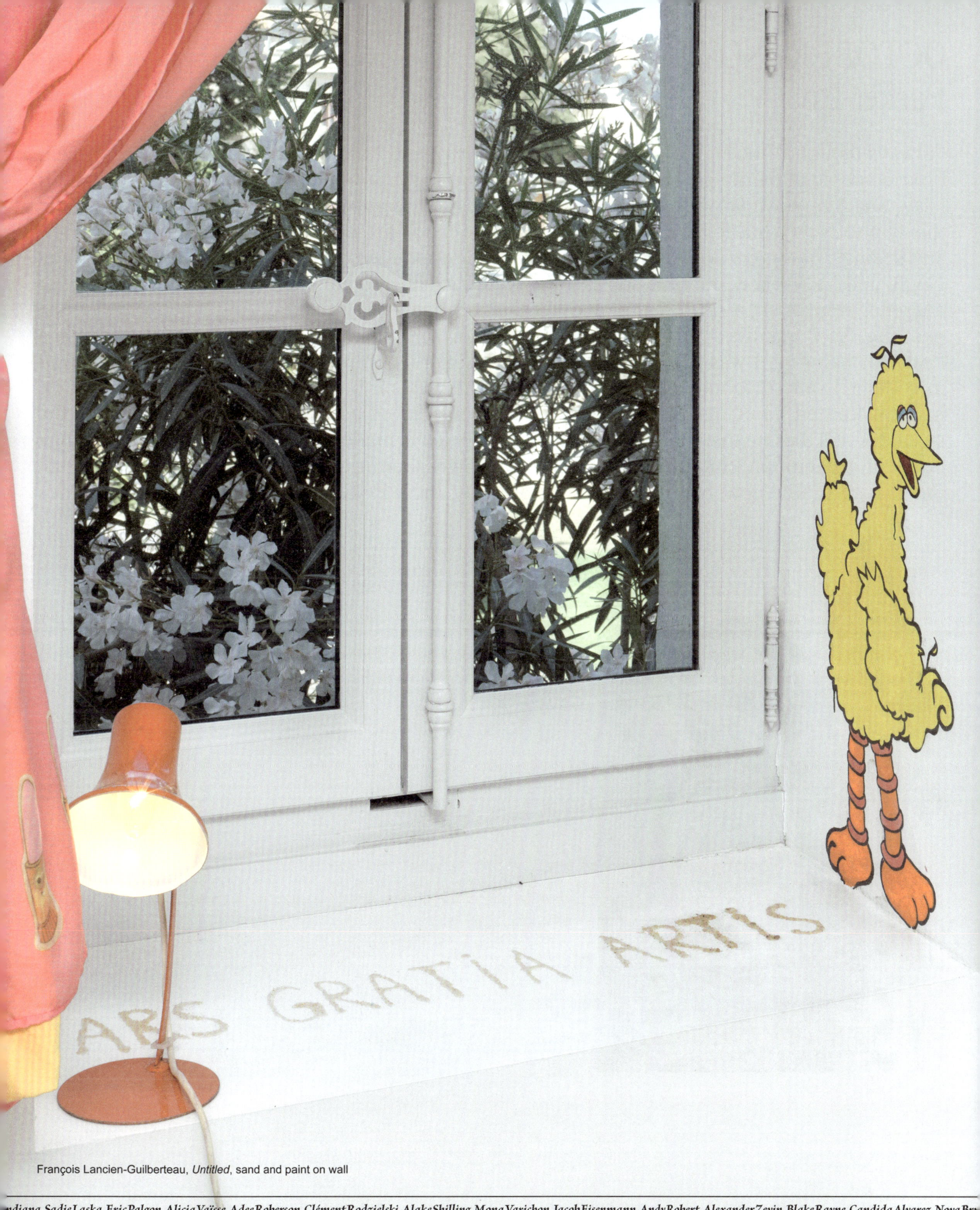

François Lancien-Guilberteau, *Untitled*, sand and paint on wall

Parker Ito

I always thought Vincent van Gogh was kind of corny, and I didn't really like his art very much. I like a couple of paintings. I've been to the museum in Amsterdam, but I don't remember at all. I saw *The Starry Night* when I was, like, eighteen. I didn't grow up going to art museums. I did this trip to New York for the first time and saw so much art, and I remember going to MoMA and seeing *The Starry Night*, and I was kind of disappointed. And my aunt is really into Van Gogh, and I think the first time she saw the painting, she had gone with a friend of hers whose daughter was an art history major, and her friend's daughter started crying when she saw the painting. So I was like, "Holy shit," like, you know, "This is gonna be amazing." And when I saw the painting, I was just like, "Oh, that's just another painting. It's not that exciting." And in college, I saw somebody on Facebook posting about their uncle or something, and the uncle had this knitted Van Gogh *Starry Night* sweater, and I loved how it looked. And so I found the sweater—it's the one that I left at the residency—which is made by this company, St. Croix, that does limited-edition knitted sweaters of well-known paintings every season. That Van Gogh one is hard to find now, but it just came up on eBay and was kind of expensive. Being in Arles

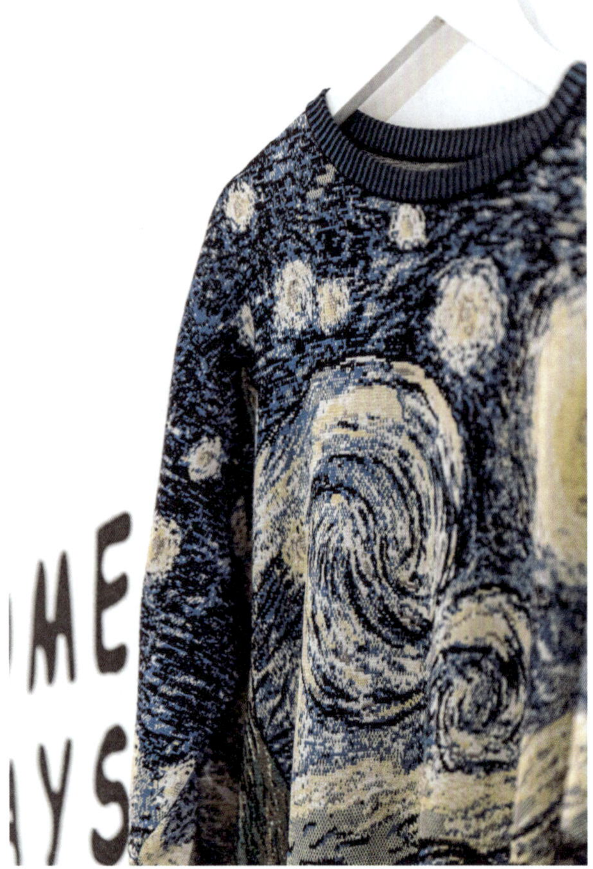

Parker Ito's Van Gogh sweater

didn't really change how I felt about him. I think my knowledge of him changed a lot because I didn't know that he was so obsessed with Japanese culture. I know that was a whole thing in Europe at that time, but he said some really funny shit, like that Arles was the Japan of Europe because the light in Arles was really similar to the light there. He never went to Japan, so I'm not sure how he knew that. Even the Yellow House, I'm pretty sure, was all based on concepts that came directly out of Japanese philosophy and art. So that was a huge thing I was unaware of that I discovered on my own. I went to Las Vegas after I was in Arles, and I saw the "Van Gogh Experience," and I still think he's kind of annoying. The lesser-known paintings are some of the better works. I mean, I love the *Skull of a Skeleton with Burning Cigarette* painting—that's a pretty well-known one. There's one painting, maybe at the Norton Simon Museum in Pasadena, that's pretty good. Laura Owens did that whole talk about the way that he kind of sits in culture, that the idea of an artist is filtered through Van Gogh. His shit is kind of everywhere, but doing the residency didn't really change how I felt about him.

Laura and I first met, I think, in 2014. I of course knew her work. Her show *12 Paintings* at 356 Mission, Los Angeles, had just happened, which was a major show in LA, so everyone was talking about her. I had dinner with her at Speranza, which is a restaurant I don't really like. Two really memorable things about that dinner: One, Val Kilmer had been at my studio earlier that day and it came up in conversation, and she was sort of making fun of me, like, "Oh, you

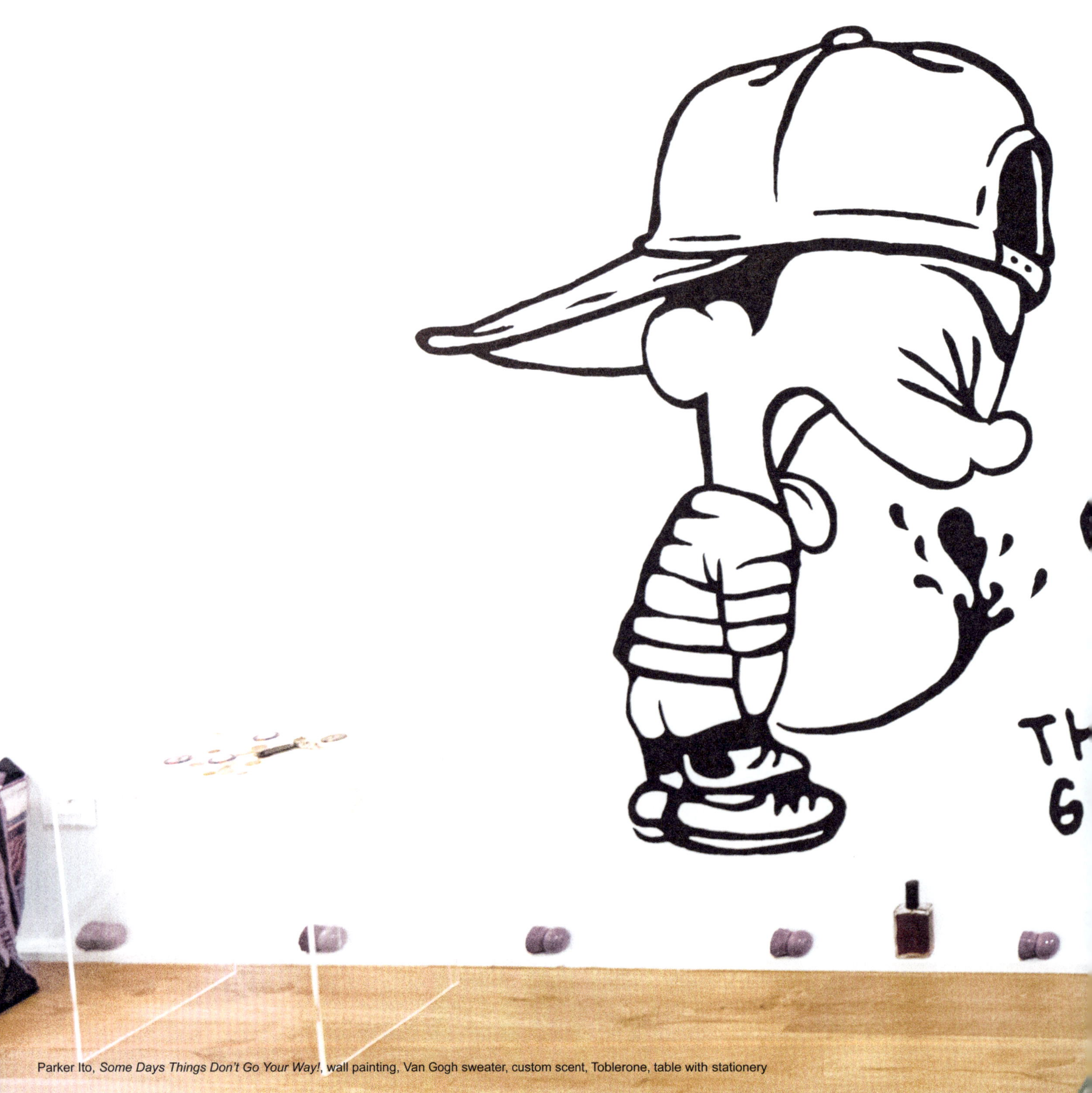

Parker Ito, *Some Days Things Don't Go Your Way!*, wall painting, Van Gogh sweater, custom scent, Toblerone, table with stationery

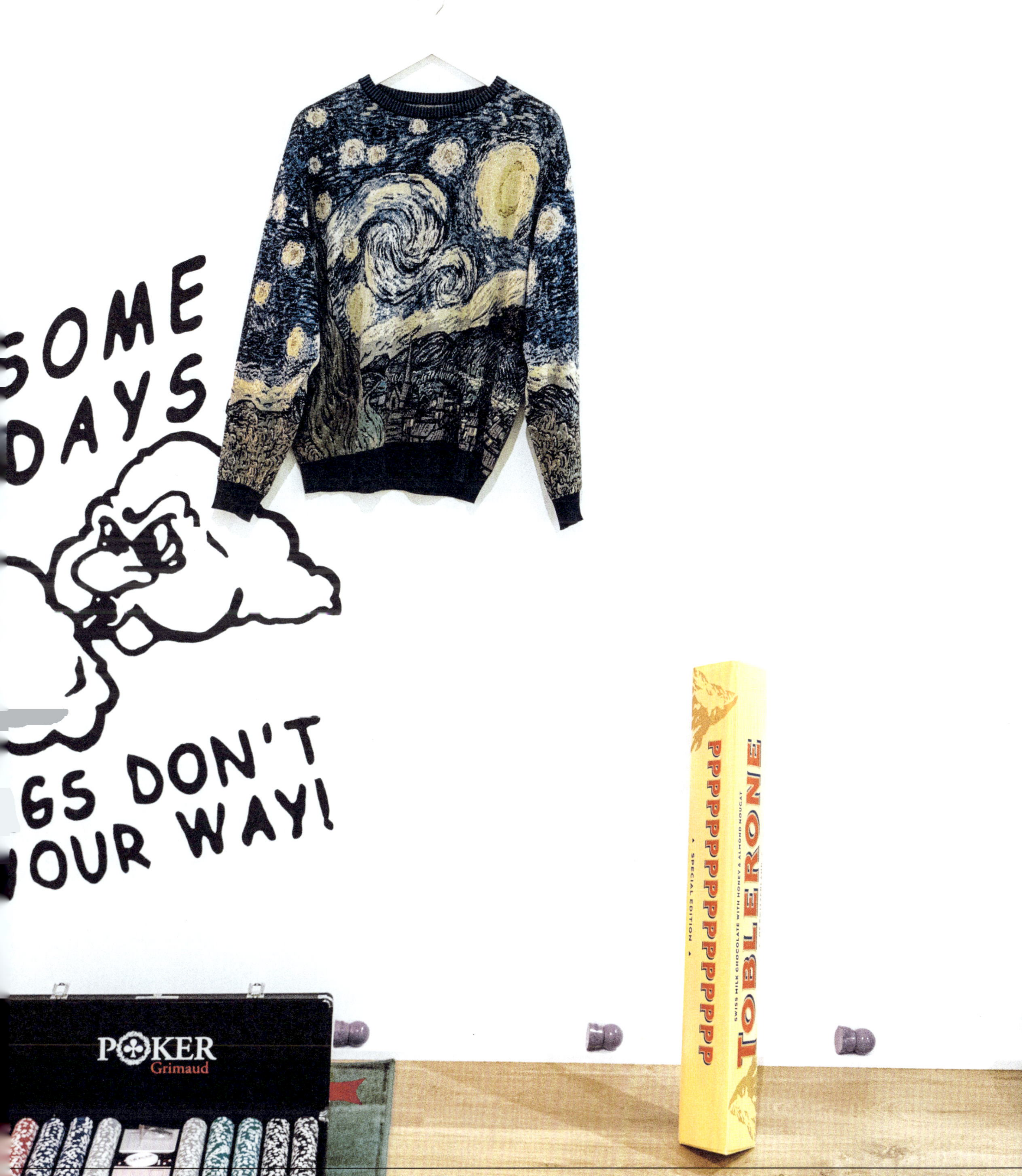

SOME
DAYS
GS DON'T
OUR WAY!
POKER
Grimaud
TOBLERONE
SWISS MILK CHOCOLATE WITH HONEY & ALMOND NOUGAT
SPECIAL EDITION

think that's cool, that Val Kilmer came by your studio?" Two, I used to be really picky food-wise, and am still a little bit picky, but I used to be really crazy. I ordered spaghetti with just tomato sauce—that was it. And she also made fun of me for doing that. She said, "Oh, you eat like my children." And then I would just see her around, and we became friends. My very first time in Arles would have been in 2019, and I knew Laura was doing the show at the Fondation Vincent van Gogh Arles. She set up a walk-through with Julia Marchand at the Fondation Vincent van Gogh, and there was this really cool show of this Georgian painter, Niko Pirosmani. I think the plan had been, like, a year from then, Laura would do her show, but it got postponed because of COVID-19. And then all of a sudden, she was living there, and I visited for her opening at the Fondation. There were a bunch of people there that I knew, and people were talking about this residency. I didn't really understand what it was or that Laura had set it up herself. I said something to her, like, "Oh, I want to do this residency. Who do I gotta talk to?" In Laura fashion, she was like, "I don't know, somebody at this party, but it's not me." But everyone I asked said it was Laura's residency and you have to get her to put in a good word for you. So I realized she had set up this whole project about continuing the idea of the Yellow House, expanding on it, inviting artists to live there and create this living, breathing artwork. The next day, I went to the house, and I realized it was a big thing that was a lot more involved, so I told Laura I wanted to do it, and I started my residency in October 2021.

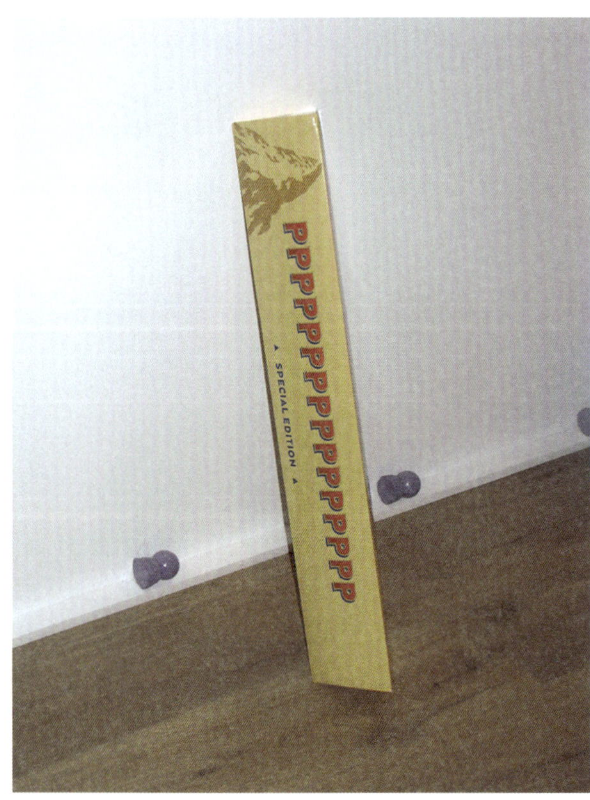

Parker Ito, *Some Days Things Don't Go Your Way!* (detail)

I had seen pictures of the house on Instagram, but I didn't put together that it was a cohesive project that had a specific purpose. And I was super excited by that because I'm into installation and site-specificity, so it was perfect for me. I was the fourth artist. Not the first international artist but the first American artist; the first artist that actually had to fly into France. So my thing felt a bit different. COVID-19 was still happening and the house was pretty fresh when I did it. I basically tried to take up as much space as possible. I really wanted to do a lot more and had all these aspirations to do so many things. But I ran out of energy and realized I couldn't complete everything. I think I did something on every floor, but I wanted to do more. I really wanted to make a wall-ride ramp. I wanted to skate in the house and set up the ramp in each room—get the marks from the wheels on the wall. It became this issue, though, of getting the materials; there's no skate shop in Arles, and I don't know how to make a ramp. It sounds really American to say "I wanted to stand out and be different," but I think it would have brought a different energy to the house than a lot of the stuff that's there. Gabriele said something about how everything in the house was sort of precious, and I wish that I had skated in the house. Most of the works I did make in the house came from realizing that Van Gogh was fetishizing Japanese culture. That was a thing that existed in my work outside of Van Gogh, but it aligned with some of the stuff I was making. A lot of my work was inspired by just being there. Some of it was kind of quotidian, like, I don't think it's there anymore, which I'm really sad about. There was a bag that I stuck on

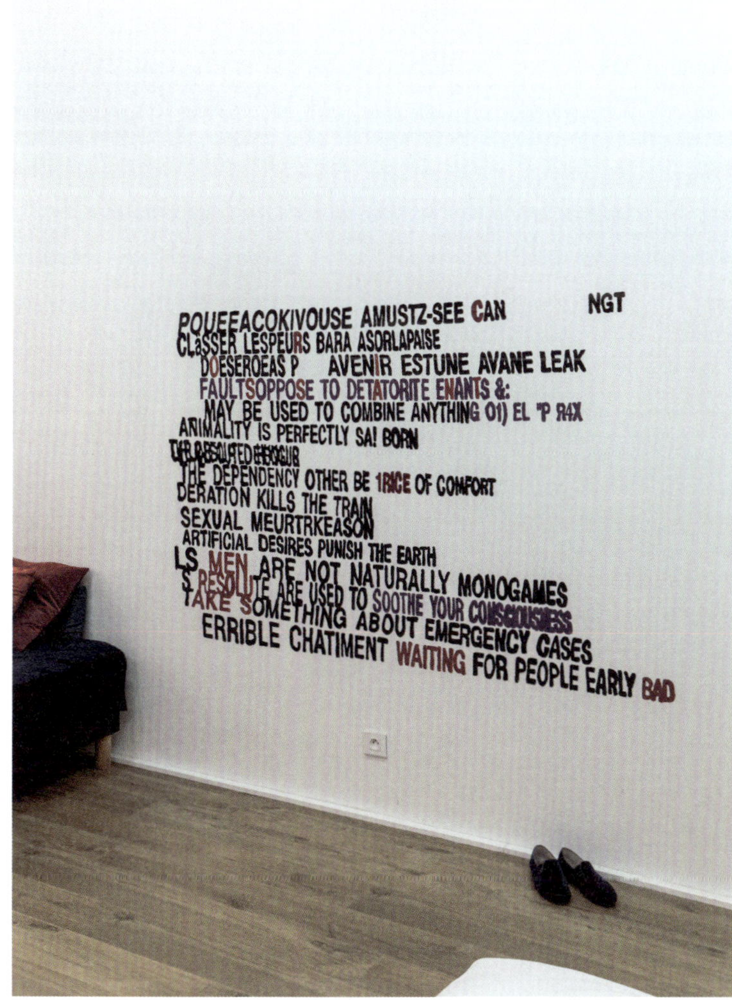

Parker Ito, *The Ineffable Ecstasy of Art*, wall painting

the roof. It was the bag that I used to get groceries—one of those reusable, plasticy grocery bags with an Aix-en-Provence theme, so it had lavender fields on it. There was a ladder that they had left in the house, so I stuck it out the skylight of the very top floor and crawled out onto the roof. It was kind of scary because the roof is not flat, and it's that old kind of tile, so it could break, but it was nice up there. There was a wire on top of the building that I attached the bag to. The title of the piece was *Capturing the Mistral*. That was another thing, this mistral—I didn't really know about that. But then, you know, it's depicted in *The Starry Night*—it's the swirls in the sky, and it's something that's very particular. I remember, when Laura gave a talk about Van Gogh, she showed a movie clip where an actor playing Van Gogh is in a field trying to paint, and the mistral sweeps up all of his art materials. Maja Hoffmann was in the audience, and she started laughing, and she was like, "Mistral!" I didn't go on the roof when I went back, so I actually don't know if the bag is still there. You could see it from the park. It could have just blown to the other side, but it also could have just blown off. I had never really lived in a space for that long, engaging with it in that way. So it was a somewhat unique experience. I don't think I've really done anything else like that. It's funny how everything I made somehow got covered up or thrown away. But I was up for the challenge of engaging with the space and making something for it, something that belonged there. It was total immersion in this thing. I was just trying to push it to the limit, in terms of what I could do in the time I had.

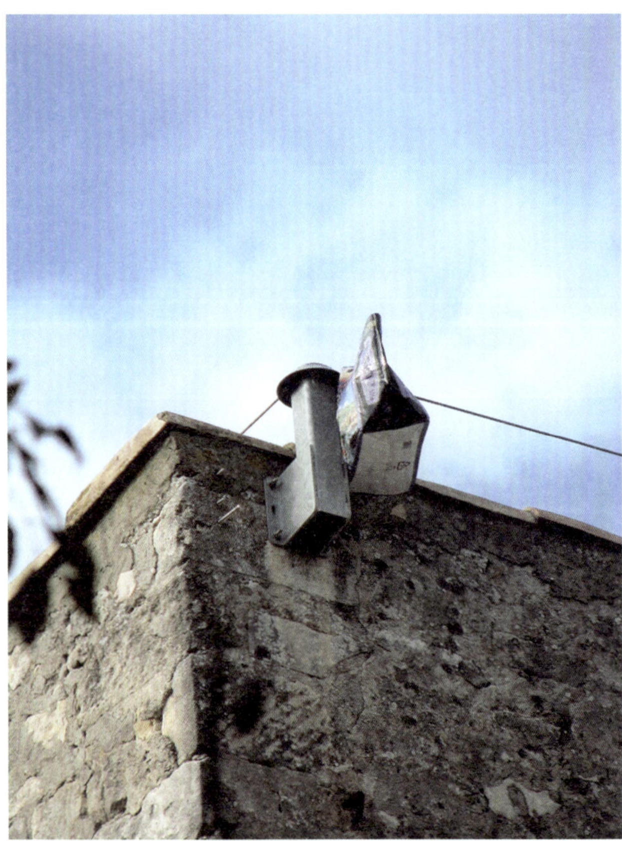

Parker Ito, *Capturing the Mistral*, tote bag attached to wire

I think only one person asked me if it was OK to cover up my work, and that was Elliot Kaufman, when he painted the *Les Misérables* thing. Naoki Sutter-Shudo had told me that he had covered up my thing, but it was almost like he did it because he—he was really funny. He was like, "Oh, it was in the bedroom, and I just couldn't sleep with it on the wall. It was annoying me, so I had to put this thing over it." And I was like, "OK, yeah, that's fine. Whatever." There was a thing with Julie Beaufils's windows and these orchids where I damaged her painting. I put an orchid with my cast flower clips I had brought on the ledge with her painting, and it messed up the painting, and she had to fix it. But to be honest, when I was there, they were doing some sort of construction on the house, so there was stuff going on, and I'm pretty sure a lot of the detritus from that installation was left on top of that section where her paintings were. So I just assumed it was a place where you could set stuff. Mona Varichon accidentally threw the orchid away with the clips still on it. I think I also left the window open one day and it rained, and the piece that had the sand on it got a little messed up too. It's funny, 'cause I feel like, when I showed up, there were several people who were like, "Oh, you can't do anything over here because this person's coming back and is going to hang something here." Artists have very different personalities, and some people are more touchy about contamination. I'm definitely someone who's more wanting to mix it up, so I feel like I was the person that annoyed everyone, in a way. Everyone sort of responded to that by being like, "No, fuck you. We're gonna cover up what you did." I mean,

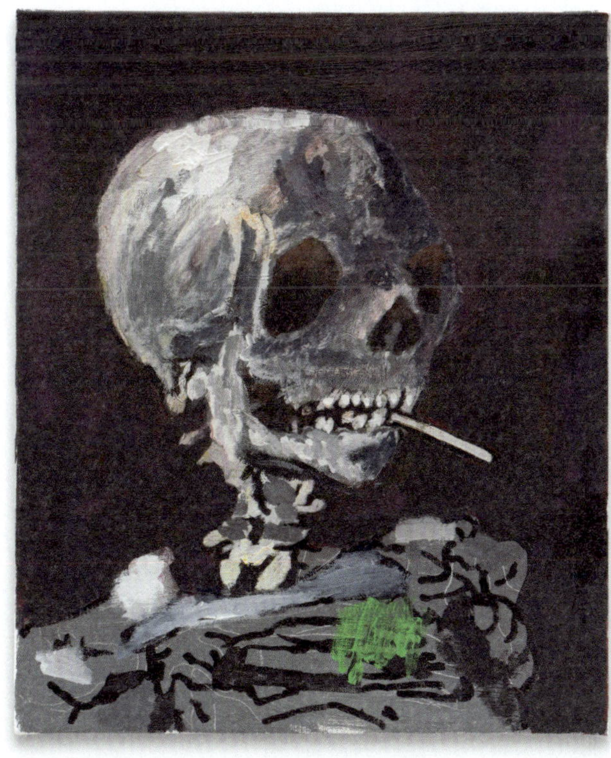

Parker Ito, *Smoking*, paint on canvas

not totally, but almost everything I'd made in the house got moved or covered up. When I was there, it seemed somewhat rigid, in that they were like, "Save this space for this person. They've already claimed this wall. Don't move that painting," you know? So I kind of thought, "Oh, if I put down stuff, then it's kind of fixed," you know? But that was not the case at all.

When I came back and saw the final version of the house, some of it I was more into than other stuff. Some of it I liked, and it felt like, maybe, the point of the project is that works exist in a gallery space in a certain way, and you don't have to be confronted by works on a daily basis in the way that you do when you're living with art. To me, the desire to modify this thing felt really important to the project, in a way. Like, certain things became kind of edgeless, where you don't know who did what, where one artist starts or ends. I liked that a lot more than "this is *my* little section, this is *my* little section." Had I known people were gonna respond to things the way they did, I probably would have responded differently, initially. I was just so early on, and so many more people came after me, you know? And the house is only so big; there are only so many walls. It's hard to tell who's trolling you versus who's collaborating, or where it's antagonistic and where it's not. The day I showed up for the show at the Fondation, Laura was like, "Oh, by the way, I also covered up one of your things." So I kind of slowly got news that this thing had been covered, then this thing had been covered, and then it was like, OK, now just about everything I've done got covered. But, to be fair, I guess, the tone of some of the stuff

I made was probably kind of antagonistic. That was not the goal, but kind of by default, because I was engaging with the way that Van Gogh had fetishized Japanese culture. Maybe there was some sort of criticality—I hate saying that, and I don't even care about that—but the work was definitely taking a more antagonistic tone toward the legacy of Van Gogh than I think a lot of the other works were. The whole "yellow fever" thing in the upstairs room with the French maid hookups girl was definitely a bit more antagonistic than some of the other stuff that was more a celebration of Van Gogh. I think a lot of European artists did the residency, and so that relationship is just very different. Specifically because I'm Japanese American, and that's going to make it a different thing. So I was the annoying one. I don't even know if the discourse of being Asian American is one that most Europeans would consider. Maybe I'm completely wrong? The Fondation posted something on Instagram about my *Yellow Fever* wall painting, and it seemed like they had no idea what "yellow fever" means, which was very entertaining for me. There's this whole thing about the Flashe paint—it was all left there from Laura, and there's a color in Flashe that's called "Japanese yellow light," or something like that. If that was a color in America, people would make a big deal about it or be like, "This is a problem." Europeans are just like, "Yeah, it's Japanese yellow. Whatever."

I was there alone most of the time, which was fucking weird because that house is huge. I get really creeped out easily, so I was super scared all the time. Also, the way the street is set

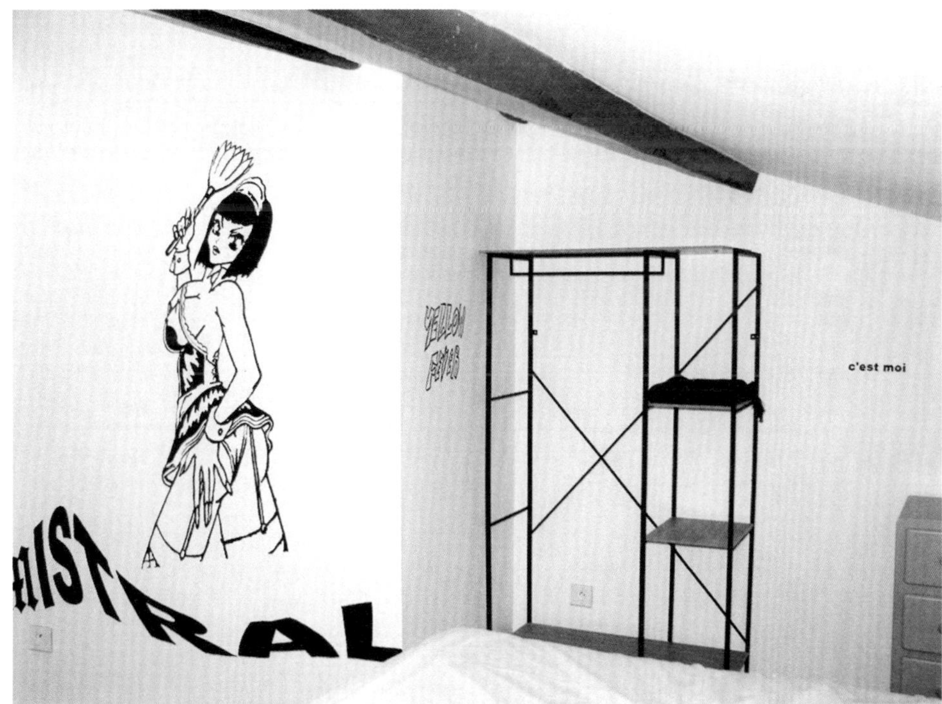

Parker Ito, *(Mistral) Yellow Fever – C'est Moi*, wall painting

up—when people would walk by and talk, it sounded like they were in the house. So I'd always be like, "What the fuck?" I'm very introverted, and I kind of keep to myself. I did a couple of things, though. I went to a Halloween party with some people who are now friends of mine—the woman who runs Sans Titre Gallery in Paris, Marie, and her boyfriend, Romain. Her family has a home there; I met them through one of the High Art gallery guys. As for other townspeople— no one. I barely spoke to anyone at LUMA except for Julie Boukobza. There were three things I did a lot of: play poker on my phone, work out, and make art in the house. There's a sports park outside of town. They had a pull-up bar and a track. I was good at calisthenics and jumping rope at the time, so I'd spend about an hour and a half or two hours a day working out there. I didn't eat out a lot because I hate speaking French and didn't want to deal with that. Also, everything was closed because I was there in the fall, so the city was drastically different than in the summer. I was in the house a lot, and I don't really cook, so I'd buy these premade soups and eat them cold, and a lot of yogurt.

I didn't feel community locally. But I would say that maybe a quarter of the people that did the residency, I was friends with. I'd met Miriam Laura Leonardi before in LA, playing poker, because of Bel Ami gallery and Eric Kim. So when I came for Laura's show, I traveled from this residency I was doing in Como, Italy. Gabriele Garavaglia came and visited me in Como because the city that he's from is pretty close to there. And then I drove back with him to Switzerland

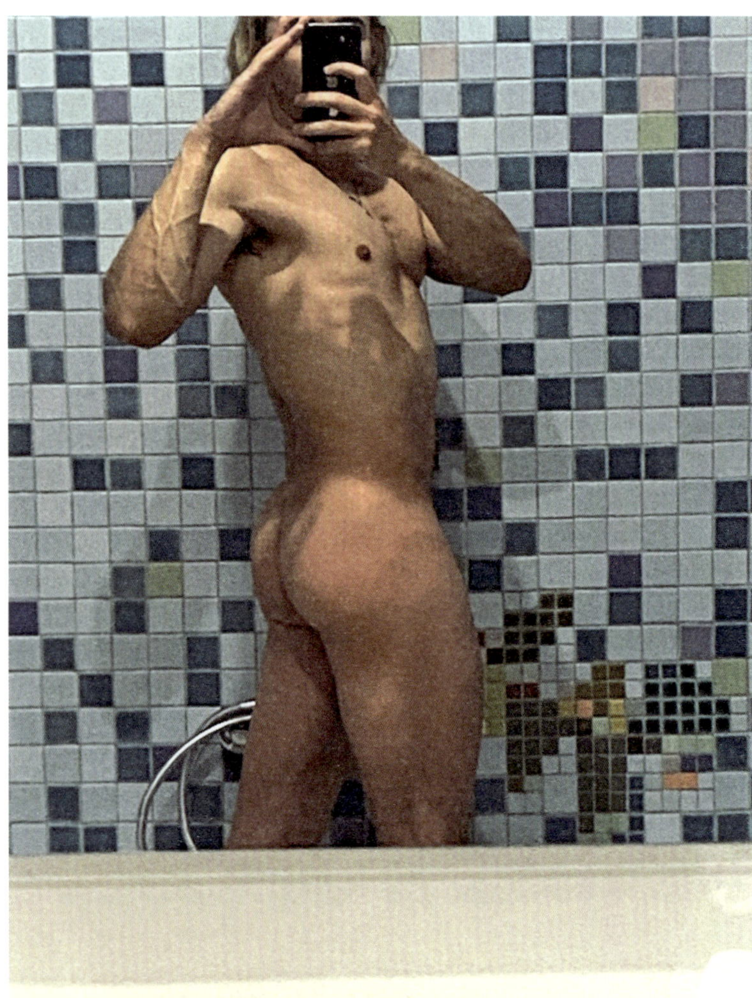

Parker in the bathtub

and spent time with him and Miriam. I don't want to say community is something I don't care about, because I do. But it's not why I make art, and it's not why I engage in art, to be a part of a community. I think because I'm quite introverted, I just keep to myself. It's not, like, something where I was like, "Oh, I'm going to do this residency and be part of this community and be really active and meet everyone." So that's definitely not as important to me. But I know that's really important to Laura and that everything she touches becomes like that. So I do feel like, via her, I am connected to this thing and this project. And going back to Arles for the show at the Fondation and seeing everyone together, you definitely get a sense of that. There were people I didn't really know very well who I got to spend time with and become a little bit closer to. But I'm at a point where I don't really feel like I'm part of the art world in the way that I used to be. And so all of these things are not as important to me—they were never super important to me. I know Miriam and Charlotte Houette had events in the house, and I just had no interest in doing that. I just like making art. That was my whole thing: I just want to be in this house by myself and try to make as much as I can.

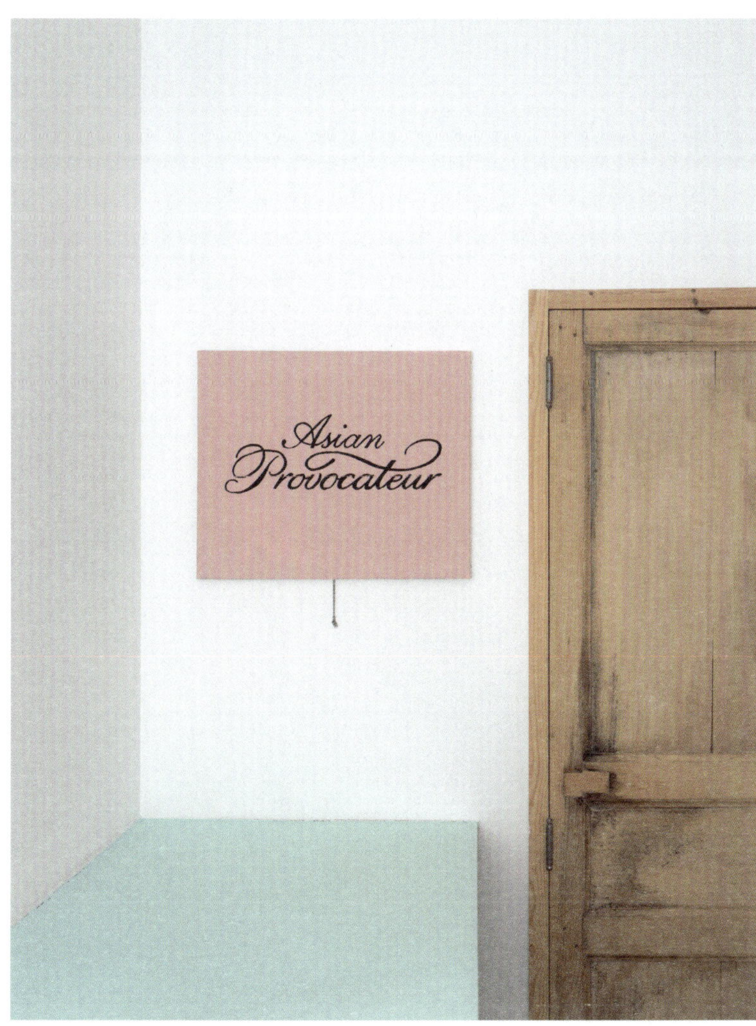

Parker Ito, *Asian Provocateur*, paint on canvas, necklace

NOVEMBER–DECEMBER 2021
Julien Ceccaldi

When I was seven, we lived for four years in the Oise department near Paris, and at the Musée d'Orsay, they have the Vincent van Gogh painting *The Church at Auvers*. My dad is not really a painter, but as a hobby, he wanted to do a replica in a kind of paint-by-numbers way. He gave up after a few months because that's not the right technique—it would take forever to paint it pixel by pixel. Later, he made a digital 3D model of *Bedroom in Arles*. That one was a success, although you couldn't move the camera too much. He didn't want to take liberties with the information that's not visible in the image, and it's a narrow room anyway. My parents like art that is sanctified by art history, so my relationship to Van Gogh is seeing his paintings in museums as a child.

One of the first times I met Laura Owens is immortalized in an *Artforum* diary. There is a photo of us, around the time of one of the three Paramount Ranch fairs, at an opening at Château Shatto, Los Angeles. We must have met before that night—maybe once or twice prior—because we're hugging very tightly in the photo. I think we got closer after she did a show at Gaga Mexico City. There's sisterhood among Gaga artists.

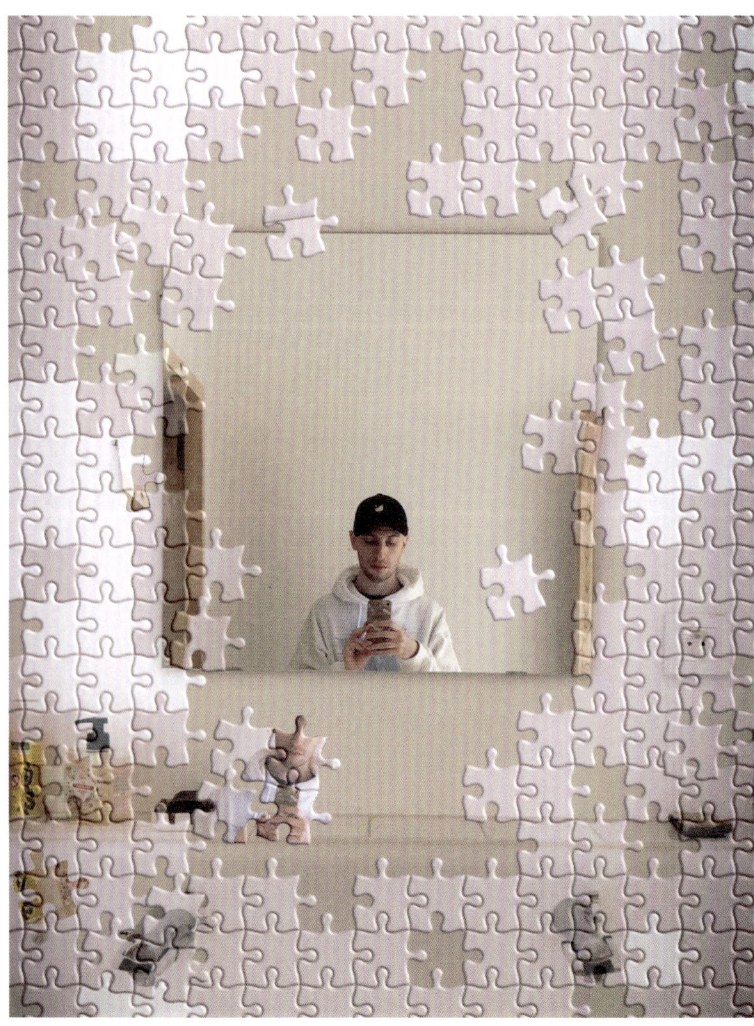

Julien Ceccaldi, selfie with digital frame

I'd never done a residency before, and I didn't see any photos of the house in advance, so I didn't know what to expect. I pictured a small, dark, wooden studio, like Van Gogh's Arles bedroom, a fraction of the size of what it turned out to be. I was already traveling to France around Christmas to visit family, so I asked if I could go in the winter. I assumed the historic building would be cold, so I thought, Oh, I'll only go for two weeks. Looking back, I should have stayed longer. I would have if I'd asked what the house looked like.

The small town we moved to in Picardy when I was young was a bit like Arles. It also had Gallo-Roman ruins, cobbled alleys, and a fountain in front of the city hall building like in Disney's *Beauty and the Beast*. So it was familiar territory, walking past medieval buildings on the way to get the daily baguette. Maybe we even visited Arles during that time. One summer, we drove south to see the Lascaux caves, then through Camargue to see Avignon, so there's a chance.

I didn't know the house would have more than one floor, let alone four. I thought it'd be a small apartment. It had the biggest studio I've ever worked in, with its own bathroom. I was shocked. I don't remember the last time I went downstairs to get from the bedroom to the kitchen.

The works that first caught my eye were the window frames and chairs by Julie Beaufils. That inspired me, and I thought, Oh, I'll probably do something in that vein—use what's already here as material. And then I saw Parker Ito's drawings and realized no wall is off-limits, no room is off-limits, you can draw anywhere. Really anywhere. But I didn't want to go too guerrilla-style.

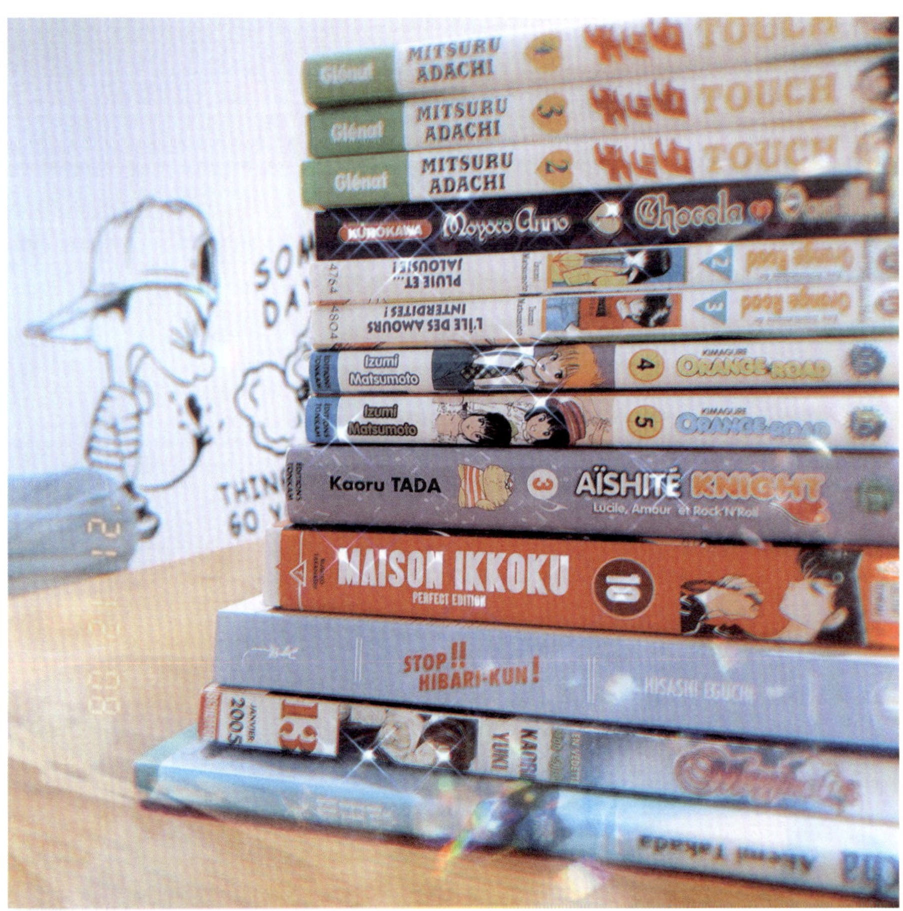

Julien's books

diana Sadie Laska Eric Palgon Alicia Vaïsse Adee Roberson Clément Rodzielski Alake Shilling Mona Varichon Jacob Eisenmann Andy Robert Alexander Zevin Blake Rayne Candida Alvarez Nova Bry

I guess I could have drawn, like, inside the cabinets or on top of Laura's pretty mosaic. I guess no one would have stopped me. It seemed wiser to paint on a white wall—it's like a blank canvas that's right here, nothing too complicated or hidden. Laura implied it was totally fine if I did absolutely nothing during my stay. So I didn't go into the residency thinking, OK, how am I going to change the house? I needed a vacation. But then I noticed that everyone before me had left a trace. I figured I would feel guilty spending my two weeks just lounging on the couch. I felt like it was kind of expected of me to leave art behind. I was told the house might end up being visited like a museum, so I conceived the chairs and the wall with an audience in mind. I thought of the mural as a gift to the house and its visitors that no one could own or even properly see in pictures. During the residency, I painted two canvases, two chairs, and a character on the staircase wall. I knew there was a chance someone would go over my wall, but it was left untouched. I had also assumed the chairs would stay in the kitchen, and they were moved downstairs to the studio, which doesn't make a big difference. I don't know where the paintings ended up; I think near the chairs.

Since I didn't arrive in Arles with a plan, I first played around with some leftover stretched canvases from Parker and Laura's Flashe paints, which I use at home too. By the time I set my mind on specific projects, like the chairs and the mural, there was no time to order paint markers or fixative spray, which I couldn't find in Arles. But that was good because I got to do a field trip, for a day, to Nîmes, where there's a Rougier & Plé art supply store. I took my courage and went on a one-hour train ride toward the unknown. I walked through the historic city and spent an hour at Terre-2, an amazing manga bookstore. The owner told me stories of pre-internet fandom—organizing for conventions, mail ordering imported stuff from Japan via ads in magazines, stuff like that.

The murals I've done before were in the context of gallery exhibitions, where I would articulate smaller works around a giant image that was the focal point. And I thought, for once I would do a mural that's not easily photographed, that's meant to be enjoyed by the people who are there in person. No photo will translate the experience because there's no proper angle to photograph it. The area is too narrow.

The idea behind this character painted near the front door is to have a little friend to welcome you and accompany you up the stairs to the light switch for the main living area. It can be a bit lonely and scary to be alone in a four-story house. I was planning on keeping this a secret, but it's also a nod to the time a gentleman caller came over and asked if I could open the door naked. So this wall painting is also a secret commemoration of the time I walked upstairs naked, kissing this man all the way to the second-floor bedroom. But I also wanted it to be a guardian angel for the house. The image is not inherently sexual; the genitals are hidden. It's also a friend who points you to where the light is if you're alone in the dark. You know, it's inspired by Michelangelo's Sistine Chapel ceiling—a "let there be light" kind of a vibe. There's a goofy aspect to the character, but it's more or less an alter ego for me and also like a phantom.

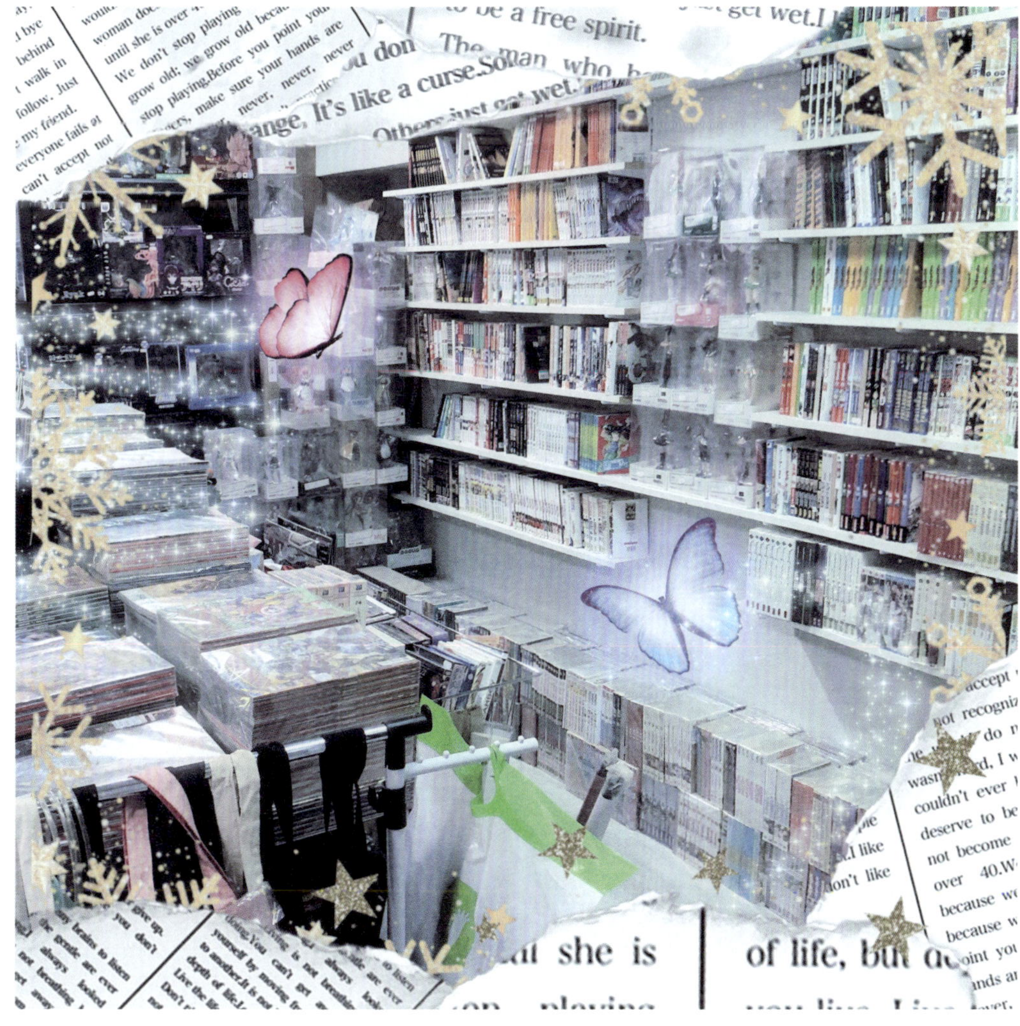

Terre-2 bookstore in Nîmes

udiana Sadie Laska Eric Palgon Alicia Vaïsse Adee Roberson Clément Rodzielski Alake Shilling Mona Varichon Jacob Eisenmann Andy Robert Alexander Zevin Blake Rayne Candida Alvarez Nova Bry

One of the first murals I did was painted directly on the big wall at the gallery Jenny's in Los Angeles. A collector bought it, and they flew me to their Paris apartment to redo it in their living room. Their wall had different dimensions and many irregularities, like two door cutouts. I changed the appearance of some characters so it would be more fun than attempting an exact replica. The second mural I sold was also originally painted directly on a wall, and it had to be reproduced for the collector as well. In both cases, I ended up painting on walls made of removable panels, which does defeat the purpose and goes against the concept of an ephemeral wall painting. But I do understand wanting the work to survive a home makeover or a real-estate upgrade.

My hope was that, after Julie Beaufils's chairs, I would paint a couple, leave some for the others, and, by the end of the residency, the whole set of eight would have been customized. I have drawn on unconventional surfaces before: T-shirts; lockers at Lomex, New York; a punching bag at Gaga; so it's not entirely out of my wheelhouse to draw on furniture. I didn't go far out of my comfort zone. I approach different surfaces with the same painting tools, whether it's a wall, an object, or a canvas. I usually depict a character contained within an object or a surface, but in this case, the chair is turned into a character itself. After the residency, I went on to make more chairs in that same style. They're so cute. The whole chair transforms into a person, and it's a little funny that you sit on their faces. I wrote a comic called *Human Furniture*, so the chairs tie in with that a little too.

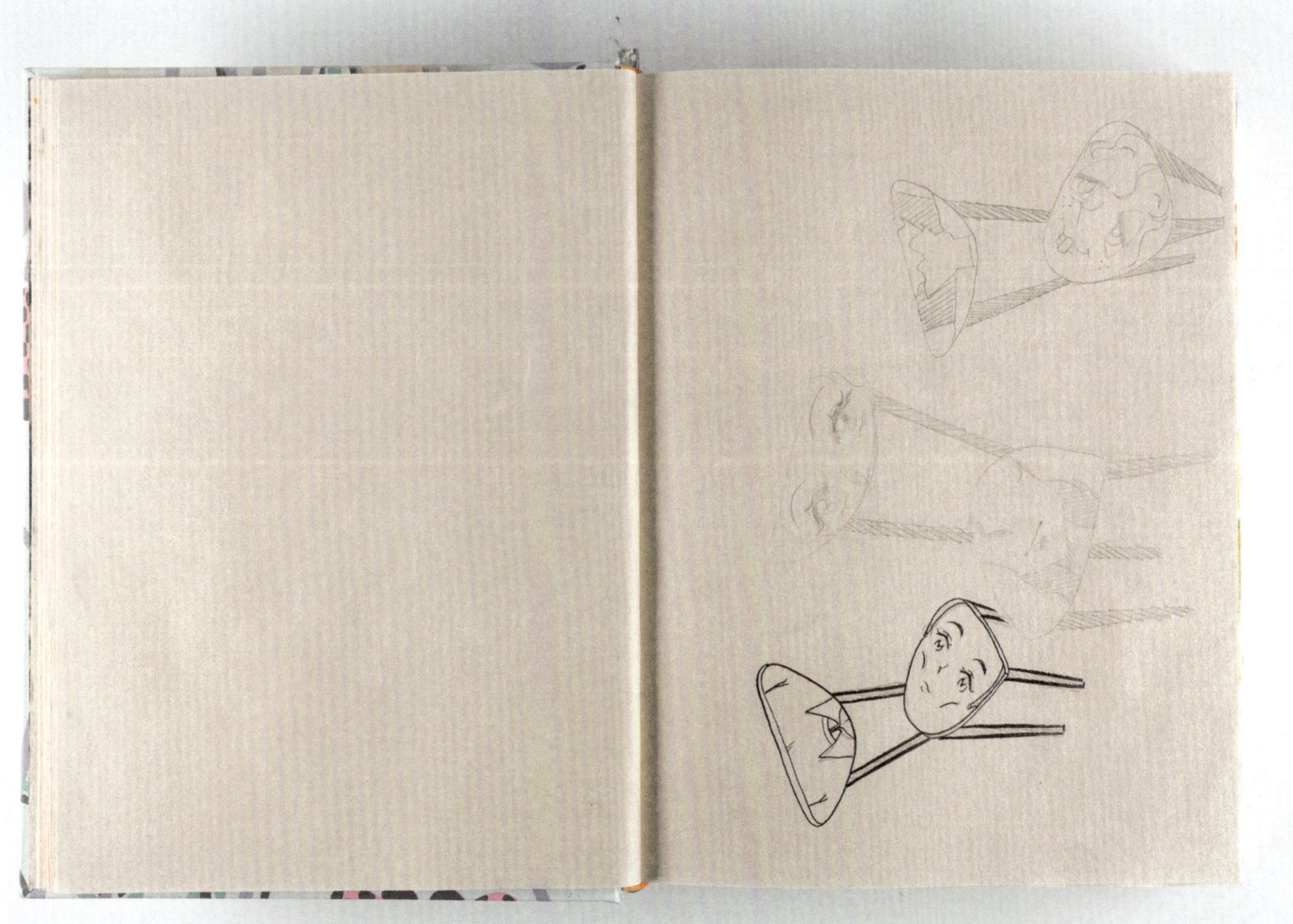

Julien's sketches of his chair designs in the guest book

ura Owens Julie Beaufils Miriam Laura Leonardi Gabriele Garavaglia Charlotte Houette François Lancien-Guilberteau Parker Ito Julien Ceccaldi Alvaro Barrington Naoki Sutter-Shudo Asha Sch

Unless you count hookups, I wasn't very social. I mostly read manga on the couch. But there were a few things I did. I arrived the night of the opening of the *Breathing One's Breath* exhibition at the Fondation Vincent van Gogh Arles. It was too late to attend the opening, but I made it in time for the big dinner at the very glam Jules César Hotel. I hadn't met Julie Boukobza; I was looking for her without knowing what she looked like. Luckily, I recognized Julia Marchand and sat with her at the same table as Julien Creuzet, who was doing the other LUMA residency. It happened very fast. I arrived late by train, hadn't recovered from the shock of how big and tall the residency house was, and then was in this opulent, Roman-style hotel designed by Christian Lacroix. I followed the crowd to a bar and got a sense of the Arles scene. Besides that, I had brunches with Julie Boukobza, and I hung out with Julia Marchand too. She invited me over for a very French wine-and-cheese with crackers and olives. It was fun to see her years after we'd met in Geneva. Her friend was a big Mylène Farmer and Alizée nerd, like me. I also remember a cute dinner with Laura and Nova Bryan. And then there was an evening we spent with Julie and Julien Creuzet at Maja Hoffmann's house. So that's maybe, like, five social nights out of fourteen.

The first thing I do in any French town is hunt for second-hand manga. I can't get enough. It's my chance to stock up on vintage titles I can't find in English. It's the second-biggest manga market, behind Japan and ahead of the US. So on my first day, after the mistral almost took me out when I went for a walk by the water, I checked out all the bookstores. And almost every day,

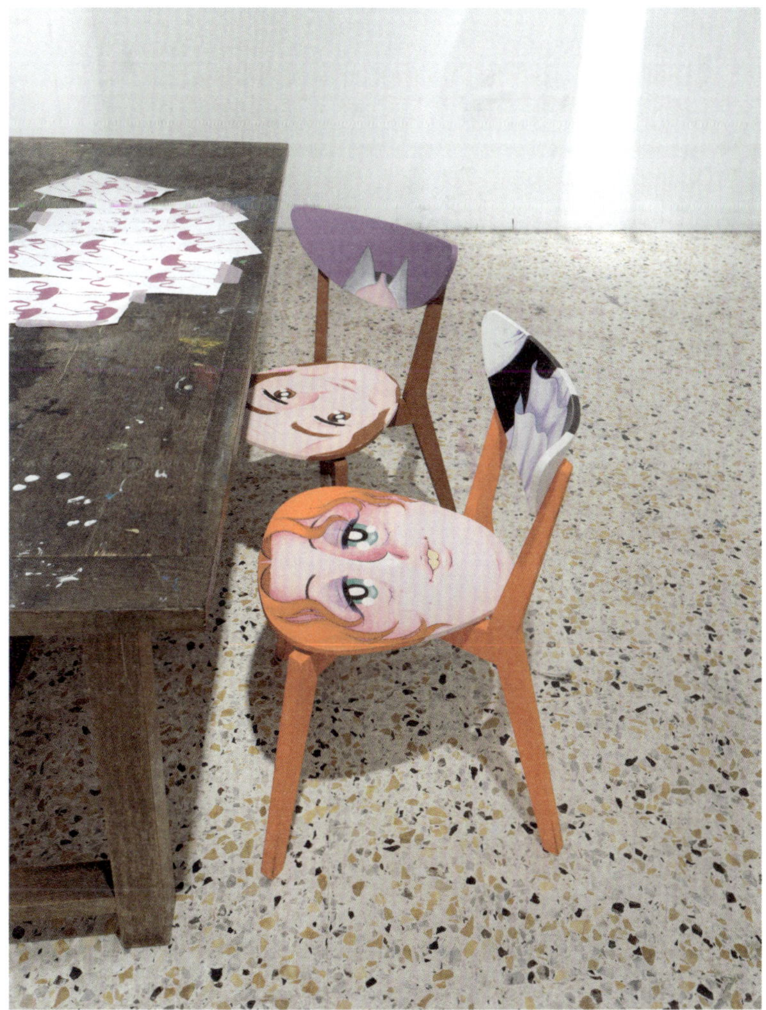

Julien Ceccaldi, *François* (top) and *Charlotte* (bottom), paint on chairs

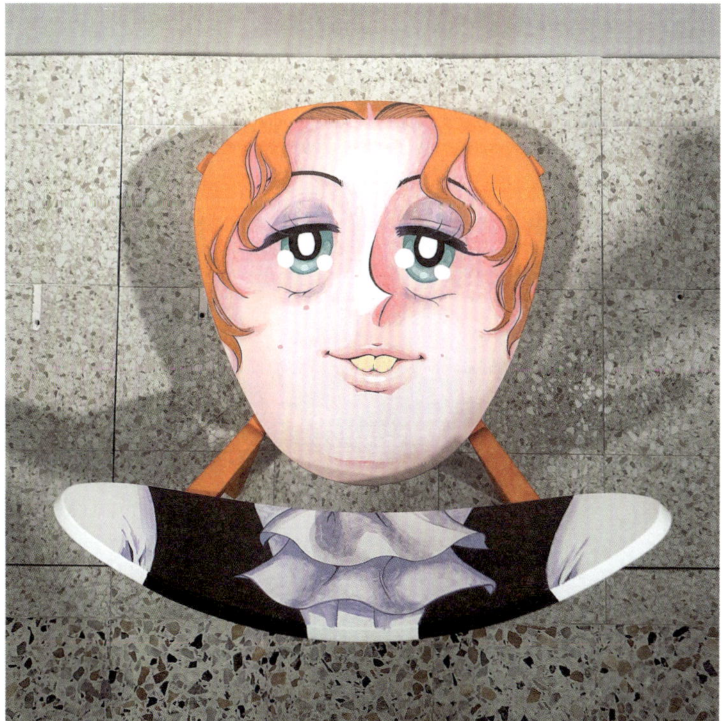

Julien Ceccaldi, *Charlotte*

liana Sadie Laska Eric Palgon Alicia Vaïsse Adee Roberson Clément Rodzielski Alake Shilling Mona Varichon Jacob Eisenmann Andy Robert Alexander Zevin Blake Rayne Candida Alvarez Nova Brya

I would buy cheese at the cheese shop. I had never frequented a cheese shop before. I'd also hunt for bakeries and pastries. I found all the spots. I guess I also found a place to buy a vegetable for a salad or something.

I also visited some houses and met locals via Grindr. One ran a quirky bed-and-breakfast in a small, converted medieval dwelling; another, who lived past the Monoprix supermarket, was looking for a human footstool. That wasn't nearly as fun as visiting Papyrus 2000, the most old-school stationery store, just around the corner from the house. They sold backpacks and pencil cases by brands I recognized from the nineties, like the girly, preppy Chipie or Naf Naf, or Poivre Blanc, which is more for the skater/surfer type. I hadn't seen those objects in years.

Besides my trip to Nîmes, I remained within walking distance from the house. I saved the touristy stuff, like the ruins and museums, for my final days when my parents came to visit, and we did all that together. They documented me painting the naked figure on the wall and they were very proud. I get emotional remembering that day.

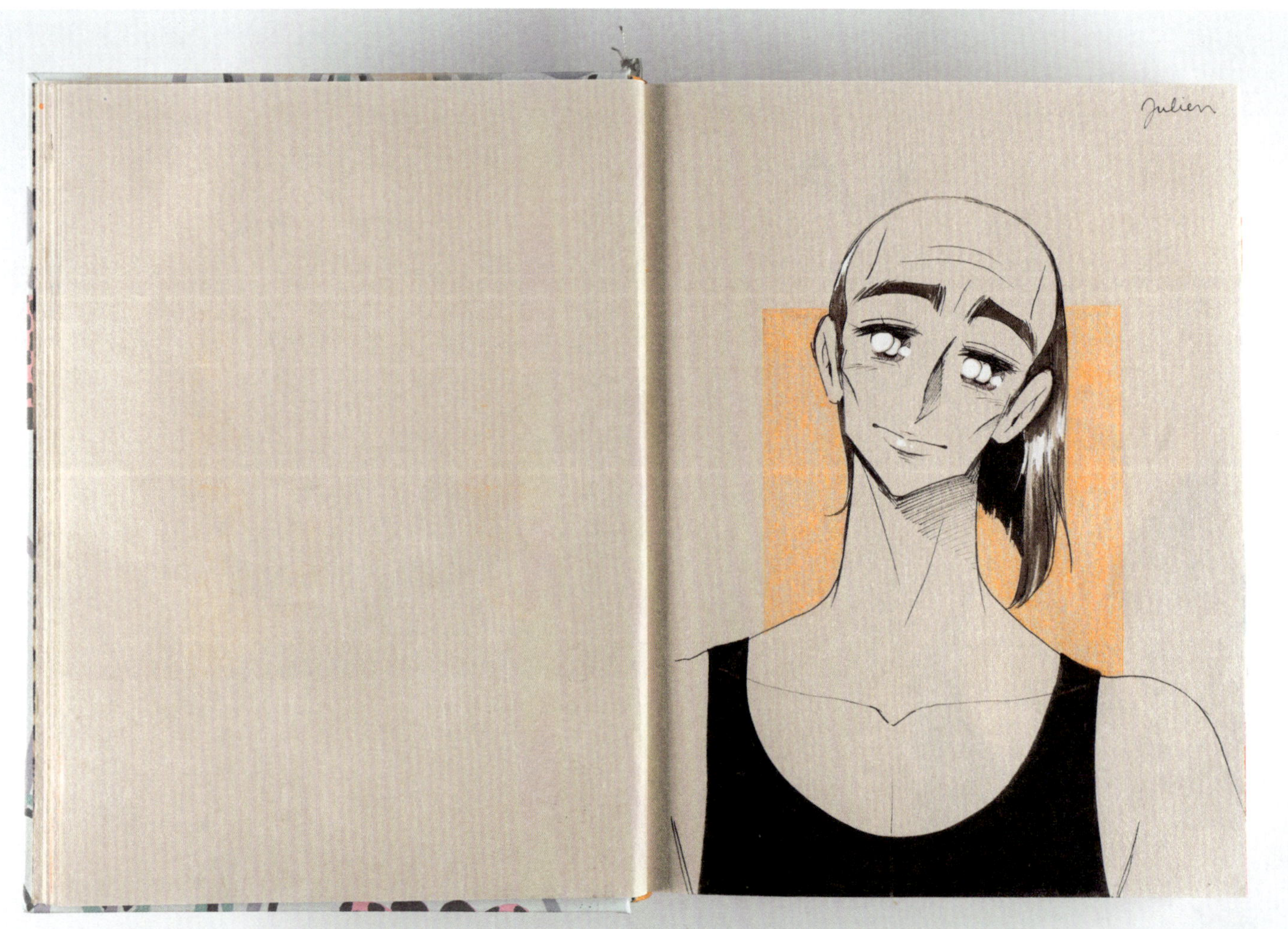

A pencil-and-ink drawing by Julien in the guest book

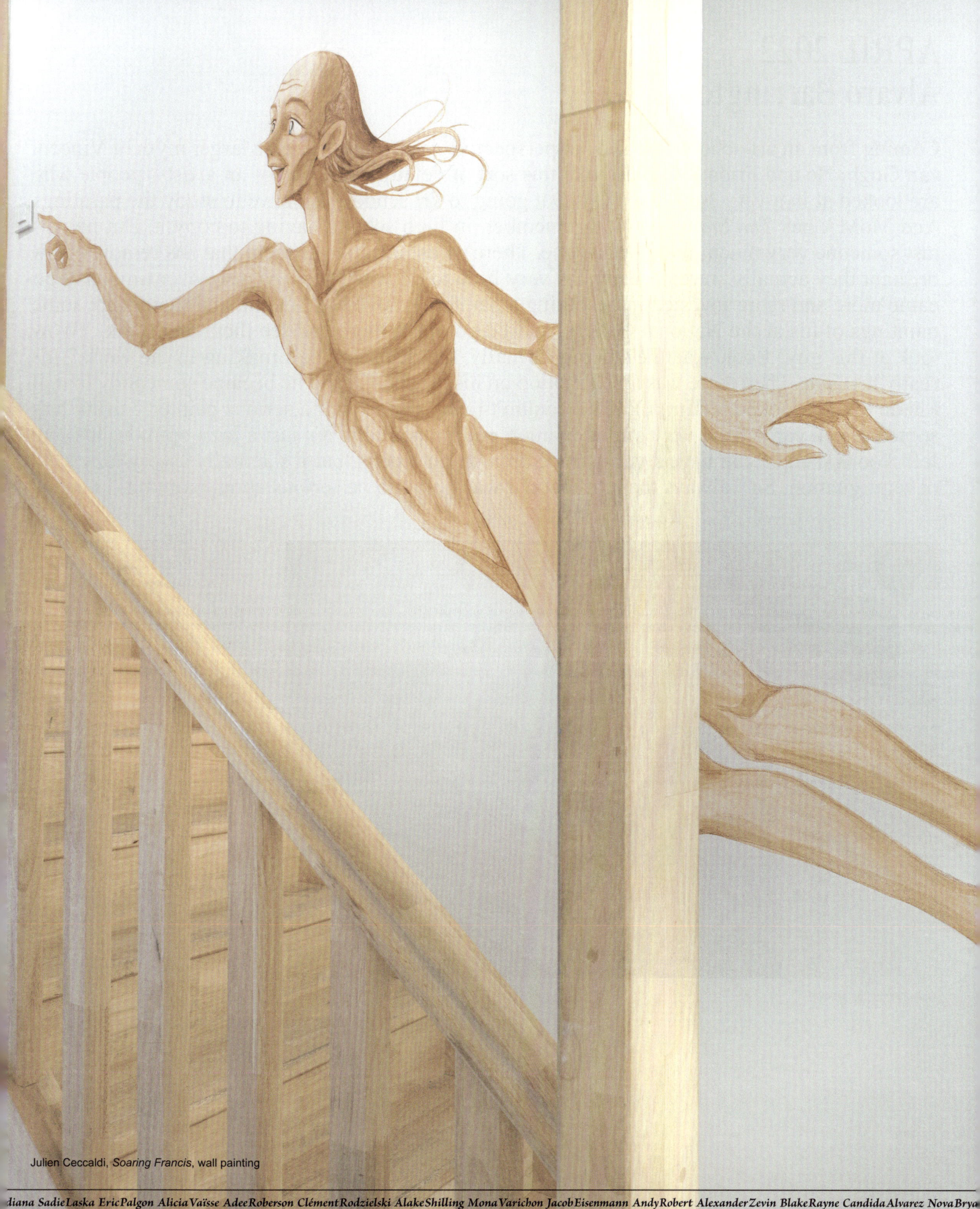

Julien Ceccaldi, *Soaring Francis*, wall painting

Alvaro Barrington

Coming from an art-school nerd kind of perspective, you know, there's a larger myth of Vincent van Gogh. He and Frida Kahlo are like this sort of default definition of an artist—people who are looked at in a very particular way. But going to art school, you have to study the paintings. And MoMA has *The Starry Night*. I remember, in high school, having to copy it. But he was just someone very much in the Frida zone. There's this narrative of them that has removed how brilliant they actually were; it really has very little to do with them. And so, over time, as I became more and more invested in becoming a painter, I moved to London and there were some paintings of his at the National Gallery, and I'd go down there and see them and think, "Wow, look at this guy! Look what he's doing formally, the decisions he's making in the work." It's really brilliant. Then there was an exhibition on his notebooks and he became somebody that, if I hadn't really looked at him, I knew I couldn't really call myself a serious painter. I think he's someone you can have a very strong opinion on, but actually, it's just a lazy opinion. It's like Jeff Koons. People can have a very strong opinion on Koons, but it's actually a very lazy kind of regurgitation. So I always thought that if I was going to be serious about painting, I needed

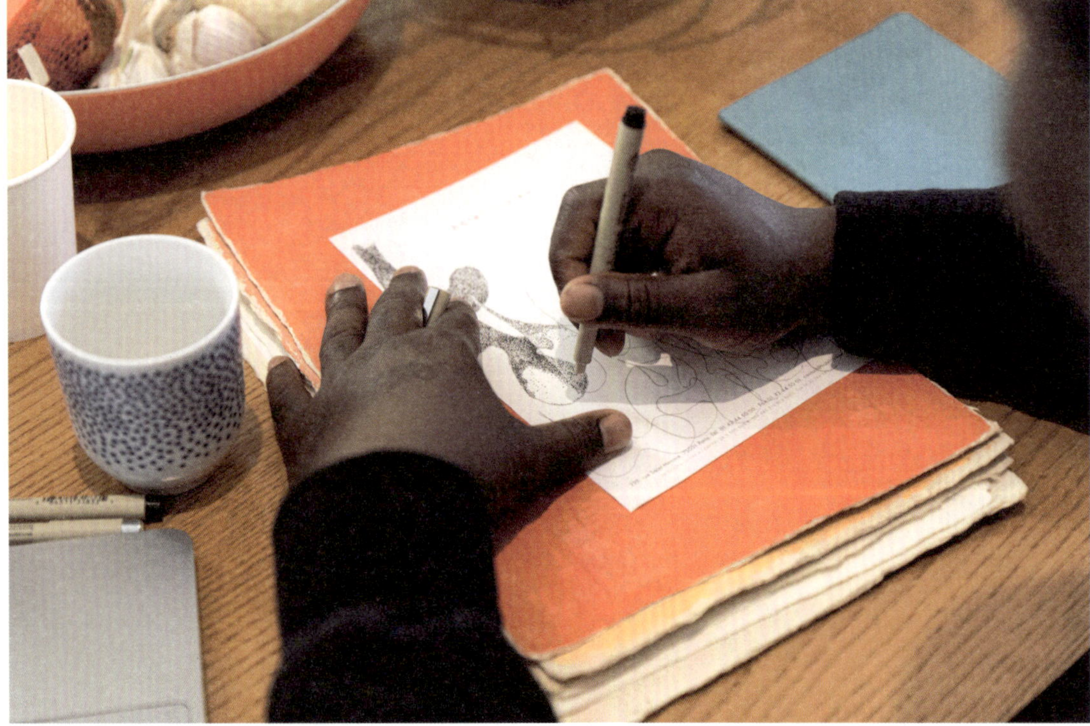

Alvaro Barrington drawing

to explore what he was doing. And then there were times that I found myself trying to do things that he was doing in painting.

I knew Laura Owens because she did a talk and visiting crits at Hunter College when I was a student there. I remember she did the Whitney Biennial, and it's like—with all the Whitney Biennials, there's always, like, maybe two or three people that you go, "That's it." You know? Like, there was the Sterling Ruby Whitney Biennial, there was the Amy Sillman and Laura Owens Whitney Biennial, Henry Taylor a couple of years ago—so there was a moment. She was going into these veins of history that I was thinking about. And then everybody was doing drop-shadow paintings, like how she used to do. You go to school, and then everybody's doing drop shadows after they saw her. So I came to London, and she did a show with Sadie Coles, and I went, like, seven times for the show. One of those times, she was there, and we talked about New York. Then she introduced me to Sadie, and then Sadie and I started showing together. And that kept Laura and me in conversation more than we would have been.

I think the residency invite was casual. I think I was between, like, three shows all happening. So she's like, "Hey, if you just want some time away, you know, you should think about this." And she was talking about how great it was for her to be away. I think it was after the pandemic had started. She was saying how wonderful it was for her to be in Arles by herself and how inspirational it was. My timeline is all fucked up; I don't know if I did the residency before Laura's show in Arles or after. I can't really remember. But I think it was after. Then I found myself in Arles several times. It was the opening of LUMA, it was a bunch of stuff, you know? It's all just one long, extra-long week for me, even though it was probably several months.

The house was, like, wow, what a fantasy. You know? It has this very romantic feeling, what you think of as a house in the South of France. It's up a hill, it's in this corner pocket, it's around the corner from this huge former coliseum. It's like, the whole thing was a vibe. It just added to what Arles was. And what LUMA was—what Maja Hoffmann was trying to do. It really reminded me of this idea that Van Gogh was trying to create an artists' space. And obviously, what Laura was trying to do in Los Angeles is what I'm trying to do here in London and New York. So it's like an inspiration everywhere. I mean, most artist studios are private spaces, right? And I remember going out to Los Angeles to visit Laura, and it was like a private-public studio. She was doing exhibitions there, it was public in that it had a bookstore, all of these things. So it was her studio, but it was also a public space. Growing up, Andy Warhol was a huge hero for me. But also with what today gets called "street art" or "streetwear"—art started for me in a public place before it became private. And I just thought, "My studio sort of needs to be a public space," you know?

I invited two of my university friends, Dorus and Fleur, and they actually stayed at the residency longer than I could. So it was the three of us there. Then there were LUMA's resources, and at

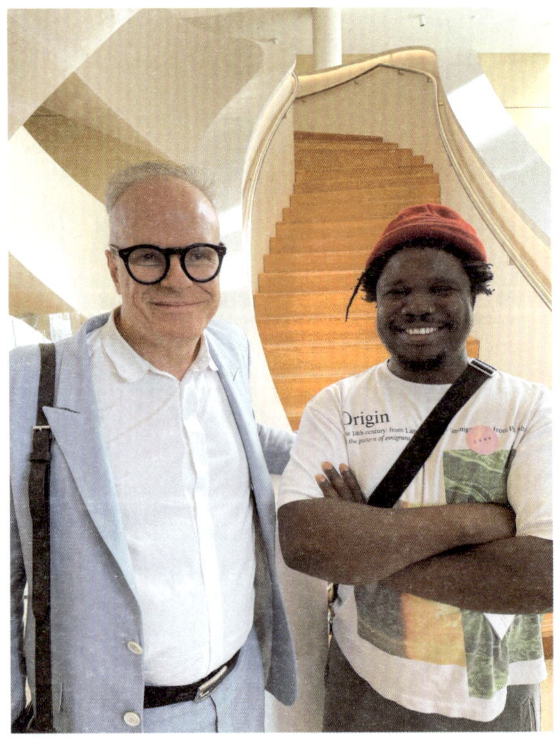

Hans Ulrich Obrist and Alvaro

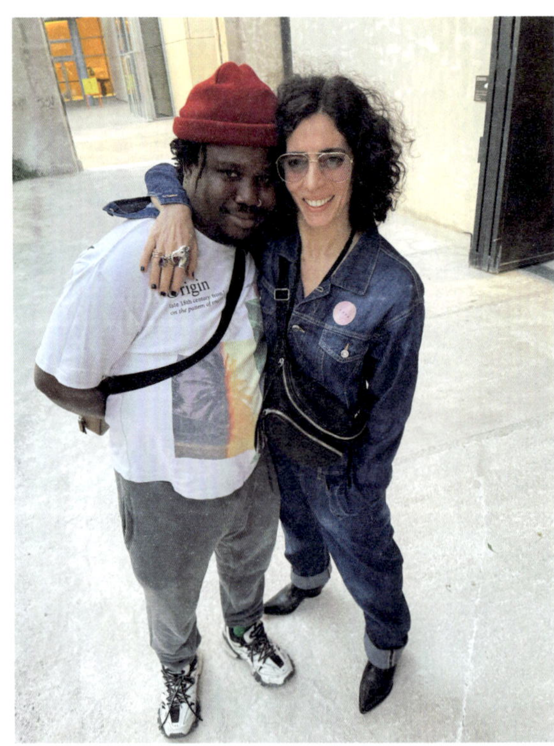

Alvaro and Maria Hassabi

the time, a lot of it was under construction. So we were talking through some of the innovations they were trying to do. I think you're starting to see it built out, now. Theaster Gates did something there last weekend. I think they opened a space for pottery and ceramics. All of that was underway at the time. Martino Gamper did the Réfectoire restaurant, so we were able to meet some of the people who worked with him. It was interesting, like a meeting of friends, friends of friends, and extensions of friends. It felt like a place that was its own thing, but also like Paul Gauguin coming in, you know? And it also reminded me of the exhibition that Laura did with the wallpapers, thinking about Gauguin, thinking about the sunflower paintings as wallpaper; it was all very inspiring.

I make wherever I make, so kind of all over the place. Actually, I don't really remember the work I made because it was all such a blur. I remember doing the clock, but I don't remember what work I was actively making. It was a long year of making, making, making. The clock was just something I was doing. I liked the idea of the wallpaper and how ephemeral it was, and I just thought it was also quite stupid. Because I was doing two or three exhibitions at the time, it was an opportunity to not do anything that was about anything.

In the house, there were some people whose work I knew, so it was good to see them and what they did. But, to be honest, for the most part, it was more about the people as opposed to the house. The works are nice, but I think I became more interested in the people behind the work

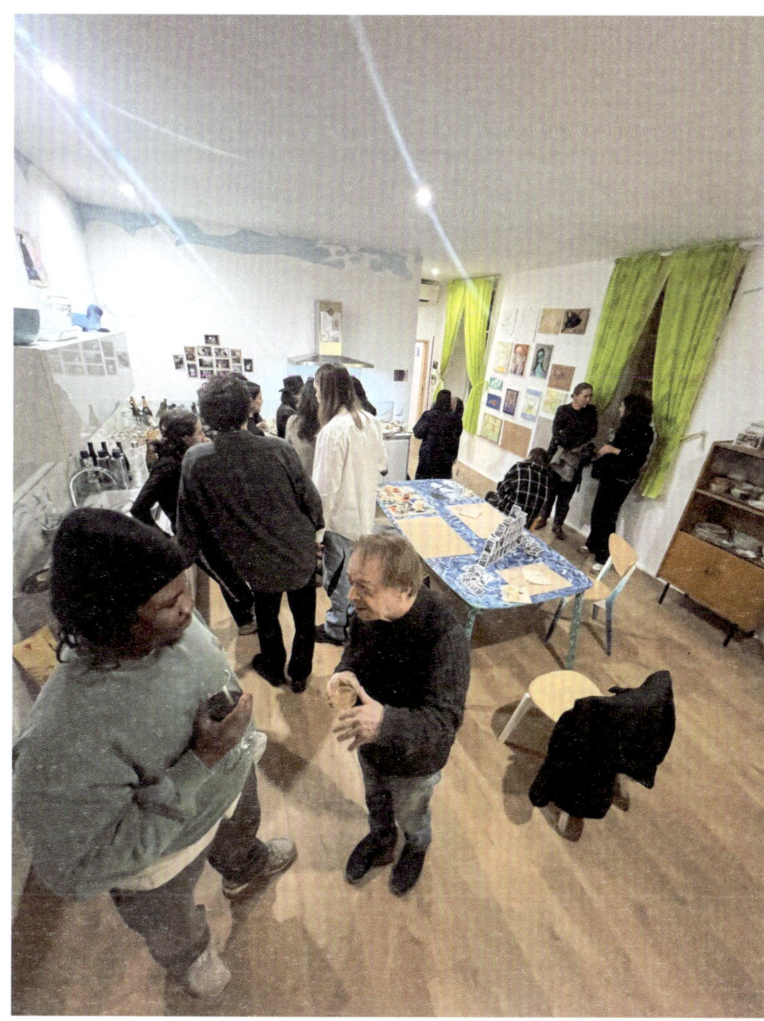

Alvaro and Gary Indiana

than the work itself. We'd say hi or grab a coffee if we saw each other again. Making things into common experiences is really interesting.

It made me live with Van Gogh in a more intimate way. It wasn't just about him for me as a fan; he became more integrated into my process. Now it feels like part of a digested way of making decisions. If I had to unpack where the possibility of those decisions came from, it would definitely be like, "Oh, that was a moment that happened in the residency." But it's sort of digested a bit more. I also see Willem Dafoe now, and go, "He was way too fucking old to be playing Van Gogh."

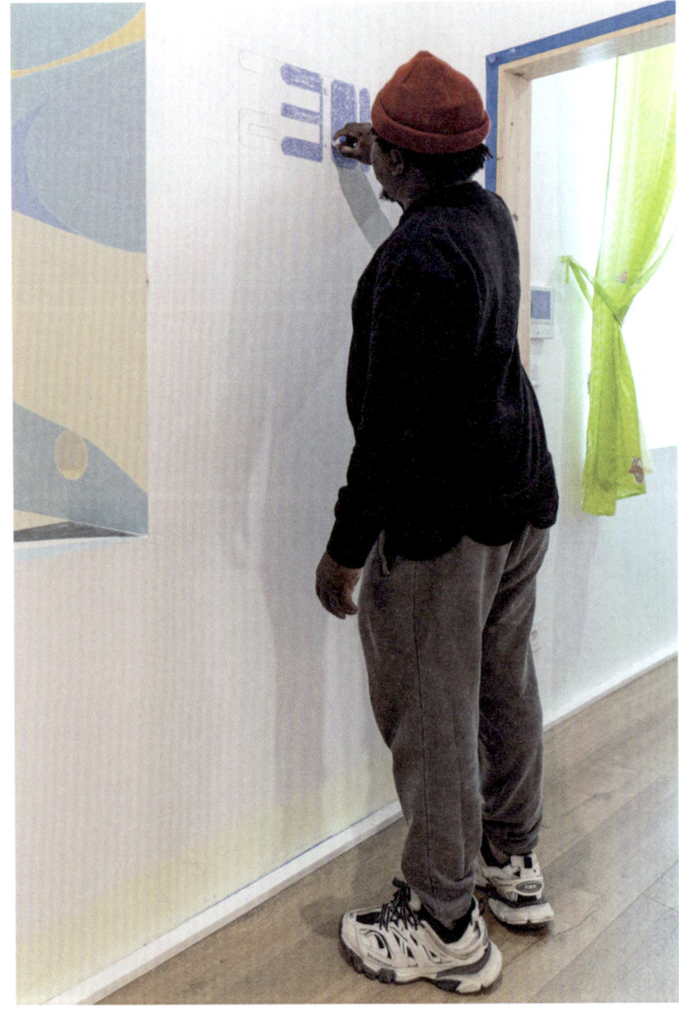

Alvaro working on *3:01 in Arles*

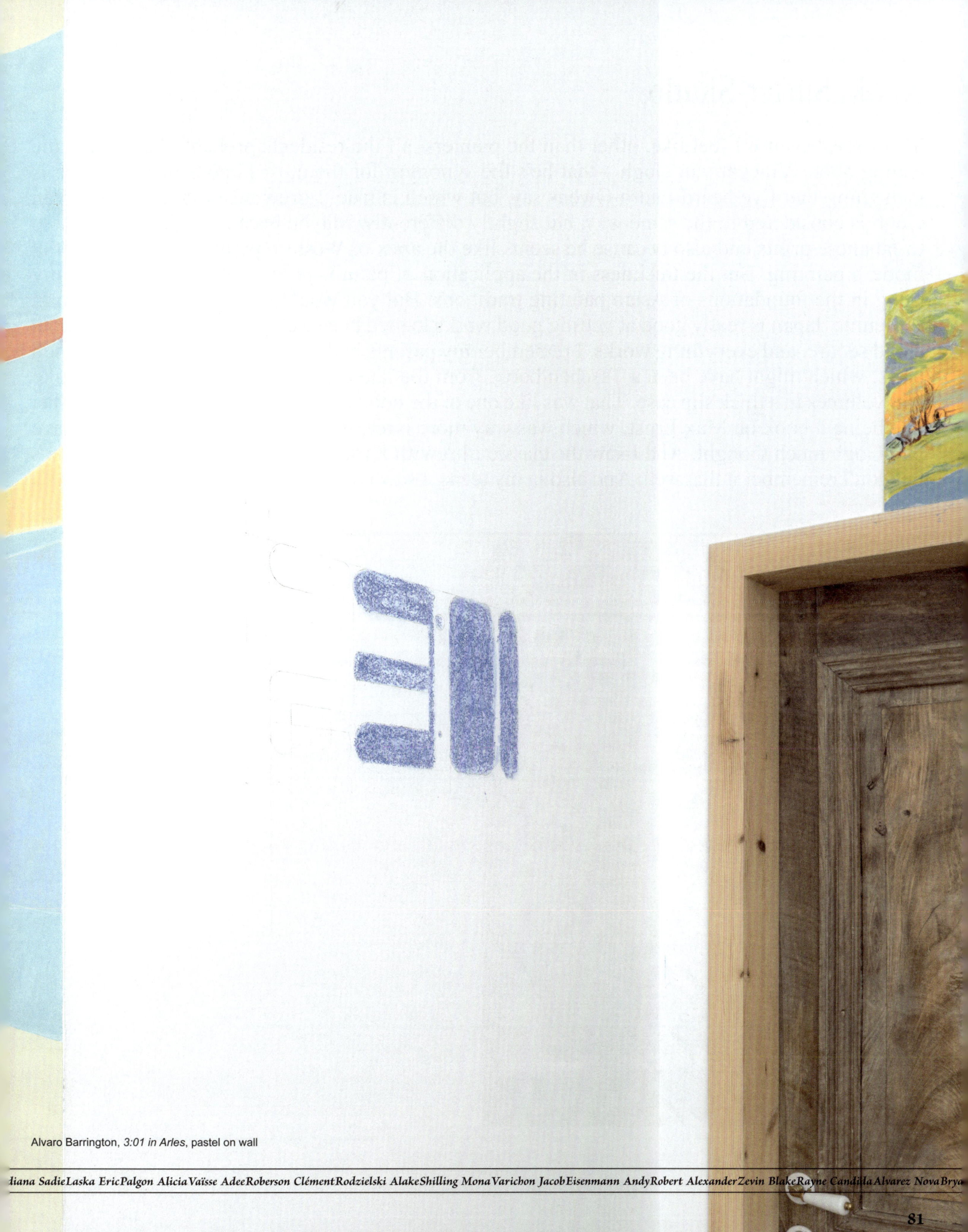

Alvaro Barrington, *3:01 in Arles*, pastel on wall

liana Sadie Laska Eric Palgon Alicia Vaïsse Adee Roberson Clément Rodzielski Alake Shilling Mona Varichon Jacob Eisenmann Andy Robert Alexander Zevin Blake Rayne Candila Alvarez Nova Brya

MAY 2022
Naoki Sutter-Shudo

It's funny, because I feel like, other than the painters, all the residents probably have the same feeling about Vincent van Gogh—that he's the synonym for the most famous artist. Which is something that I've heard Laura Owens say, but which is true. I grew up in Japan, where Van Gogh is considered in the same way, but slightly differently. Maybe because of his relationship to Japanese prints and also because he seems like the apex of Western painting or the advent of modern painting. But the thickness in the application of paint is completely antithetical to anything in the foundations of Asian painting traditions. But you would see Van Gogh in Japan in museums. Japan is really good at getting good works loaned because they're super serious about it and secure, and everything works. I remember my parents had a really big, box-like Van Gogh book, which might have been a Taschen book, from the late eighties or early nineties. It's, like, two volumes in a thick slip case. That was like one of the books that I enjoyed looking at, the other one being a book on Max Ernst, which was way more interesting to me. But it's not like I gave Van Gogh much thought. And I saw the classic film with Kirk Douglas when I was in my teens but don't remember it that well. And also in my teens, I saw the sequence from Akira Kurosawa's

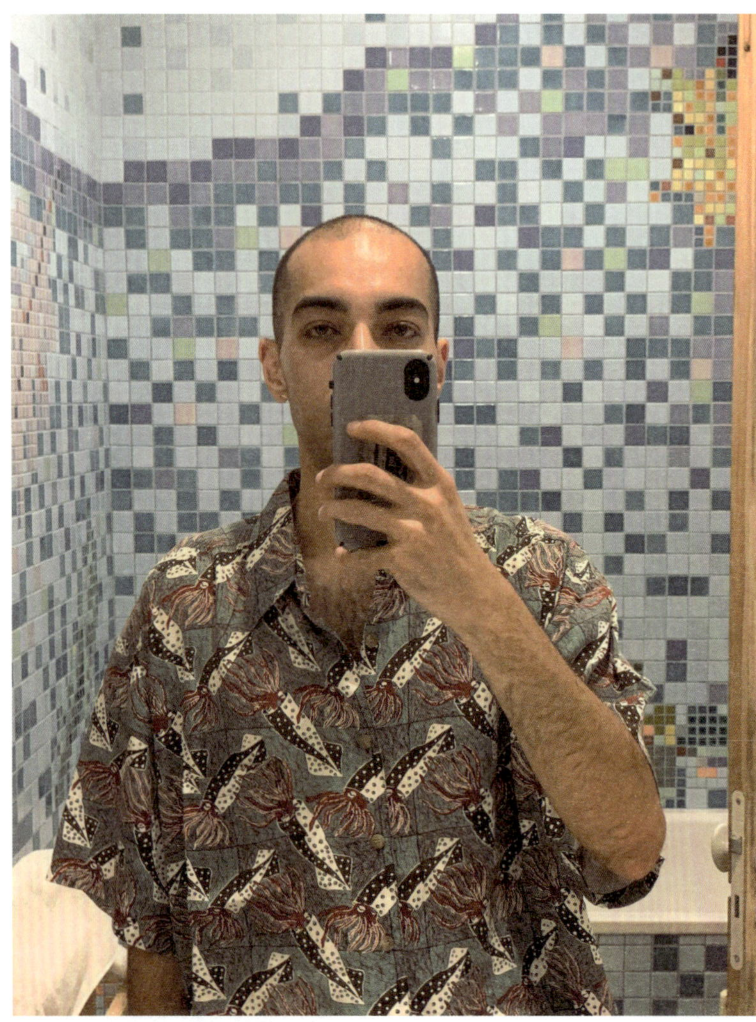

Naoki Sutter-Shudo, mirror selfie

Dreams—Martin Scorsese playing Van Gogh. And I was into Kurosawa films, especially *Dreams*, because the visuals are so crazy. I also read Van Gogh's letters to his brother in my teens, when I was trying to get my hands on first-person accounts of an artist's life. But I wasn't really thinking about Van Gogh that much. You know, it's kind of like Salvador Dali. It's taboo to be into Dali, but, like, every time you see a Dali in person, you're like, "Wow! This is actually crazy." And Van Gogh feels that way to me. In a way, the photos don't do it justice. When you see a real Van Gogh, you're like, "Oh my God, yeah, this is really something." I remember my dad had this anecdote of Van Gogh paintings being discovered in barns, patching up, like, a broken window or something—like, people did not really care. So that whole myth about the struggling artist who's not recognized in his own lifetime was probably a good sort of thing to have in the back of your head, ingrained in you when you're a kid, so you don't have these expectations, like, "As an artist, I'm gonna buy the sickest house and party with collectors." That cliché is nice on some level. Now, in 2024, it feels nice to be like, "No, artists should be struggling."

The first time I met Laura was around the time she opened the *12 Paintings* show at 356 Mission, Los Angeles, which was the first time I was ever in LA. I was a student in Paris at the art school there, and I came to LA on an exchange program and stayed six months at ArtCenter College of Design, Pasadena. This was before Laura was involved with that school. I went to 356 Mission to the *12 Paintings* show, which was probably one of the most important shows I've ever seen

diana Sadie Laska Eric Palgon Alicia Vaïsse Adee Roberson Clément Rodzielski Alake Shilling Mona Varichon Jacob Eisenmann Andy Robert Alexander Zevin Blake Rayne Candida Alvarez Nova Brya

in my life. There's only a few shows that really mark you in a certain way, and this was one of them. It made me think about painting in a completely new way, as someone who was only interested in looking at paintings but not making them. The climate at the time, when I was in art school in Paris, was very anti-painting. The painters and the non-painters were completely separated in a way where people were saying "painting is dead" unironically. Like, "There's nothing more you can do with painting." But seeing, in Laura's show, the level of technology involved in making these massive things that were between many genres and techniques, and the sheer scale of it, and getting a space to make a certain work—that way of thinking made me think of Mike Kelley, who had passed away perhaps six months before I came to LA. Mike Kelley was an artist I've always loved since high school, and my interest in LA was through Mike Kelley and his circle: Paul McCarthy, Jason Rhoades, Jim Shaw, and other figures around that. And the music thing. When I went to the *12 Paintings* show, but more so when I went to 356 Mission when it first opened, it really felt like this was probably the feeling when Mike had three studios and organized things like screenings, and everyone had a link to it, and it blended all these different things, like music, art, cinema, fashion, and socializing. I met so many people at 356 Mission that I am still friends with. My wife, Alexandra Noel, worked there as the event photographer. So I guess I met Laura kind of marginally in 2013. And then, when I came back in 2014 or something, I think I asked her if she wanted to do a show at Shanaynay, which was a

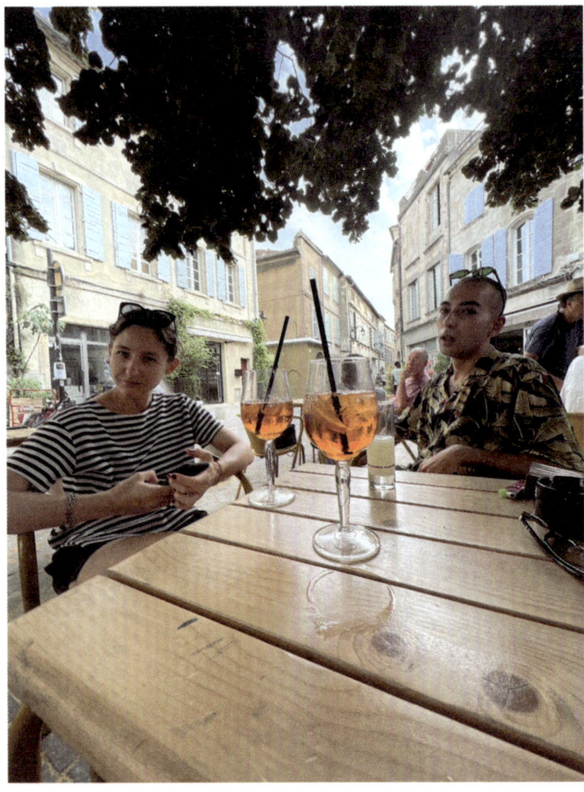

Naoki and his wife, Alexandra Noel, at Café de la Roquette in Arles

very tiny space I was involved with in Paris. I think we sat down upstairs in her studio, in this giant room that had nothing but two couches, while people were silk-screening stuff next door. It was kind of my fault that the show never happened, because I think we discussed budget stuff and we never had a budget. But I was a fan by that point. And then, when shit started getting crazy with 356 Mission and people were protesting, I remember talking about that a little bit with Laura, because I would still come and be like, "This thing that's happening outside is bullshit. It's so stupid." And I stand by that. And then also, through Asha Schechter, I guess I got to know Laura more, but, you know, she's such a busy person and a strange person too, so I don't really hang out with her.

When Laura invited me to the residency, she was talking about how it was a very open-ended thing with no conditions or constraints like having to make work to decorate the house, although that was kind of implied because of how, like, she was talking about the Jean Cocteau house. And I remember we discussed the chapel that Henri Matisse designed, and the hotel La Colombe d'Or, and all these legacies. But I typically like to take my time when I work on artworks, so I remember her telling me that I should just use that time as a writing residency, which is another thing I do. It was during COVID-19 when we were talking about it, so she couldn't officially invite people who weren't European citizens, 'cause it was complicated or something. So she was like, "You should come, and Allie too since she can't be invited officially, and you guys can

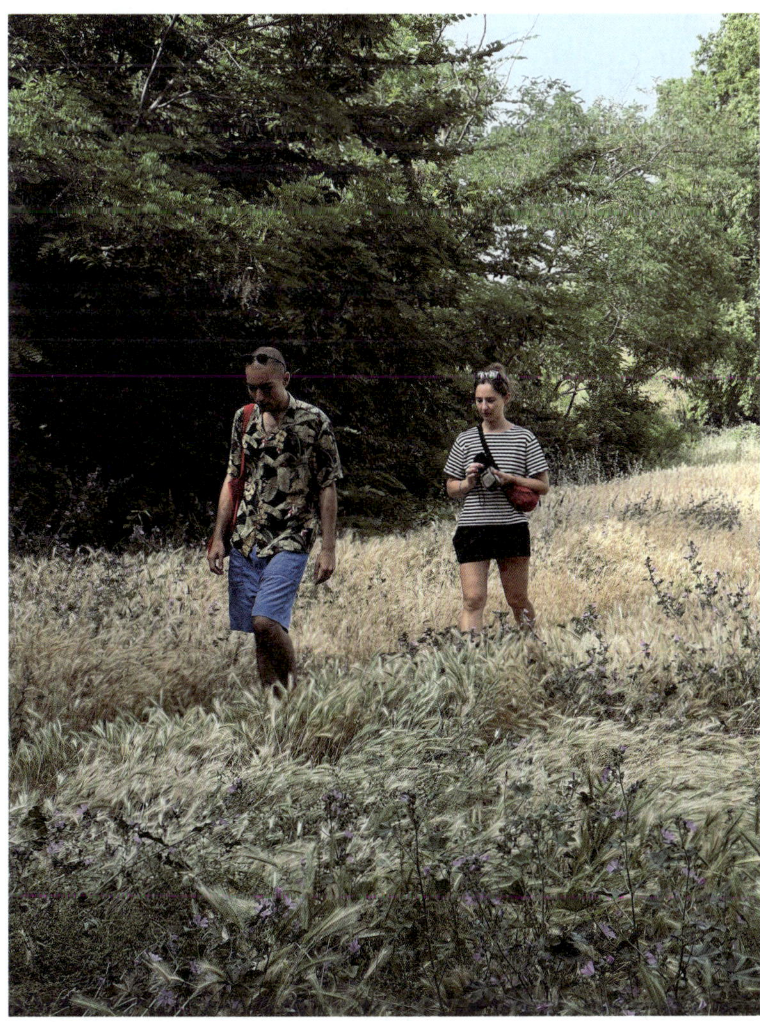

Naoki and Alexandra

do the residency together." When I went, Allie was busy, so she couldn't come the whole time. I went with the intention of maybe writing. When I went, I was already in Europe doing other projects, like a show with Mona Varichon at Alienze in Vienna, and then I was in Paris a little bit, and then went to Arles. So it was nice to have that moment in Europe, seeing my friends. Most people who had done the residency by the time I went were people I knew, so having each person's feedback and stuff in person while I was in Paris was cool. But it's not like I brought any specific material to make a specific thing for the house. I just brought books.

I had been to Arles. I went once for the photo festival, the Rencontres d'Arles, but it had been a while—maybe fifteen years ago. When I arrived, the house was still pretty minimal in the sense that the interventions were not as bold as I thought they would be. Some were, but things weren't blending together. You could see that this person had made this, or see a weird object that someone left. But it wasn't an overwhelmingly total environment. The appliances and furniture kind of felt like an upscale Airbnb a little bit. I'm not necessarily saying this in a bad way; like, I thought it was kind of true to its thing. You could tell it had been redone and furnished rather quickly to be as functional as possible, but maybe not to be have the most insane details.

When I first got there, they were, like, bringing all these vegetables in, which is something they did for the residents. And then I remember getting stressed about it, like, "Oh my God! This is so many vegetables. I have to eat them really quickly." So I tried to find the best bakery

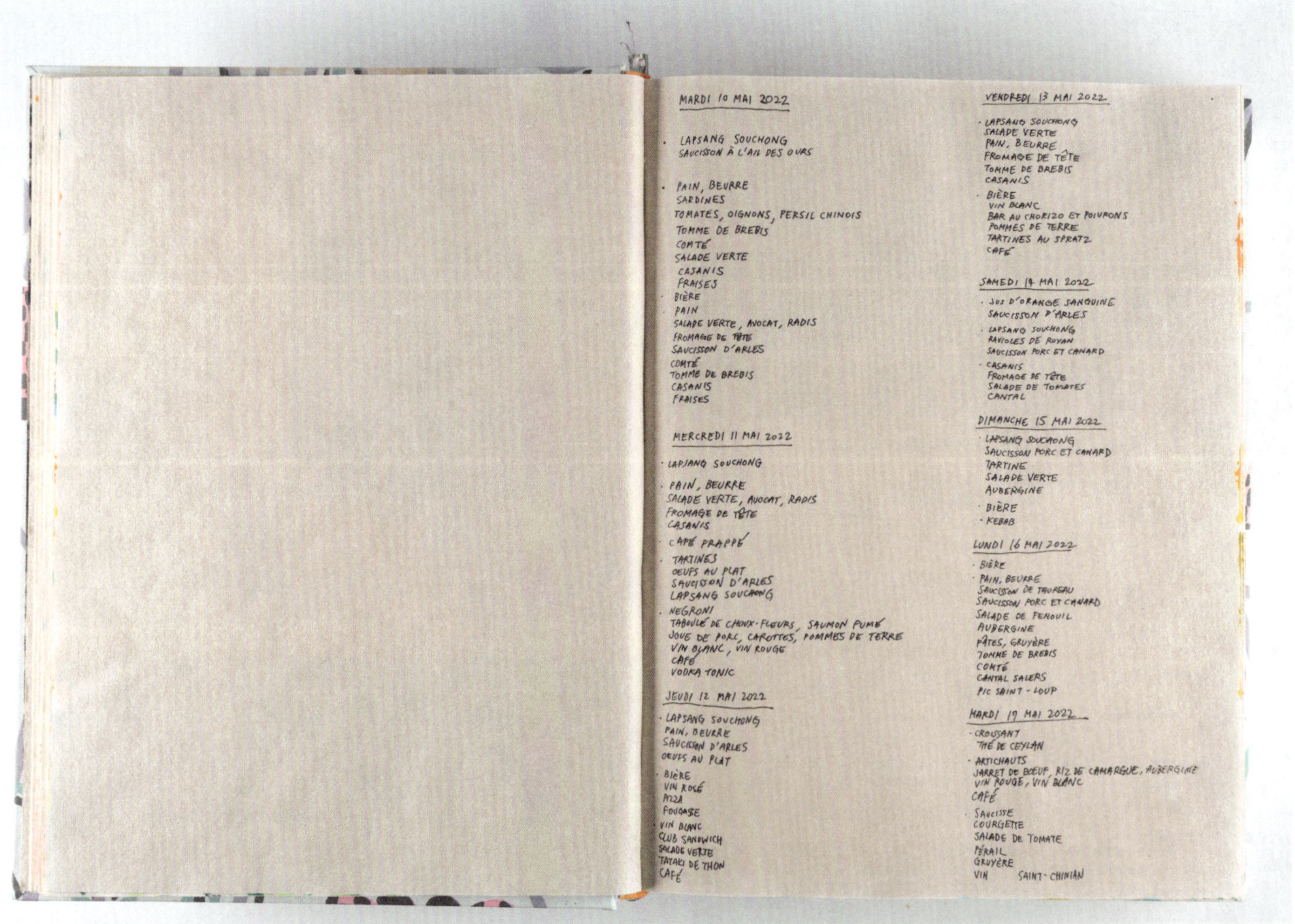

Naoki's food log in the guest book

and charcuterie and cheese, and I quickly found really good places nearby. So I was kind of set, and I was like, "Oh, how nice is it to eat like this." The first day I was there, I saw Lily van der Woodsen, A.K.A. the actress Kelly Rutherford, and this was a very important thing for me. She played the mother of Blake Lively on the original *Gossip Girl* TV series, and she used to be my profile picture on Facebook. I've written poems about her, and I also made a book that is mostly close shots of her face from red carpets and stuff. But I saw her walking on the street in a flowy, white dress, and at the same time, I was on the phone with Julie Boukobza, who was telling me I had set the alarm for the house wrong or something. So it was beeping, and I had to go back immediately, so I just saw her in passing. But that was the last place I would expect to see her, and was a very important vision that happened to me the first day I was there.

Another interesting thing is, I had talked to some friends in Paris who were involved in anti-gentrification conversations, anti–private foundation, tax evasion, all that discourse. They had painted a picture of Arles that was not necessarily as serene as it seemed. I was thinking about it before I arrived, and as soon as I got there, I wasn't really feeling any of that. I was talking to a lot of local merchants and people, and everyone was mostly happy to have all this culture around and these new places to work, and sort of felt pride. But of course I did not talk to young people with no money or anything. I don't know. I mean, it's a special thing when you're there under, like, the LUMA umbrella; that had a lot of advantages, for sure.

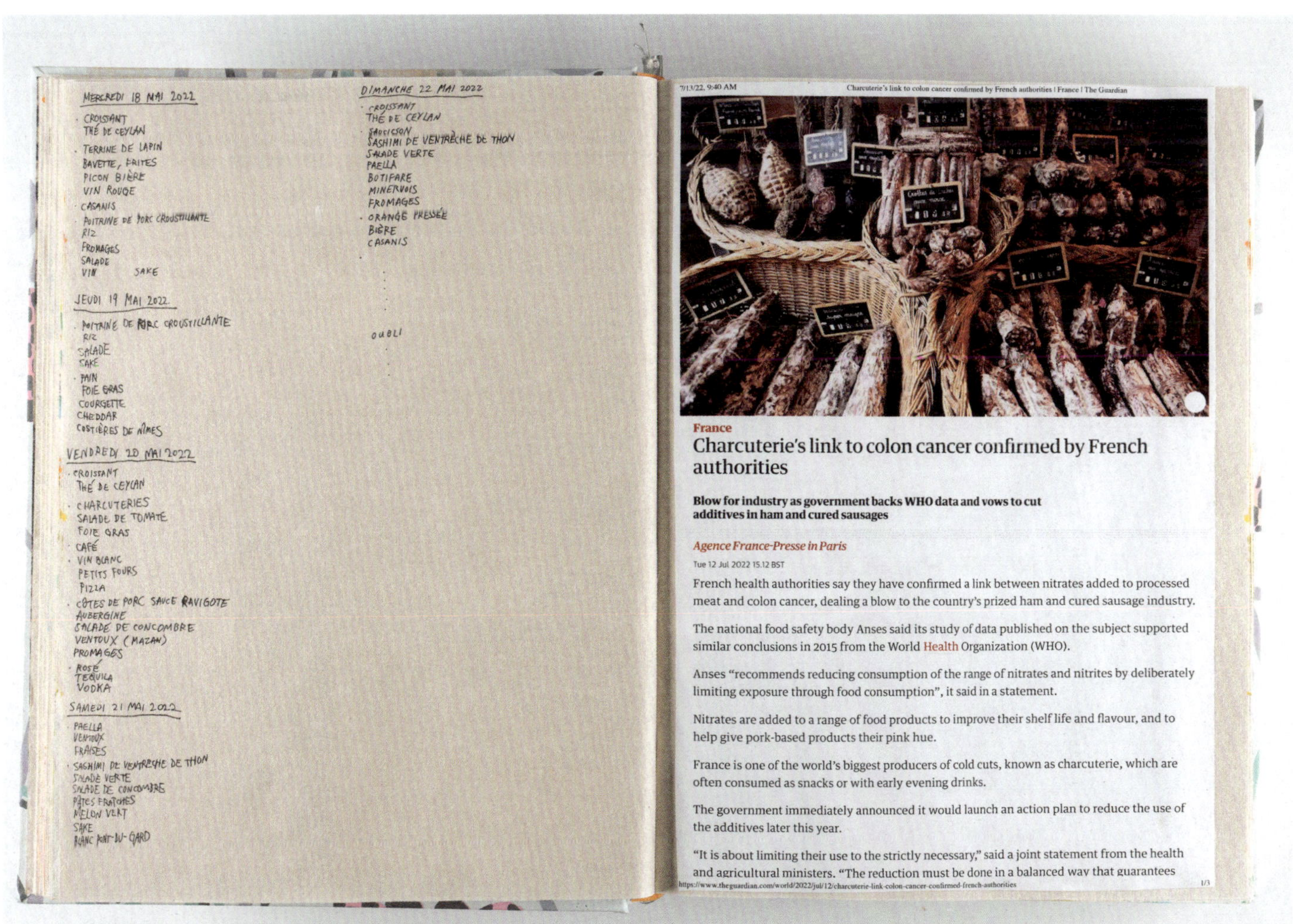

France

Charcuterie's link to colon cancer confirmed by French authorities

Blow for industry as government backs WHO data and vows to cut additives in ham and cured sausages

Agence France-Presse in Paris

Tue 12 Jul 2022 15.12 BST

French health authorities say they have confirmed a link between nitrates added to processed meat and colon cancer, dealing a blow to the country's prized ham and cured sausage industry.

The national food safety body Anses said its study of data published on the subject supported similar conclusions in 2015 from the World Health Organization (WHO).

Anses "recommends reducing consumption of the range of nitrates and nitrites by deliberately limiting exposure through food consumption", it said in a statement.

Nitrates are added to a range of food products to improve their shelf life and flavour, and to help give pork-based products their pink hue.

France is one of the world's biggest producers of cold cuts, known as charcuterie, which are often consumed as snacks or with early evening drinks.

The government immediately announced it would launch an action plan to reduce the use of the additives later this year.

"It is about limiting their use to the strictly necessary," said a joint statement from the health and agricultural ministers. "The reduction must be done in a balanced way that guarantees

https://www.theguardian.com/world/2022/jul/12/charcuterie-link-colon-cancer-confirmed-french-authorities

Naoki's food log and a printed-out article from *The Guardian* in the guest book

So my dad lives perhaps, like, three or four hours away by car, so he drove to visit me. He had a desk that he brought in his car and also has this camera that I have that I didn't bring, the Mamiya RZ67. I ended up installing the desk in the main bedroom and it's still in the house. But he came, and we spent a lot of time going to the market and eating and cooking. I'm kind of reticent to really call the things I put in the house "pieces." But, you know, something that has always been interesting to me is art in a domestic context. And also things that don't necessarily need to be art, but the sort of blurry line between art and decor, or something that can be both, or something that adds to the space. This is also my interest in sculpture. Charles Ray was talking about how sculpture is something that makes you aware of the space you're in. Most of the things I made were completely motivated by the space of the house itself. There were these murals in the main bedroom that I could see from the bed when I was reading, which is something I like to do, even during the day. And there was this mural with a lot of text that was Google-translated or something. The text was distracting me from being able to fully focus on reading a book, so I wanted to cover it up—not in a permanent way but just for the duration of my stay. So I went to the market and got a bunch of fabric and sewed it to make this random patchwork thing. I also used fabric that I got from the Atelier LUMA, which I visited one day, thanks to Julie Boukobza. I wanted to document it, so I have a trove of pictures, mostly close-ups of random things. That was a very interesting moment, when I spent a whole day in the Atelier and then, later, in the

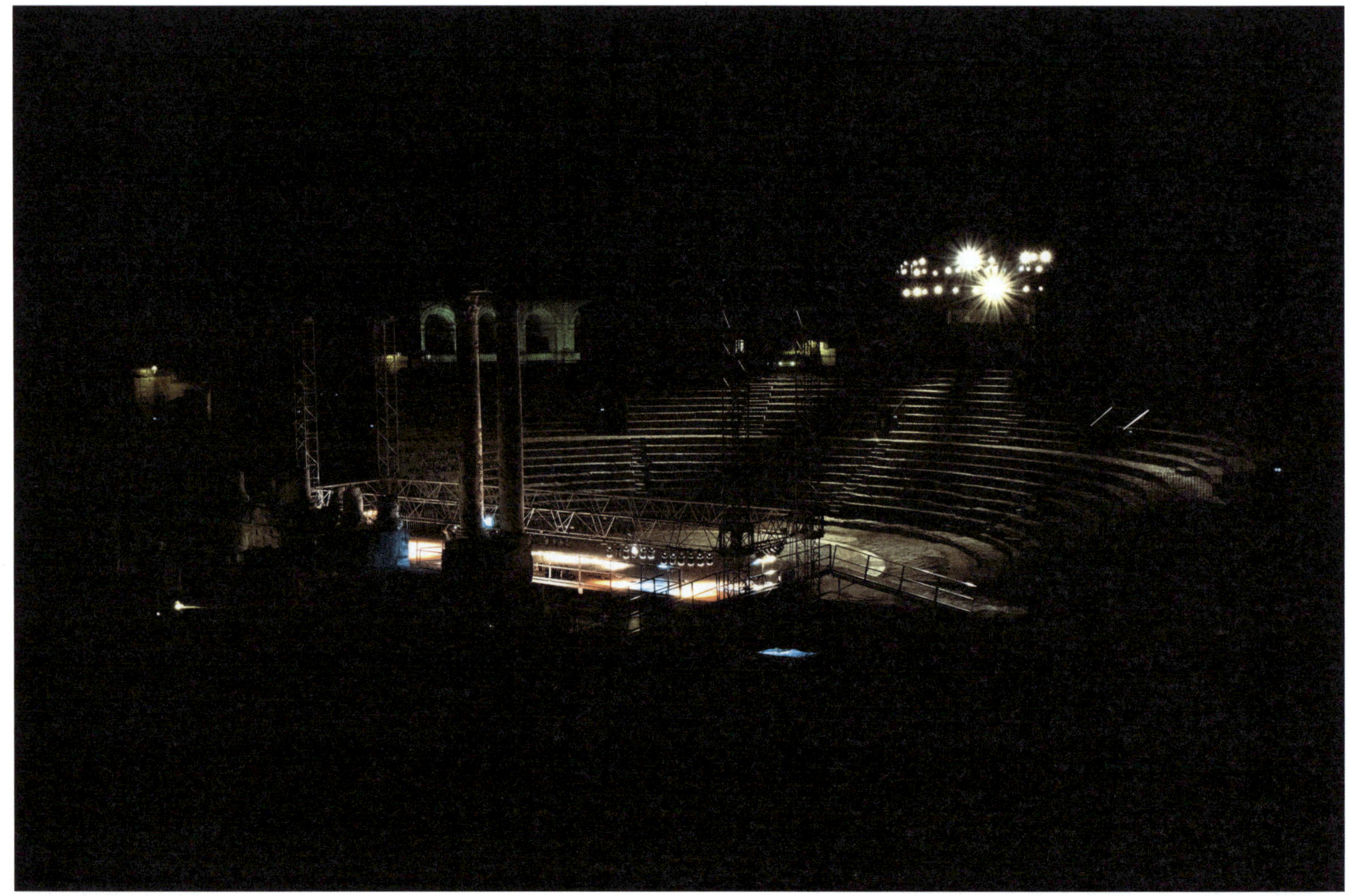

Roman Theater, Arles

offices of the curators—to really see what LUMA does for all these people interested in crafts, coming up with new materials that use local things, seeing other people who are working there on residencies. And they gave me a bunch of extra material, which I then reused for the patchwork thing to cover Parker Ito's mural. So that was the first thing I made, and it wasn't really art. The aesthetic decisions of that fabric thing were not motivated by a desire to express anything innate in me or an idea, but were purely responding to the colors around that room already and using what was at hand. So a quick solution, a cheap fix. Because the house is, like, a typical sort of bourgeois dwelling where you can feel—with the heights of the ceilings on each floor—what was the kitchen or what was the main area. I loved that the staircase was this big, open space that spanned almost the whole height of the house. Initially, the thinking behind that rope was to make a sort of bell; like, in Japanese temples, you ring a bell when you go to the front and pray or give money and then bow. In Shinto temples, you have these big bells with a rope that you shake, and it rings the bell. I felt like the house needed something to announce your arrival, especially if it's a communal space with multiple people—you might be upstairs and not hear the doors open. So I decided to do a bell that you can ring from the bottom when you arrive. So I did that, and then also made loops around the rope so you could potentially hang things, like charcuterie and things to dry. This is sort of like a riff on this Haim Steinbach work. He made a piece in an Italian village, I think, where he had tons of the salami they make locally hanging

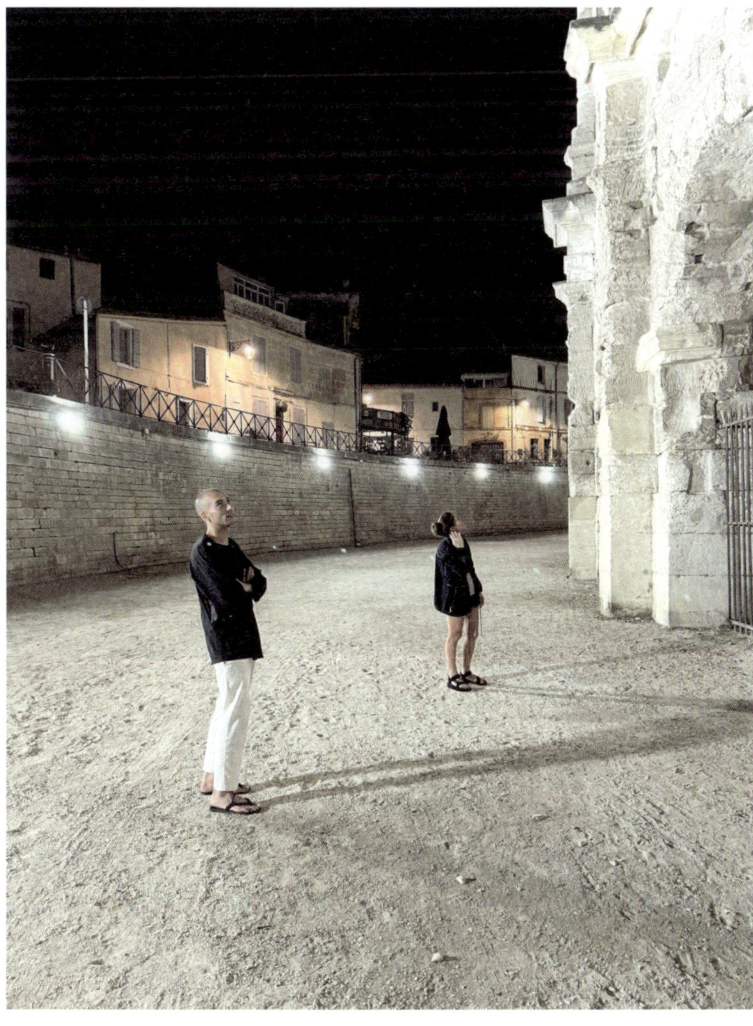

Naoki and Alexandra at the Arles Amphitheater

diana Sadie Laska Eric Palgon Alicia Vaïsse Adee Roberson Clément Rodzielski Alake Shilling Mona Varichon Jacob Eisenmann Andy Robert Alexander Zevin Blake Rayne Candida Alvarez Nova Bry

from the ceiling. And, you know, Arles is famous for the *saucisson d'Arles*, which is a traditional sausage that they make. I hear it used to contain donkey, but it also is a mixture with bull meat. So the rope was to be able to hang all these sausages I wanted to try. At the market, there are all these different vendors who come with sausages from elsewhere, so I felt like I needed to be able to hang them and keep them. And also, you can kind of hang anything, like, if you want to dry a T-shirt or something. So it became that. My dad helped me make it, because he's much better at knots and ropework than I am. He showed me how to do it, and we went to a boating store to get stainless steel hardware for the top. The bells themselves came from the flea market. I also made a chair, which seemed like a sort of tradition—people staying there and painting a chair. So I did that just based on paints that were left at the house and some paint I bought. I think I might have left a few little things that were not really works, but, like, interventions or something. Before arriving, I was in Vienna for a week or so, and I saw my friend Soshiro Matsubara. He's a Japanese artist who lives in Vienna. I went to his place, and he gave me these little ceramic balls that he had made as a test. I think I left those with some other balls, like, marbles or something, that were already in a plate. And I thought that was a way to have the presence of someone else.

So my dad was there for like a week or something. Then my friend Mathieu Joubert came and stayed with me. He's from the South also. Our routine would be to go eat or cook something from the market, and then go see LUMA or some art shows or local museums or Van Gogh's *Les Alyscamps*, where I went several times. And then we'd stay in the studio when it got hot out and make a few things. I was sketching and he was making paintings based on local plants and flowers that he found. He made several, and we installed one in the living room near Laura and Charlotte Houette's paintings, which both featured flowers and were all similar in size. So that was also leaving a trace of what happened in the house. The works I made were for the house. They wouldn't exist outside of it. There was a thing that I ended up not doing. I brought this collection of T-shirts from LA—merch shirts from restaurants and bars, some still being sold, some vintage that I had been collecting. Because of the house's connection to LA and also to Arles as this new touristic destination, I thought it would be funny to leave these clothes there as a sort of uniform, or work clothes, that anyone in the house could wear and be in two places at the same time. Or have the memory of all these LA places that I know, that Laura knows, that Asha knows, that Mona knows, Miriam Laura Leonardi, Parker— a lot of the people in the house would know. So I brought those shirts and was trying to find a way to make some sort of structure to house them, something where they would be for the house, but I ended up not doing that in the house and did it for the show later, in a different way.

Van Gogh's idea for the Studio of the South never really worked. Unlike the Studio of the South that did work. If I remember correctly, I think Paul Gauguin was like, "OK, fine. I'll come." But I think Van Gogh really thought that he would create a whole hub, which was a completely modern and kind of innovative way of thinking, and was what happened later with all these communes

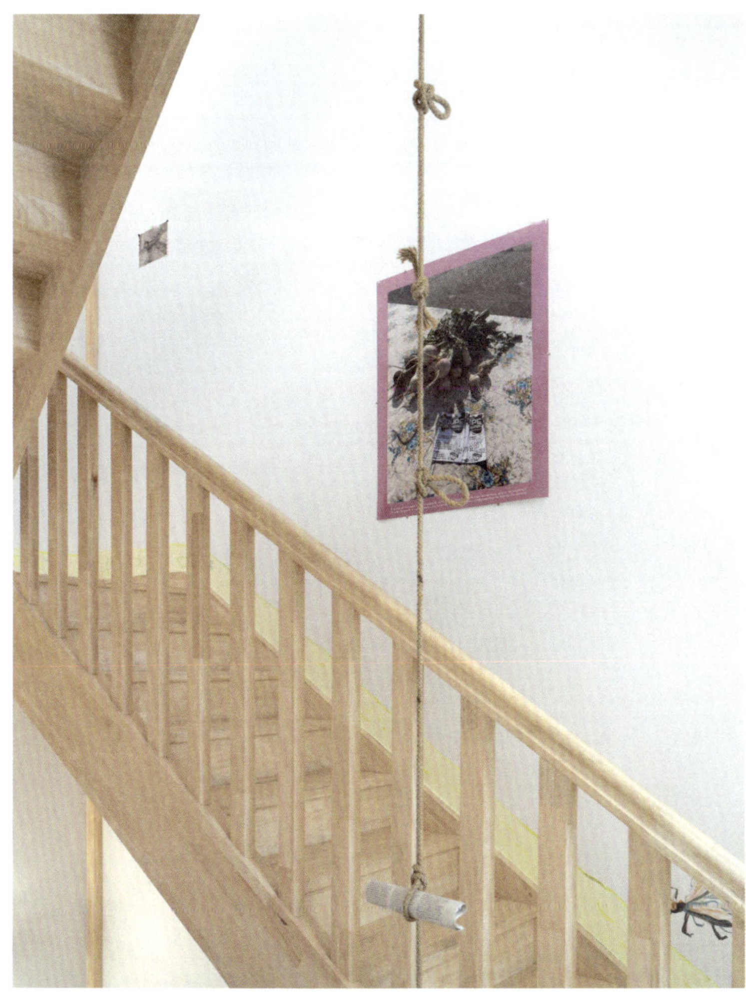

Naoki Sutter-Shudo, *Untitled*, rope from Atelier LUMA, stainless steel, soap, sausage, various objects to be hung by inhabitants as they wish

in places like Hudson, New York. But what was interesting with the Studio of the South was having all this layering in time as opposed to everyone being there at once—seeing and knowing the timeline, seeing who made what and how it changed and the additions. Of course you're not gonna make the same thing if you're the first person there or the last person there. And knowing most people who had been there before me was like being surrounded by familiar presences. For example, seeing Julie Beaufils's painted windowsills, which were so nicely done—probably because it was early on—but they were probably the most true to the spirit of what the house could be, in terms of slowly decorating, really precisely. But then, of course, it changes; you have other types of murals that don't necessarily all match, and that dissonance is fun also.

When I came back and saw the house again, it was pretty full. But it could be even crazier, is what I thought at first. Seeing things move, like that natural evolution of, "Oh, this thing was not here, or this thing was here and now it's in this other room," or something like that, was cool. I feel like there's a few things that could have been specifically commissioned for the house. For example, the main bedroom could have had a really nice lamp sculpture hanging in that beautiful, tall ceiling space. Kind of like the interventions of Laura's, like the backsplash in the kitchen, the bathrooms that she designed, the curtains—those were really nice. So more in that spirit. Artists don't want to consider themselves decorators, but sometimes they should, is what I think. It's funny, too, to see the personal sort of inclinations or personalities manifest so much more obviously than

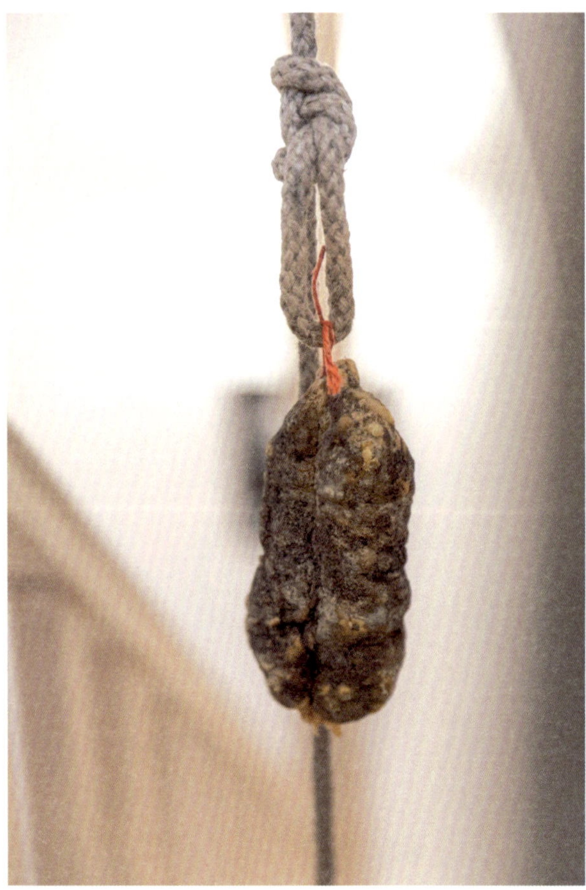

Naoki Sutter-Shudo, *Untitled* (detail)

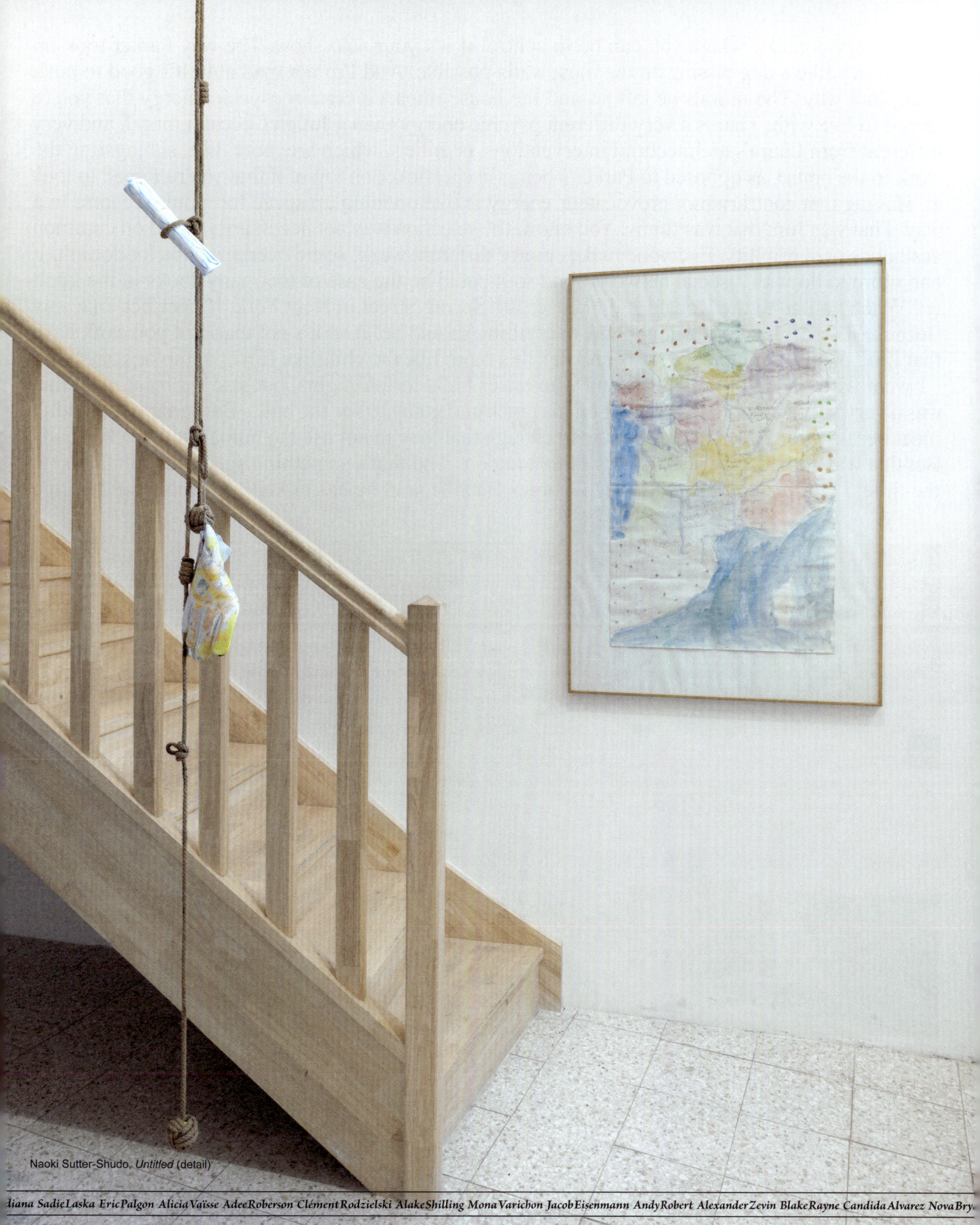

Naoki Sutter-Shudo, *Untitled* (detail)

in a gallery context, where you can be in control if it's your solo show. The way Parker took up space—it's like a dog pissing on the most walls possible. And I'm not mad at it. It's good to push back, in a way. The murals he left around the house impart a certain psychic energy that you're forced to live with. That is a very different psychic energy than a Julien Ceccaldi mural, and very different from Laura's architectural interventions, or Julie's, which are more, like, subjugating the work to the house, as opposed to Parker's being like a sticker on top of it that you're forced to look at. Having that contrarian or provocateur energy is like opening up space for more freedom, in a way. That was fun; that was funny. You know, the selection was not necessarily based on common aesthetics or sensibility. Everyone makes pretty different work; some overlaps but a lot doesn't. It had more to do with a social network. And so it could be the case of too many cooks in the kitchen. When you go to the Donald Judd house, 101 Spring Street in New York, it's perfect, in a way. Because it's one dictator deciding how everything should be. And it's not that. But you can't have that if no one is living there year-round. It's this more like the childlike fun of camp or something.

I went with my dad to see his friend who raises bulls for bullfights, but also for meat. And that was a very special moment—driving on his ranch and going to see the bulls. But some you couldn't meet because you have to keep them wild enough that they're not used to human contact, basically. But that was something that was very of that region. And that's something special about it. And at the time, I was reading or translating Georges Bataille, and he has talked a lot about bullfighting

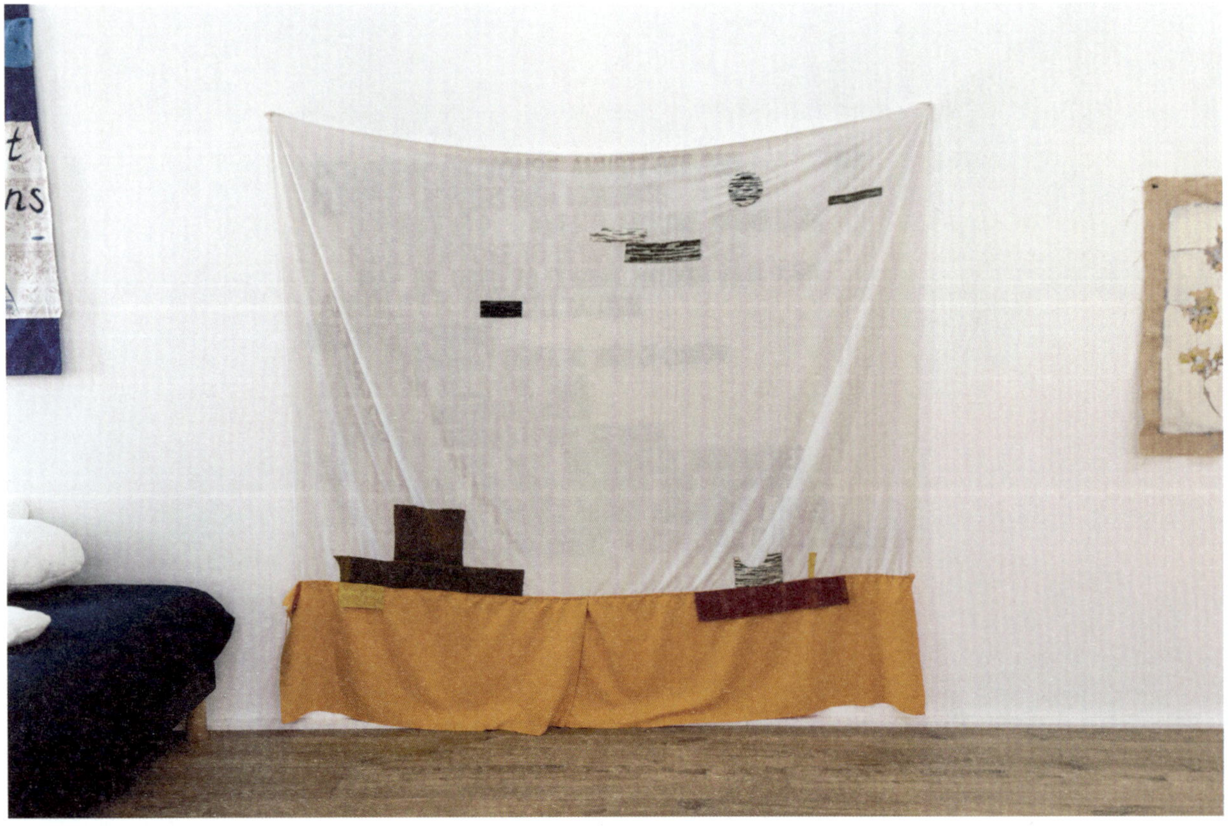

Naoki Sutter-Shudo, *Tenture censure (Parker Ito)*, fabric from Atelier LUMA, steel nails

and the sacrificial aspect of it. And I had other books by Michel Leiris, who talks about bullfighting specifically in Arles. And I know that Georges Bataille saw some bullfights in Arles and has written a lot about that practice and tradition in an intellectual and also erotic way that is not from a political position—whether it's OK, or is it animal abuse or not, etc. So those were things I was thinking about a lot, especially as you're keenly aware that the region of the Camargue and around Arles is a very unique ecosystem that is able to sustain itself. Not that it has become, like, a playground or retreat for the wealthy, but you're aware of the ecological issues that are getting worse and worse— I think about that all the time. But thinking about that as you're in this old city, and also going to see how bulls are raised, and then seeing the transformation into a hero fighter or meat—all these things were interesting. I didn't see any actual bullfighting because it wasn't the season yet.

But another thing, going back to Georges Bataille—like, there was this rumor that he worked as a house painter and painted this building that's, like, on the other side of the river. This modern building that's by the river—it's like a 1960s or 1950s modern building. And that was an anecdote that someone told me, and then I tried discussing it with this bookseller in Arles, who was like, "I don't think he would have done that," and I'm like, "That's true, because he was a librarian, not really a house-painter type." But, like, he might have taken some odd jobs—who knows? He was not very rich his whole life. But that also was a layer of mythology or something. So I did take some pictures of that building, which was funny.

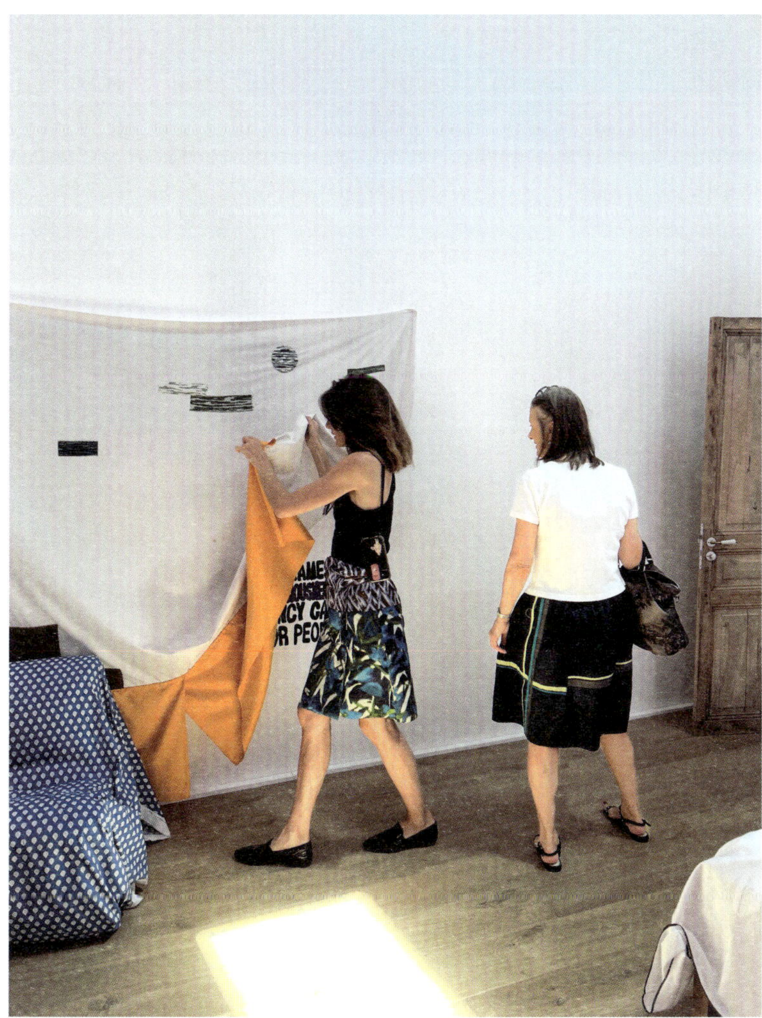

Julia Marchand and Bice Curiger viewing *Tenture censure (Parker Ito)*

diana Sadie Laska Eric Palgon Alicia Vaïsse Adee Roberson Clément Rodzielski Alake Shilling Mona Varichon Jacob Eisenmann Andy Robert Alexander Zevin Blake Rayne Candida Alvarez Nova Brya

Asha Schechter

For a long time, I had the standard American idea of Vincent van Gogh—a guy whose art is on tote bags and is the cliché idea of the eccentric, suffering artist. I had seen *The Starry Night* as a teen at MoMA in New York, but I grew up in Northern California, and I don't think there are as many Van Goghs there. The main museum I went to when I was in art school was SFMOMA, but I don't remember a Van Gogh. My friend Trevor Shimizu would always say that he and Van Gogh had the same birthday and that meant it was his destiny to be an artist, which added to the mystic idea of Van Gogh. I started thinking about Van Gogh more when Laura Owens began working on the show at the Fondation Vincent van Gogh Arles—thinking of him as an artist outside of the mythology. But because I never took a painting class and my education was all in photography, it was never anything I had to work through as I became an artist. I imagine when you train as a painter, you try to understand what is important about his work. As Laura prepared for her show, she had life-size replicas of Van Goghs printed out in her studio in Los Angeles, and seeing them all together, I started to think more about what this kind of brush stroke meant and the subjects of his paintings.

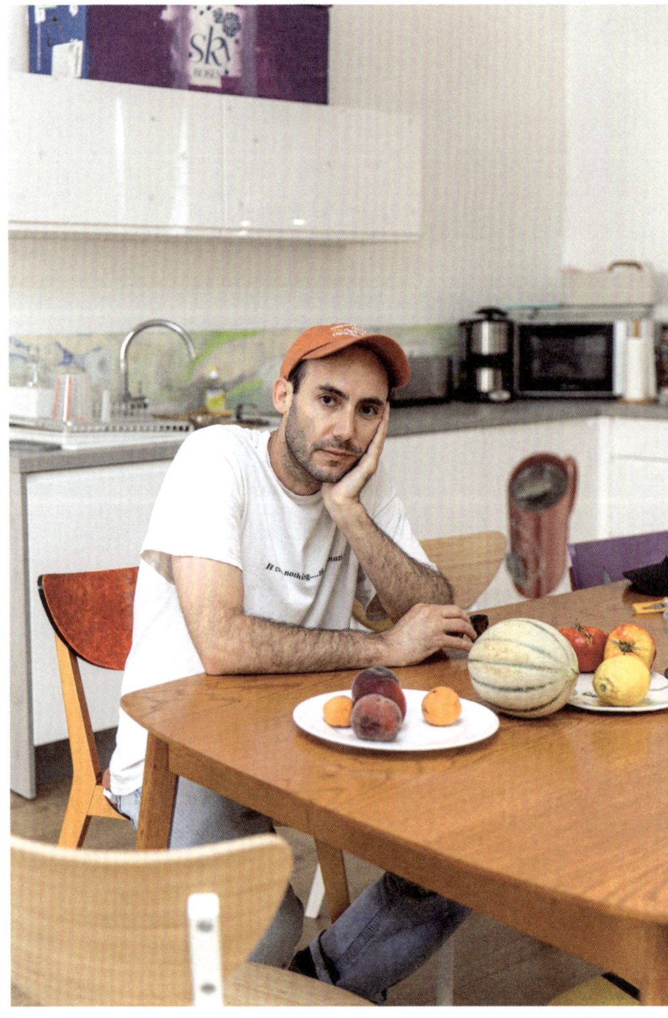

Asha Schechter in the kitchen

I met Laura in Los Angeles in 2011 through multiple people, kind of all at the same time. One was Eric Palgon, who had been her student. Around the same time, my friend Leah Glenn was Laura's student in the grad program at UCLA. And I was also getting to know Wendy Yao, who was close with Laura. So we kind of met through all those people at the same time. At an event at Ooga Booga, which is Wendy's store, I saw Laura, and we realized we both liked tennis. So we started playing and became closer through that. I got a studio next door to 356 Mission, where her studio also was, and she and Wendy invited me to have an iteration of The Vanity, a gallery that had been in my apartment closet, in a closet inside of 356 Mission. Early on, Laura and I made a poster for Ooga Booga that was about this theory that a Bob Dylan art show at the Gagosian Gallery was actually Richard Prince pretending to be Dylan. So there's always been a mix of being friends and working on projects together. Over the years, I would occasionally help her in her studio. I worked on the catalogue for her Whitney show in 2017, so became very familiar with the trajectory of her work and her approach. And in 2018, we started a collaborative publishing and design company called Apogee Graphics, so a lot of our shared ideas have since gone into that.

Before I came to Arles, I had never been to France. My first time was in the summer of 2021 for Laura's exhibition. Alex Zevin and I shared a cab from the airport in Marseille. Arles has small streets that are blocked by mechanical bollards. We stopped at one to wait for it to retract,

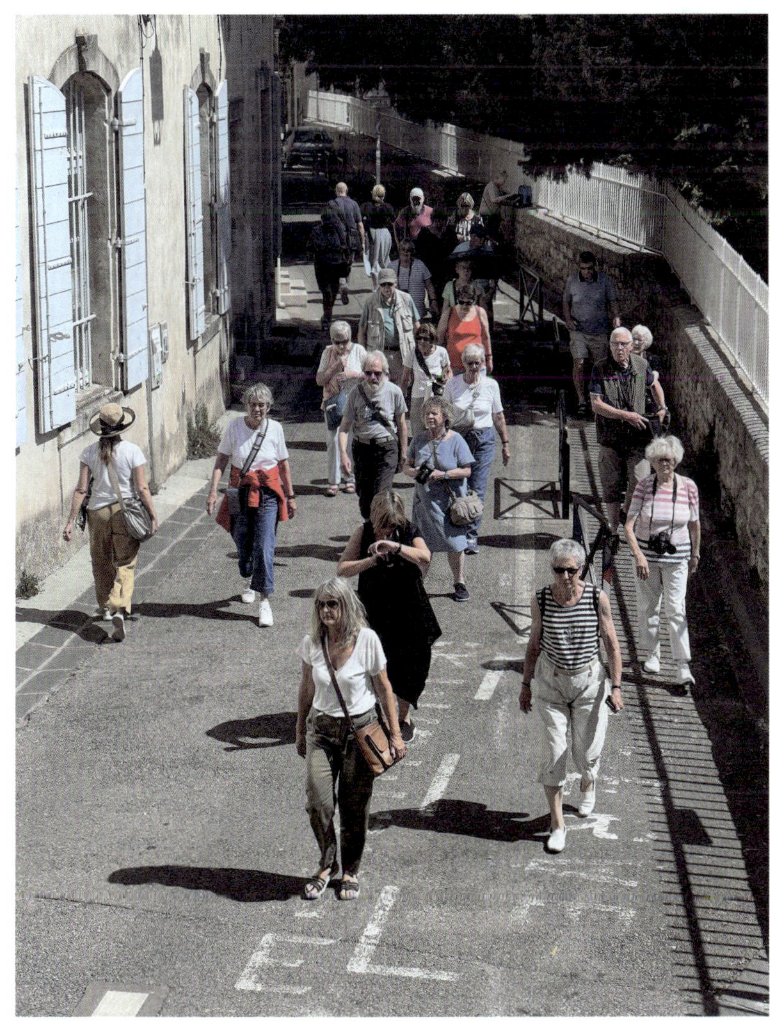

A tour group outside the Roman Theater, Arles

and immediately this cyclist being chased by the police crashed into the cab we were in, got up, jumped back on his bike, and sped away. It was a funny first impression of what is usually a sleepy town. Alex and I went directly to the museum where Laura was installing her show. There were three or four curators, and Laura asked what we thought. Me and Alex started making install suggestions, and I think the curators were like, "Who are these people and what are they doing?" I'm sort of used to doing that with Laura when she makes a show, but I don't know how welcome our contributions were. I had nothing to compare Arles to because I had spent no time in France. It's a little bit like a caricature, especially in the summer. It's so cute, and everything is flowers and sidewalk cafés and cobblestones. It's more user-friendly to a non–French speaker like myself than other parts of France because it's so touristy. After being there for twenty-four hours, you start to recognize everybody. You sit in the main square and you'll see the person who works at the coffee shop or the museum walk by.

I loved the Saturday market. It was summer when I was there, so there were a lot of stone fruits and berries. There was one farmer who grew Japanese vegetables and herbs and had a van with cute drawings all over it. And a grouchy woman in the *bio* (organic) section who had really good peaches and apricots. There was a pasta vendor who had these giant lemon-ricotta raviolis that you could fry. I also liked the coffee shop, where a guy made espresso drinks and sold beans. With a translation app, we figured out how to get the right grind to make cold brew.

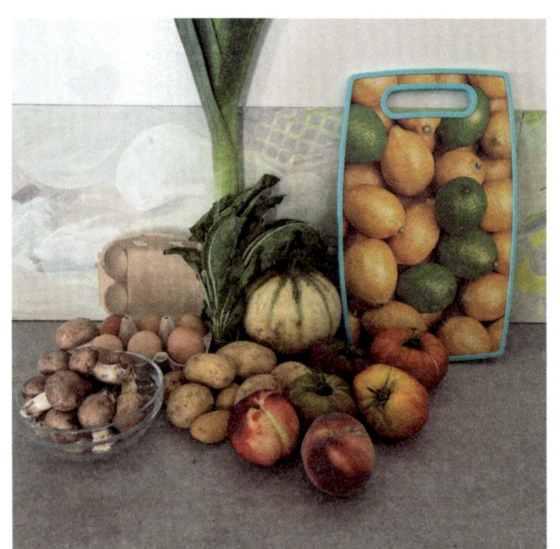
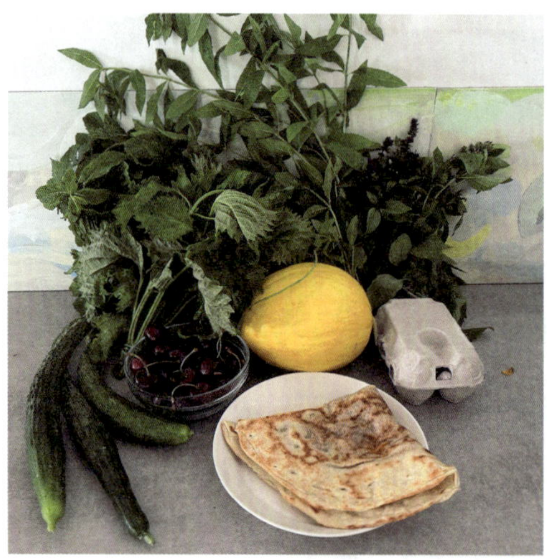
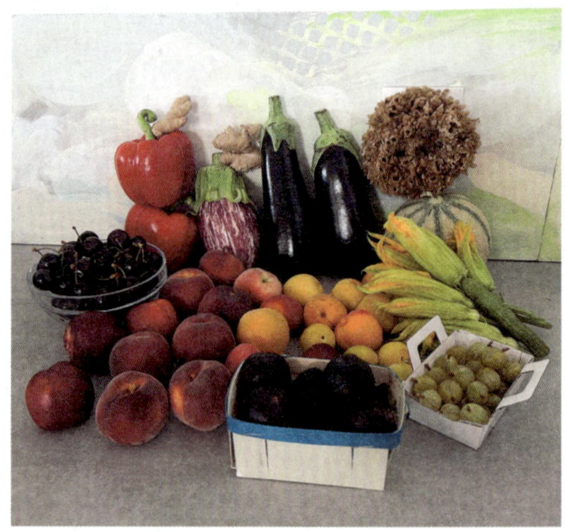
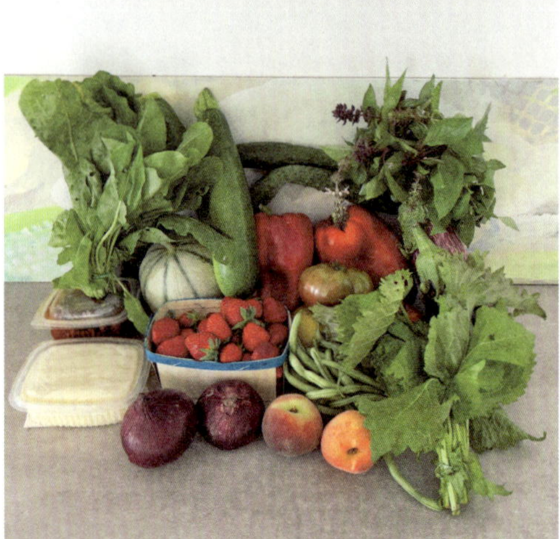
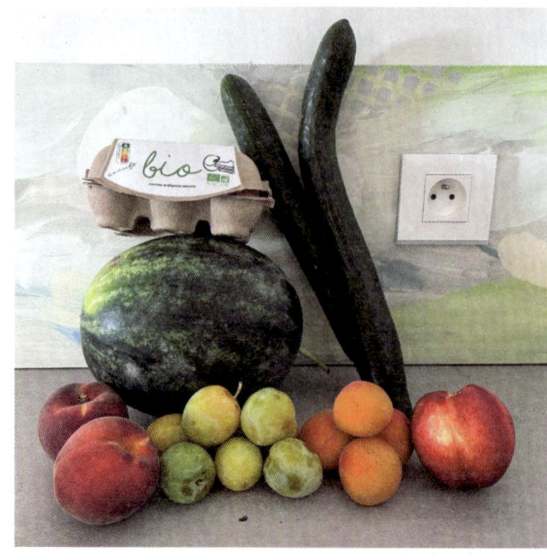

Produce from the Arles markets

It was so hot while I was there, and I wanted to make iced coffee, which was not really available. I went to the Biocoop grocery store and the cheese shop a lot. I was a bit anxious about going to restaurants by myself, because I don't speak French and don't love dining alone. So I cooked a lot. I accidentally made a massive batch of ratatouille and ate it for a week. In Arles on Sunday and Monday, a lot of shops are closed, so I would get really stressed out on Saturday, stocking up for the upcoming food drought.

I had first seen the house in 2021 when there was not much art yet. It felt really open at that point. I was into the possibility of it; I like art in specific architecture more than a typical gallery, and the idea of making something for a space like that was compelling. When I came back for my actual residency, more people had been there, and nearly every wall had been covered. So I was figuring out how to work around the limitations and questions of aesthetic harmony versus dissonance. Does one try to make something that's nice and fits in with everyone else's art or to make something antagonistic to the circumstances? There were some things like Julie Beaufils's windowsills, Naoki Sutter-Shudo's rope, and Laura's tiles—elegant works so perfectly integrated into the house that they were sort of unquestionable. Whereas other things felt more antagonistic to the circumstances of the house or the other art. I came right when Naoki was finishing his residency, and he had covered up one of Parker Ito's works and introduced that possibility. There were no clear instructions of what one was meant to do.

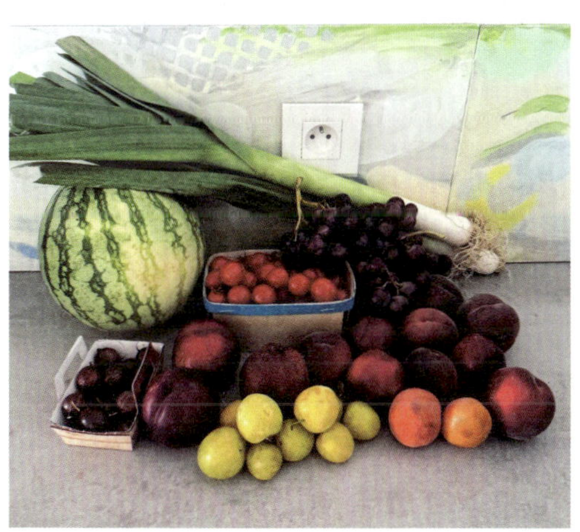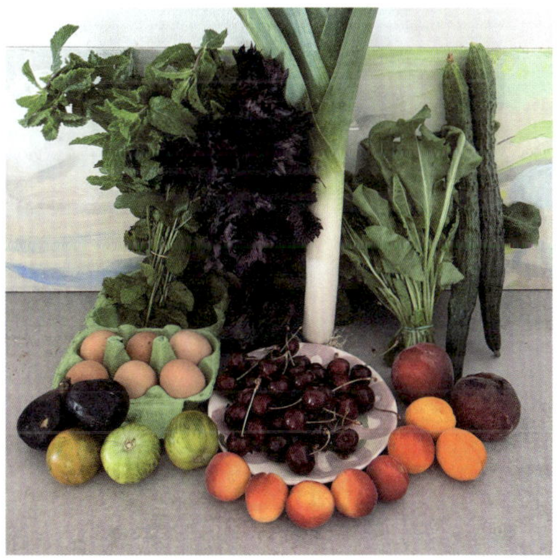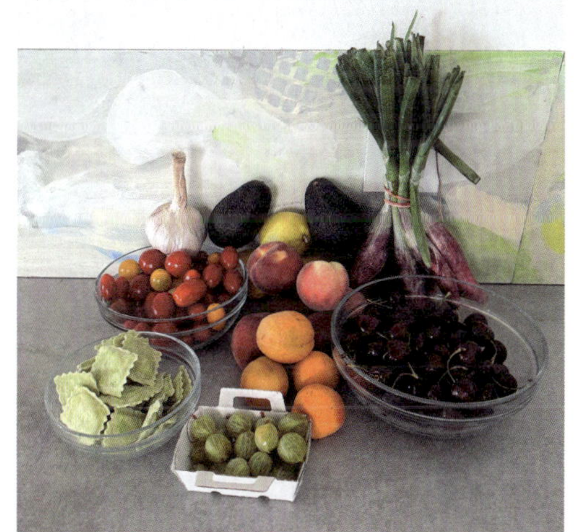

I was there for six weeks, and I used the time in a few ways. I made some book dummies of older work. At that time, I had been making photographs in Luther Burbank's Gold Ridge Experiment Farm in Sebastopol, California, for a few years, and I had never really edited them. So I spent a lot of time in the studio editing and organizing those pictures in a way that I didn't have time for before that. Doing that, Van Gogh was on my mind—working on images of nature that were heightened by a stylized representation. Toward the end of my time, the Rencontres d'Arles happened, which is this photography exhibition spread over many venues across town. I wrote reviews of the exhibitions and glued them in the guest book. I have a complicated relationship with photography. I teach it and I studied it, but most of it, I think, is bad. This is true of all art, but photography has its own particular demons. That photo festival had so many egregious examples of ethically questionable and formally impoverished photography. There were some great historical shows, but generally it felt like most of the festival had a very outdated idea of photography, which I tried to articulate in my reviews.

In terms of my pieces for the house, the work I was making then was large prints on adhesive vinyl of 3D-rendered objects, affixed directly to the wall. I had a sense of the scale of some of the spaces in the house, so I brought tall works to fit the high ceilings. I'd been making images of paper straws, and they can occupy a lot of visual space without taking up very much physical space. So I printed a few in different sizes in New York, and they rolled up to the size of a

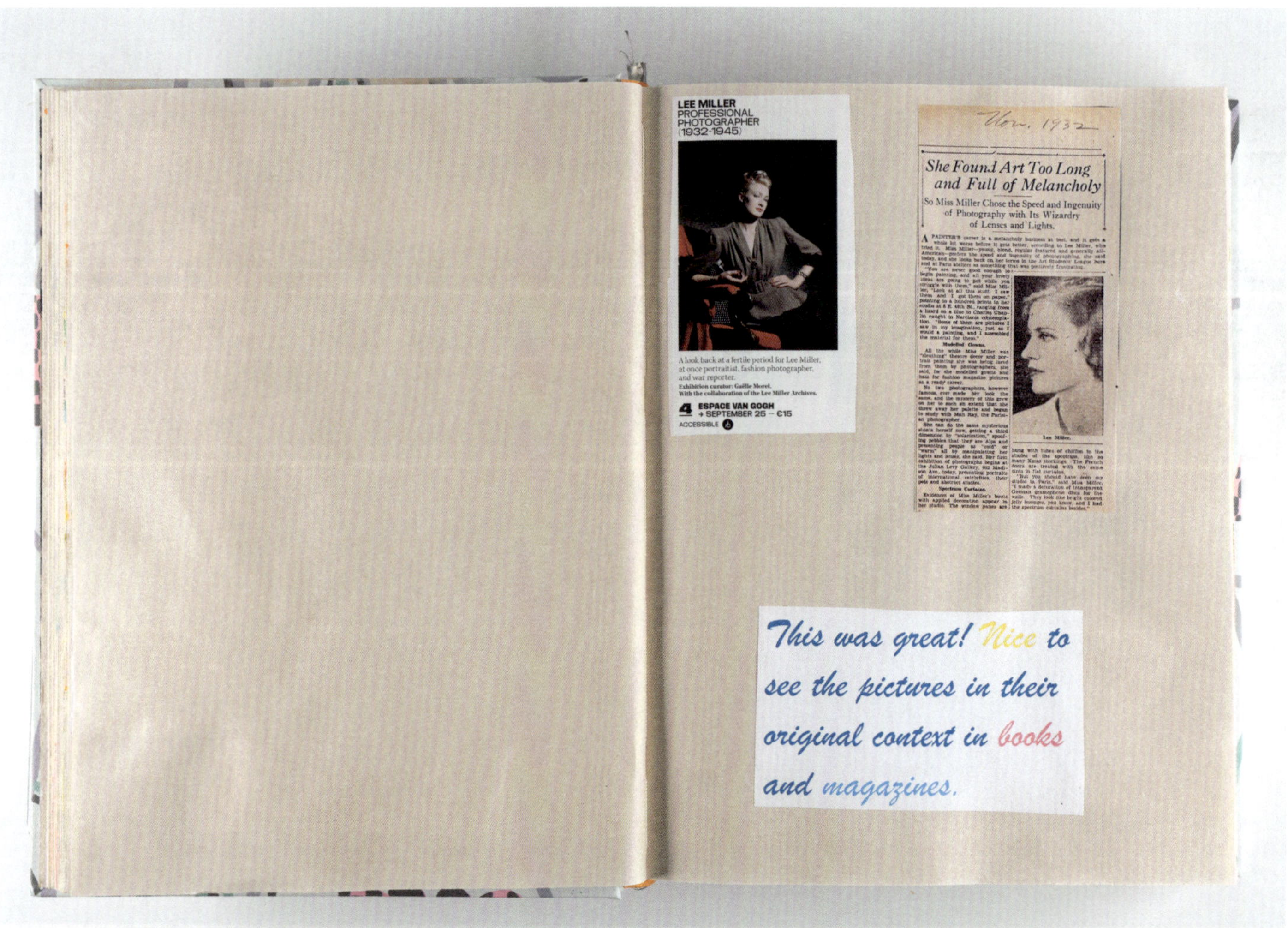

Asha's review of the exhibition *Lee Miller: Professional Photographer (1932–1945)*, part of the Rencontres d'Arles, 2022.

Coke can. I brought them with the idea that I would see how they worked with whatever else was there. I had a straw with cartoon elephants printed on it that kind of matched the marks on Laura's curtains, so I installed that next to those. I tried to install it by myself with the leaning ladder that was there. I put it against the wall and was at the top, nine feet above the floor, and as I was sticking the straw, I started to feel the ladder sliding down. I kind of rode it down the wall, and right before it hit the ground, I jumped in the air. My friend Daphne came to visit a few days later, and I waited and put it up with her, because I didn't want to crack my head open and die alone on the floor of the bedroom. I also had a straw with different fruits on it, which looked like this produce bag at the Arles market—a nice echo. I put that one high in the hallway using a very tall ladder this guy from LUMA brought. He didn't speak English, so it was an exercise in nonverbal communication. Sometimes the vinyl works don't stick properly, so I wanted to print a work more permanently onto a surface in the house. I realized I could remove one of the kitchen cabinet doors and UV print directly on it. The 3D-modeled works are rendered in a virtual model of a space. So for that one, I put a teacup in a virtual model of the kitchen, the room it would be installed in. On the surface of the liquid there is a reflection of the table with my hat on it, the chairs that Julie and Julien Ceccaldi customized, and the rest of the room. This reflection is an image of the specific moment that I was there. It's a kind of portal to that stage of the residency. I found a place to print the door in Marseille, and I sent them the file. When I asked if they could

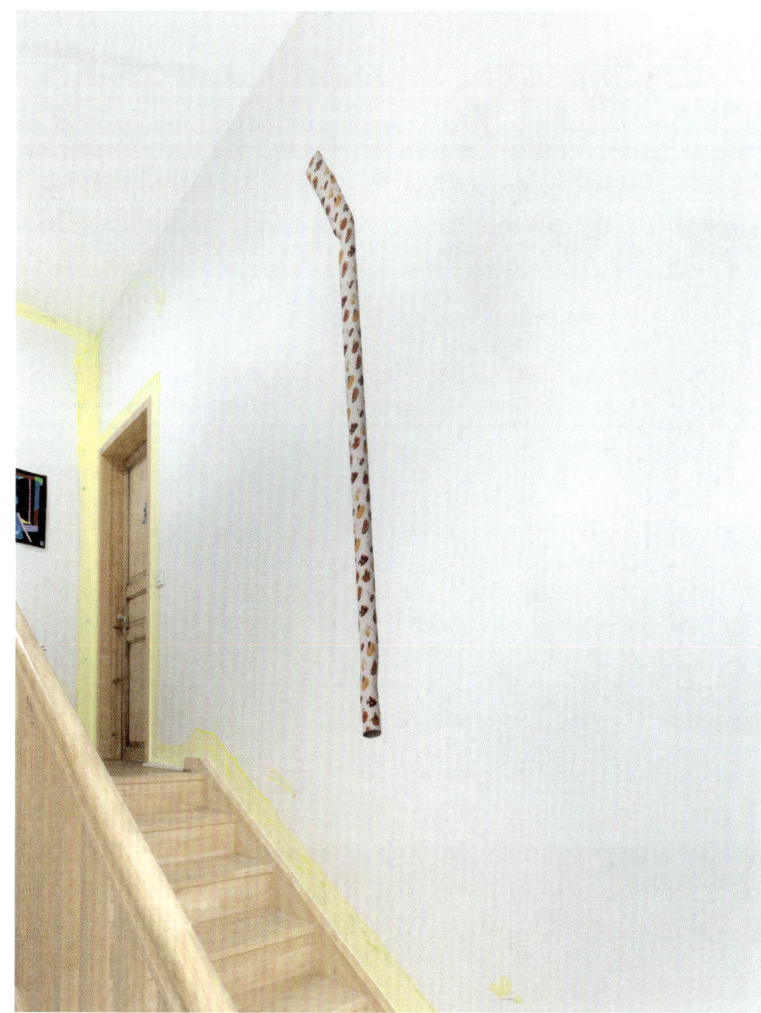

Asha Schechter, *Ecostraw (Fruit)*, inkjet print on adhesive vinyl

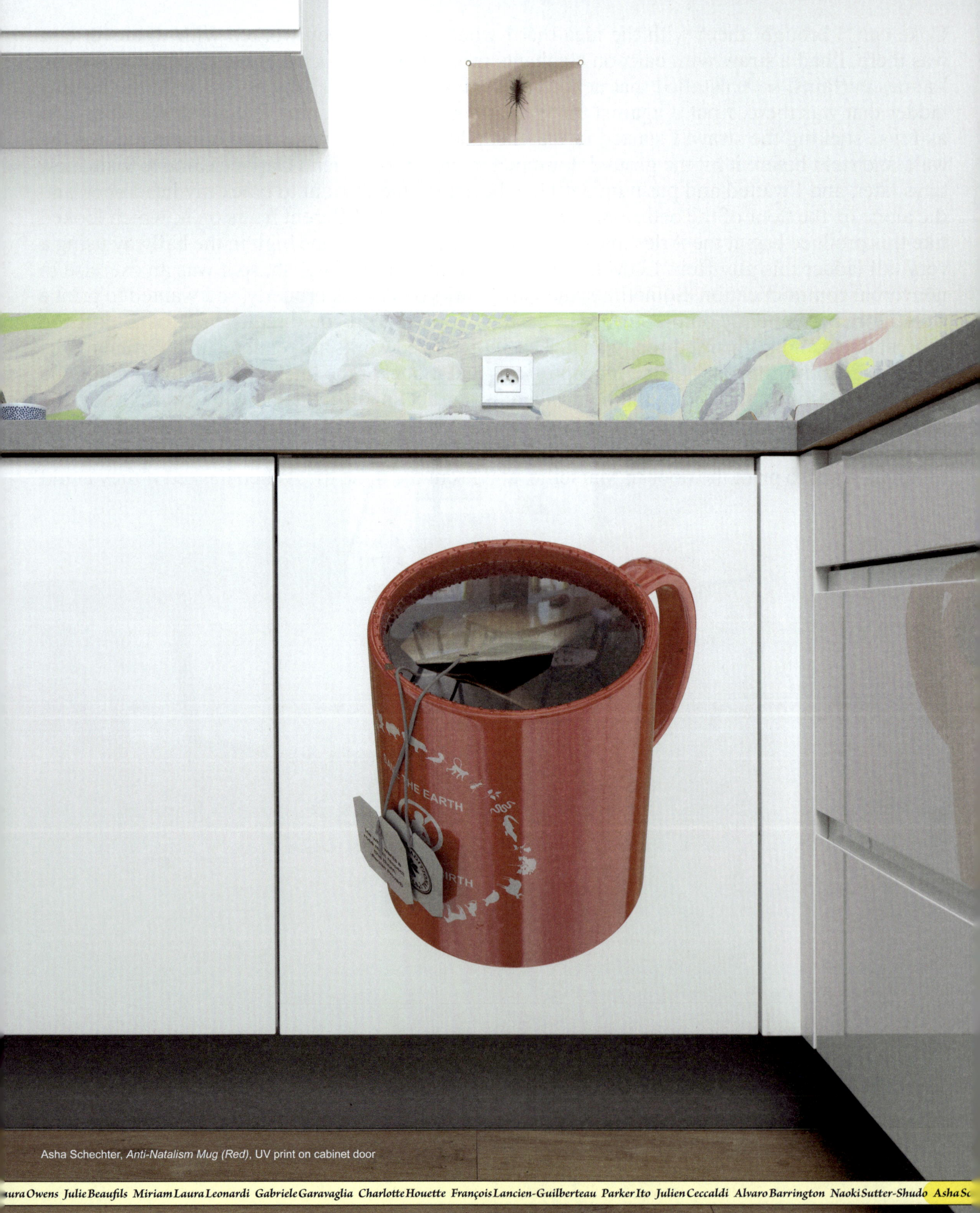

Asha Schechter, *Anti-Natalism Mug (Red)*, UV print on cabinet door

them the file. When I asked if they could send a photo of a test print, the guy replied with a lowercase almost-haiku that said:

no time
i am very busy
i'll try

I removed the cabinet door, and it and it weighed, like, forty pounds. It was extremely hot out, and I carried it wrapped in paper through Arles to the train station. So I'm sweating, and I get on the train and go to the train station in Marseille and take a taxi to the print shop. And this guy Sam takes me to the back area, brings up my file, and prints one test. We made a slight change to the file, he printed it, and it looked good. It was, like, seventy euros, extremely fast, cheap, and really well done. We packed the door back up, and I decided to walk to this restaurant that I've been to before. So I walked with the heavy door for twenty minutes or so, sweating and feeling crazy, ate lunch, took the train back, and put it back on the hinges. The other thing I made was a blanket printed with a photograph of a sunflower I made in California, ordered from an online print-on-demand place. I wanted to contribute something useful to the house; I saw how people had made functional objects, like cups and ceramics and the tiles Laura made. So I made a blanket that kind

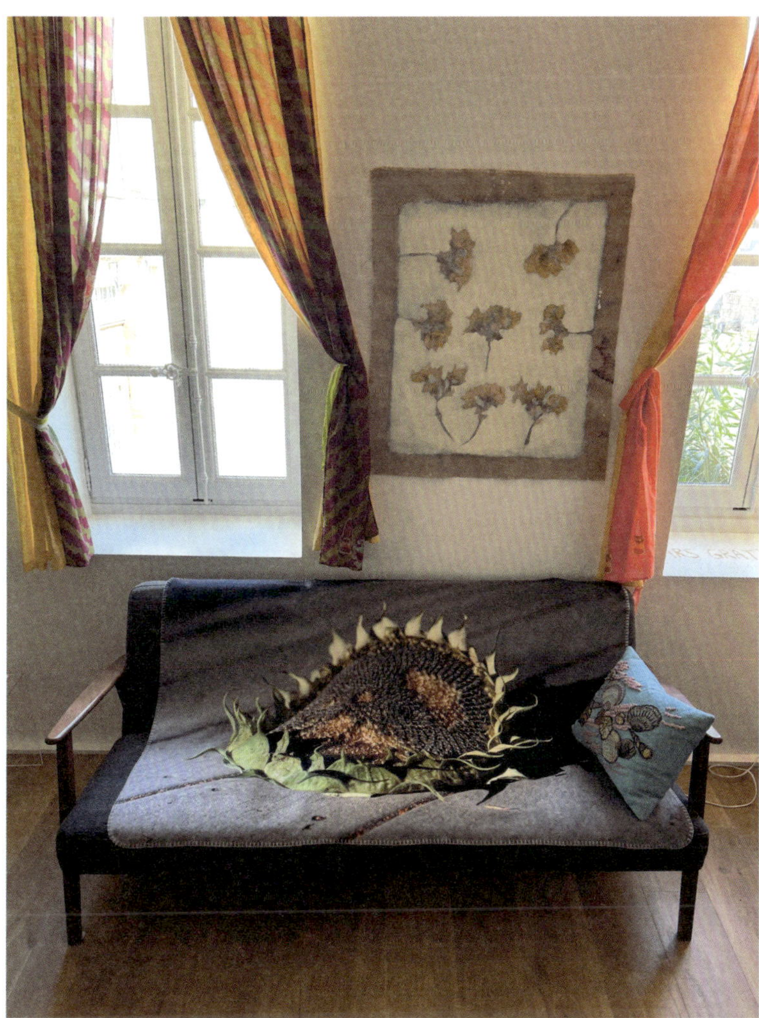

Asha Schechter, *Sunflower Blanket for Vincent*, print-on-demand blanket

of engages with the Van Gogh merch industry, the sunflower thing, Arles, and Provence. I had fantasies of doing a coffee shop once a week where I would bake, or an iteration of my gallery The Vanity, but I didn't get to those things. When I was there in 2021, Charlotte Houette and François Lancien-Guilberteau were doing the ciné-club, and I screened Gregg Araki's film *Nowhere*, and we had pizza, teen-sleepover style. I thought it was nice how they made a social space in the residency. I didn't realize that LUMA was so focused on Relational Aesthetics, so the idea of doing a coffee shop as an artwork in this town where you have works by Rirkrit Tiravanija, Pierre Hughye, etc., is kind of funnier now than I realized at the time. It could have been read as parody.

I didn't know many of the European artists very well. I knew Mona Varichon and Miriam Laura Leonardi. The summer before, when Charlotte and François were in residence, I met them, and they invited me and Alex to stay at their apartment in Paris for the remaining three weeks of their residency and look after their cat, Michel. That was so nice and made that first trip to Paris really great. At Laura's opening, I met a lot of the other artists who would eventually do the residency. So there was this kind of imaginary community that formed among all of the residents. In Arles, I met some people who lived there, like Julia Marchand, Bice Curiger, and Margaux Bonopera, curators at Fondation Vincent van Gogh; Clara Murray, who works for a photographer in town; Alicia Vaïsse, who eventually did the residency; some of the LUMA people that worked in the Atelier; and Julie Boukobza, who showed us all around. But any semblance of artistic community was really

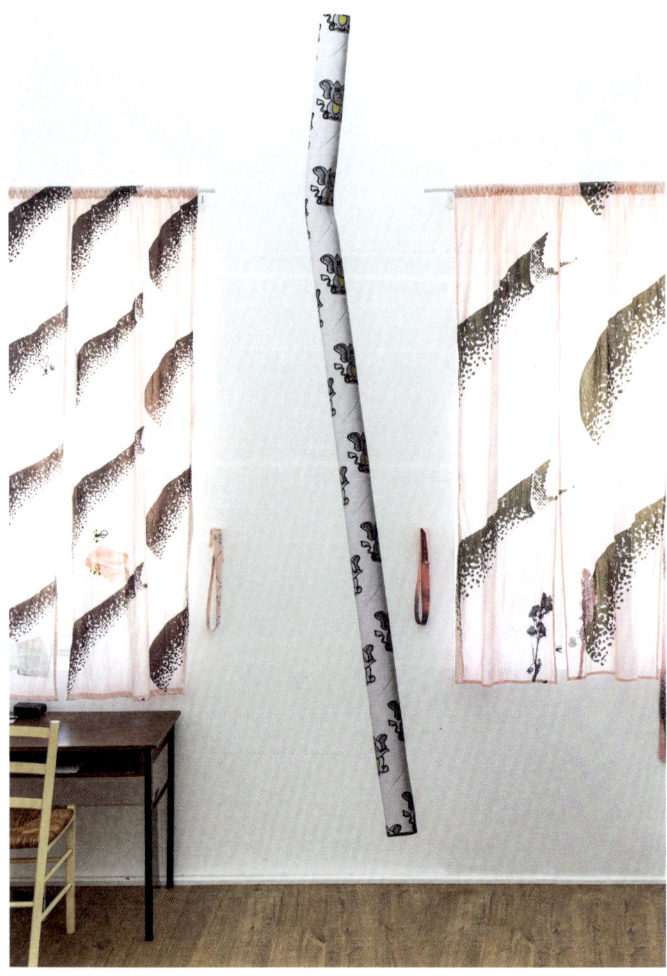

Asha Schechter, *Ecostraw (Elephant)*, inkjet print on adhesive vinyl

formed in this kind of expanded imaginary way between the residents, one after another, where you're living with their contributions. There were some moments around Laura's show when a lot of us were there at the same time, when you felt more of a communal experience. And there were a few more social moments within my time there. A friend of mine, Cooper Jacoby, had a show at High Art in Arles when I was there. So when that opened, he and his wife Stephanie Seidel, who's also my friend, stayed. I had the High Art people, like Anna Frera and Jason Hwang, over. A few other friends came through—Ian James and Patricia Fernández and Luna from Los Angeles and Daphne Correll from Berlin—and they stayed at the house with me. The house was so big, it was easy to host people. When Naoki and his wife Allie and I overlapped, it was fun going out and walking around the amphitheater, looking at stray cats, having a spritz; it felt a bit like the fantasy of Provence. But most of the time when I was there, I was in the studio alone, projecting the NBA finals on the wall and working in Photoshop. It was a weird mix of being hypersocial and then a chunk in the middle that was the longest I've gone without talking to someone in real life. Most of the community I engaged with was more the international art world than the local scene—that's the pitfall of not speaking French. It made it harder to connect to people outside my bubble.

I imagine that if it had been a structure where everybody who did the residency was there together and had to make all the art in a month, the house would look very different. The single artist at a time maybe speaks to the mythology of Van Gogh and what he desired, with the Yellow

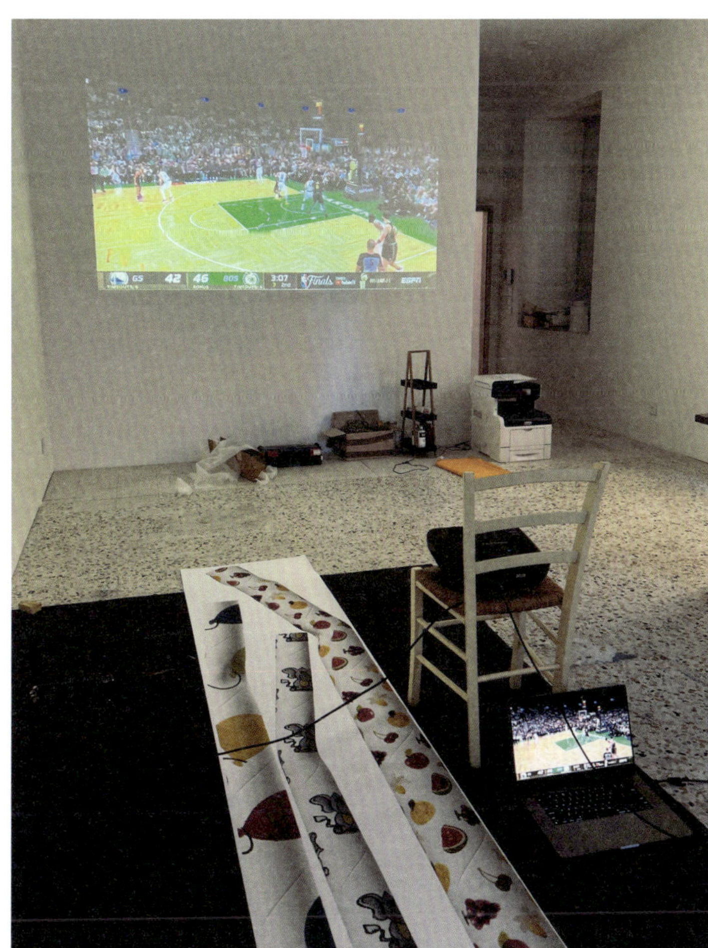

A projection of game four of the 2022 NBA finals, Golden State Warriors vs. Boston Celtics

diana Sadie Laska Eric Palgon Alicia Vaïsse Adee Roberson Clément Rodzielski Alake Shilling Mona Varichon Jacob Eisenmann Andy Robert Alexander Zevin Blake Rayne Candida Alvarez Nova Brye

House being at odds with that. He's the ultimate lone, heroic figure who sacrificed everything for his art, but maybe what he really wanted was to impress his friends and have a community where he could make art, make a living, and have a comfortable life. It's a funny thing—his desire was to be stable, but he became the model of chaotic, artistic instability. So the house is this weird version of both of those things. It's probably the biggest house I'm ever going to "live" in; there was a glimpse of luxury, but only for a short amount of time. It was interesting to think about collectivity and individuality and how those ideas express themselves. Both in obvious collaboration, like the ciné-club, or unplanned collaboration, like Naoki covering Parker's work or me reflecting Julie's and Julien's chairs. To make something for a situation where you're in conversation with the space and all these other artists, that accretes over time, is out of the ordinary.

The final form of the house was a cacophony. Questions of aesthetic harmony had mostly been done away with. But as people have mentioned, it could have been crazier; it was still relatively tame. Someone could have poured bronze into the toilet so it didn't work anymore. Or had a huge party and left the residue behind. I wonder if that was partially because there were no spoken rules, nothing to push against. I suspect the main reason is because everyone who did the residency is friends with Laura and thought it would be disrespectful to her. No one painted an entire wall, aside from Charlotte's bathroom mural. Over the course of the time I visited the house, I saw the Gustave Moreau house and Henri Matisse's Chapelle du Rosaire, and went to

Venice and saw all these Giovanni Battista Tiepolo works in churches. I was really affected by those experiences, and I arrived at this feeling that this is when art is most meaningful: when it's part of life and incorporated into structures that have other functions. Seeing the house in the end, I was left with a lot of questions. Who is it for, and what is it going to be? If it stops being a house where people stay, what is it?

The residence is an example of the way Laura approaches things, where she engineers situations and then sees what happens within them. 356 Mission was like that, and our publishing project is a bit like that too. The projects take on a life of their own. And I feel like that's what happened in Arles. What's different between the original Studio of the South and Laura's is that the original was so much hinging on Van Gogh's presence and an expectation about what would happen. Laura, I think, is more invested in producing a space for people whom she trusts and supports to do something. And I don't really feel like she's that invested in outcomes, in the way that most systems and opportunities in the art world are. She said, "Do whatever you want when you're there…You can just read the whole time." And that's very different from a lot of the circumstances you encounter as an artist, where there's an expectation of productivity or a product that is beneficial to somebody else. That was the most generous part of this invitation—you could just go there and do whatever you want.

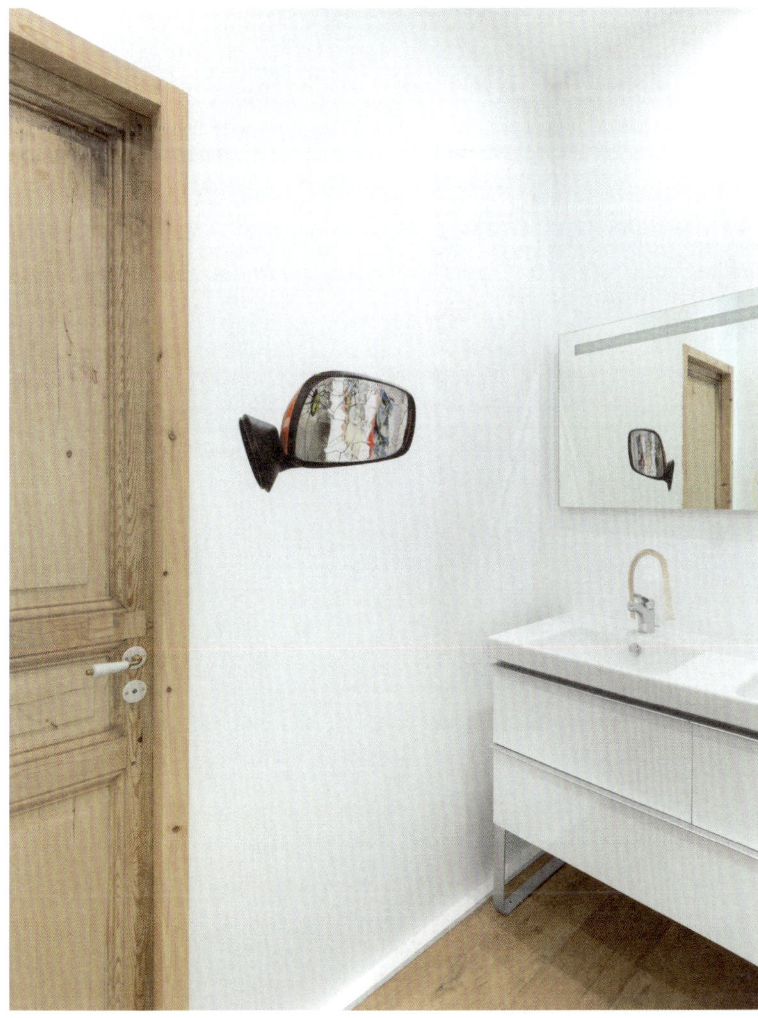

Asha Schechter, *Prius Mirror from Baby Barcelona with V's Grasshopper*, inkjet print on adhesive vinyl

Gary Indiana

I always liked Vincent van Gogh's paintings, but I didn't know that much about his life. I knew his brother was the only person who ever bought a painting from him and that he never had any money. I wouldn't call it a cautionary tale because, obviously, if it was, I missed the caution of it. But I always thought of him as a sort of wonderful, tormented person. Like Antonin Artaud or some of these people that I like, not because they're mad but because they managed to make something wonderful out of their madness. I don't think madness is very good; it's not attractive, you know? I mean, I am afraid of insane people. But from what I know of him, he never seemed to me like an insane person, just a really tormented person. I'm very sympathetic to people that end up in mental institutions because institutions are not nice. I think maybe he was lucky in some ways; he had sympathetic doctors. But as a general rule—I mean, it's insane people without money that end up in horrible situations. He was an artist too, and even in his time, I think, he was respected as such.

My first time in Arles had been the year before for Laura Owens's exhibition at the Fondation Vincent van Gogh Arles. Laura had rented an apartment, and I was there for about a month. My

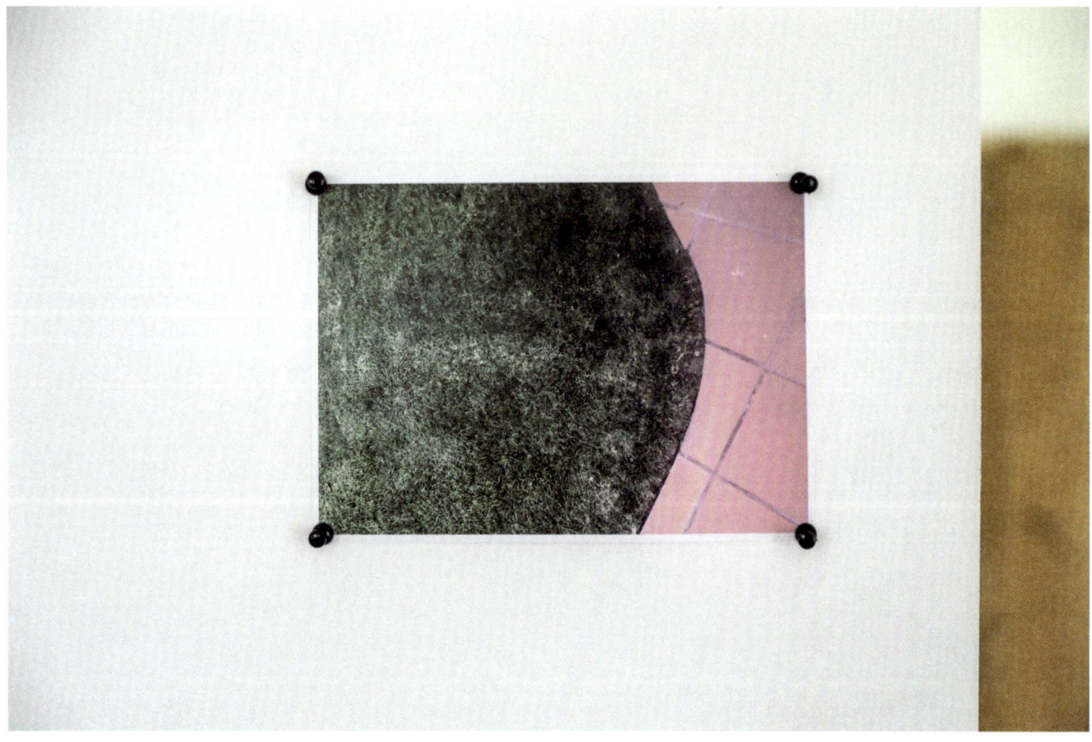

Gary Indiana, *Untitled*, inkjet print

initial impression of Arles was that it was gorgeous. I love little French villages. It just was completely charming to me. The pace of it was so much more agreeable than Paris and certainly more than New York City. I loved the feeling of the city hall—I fell in love with the ceiling. I took a million photos of that ceiling. One of the pictures I took of the city hall is in the house. I put a Paul Éluard poem right on it. It was a poem that he wrote in Saint-Alban. And the amphitheater that you can see right out the window of the residence—there were a lot of concerts that were annoying. They were OK, but I didn't go in to see any of it because I could see it from the window.

When I was doing the residency, it was very different from the first time I was in Arles because it was so hot outside. Hot enough that, at my age, you don't go outside. You could just keel over and croak. So I spent almost all my time indoors. I would go out first thing in the morning. Even if I didn't sleep the night before, I would go out before nine o'clock. I would get my baguette if the market was that day; I'd run down there and get a bunch of stuff: my cheeses, my vegetables. I'd get all of that really early and haul it all back to the residence, and then I wouldn't go out again until late in the day when it cooled a little bit. It was so hot I couldn't function; I just ran the air conditioning around the clock. When I was doing the residency, my friends Lily and Matt, an English couple who live in New York, wanted me to meet Lily's father, who resides somewhere nearby in the South of France. They came to Arles to have lunch with me. The father knew this woman who lived on the street parallel to the residence, and we had coffee at her

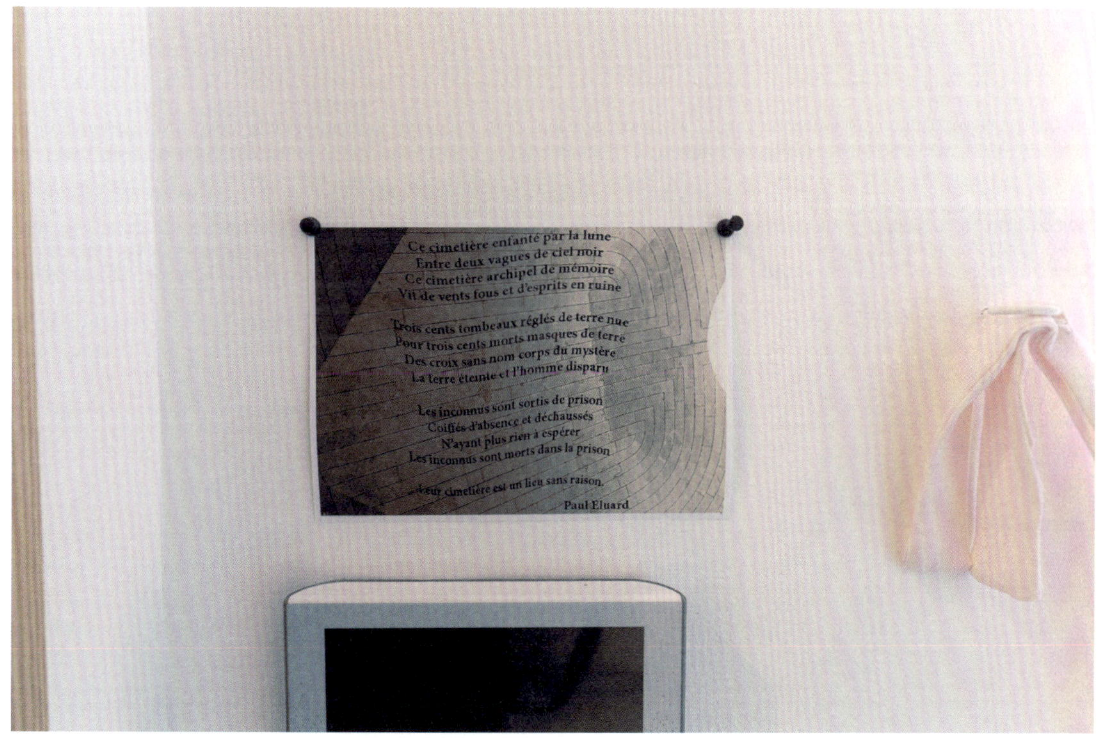

Gary Indiana, *Untitled*, inkjet print

place. I mentioned that I was using the air conditioning all the time because it was so hot. She said, "Well, you ruin it for the rest of us because air conditioning heats up the street and makes it worse." She was accusing me of some criminal use of air conditioning.

While I was there, I met a number of people that worked at LUMA, like Simon, Julie, Bice and Jacqueline, and their dog, Schatzi. It was really nice to see Bice; I hadn't seen her in, like, thirty years. I used to do things for *Parkett* in the early days, and I think I stayed with her once in Zurich for a day or two, or she found me a place to stay, or something. I love Bice; I always thought she was fabulous and still is fabulous.

When I began the residency, I had great plans for making a lot of paintings. I was inspired by the fact that Laura had hung one of my paintings in her house—one of the ones I did at 356 Mission, Los Angeles. But I didn't, really. I made one painting and put up some photos. I had also hoped to get some writing done. The way I conceived of the work for the house and installed it was based on using photos I had taken in Arles. I wanted the photos to be in Arles, but later I realized that a couple of them weren't. They were taken in LA, but you wouldn't be able to tell that. I wanted to put photos not all together but just in discreet places so that people's sight lines would go to those photos. If they walked into a room or they were going up the stairs, they would see those photos. With a lot of them, you wouldn't very specifically know they were taken in Arles, but they were. I wanted it to feel like there was some connection between the photos and the location. The other art

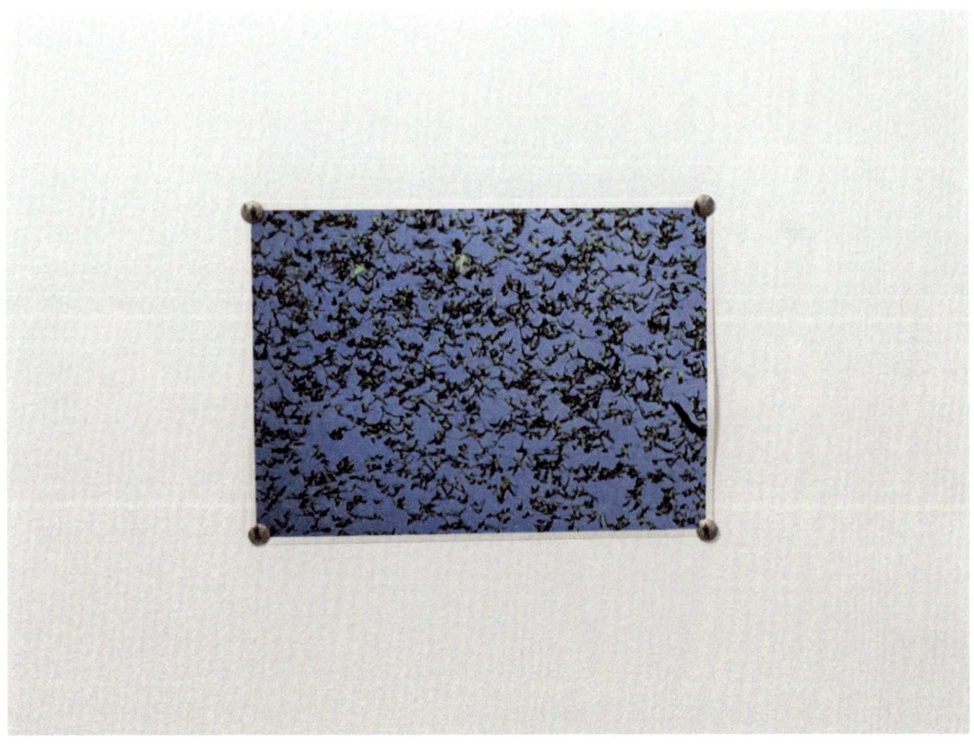

Gary Indiana, *Untitled*, inkjet print

in the house guided my approach, to the extent that I had to avoid other people to find spots where there wasn't anything. There was that one guy who had painted huge things all over the place. So one whole wall was out of the question. I did put one photo at the end of that wall. I wanted to do the stairwell; I wanted to put things in strategic locations, but not really obtrusive things, so people would go, "Oh, there's that." It's a very modest sort of work. When you walk into a place and you see that somebody's covered a whole wall with some stupid cartoony bullshit, It doesn't make you want to make a big statement. It's like, how can I compete with this idiocy?

Living in the house was great. I had five floors all to myself. You settle into a routine. No matter where you are, if you stay anywhere long enough, it turns into a rut. But the remarkable thing that summer was how oppressive the heat was. It was something not to be believed. You know, I'm sure it's gonna be the same from now on. I had the impression that people were really suffering, and not just old people. It was that bad. You also had the fires, which weren't directly in Arles, but I think they probably heated Arles up a lot more than my air conditioning. I was with Julie—we took the train down from Paris together, and then a car picked us up in Avignon, and that's when we saw the fires. The sky was full of smoke and helicopters, and some of the roads that we were trying to take to get to Arles were blocked by different fire departments. It really was so dramatic and scary.

I would go to the Actes Sud bookstore all the time. I love that bookstore. I would go to the sandwich place that had a window just around the corner. I would get a sandwich every day. That would be

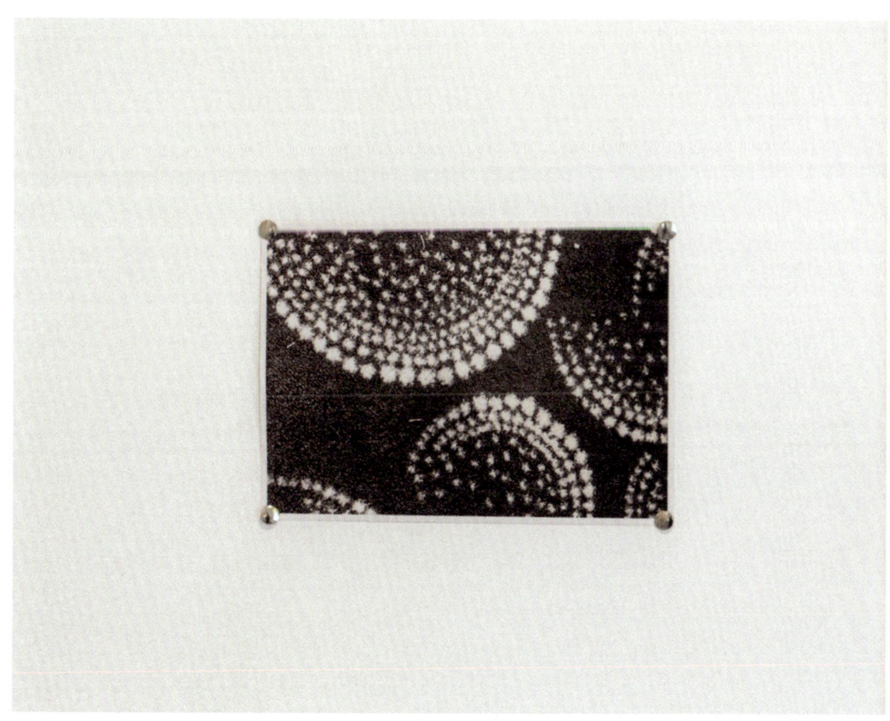

Gary Indiana, *Untitled*, inkjet print

my lunch or my dinner or whatever. And of course I went to the Carrefour quite a lot and the cheese shop nearby, which is wonderful. And the market is so wonderful. The Saturday market—that's a whole trip. I love France because you still have these markets where they're selling every kind of thing you can eat, and it's all good, it's all fresh, it all just came from the farm. I'd get different cheeses, maybe some prepared things, like Vietnamese noodles. I would get tomatoes because the tomatoes tasted like tomatoes. Not like any tomatoes we can buy in this country.

I was a part of it. And to me, that was the joy of it—that I was part of the residency. It's maybe hard to explain, but I felt the same thing when I did the show at 356 Mission. I was living upstairs at the gallery for a month, and when I came downstairs, there were all these people that worked there whom I could have coffee with and say hello to, and I could also go upstairs and be completely alone. And it felt good to be part of something, like a community of some kind. You know, I don't have that in New York anymore. I think I have more of it in LA, but the exigencies of staying in LA are prohibitive at this point. When I was in Arles, I was alone all the time, but that was OK. People get to know you—the people who you buy sandwiches from and who serve you in a restaurant and the people from a store—they get to know you, and they're very friendly. You know, Americans are so weird about the French. I've been going to France practically since I was a kid, and I have never found the French to be the way Americans think they are. I've always found them really friendly. I was happier in Arles than I normally am here. I'm a very solitary person. I don't have any life partner, I don't have any boyfriends anymore, and when you're by yourself all the time, you kind of develop into this…I don't know. I was happier there than I am here, happier to walk outside—even though it was really hot—to go to the store to buy things. It's all pleasurable, intensely pleasurable. Here, it's just like, I have to buy milk again, I have to get eggs again. I have to do this, I have to do that, just to keep alive. Whereas, I felt like, nobody's gonna let me starve in France. The dailiness of sitting in a café—to me, that's genius. It's why I love Paris so much. I spend all my time in Paris sitting in cafés and shopping, which I hate doing in New York. I just found the quality of daily life so superior; there's just more plea-sure. I mean, it would never occur to me here, for example, to go walk along the river. I hate the river. It's been used up. It's a qualitative difference. And it's something that I've experienced not only in Arles and Paris but in Zagreb, Athens; any place in Europe, to me, has a better quality of daily life than here. Because everything here is transactional. Everything is about money here. And even though, let's say, under the surface, that's true everywhere, but in France, the idea of taking pleasure in eating food, taking pleasure just sitting in a café, having a coffee without any purpose, just simply to sit and live with your thoughts—I find that infinitely more possible anywhere in Europe than here. I wish I could get that feeling back about New York. I'm trying to rekindle some interest in this city, but I think this city has ruined me. It just ruined me.

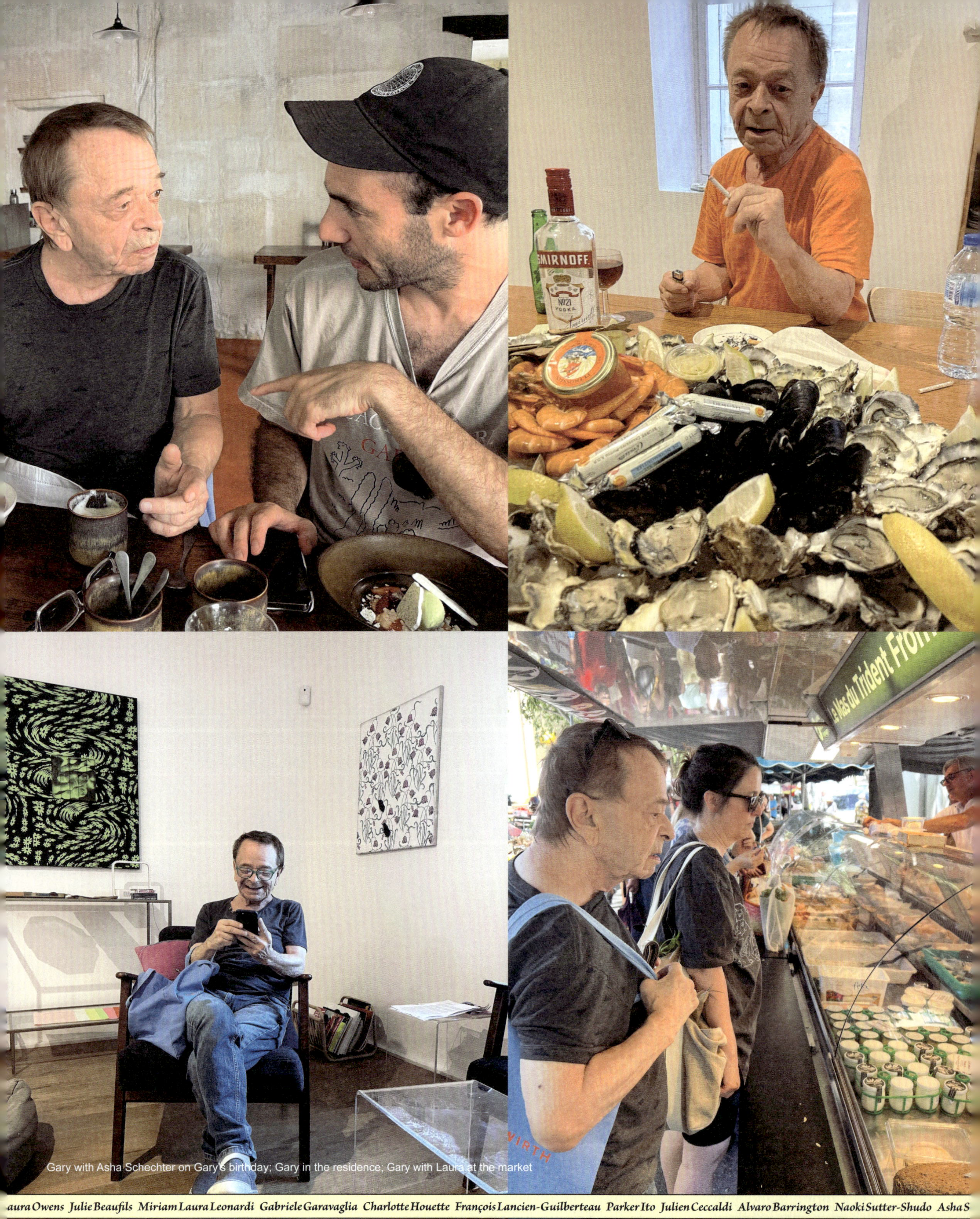

Gary with Asha Schechter on Gary's birthday; Gary in the residence, Gary with Laura at the market

114

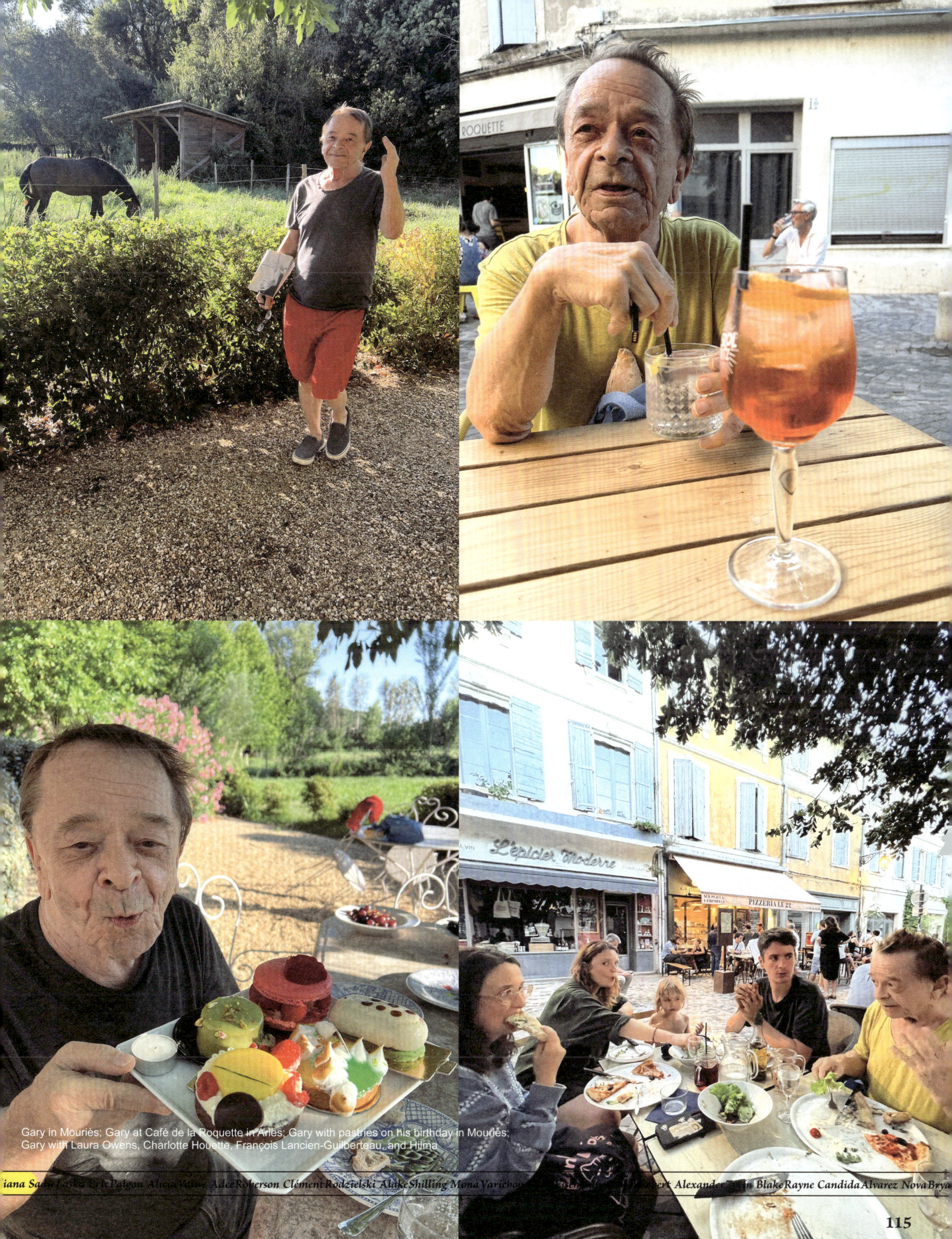

Gary in Mouriès; Gary at Café de la Roquette in Arles; Gary with pastries on his birthday in Mouriès;
Gary with Laura Owens, Charlotte Houette, François Lancien-Guilberteau, and Hilma

AUGUST 2022
Sadie Laska

I did not really think about Vincent van Gogh very much. I mean, of course I was quite aware of his famous paintings and had seen some of them and liked them, but he wasn't an artist that I was studying or thought about when I made paintings. I learned about him in art history classes, but I didn't really think about the fact that he lived in Arles too much. Being there didn't really change the way I thought about Van Gogh, maybe because I thought of him as more, like, out in the fields or something, and we were kind of, like, in town. But I did enjoy the legacy of the city and just how old it is. We definitely don't experience anything like that living in the United States.

Laura Owens and I have a ton of mutual friends, and my partner, Eric Palgon, is a very good old friend of hers, and so I really got to know her through him.

Arles is such a small, medieval old city. I guess it seems a little different from the other places I've been in Europe because of how preserved it is, historically. It felt like we were really staying in ruins, so that was cool. The residency terms were pretty vague for us. It came from a casual talk with Laura, and then we did it. I felt like we didn't really, truly know if anything was expected of us or, like, what our plan was to do there other than maybe just be there. And then

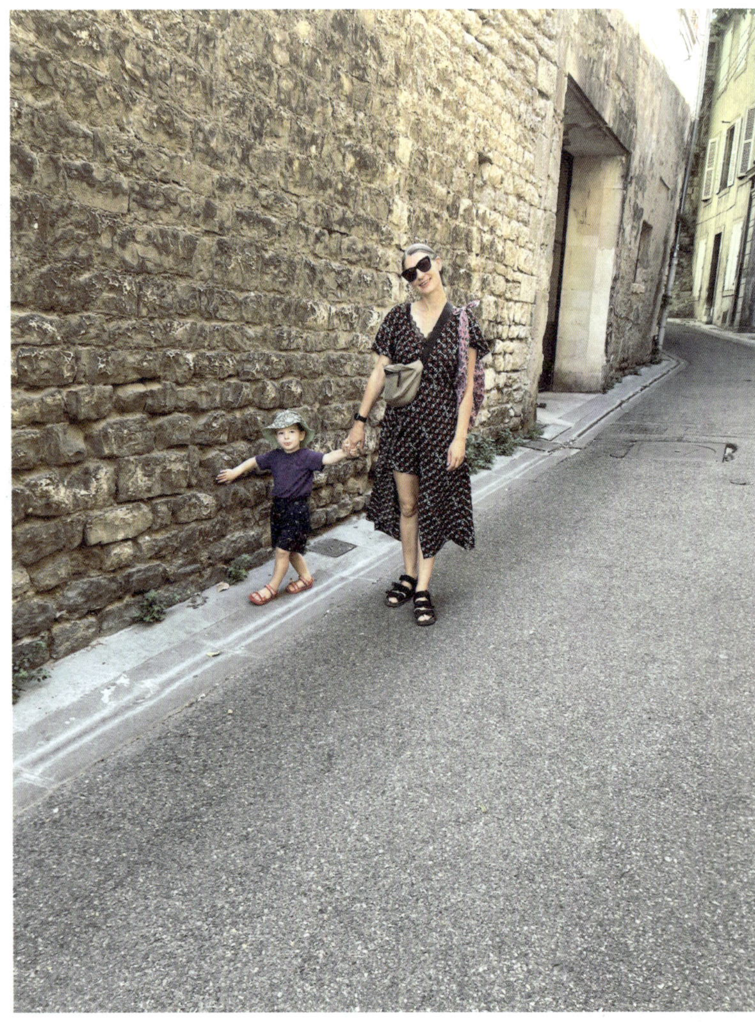

Sadie Laska with her son Cosmo

we understood more when we got there. When we arrived, I thought the house was really cool and great, and I was excited that we got to stay in it. Of course, some of the artworks we liked more than others, but it was fun to see what people had done while they were there. And then, we immediately started thinking, like, What are we going to do? I cannot remember everyone's name, but I liked the paintings in the windowsill the most, I think, and Laura's tile pieces in the bathroom were amazing. I loved the curtains the most, I think, because I'm working with fabric pieces, and I thought, I should make curtains—these are fucking awesome.

We were some of the crazy people who brought our child with us. He had just turned three. And so we were kind of overwhelmed by just being in France and trying to find a playground and food that he eats and doing stuff like that. He would only eat boxed mac 'n' cheese, and I was going to every store, trying to find that. So it did take us a minute just to get our footing there. I wish that we had stayed longer. So it was really, like, the last week that we were there that we thought about the artwork, to be honest. I just sort of expanded on the works I was making. I had been making these pieces with found and prebought flags. I didn't have anything with me to make art, so I went to the market, and they have all those vendors, and I bought sewing supplies and fabric glue and fabric paint and scissors. I found these guys that sell flags, and I bought a bunch and cut them up. I used French flags and earth flags, and I bought this great traditional fabric from the Provence region. I wanted to include that fabric because it's so specific to this place. So I made these collaged flags. And I also, found at a bookstore a book of rebus puzzles that was in French, and I did get kind of obsessed with it because I couldn't figure out what the rebus puzzles were saying. I was trying to get someone to translate it for me. I ended up with the idea of the work I was going to make—this flag work that had this rebus puzzle on it. I think it said something like, "At night I need a cap," which means, "I need a drink." But then I was, like, working on it, and I didn't like that for some reason. Then I thought of this Alain Bashung song, "La nuit je mens"—"at night I lie." It's a really famous French song. It's not about the specific region of Arles, but it talks about the Vercors massif and coves and Cadaqués and conjures the Southern French landscapes and stuff, and I was thinking about it, and I changed it to say "At night I lie," which is a nice pun—you're lying in bed but you could also be a liar. The song also has a lot of puns and double meanings, and it's about the Carlingue and the French Resistance during World War II. And men who avoided fighting in the war and lied about it later.

I painted one of the rebuses on the wall directly from the book. It means, "At night, any cap is good," and it has a donkey in it. I thought you should lay in bed and look at it because it was like "At night I lie," and so I put it in the view of where the bed was placed so you could lay there and see it. It was really interesting, that book of rebus puzzles; the illustrations for them, I think, bled into the next group of paintings that I made. The way you have these sort of logo-type images, and they're sort of layered. I had a friend come to my show this winter, and she said, "These

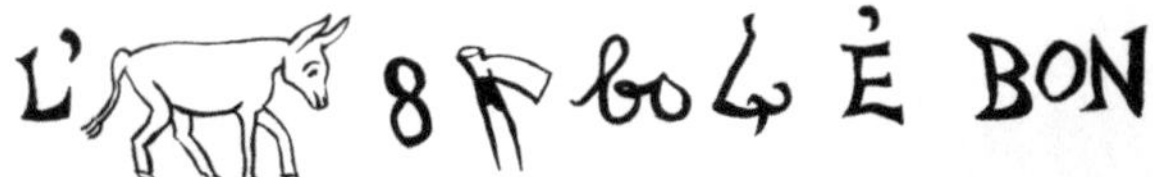

Sadie Laska, *At Night Any Cap is Good*, wall painting

look like rebus puzzles." And I was like, "Holy shit, I think they are!" Yeah, it's just, like, the visual language. Not necessarily, like, the puzzle part. And then I made another mural painting in the bathroom of that floor, based on a drawing that my son and I made together. We were in Paris, and we kept showing him Notre Dame, and we were like, "There was a big fire." And then he kept confusing it with the Eiffel Tower in his memory, and he kept saying, "Draw the Eiffel Tower on fire." So I did these drawings of the Eiffel Tower on fire. I just thought that was a funny painting to put on the wall.

We were co-parenting, so we were trying to manage who was going to watch our son and how to entertain him. And we were trying to give each other some personal space to explore, go to the studio, you know. We couldn't eat out very much because of the hours of the restaurants. We were trying to give our son dinner at six thirty, and it seemed like a lot was closed. So we were cooking a lot. I would go to the market, find food, and cook. I did the farmers' markets and the *bio* (organic) store—I love the French *bio* stores—and the Monoprix supermarket near the train station. I went there a lot and I would try on clothes. That was fun. We went to LUMA, and I was curious to see it because I had heard a lot about it and seen photos, and it's quite impressive. And it was really fun with our son. He enjoyed the architecture and the gardens, and he was playing in the pond in his underwear. So we went there a couple of times. And then we went to the Fondation Vincent van Gogh Arles. And that's about it. We also took the bus to the beach

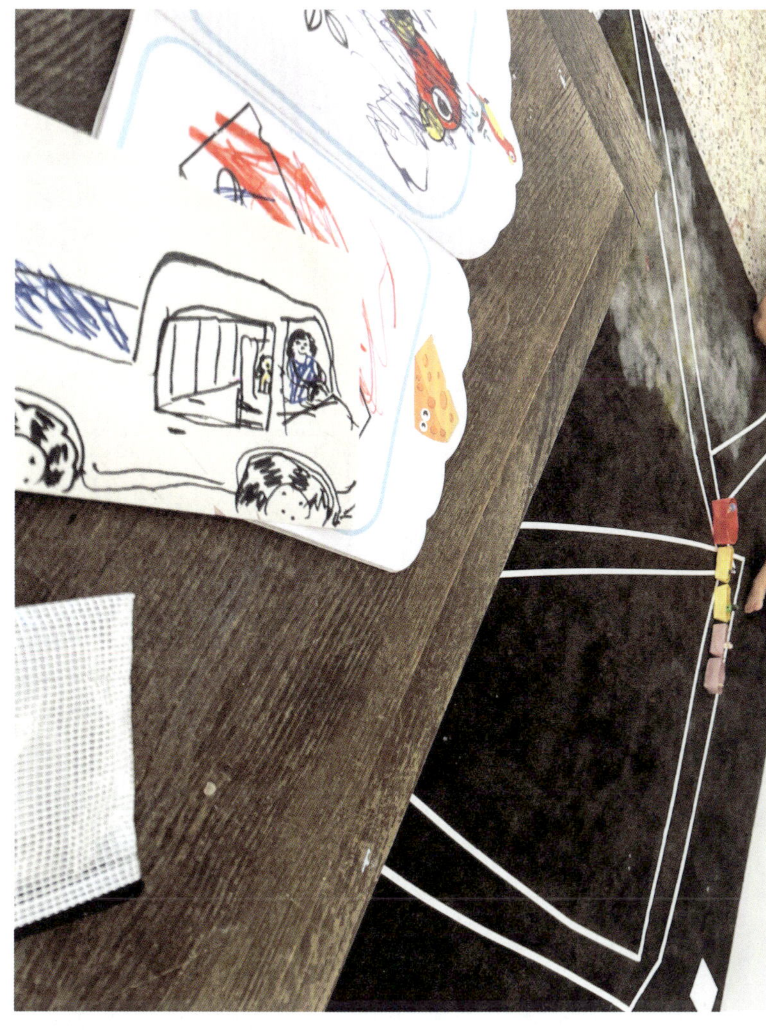

Sadie and Cosmo in the studio

…iana Sadie Laska Eric Palgon Alicia Vaïsse Adee Roberson Clément Rodzielski Alake Shilling Mona Varichon Jacob Eisenmann Andy Robert Alexander Zevin Blake Rayne Candida Alvarez Nova Bry…

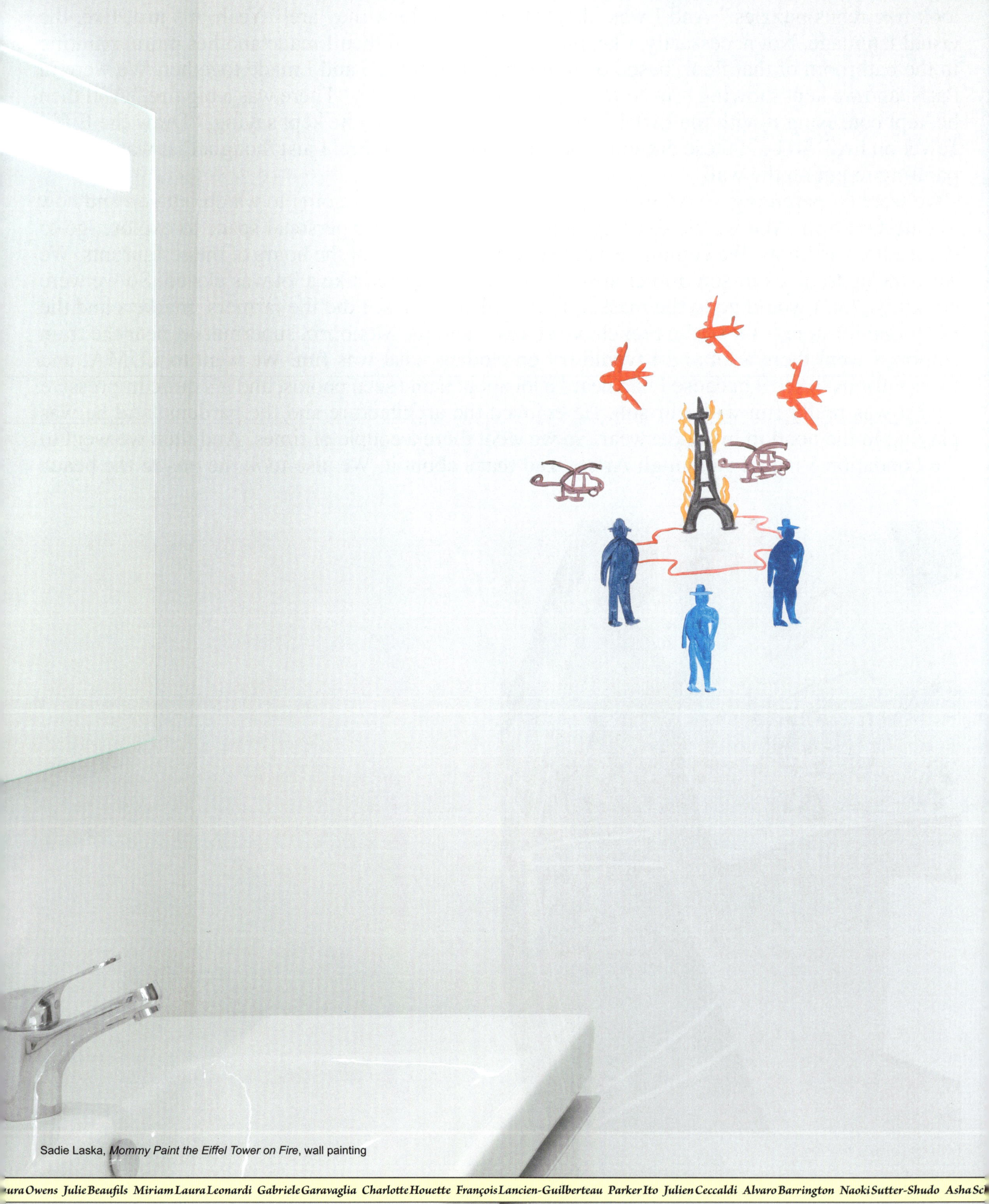

Sadie Laska, *Mommy Paint the Eiffel Tower on Fire*, wall painting

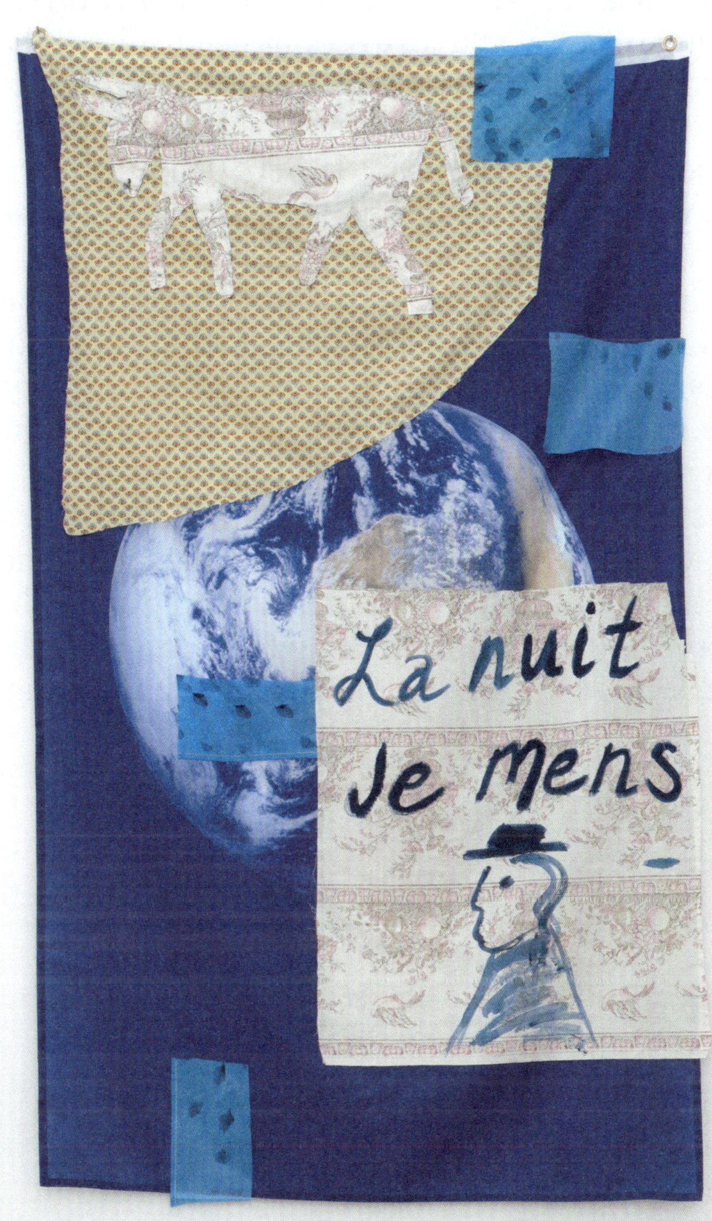

Sadie Laska, *At Night I Lie*, acrylic paint, fabric, and glue on flag

because it was hot, and we had our son with us, and we were like, "Let's take him to the beach." We went to that town, Saintes-Maries-de-la-Mer, and it was really nice. There's, like, a one-euro bus that takes you right there, so we would just get on the bus. I did that a couple of times with Cosmo, our son, so Eric could paint in the studio. We sheltered in the church there during a torrential rainstorm, and we lit candles and went into the basement to see the statue of the Black Madonna. I also took my son on this little train, le Petit Train Camarguais, which gives you a tour of the Camargue, and we saw flamingos and wild horses. I was sort of wandering around trying to entertain my son.

I had never met Gary Indiana, but I've certainly known of him for many years. And we did get to overlap and have lunch together. I was very charmed by that and thought it was cool. We knew Charlotte Houette and had spent time with her. I had met her many times, but I feel like our friendship got stronger. We had one of the shortest stays there. I think maybe it would have been better if we had been there longer.

My father died two weeks before we went, and we talked a lot about whether or not we should go. My mother and Eric—we all decided together that we should, and I'm really glad we did. I was very fucked up from it there. And it was kind of a good place to be that fucked up. I would have been grief-stricken probably anywhere in the world. And so I did appreciate being there. And I don't know if it's just because it's such an old city and I liked lying in bed and you have this

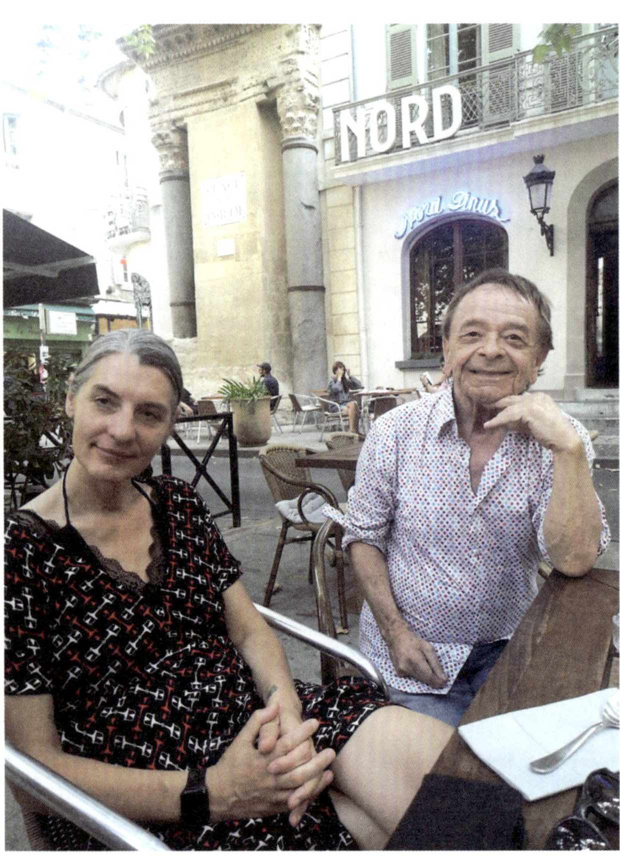

Sadie and Gary Indiana in the place du Forum, Arles

aura Owens Julie Beaufils Miriam Laura Leonardi Gabriele Garavaglia Charlotte Houette François Lancien-Guilberteau Parker Ito Julien Ceccaldi Alvaro Barrington Naoki Sutter-Shudo Asha Sc

amphitheater there—I felt like I'm connected to the ages, imagining all the people who lived on this land and died there. It made it a little bit easier, something that was really hard. Like, we're all in it together, life and death. I think the trip gave me a lot of space to think about it. And I needed that space, and I might not have had it if I had just stayed home. I will always think of my father when I think of Arles. They are sort of joined in my mind.

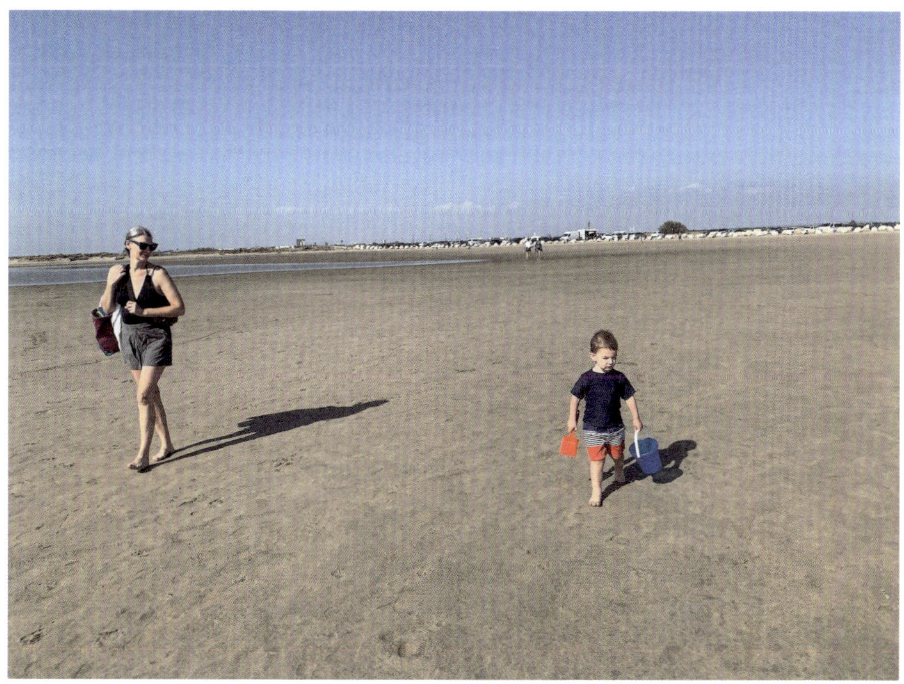

Sadie and Cosmo at the beach, Saintes-Maries-de-la-Mer

AUGUST 2022
Eric Palgon

Vincent van Gogh was not my guy. I liked Pierre Bonnard, Paul Cézanne—those were my South-of-France guys. I will say that when you see the Van Gogh at MoMA—I guess it's *The Starry Night*—it's amazing. You know, it's a shopping-mall bag or whatever, but it is really great. I'd say that every single Van Gogh painting I've seen in real life has always been good. None of it seems shopping-bag to me. They're great.

Laura Owens was my teacher in undergrad at UCLA. I took advanced painting with her two times. This was around the time of her MOCA show, and we became friends after. She was one of the most popular artists at the time in Los Angeles, and you could feel the excitement around her at the school.

I hadn't been to Arles, but I'd done a tour of the South of France and Côte d'Azur with my friend Kyle, and I had been around that area other times. Marseille, Montpellier, Aix, Cassis, Le Cannet, Nice, some places in between. I had never been to Arles. Arles is very beautiful and pleasant. It's maybe a bit too pleasant for me? Ha ha. No, it's very nice. We were there half during the peak season and half when kids went back to school, when it died down.

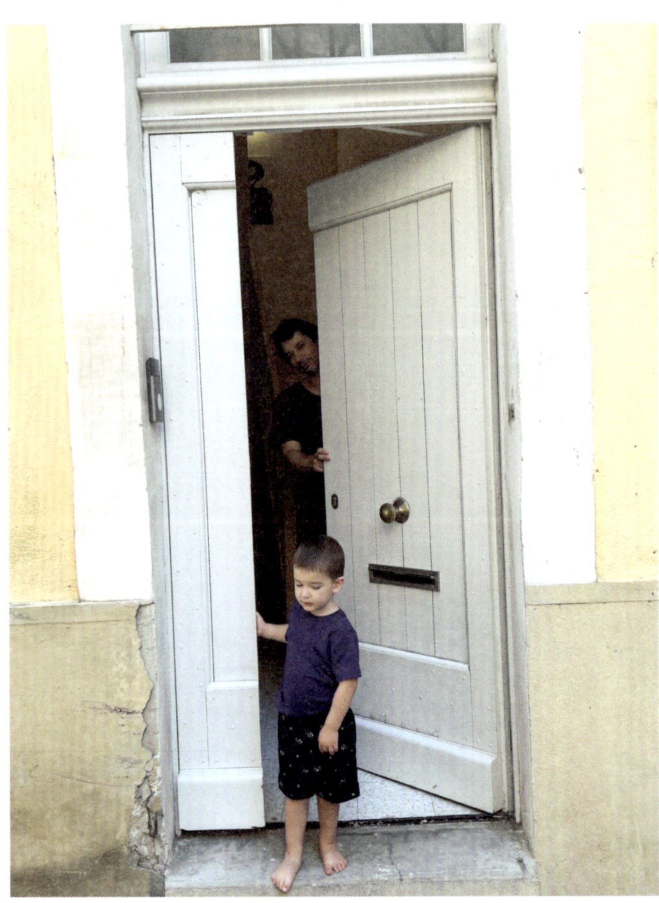

Eric Palgon and his son Cosmo at the front door of the Studio of the South

My first impression of the house was just like, man, this is too much art! It reminded me of some collector's home where they just have art everywhere. It's too much. We took a couple of things down with the idea that we'd put things back up later. By the time we went there, I think maybe someone had covered up the peeing Calvin? Or maybe that was later. But someone covered something, so covering or concealing had been introduced as an option. We loved the studio and the street and how free the house felt. I'm friends with Charlotte Houette and François Lancien-Guilberteau, Asha Schechter and Laura, and Blake Rayne and Alexander Zevin, so it was nice to see their work in the house. Laura's curtains and the tile mosaics in the bathrooms reminded me of her tiled bathrooms at her home in Los Angeles. Charlotte's Op-Art painting, her and François's books, and Asha's giant straws made me feel at home. I have known them and their work for years.

I wanted to find somewhere quiet to make an installation, but the space was pretty filled up by the time we got there. I liked seeing the painted window areas that Julie Beaufils did. They seemed sort of quiet and contained. I found a relatively unused spot: the small room or hallway space just before you enter the bedroom. The right side of the room had built-in drawers, all painted white, with a big, white, flat surface on top. The only thing someone had installed nearby was Miriam Laura Leonardi's, the *VAN À GOGO CLUB* door piece, which was relatively unobtrusive. I liked that area and decided to claim it.

During the residency, I made books using newspapers and leaves from Arles and nearby Mouriès. The hotel across the street gave me day-old newspapers. I made a book about pétanque. I made a book about the painter Shirley Jaffe, who had a show up in Paris at the Pompidou that I had just seen. I made a pressed leaf book. One maybe called *Nuit*, that had a theme of blue and some French poetic phrases. Then there was a painted poetry book on newspaper I made that was about the whole trip. That was probably my favorite book that I made there. And it sort of served as the glue for all the books. It was about our time in Arles, going to the flamingo beach, going to Marseille. It mentioned Laura, the Arles streets, and noon ice cream. I made a video of me reading it outside the residency door in Arles on our last day there. That was my favorite book. Julie Boukobza, who took us out to lunch when we arrived—it was her idea for me to make a book about our time in Arles. It seems like an obvious idea, but I hadn't thought of it. I also made a mobile, which, in my mind, had a sort of Provence vibe. It had little pieces of wood with a deep-blue color painted on. I made a plus-sign pattern on each piece that somehow reminded me of the area. The hanging wood shapes spun and floated above the books. Everything I made felt very local to me.

I knew going into the residency that it'd be hard to really get going on some oil paintings, knowing that I also had to be dad to a three-year-old. So I went in planning on making books and some type of Richard Tuttle-y sculpture. I thought, if nothing else, I could work on those at night after our son, Cosmo, went to bed.

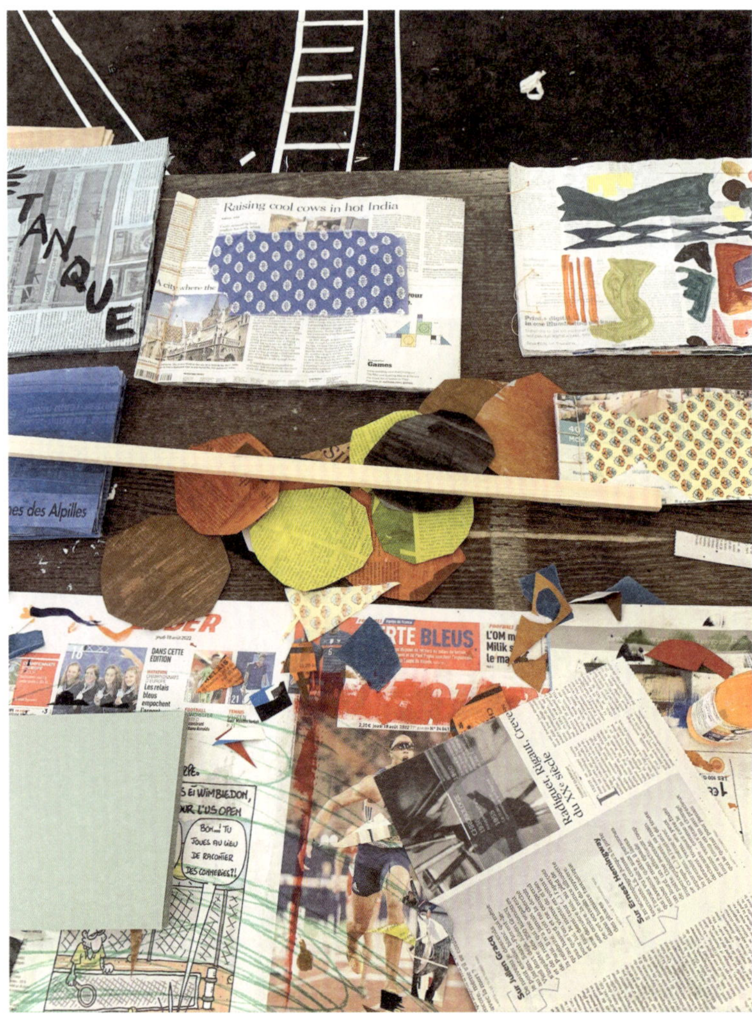

Eric's books in progress

The residency ended up being a major thing for me because of the books. The first time I made a book similar to the ones at the residency was with Laura. She did a project years ago where she invited artists to make an artist book—well, two books, really. One for you and one for her. You could just spitball any idea, any paper, any approach. She was experimenting with all these processes and her studio would basically try to make anything you dreamed of. I think I was one of the first people she asked. I dragged my feet for a while, then finally made a book for her project that I really liked. I made more books later, but Arles was the first time that I really concentrated on making a collection of handmade books. At that time, in my studio, I had been struggling with getting my sculptural works to talk to my paintings. I didn't feel like they were really helping each other. And then, when I made these books and brought that practice back to New York, it seemed to work better. I paused making sculptures and kept making books. The books allowed me to keep following my craft impulse and were a way for me to fold in the poetry. The books could be considered kind of like drawings, or an intimate thing that you hold up to your face. I liked how the books have this "reveal" quality as you turn the page. And I was trying to do that in my paintings, though you read the paintings all at once.

I think Arles was also the first time I made a painted poem book with a brush. Maybe not— I can't remember. I think rolling around in my head was a book Laura made years ago, and the Bob Dylan video for "Subterranean Homesick Blues" with the cue cards. The book Laura made

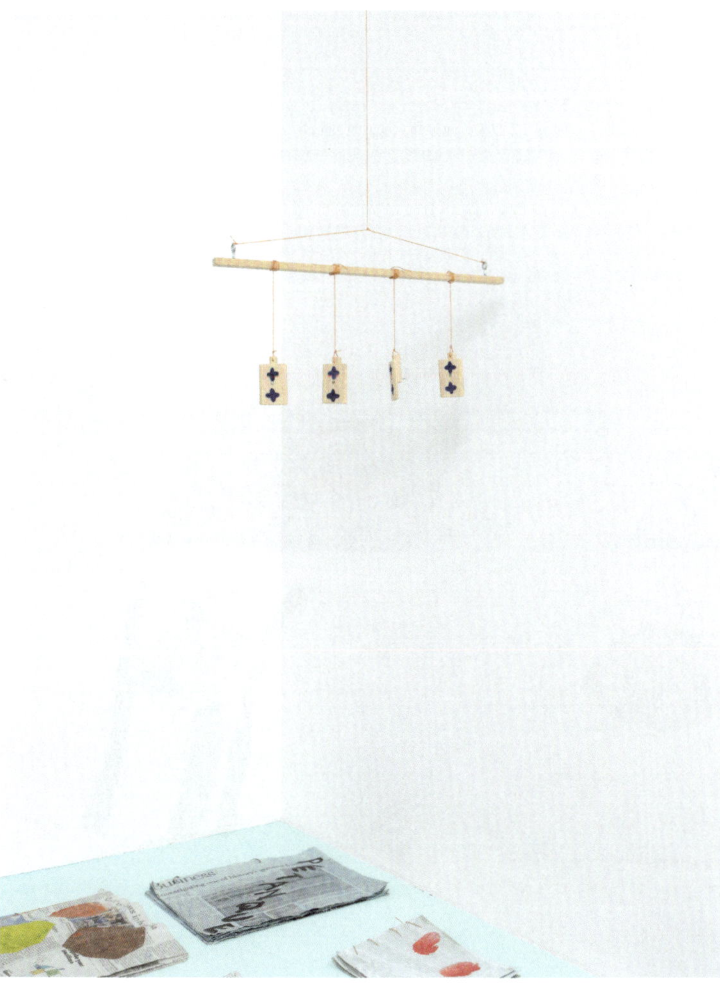

Eric Palgon, *Untitled Mobile (Provence, Arles, Mouriès, Plage de Piémanson, Saintes-Maries-de-la-Mer)*, wood, Flashe paint, nails, waxed string, eye hooks

that stuck with me was a book where she just wrote out, or painted out, the lyrics to a Kid Cudi song, "Pursuit of Happiness." It was a very simple and beautiful book and I mainly just remember the concept of it. I liked that the gesture was, sort of, "I love this song so much I'm going to make a book about it and just paint the lyrics." Maybe the book had a bunch of drawings around the text, but I mostly remember it being pretty straightforward. There's a page in my Arles book where I mention both Laura and Jonathan Richman (who has a song about Van Gogh), and I was definitely thinking about Laura's Kid Cudi book. I think the page in my book says, "Arles starts with Owens / Arles starts with Jonathan Richman." I can't think of Van Gogh without thinking of the Richman song about him. There are two really good videos on YouTube of him singing it. They're both very short. He sings, "Have you heard about the painter Vincent van Gogh, who loved color and let it show? And in the museums, what have we here? The most soulful painter since Jan Vermeer." It's beautiful.

Since the residency, I have made way more books and have embraced poetry more. My impulses in poetry and painting and sculpture are all pretty different. I think the residency helped me develop a way to put all those impulses in the same room.

We didn't meet too many other people while we were in Arles, because Sadie Laska and I had each other. We did meet someone on the last day. I had accidentally left my New York keys in Paris, and Charlotte found them and mailed them to me in Arles. But the keys never arrived, so

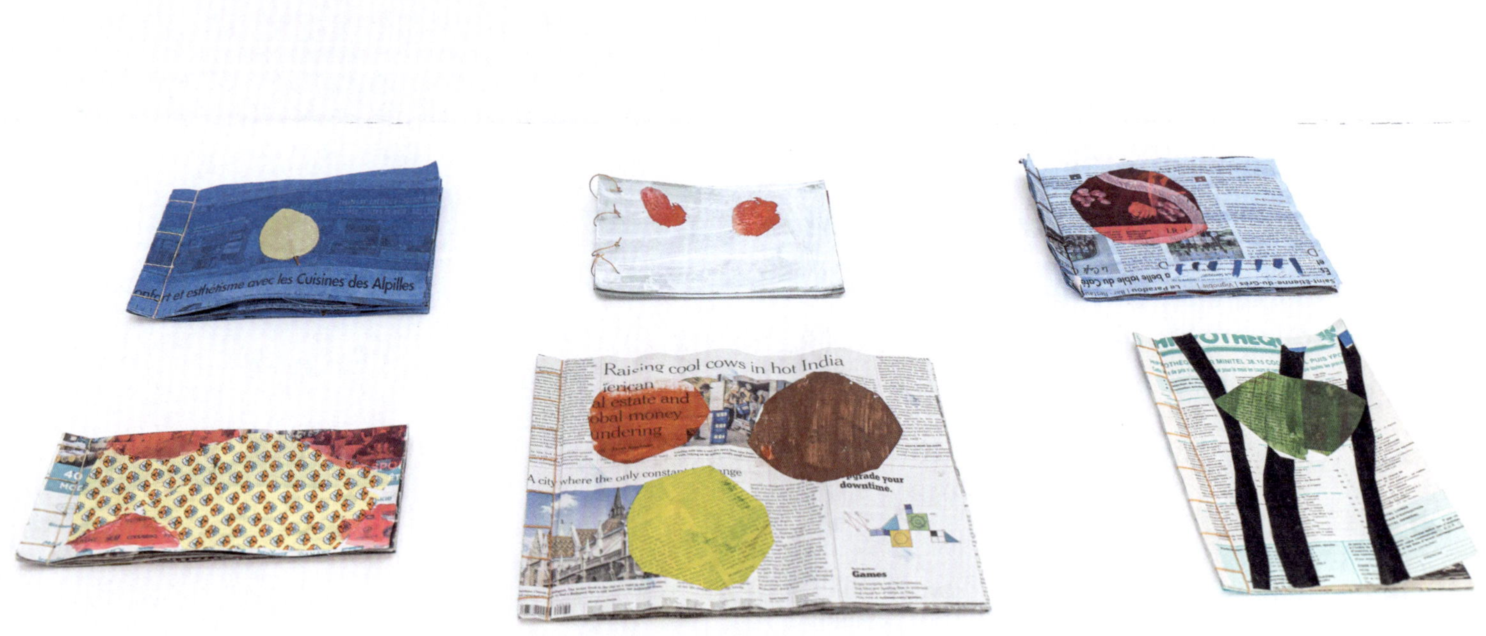

Clockwise from top left: Eric Palgon, *Is It a Leaf?*; *Untitled (Two Dots)*; *Nuit*; *Cherry Blossom Tree*; *Raising Cool Cows in Hot India (Arles leaves)*; *Google Translate > Anglais, Français*; mixed-media books

I just knocked on all the neighbors' doors, hoping they got delivered to them. I met this woman, Diana, who had a studio a few doors down. She is a painter and a photographer (I think) and had worked on Laura's big show at the museum. I don't know how she met Laura. She was very cool, and I think that if I had met her on the first day we were there, we would have met more artists in Arles, because she must have known other artists.

Cosmo had a great time. He went on the carousel and had sorbet or ice cream every day. He ran around the obelisk and down all the cobblestone streets. I remember sleeping in that upstairs room with him, where we could get the room super dark, and waking up in the morning and peeking out at the pigeons huddled in the building across the street, and watching the people milling around up in that rooftop café. In the studio, we made a maze of blue tape, and he would race cars in it. And he would make art with us. With Sadie, he made a series of drawings about a thunderstorm, and we would flip through them and tell the story. I remember when we had all his paintings all laid out in a long grid on the big studio wall.

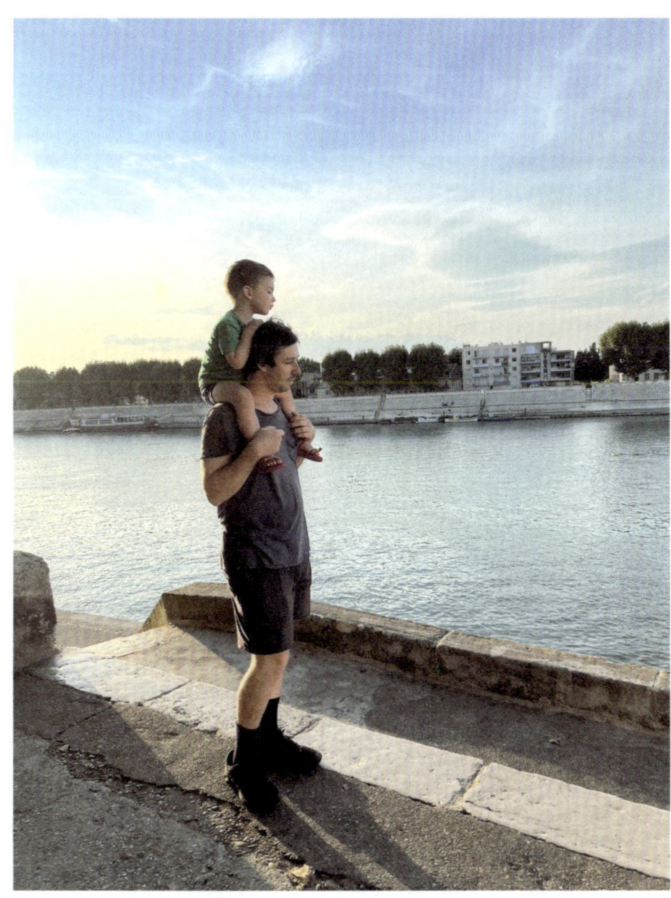

Eric and Cosmo by the Rhône

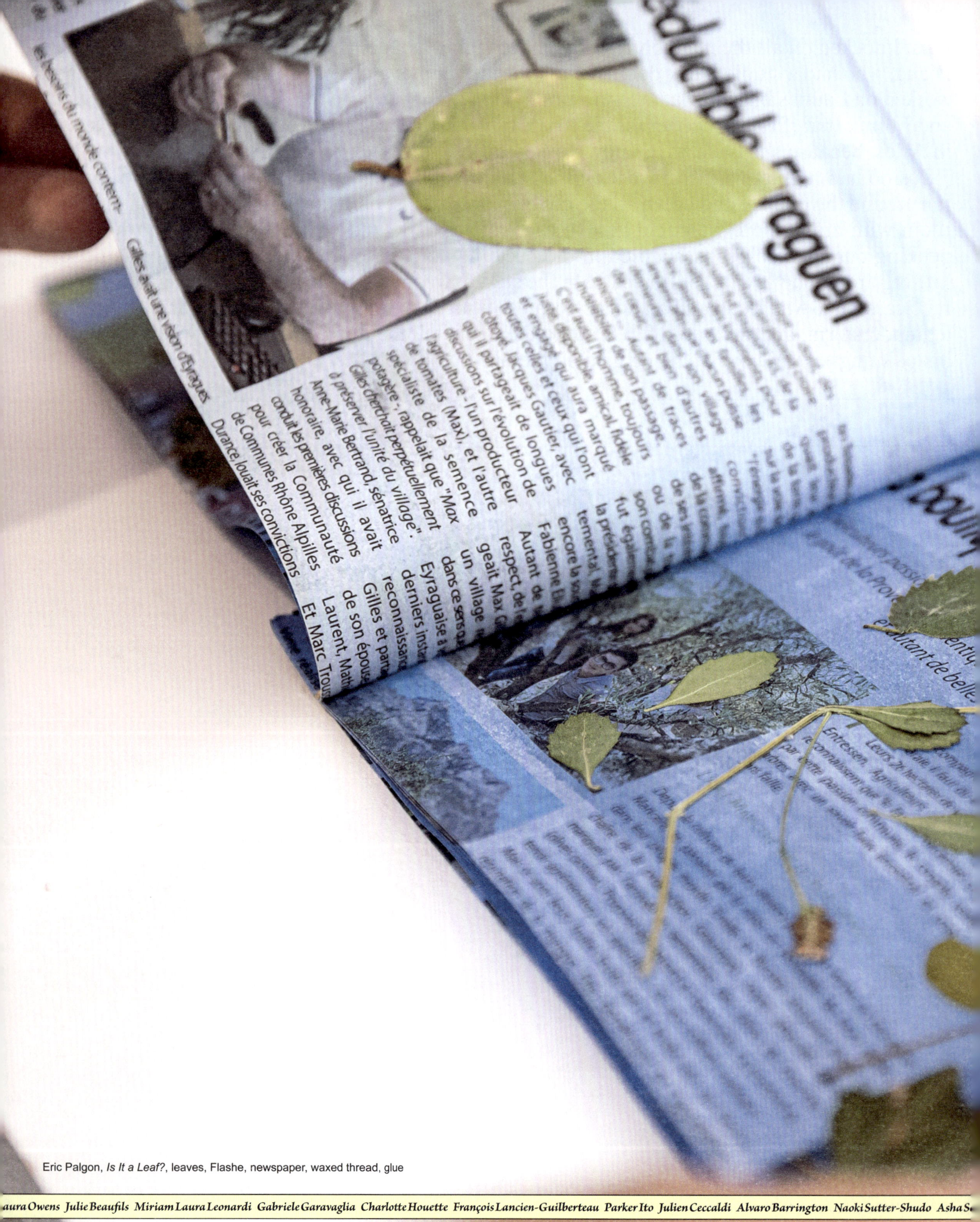

Eric Palgon, *Is It a Leaf?*, leaves, Flashe, newspaper, waxed thread, glue

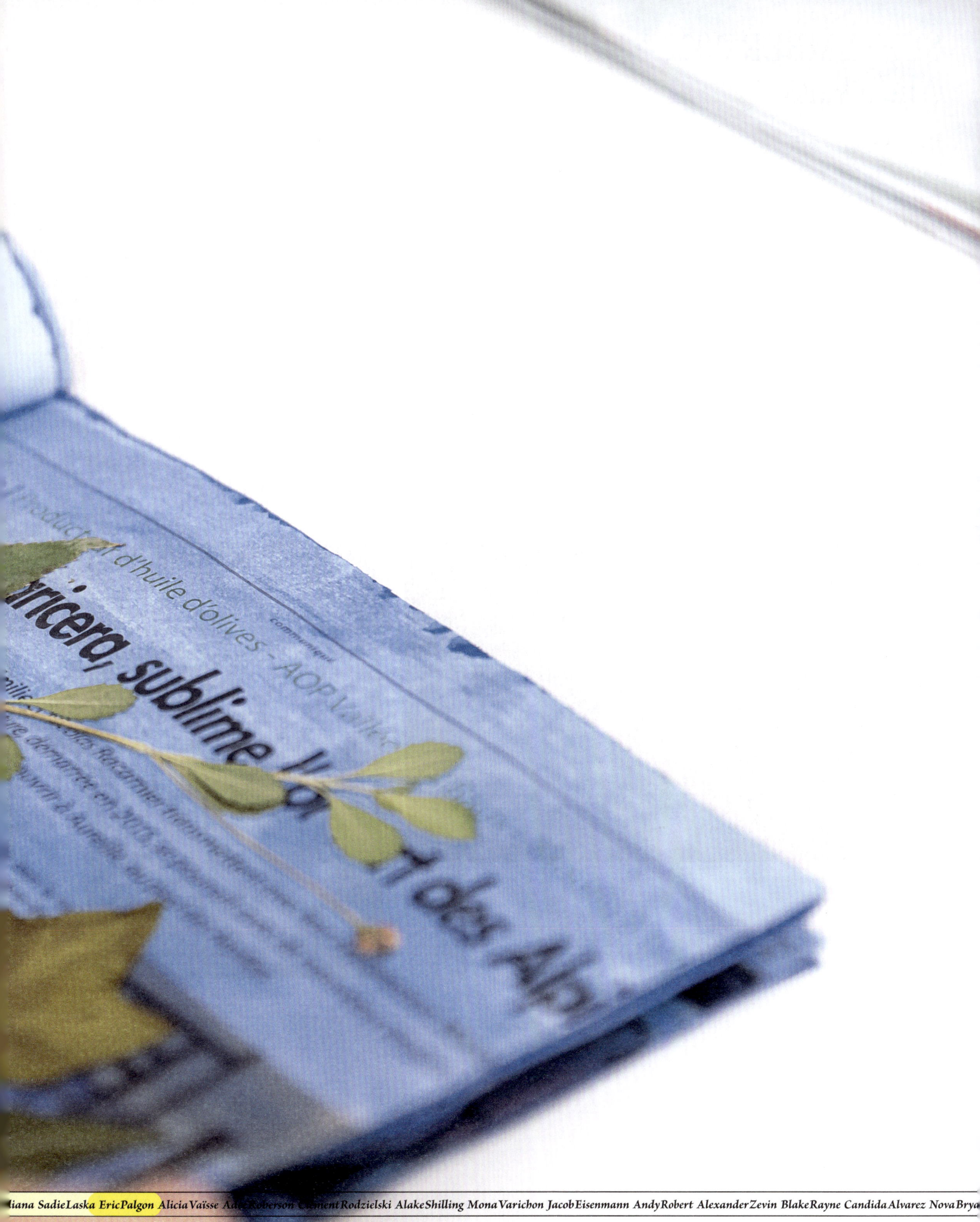

d'huile d'olives - AOP Vallée
ricera, sublime
des Alp

SEPTEMBER 2022
Alicia Vaïsse

I've thought a lot about Vincent van Gogh throughout my life. Not only because I studied art history for many years but also because I live in the South of France, an area he famously painted, and I experience the landscapes he represented every day. Additionally, I've been an art teacher at a school located at the crossroads of the Crau and Camargue regions. Van Gogh often came up in conversations as a major reference, particularly because of his understanding of nature as a subject, the unique way he rendered emotions through his brushstrokes, and his extraordinary sensitivity to colors, skies, and more. I was aware of Laura Owens's work before I met her and found it very interesting, full of beauty and meaning. I met her through Julia Marchand, long before the residency. When Laura came to France for her show, she was looking for a house and some help preparing the exhibition. Julia introduced me to Laura, and Laura ended up renting a house from my mother, next to where we breed horses, at the Haras du Coussoul in Mouriès. It is a place away from the world, separated by twenty-five healthy minutes by car from the hustle and bustle of the city. I used to live in New York, but I came back to France in 2014 because my father was sick and I was expecting a child. I looked for a job

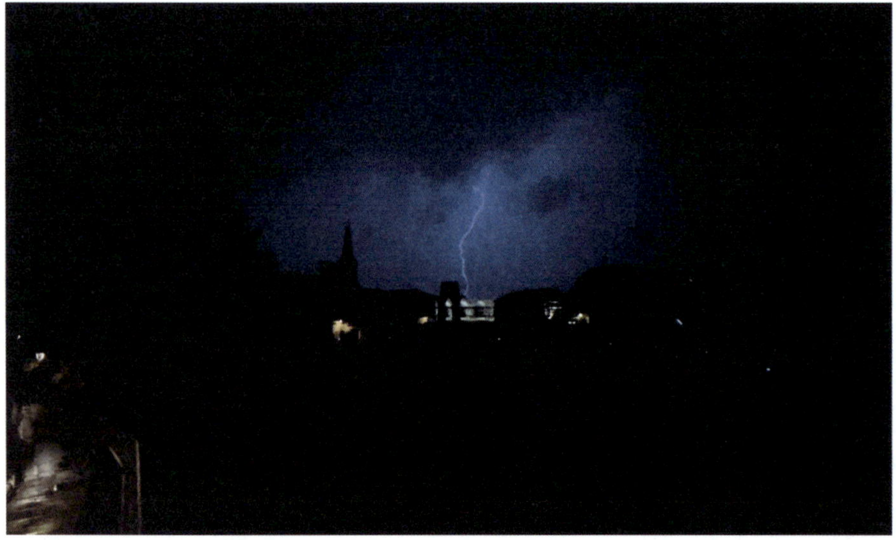

Lightning over the Roman Theater, Arles

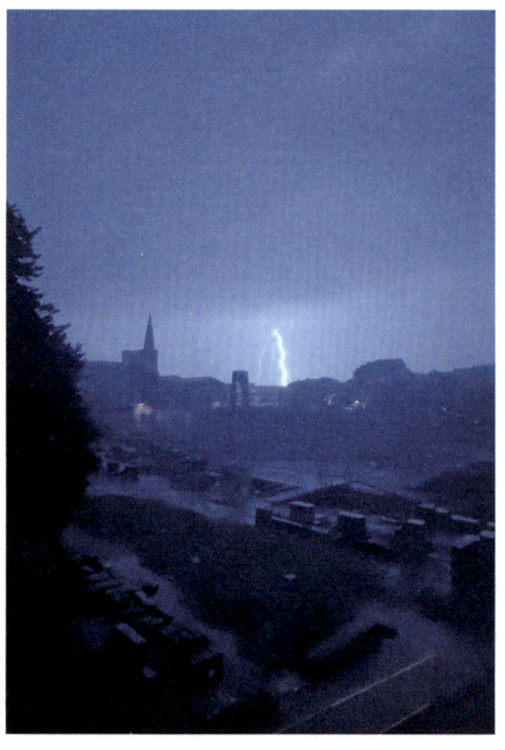

near my parents' horse farm and found one at the Domaine du Possible school, which brought me to Arles. It's an alternative school in the middle of nature. I was first hired as an English teacher but soon became the art teacher and, later, also a horse-riding instructor. I sought to connect the practice of art with the experience of animal communication, and this school gave me incredible freedom to explore very creative programs. Back then, LUMA was still under construction. Living in Mouriès, the cultural center of gravity used to be more focused on Saint-Rémy-de-Provence, but it quickly shifted to Arles thanks to the dynamism of cultural actors there. Even long ago, Arles was already famous and definitely worth visiting. I vividly remember going to Arles as a teenager with my school. I was raised in Paris, and during a school trip to Provence when I was about thirteen or fourteen years old, we stayed at an Ibis hotel on the outskirts of the city. Bored with my Parisian classmates, I ventured alone into the streets of Arles. I smoked pot with some young Arlesian people and made brilliant friends. Because my parents had a place in the South of France, I started partying there a lot in the late nineties. I would hitchhike to Arles to meet my newfound friends. The city fascinated me: its wonderful buildings, the beautiful flats hidden behind rusty doors. It was a bit run-down but full of hidden gems and wonders to uncover. It felt vibrant, with real people who stood apart from my Parisian peers—they seemed truer, less standardized than the kids I knew back home. In many ways, I think I learned more in Arles during my teenage years than in Paris. I believe

I visited the Studio of the South house before it became a residency. At the very beginning of the project, Laura took me there. It felt like a raw canvas, and the sound in some rooms was strange because of the unusual proportions and the lack of furniture. The location was amazing, with an inspiring view outside. It was also a peculiar place, between a void and an outgrowth. My impression was that it would be completely transformed. From what I understood, Laura's project was really to let artists take over and make it into something. It really was pretty much nothing when we first opened the door. It stood on a great corner with an incredible view, and it just felt like a place with no personality but so much potential. And I had absolutely no clue of what it was going to become. When I began the residency, a recurring figure in my work was the dog. I was researching *la chasse à courre*—a traditional hunt with dogs. My work often focuses on interspecies relationships, and the layers of complexity in this ancient, now largely irrelevant practice fascinated me. Painters throughout time have tried to convey the violence of it all, but also some kind of beauty in all these species colliding in an absolute drama, which was just leisure for some noble people but a matter of life and death for most participants. The vocabulary of this practice is also unique and somehow poetic. For instance, they call it *le sentiment* (the feeling)—the smell of the prey being pursued. As a woman in today's world, one might say that rings a bell. I leave that to everyone's interpretation, but in my mind, bells were certainly ringing. All in all, there is a whole vocabulary that, at the time, I found "romantic"

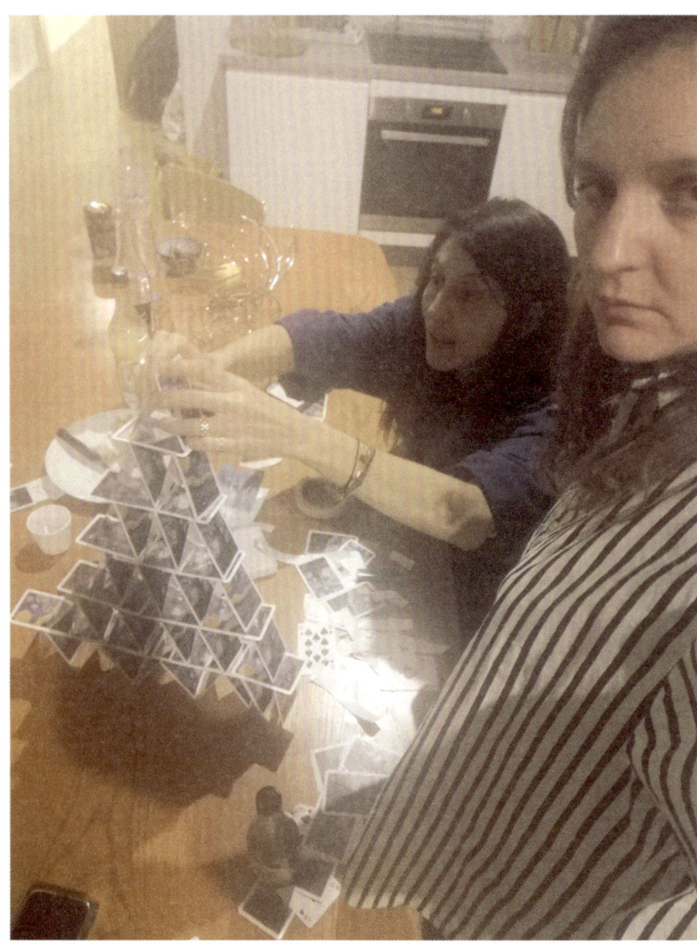

Alicia Vaïsse and Charlotte Houette making a house of cards

and particularly interesting in the realm of the art world. I thought about this pack of dogs, and the staircase seemed like the perfect place because, as you descend, the paintings appear to come alive, transforming into a kind of cinema. A bunch of nude souls running down the stairs…I also painted a dog in the basement studio, but it mysteriously disappeared. The studio walls hold hidden stories. When I was there, the residency wasn't over, so I expected things to evolve on top of the work I had added. The room at the top was already very painted when I got there, and the stairway starts with multiple paintings. There's a portrait of Mona Varichon by Nova Bryan and a painting by Jacob Eisenmann. So I thought the painting should spread down. I felt like inscribing myself in this movement. And then there's Julie Beaufils's window. The whole ensemble was very inspiring. At the very beginning of the project, Laura invited me to paint with her, no explanation given; it was to me, then, just a conversation in words and images. Laura said, "Paint!" I asked her, "What should I paint?" She replied, "I don't know— maybe butterflies and flowers." I asked for images, and she provided beautiful ones. I started painting herbs with insects and birds. Later, placing the dogs became a way to continue my work after the initial painting sessions were interrupted when the residents arrived. It felt as though the dogs had been placed by this burst of nature. Initially, it was a game with the yellow line that goes down the staircase, interacting with what was in front of the line and what was behind it. Later, I repainted the line in front of my herbs. It became a line of time. I enjoyed

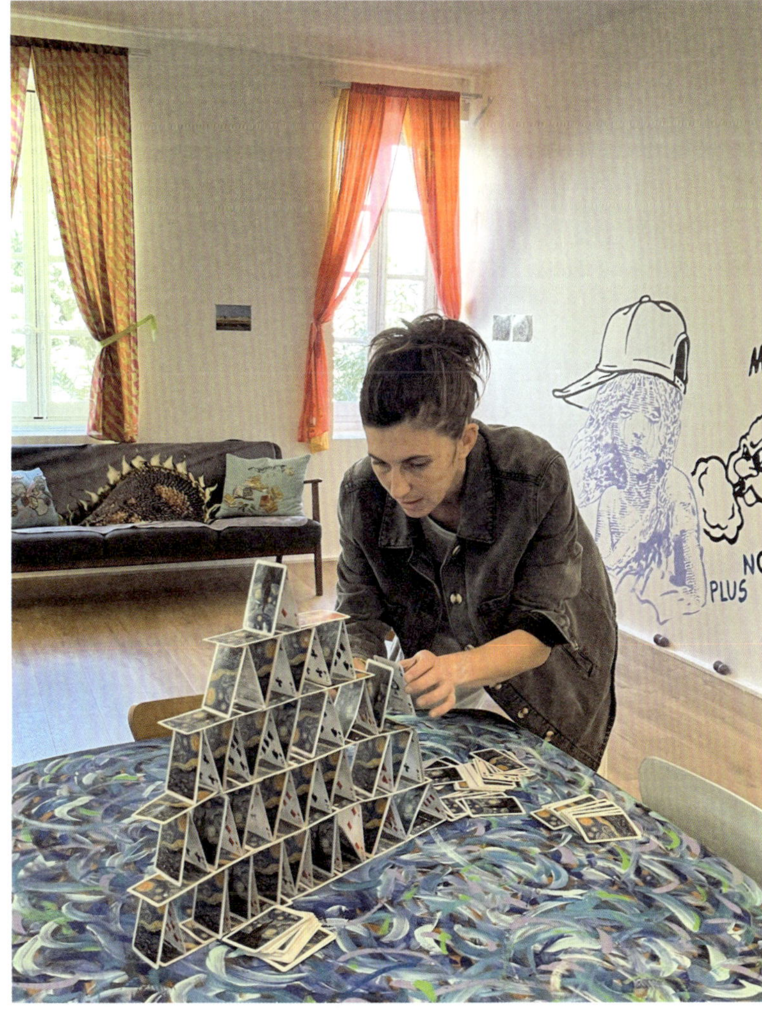

Alicia making a house of cards

diana Sadie Laska Eric Palgon Alicia Vaïsse Adee Roberson Clément Rodzielski Alake Shilling Mona Varichon Jacob Eisenmann Andy Robert Alexander Zevin Blake Rayne Candida Alvarez Nova Bry

how my blue turned green upon interacting with the line. In my mind, there's no question that a community of artists existed there. All these artists experienced a little piece of life in this house, this street, this city—a peculiar time and space capsule. Living under this sky, in this light, and having the opportunity to work there as an artist—especially as a painter—you understand…it's a feeling, whether it lasts five days or fifty. Living near Arles, Laura often introduced me to the residents, and I felt lucky to meet all these people. I saw many of these artists discovering Arles, and I think everyone felt that it has a very strong personality. It's like meeting a character. It's the same thing that has happened to so many artists before—not only Van Gogh, but Pablo Picasso, Jean Cocteau, and others. Many fascinating artists came and stayed in Arles, whether during the full bloom of summer or the discreet intimacy of the off-season. I had already worked on murals, but I had never worked in three dimensions. I started to explore that in the house. I sewed a large cloud as a dog bed and assembled it with a deep-blue rug. I was there with my dog, Maui, and I felt she was very uncomfortable. I couldn't let her sit on the artworks of other artists, so I decided to make her a dog bed. Maui is extremely important to me. She's always with me and was, somehow, a silent judge and friend during my time at the residency. Then I really wanted to create a dog chair, because I felt it inverted the language of the hunt, as if, finally, the dog was the prey—or at least the one meant to be found. As the idea emerged of a character traveling through different realities—from dreams to

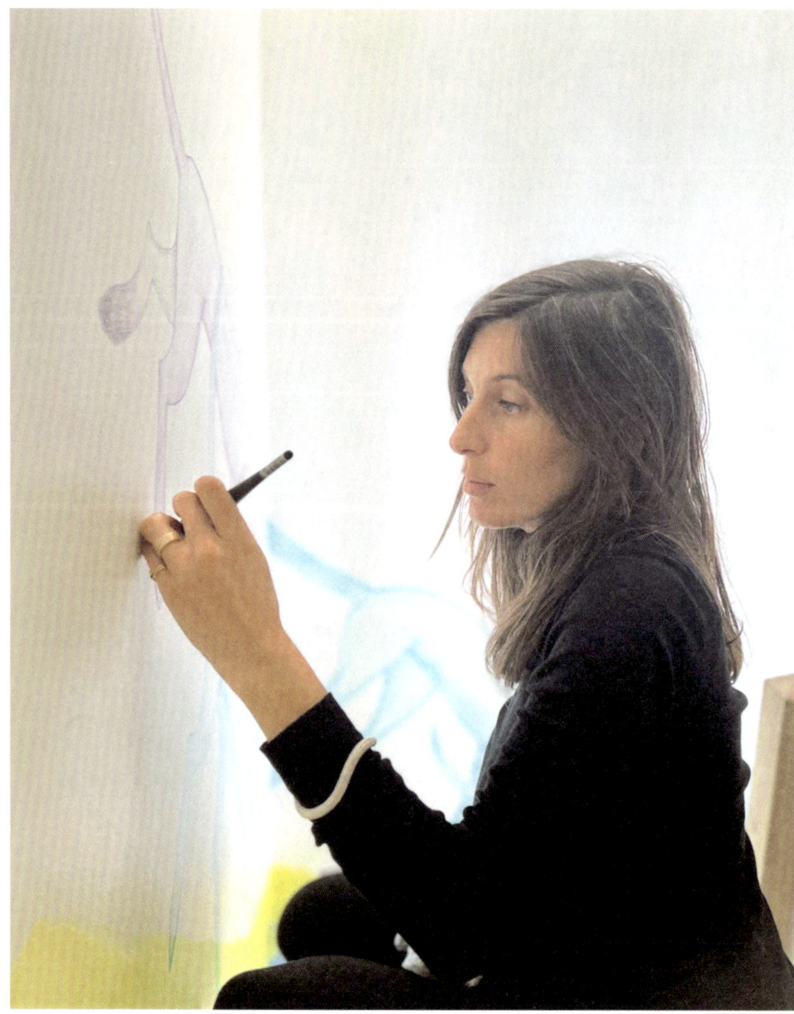

Alicia working on *Poursuite*

drawings, walls, or 3D forms—I began sewing, which led me to conceive of the 3D dogs. It was yet another way to embody these figures that haunted me at the time. When I worked on the mural, I was six or seven months pregnant. It was quite physical for me, working on the staircase. After I completed that piece, I needed to be more mindful of my health, and sewing became the right solution to continue working without putting myself or my unborn baby at risk. A problem turned into a solution. A few months after my residency, at an opening at High Art, Charlotte Houette introduced me to Blake Rayne, who told me, "There's a huge hole in your wall!" I went to see it, and there it was. Repairing it was complicated because I didn't want to repaint a dog, but I did need to do something to stabilize it. By then, the concept of the show had emerged, and the hole seemed to me like a portal or a gate, so I decided to use it. At the time, I was working on 3D dogs and wanted to interfere with the hole as little as possible. Blake had placed a golden piece in it, and I had no desire to disrupt that because the story of the hole added another dimension to the house, which I really liked. A young man working in the neighboring building went ballistic, kicked the wall, and broke through it, creating this space between the two buildings…I decided to use it, placing a piece of a 3D dog that extended into a drawing. To me, it represented a transition between dimensions. Inside the wall represented the fabric of ideas, while outside, it became 2D. When it came time to create a piece for the museum, it allowed me to create a direct transition. The dogs are eternally running through this infinite loop

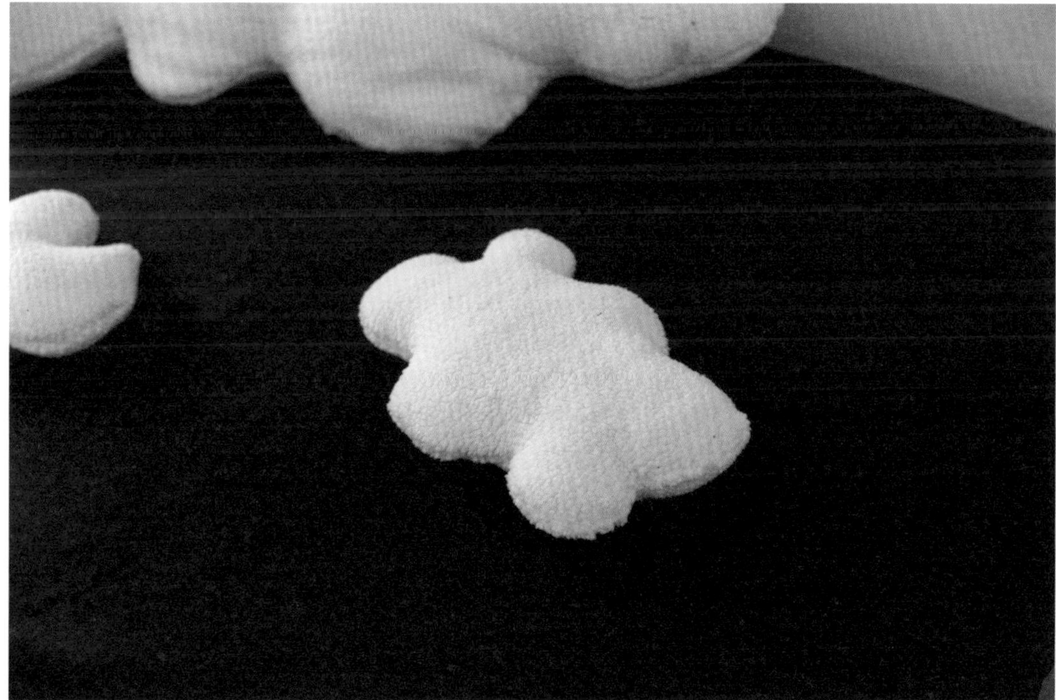

Alicia Vaïsse, *Dog Bed*, fabric

between the museum space and the house. I also didn't realize the house would be visited by the public, so I thought it was interesting to establish communication between these two spaces. In my mind, the intimacy of the residency and the public display of the show at the Fondation Vincent van Gogh Arles complemented each other. I'm not really sure where art begins or ends. Is it in the museum? In the house? It's very hard to tell. Like Miriam Laura Leonardi's intervention with her eyelashes on the cabinet, the house blurs the definition of what art should be—you're sitting on it, living with it. It's in your bedroom and your bathroom. In the Studio of the South, the art piece is the house itself as much as it is the interventions of each individual, whether temporary, like a ciné-club, or final, like a wall painting. This became even more interesting when we did a show in a museum, transitioning from something that was a living experience. It was difficult to translate into a show because how we lived in the house and interacted as artists was so intuitive. I love the world of the unspoken, and I think people can be extremely sensitive, respectful, and generous toward each other through objects. We all interacted with the work we lived with, and it was very interesting to communicate with them every day. It fueled my work and inspiration while I was there. Moreover, I made great new friends, like Gary Indiana. As he really enjoyed staying in France, we started discussing new projects for the future. I am very grateful for my time getting to know him—his finesse, wit, great sense of humor, and talent for art. In these few months, I had the opportunity to discover

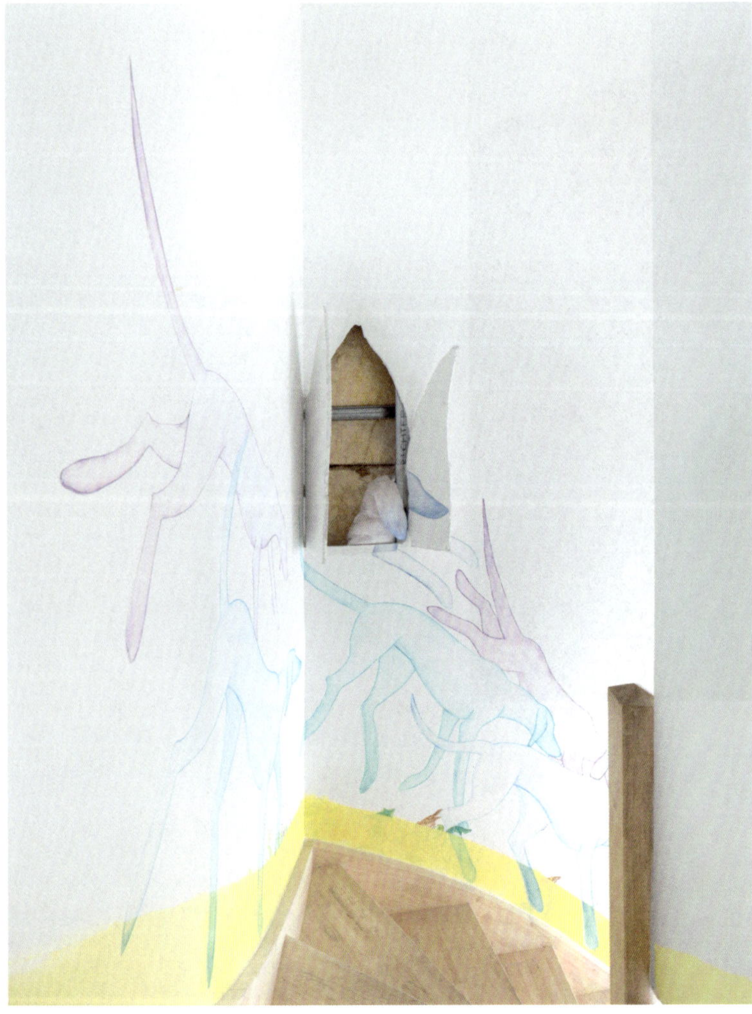

Alicia Vaïsse's *Poursuite* after the hole in the wall was made

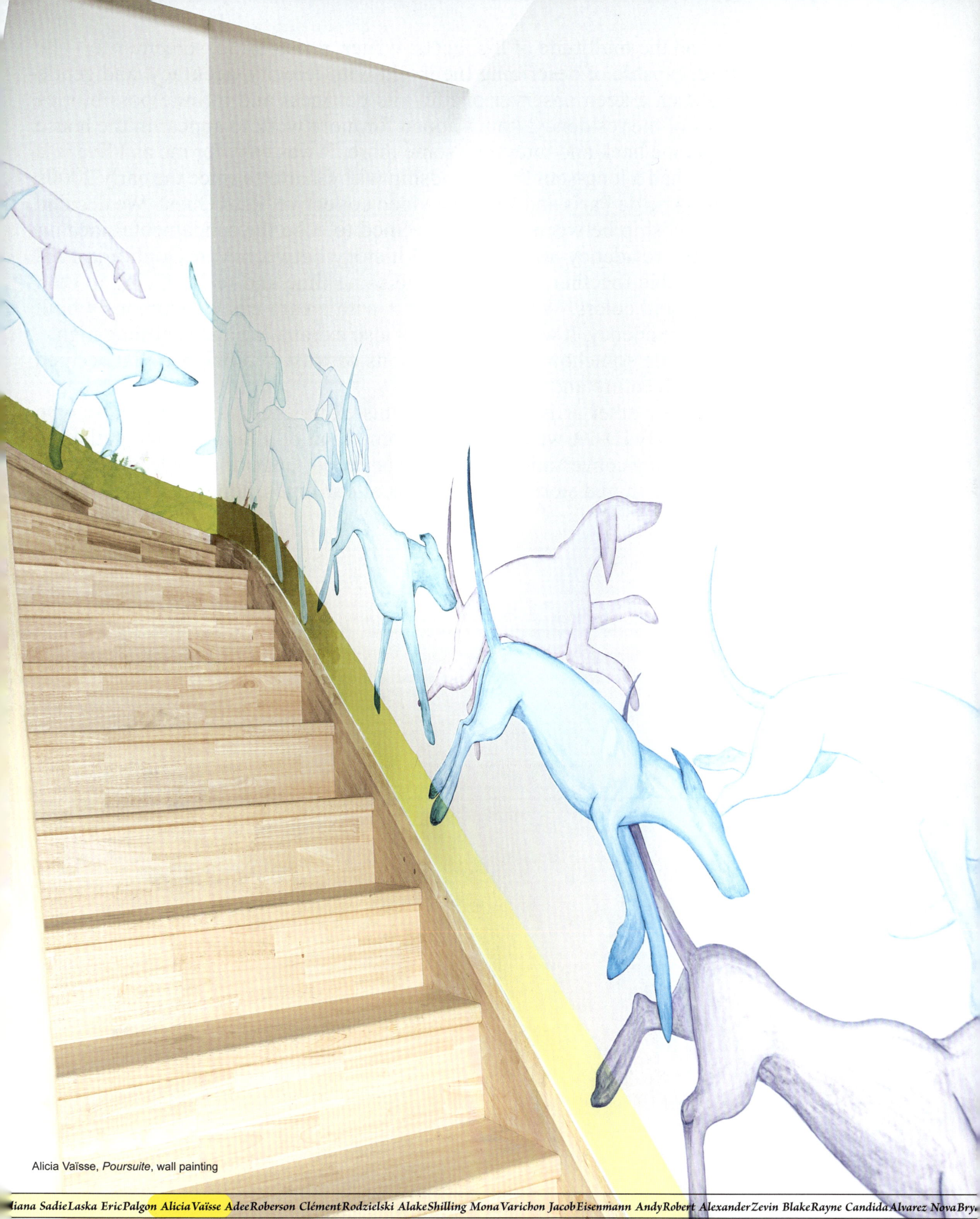

Alicia Vaïsse, *Poursuite*, wall painting

the breadth of his talent and the multitude of his facets: writer, artist, critic, screenwriter—he was a master of literature, capable of describing the world with ferocity, accuracy, and gentleness all at once. He was such a keen observer of life—its pettiness and infinite possibilities. During the last few weeks of the residency, Laura hoped for more work to appear in the house and encouraged us all to come back and intervene some more. It was easy for me as I live in a neighboring village. I have had a long-standing friendship with Charlotte since the early 2000s, when we met at the Beaux-Arts de Paris and started a video collective: Est&Ouest. We decided to create a piece about friendship between artists. It seemed to echo the fundamental idea underlying the creation of the residency and the heated history between Van Gogh and Paul Gauguin. We painted this table together, working at the same time and really trying to communicate through gestures and colors. We then topped it with a card castle fastidiously built on our very last night at the residency. It was a playful but also exhausting and very long night… The unsteadiness of this castle somehow evoked questions of trust and balance that seemed very present in this whole adventure and for its future.

I think that for me and a few other artists who shared this experience, especially those who came during and just after COVID-19, we did become some kind of a family, often gathering around Laura and Gary. So many conversations—shallow or deep—under the shade of trees that had seen much more. So many shared stories, impressions of our times, hopes, dreams, visions, and realities. Always one foot in reality and the other in its double. For a time, we were this miraculous unity. I want to believe this family will exist forever. Sometimes—actually, most of the time—what we keep from an experience goes beyond words or proof. The Studio of the South was a very interesting chapter of my life. The people, ideas, and dreams I encountered there will undoubtedly stay with me—mostly unspeakably.

With deep gratitude to all involved and in loving memory of Gary Indiana.

liana Sadie Laska Eric Palgon Alicia Vaïsse Adee Roberson Clément Rodzielski Alake Shilling Mona Varichon Jacob Eisenmann Andy Robert Alexander Zevin Blake Rayne Candida Alvarez Nova Brya

Adee Roberson

I don't think I had any sort of relationship with Vincent van Gogh. The context that I thought about him in was that some of the work was derivative of African sculpture and masks. So I knew that he had looked at that stuff at some point. Besides other things that are very commercially seen, I didn't put much thought into him.

Laura Owens is a friend, and she's always been really supportive of me. We don't see each other that much in Los Angeles, but we've always kept in touch. We met at Kathleen Hanna's house, I think, and through Wendy Yao. I had done a shirt design for Kathleen and was at her house for the release, and Wendy and Laura were there, and we all ended up talking. And then my friend Kate Hall, who I screen print with, used to work at Laura's studio too. So she invited me, and of course I said yes, because I really like her and I was really honored and stoked. I love the idea of the residency—I do a lot of residencies, and I'm always excited to see what different ones are like.

As I understood it, for the residency, it was proposed that you had the choice to do something in the house or not. Since Laura had been working there so much, offering space for other people to feel the energy of the place and that connection and see what came from it, I was really open to that. I hadn't been to France in a long time; the last time I was through I was touring in a punk band, so that was a different perspective on it, and I didn't know what to expect. But I really had a good time and wanted to stay longer. I had been like, "I'll stay for two weeks, 'cause I don't know what it's gonna give," but then I felt like it could have been longer.

In Arles, I liked that everything felt so accessible—people there were really nice. My sister came with me the first week and she was obsessed, like, "Oh my gosh, this is crazy. All the food is so good. I don't feel sick. What is going on?" She'd never been to France or anything. I was like, "Yeah, girl, this is what happens when you leave America." I did quite a bit of walking, which was really nice, and just took things in, checking out the city. I went to LUMA and they had really good stuff happening, like the Sky Hopinka show and this African photographer James Barnor. But I didn't do too much art stuff. I was mostly in my routine of painting a bit, walking, eating, meditation, and stuff like that. I really think it's beautiful there.

I hadn't seen pictures of the house, so I didn't know what to expect, but I really liked it. It's kind of a perfect situation. I hate to sound indifferent, but my impression of the art in the house was kind of like, "Oh, this is interesting, this is where people have kind of placed things." I didn't have any particular expectation or thought around it. But I knew where I wanted to do my piece pretty soon after getting there, and what I wanted it to be about. It was a reaction to the circumstances—there was already a lot of stuff there when I got there. I was there later on, so a

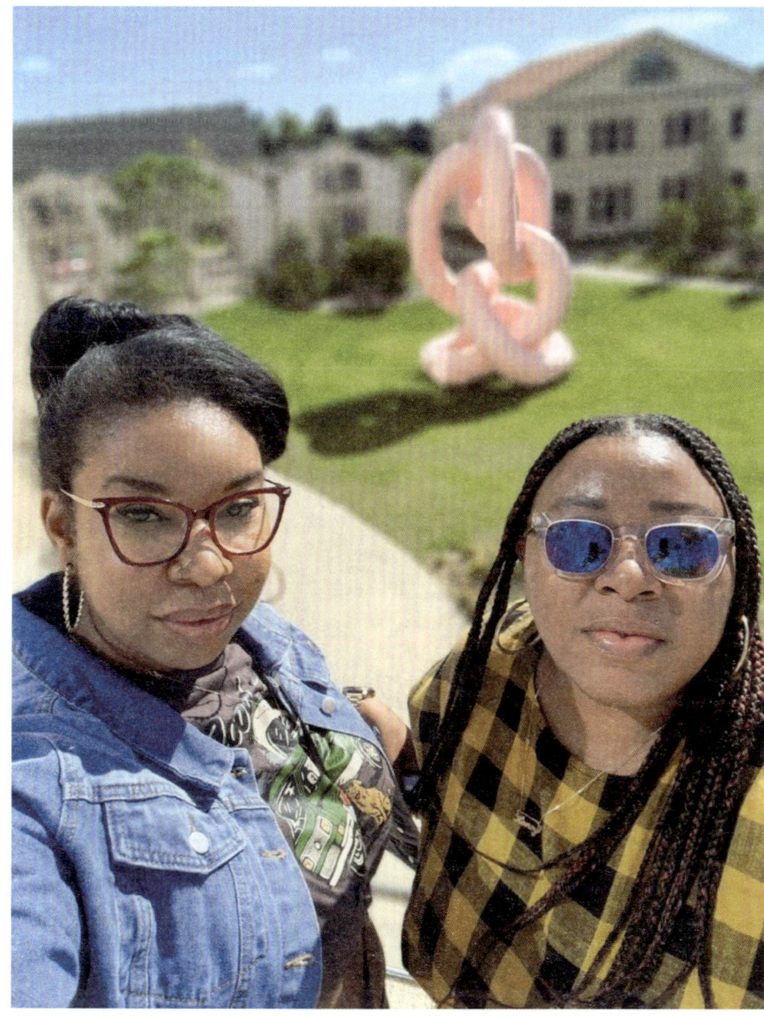

Adee Roberson with her sister Sequoia

lot of the wall space was taken up. So I had a certain amount of space that I could do something with. I knew I wanted to do some type of mural thing. I had been really into the energy of corners. I've done murals before, but none in a house or space that was permanent. But I have one in LA in Leimert Park and have done them site-specific in galleries. While I was in Arles, I was reading this book called *Dub* by Alexis Pauline Gumbs. It's kind of a memoir, kind of sci-fi, it's so hard to describe. It's kind of an abstraction of writing about Black feminist thought and also connection to the water, connection to coral, marine life, ancestors being people and also being marine life as well. So I was thinking a lot about water portals. And then, while I was there, my friend Mawena Yehouessi came. She's an amazing artist and filmmaker who lives in Paris. We had a studio visit that was really great; she looked at what I had made, and she said a lot of the colors and the shapes reminded her of—some of her family is from Benin, West Africa—and she said they reminded her of spiritual qualities and things that are connected to nature in that context. And so it was really cool to have the studio visit and conversation with her as someone who grew up in France, and get her perspective on my work there in the space. So that's how the piece unfolded. She also had a studio visit with someone at LUMA, 'cause she had done, or was about to do, something else there with her collective, so it all kind of just worked out. But I did want to make a point of connecting with people who lived around there, specifically Black people. So she came for two or three days.

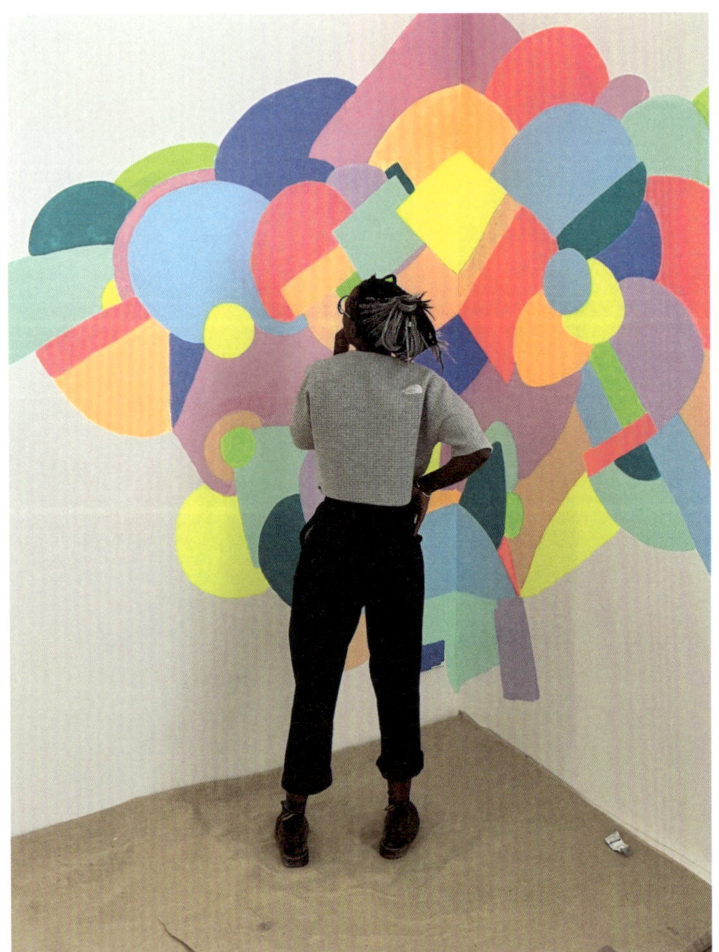

Mawena Yehouessi with *Ocean Dub* by Adee Roberson

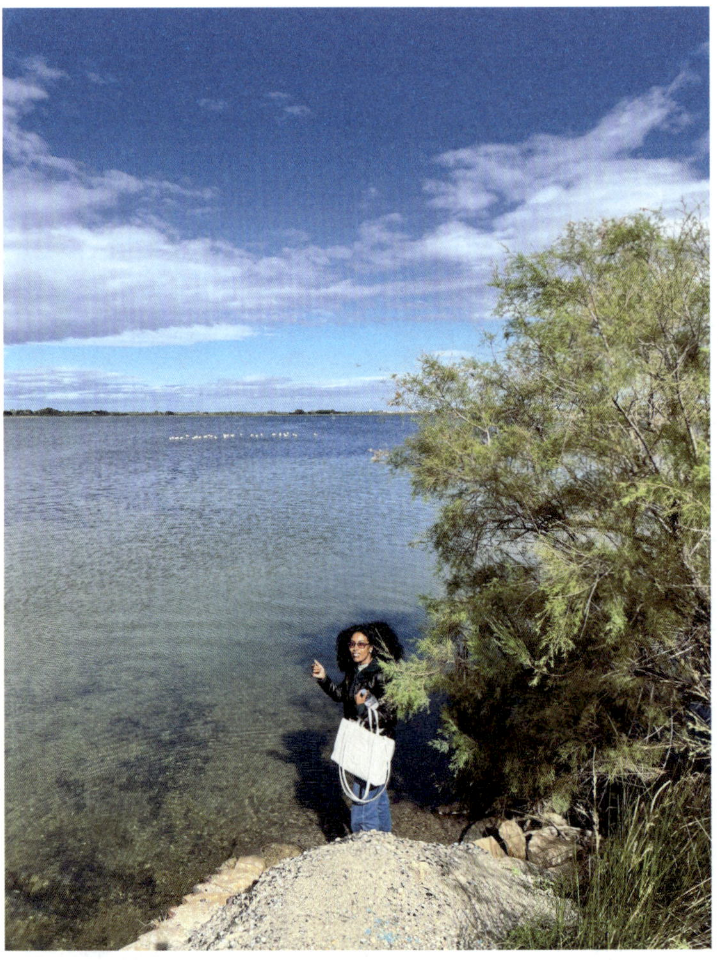

Adee's friend Atheel Elmalik near the salt flats

144

I also met Alicia Vaïsse while I was there. I really loved her work. It stood out to me in the house and made so much sense when I met up with her—it matched her vibe and energy. She was so sweet and we had a really beautiful lunch. She invited us out to her place, but I was unable to go. But it was really cool to link up with someone who lives there. I had another friend, Sidony O'Neal, who's an artist who was doing a residency at a castle, like, two hours away. So she happened to be there at the same time as me, so after I left Arles, I drove with her to her residency and then was there a few days as well. That was also in the South of France. So it was a weird time when, somehow, there were all these connections happening, which was cool. Afterward I went to Paris and met up with my friend again, so I went to some art stuff there as well. So that was good, and I had a lot of really generative conversations around the Black American experience as artists coming to a place like France, being in Europe, and what Black artists who live there are actually experiencing and what they're getting access to, as opposed to people coming from the outside. So that was a good conversation to be having.

Because my practice has so many things going on, one of the things that I think about a lot with abstraction is the amount of research and thought and planning, not that goes into actually painting the mural, but into the energy of it. So thinking about what I made in the house, there was so much energy that went into that. Books about certain experiences and poems and things like that that went into this more abstract piece. There's so much around identity politics, and

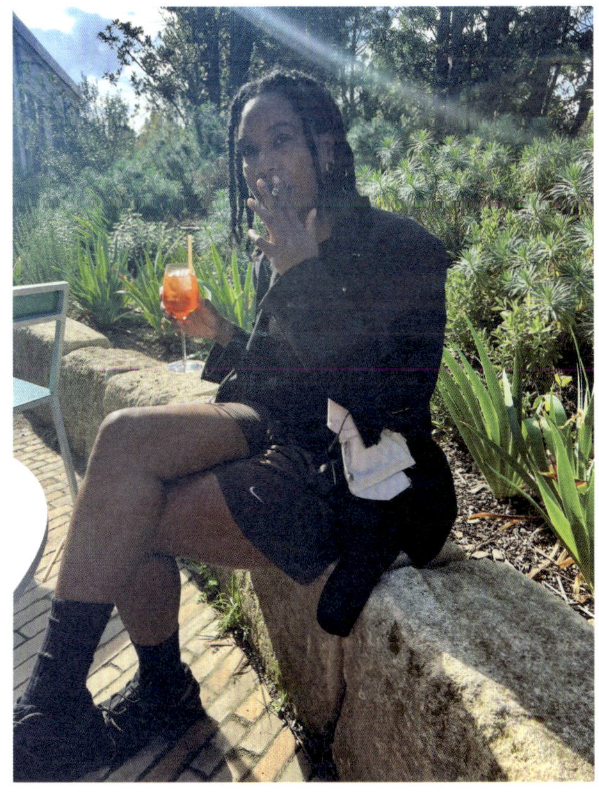

Sidony O'Neal

identity—that can be so didactic. But to me, so much of that is about embodiment and about energy and experience. And so I think that language, especially the English language, kind of takes away from that—all those experiences. The best way for me to transmute that energy or to engage with it is through abstraction, through color, shape, form, sound, archival images, collage; and working in this way that's energetically generative. My friend Grace Rosario Perkins—she's an amazing painter—we had this conversation in which she said we as artists transmute trauma and grief into beauty. That's part of our job. And for some of us, that's the work. And it definitely feels like my work is about that.

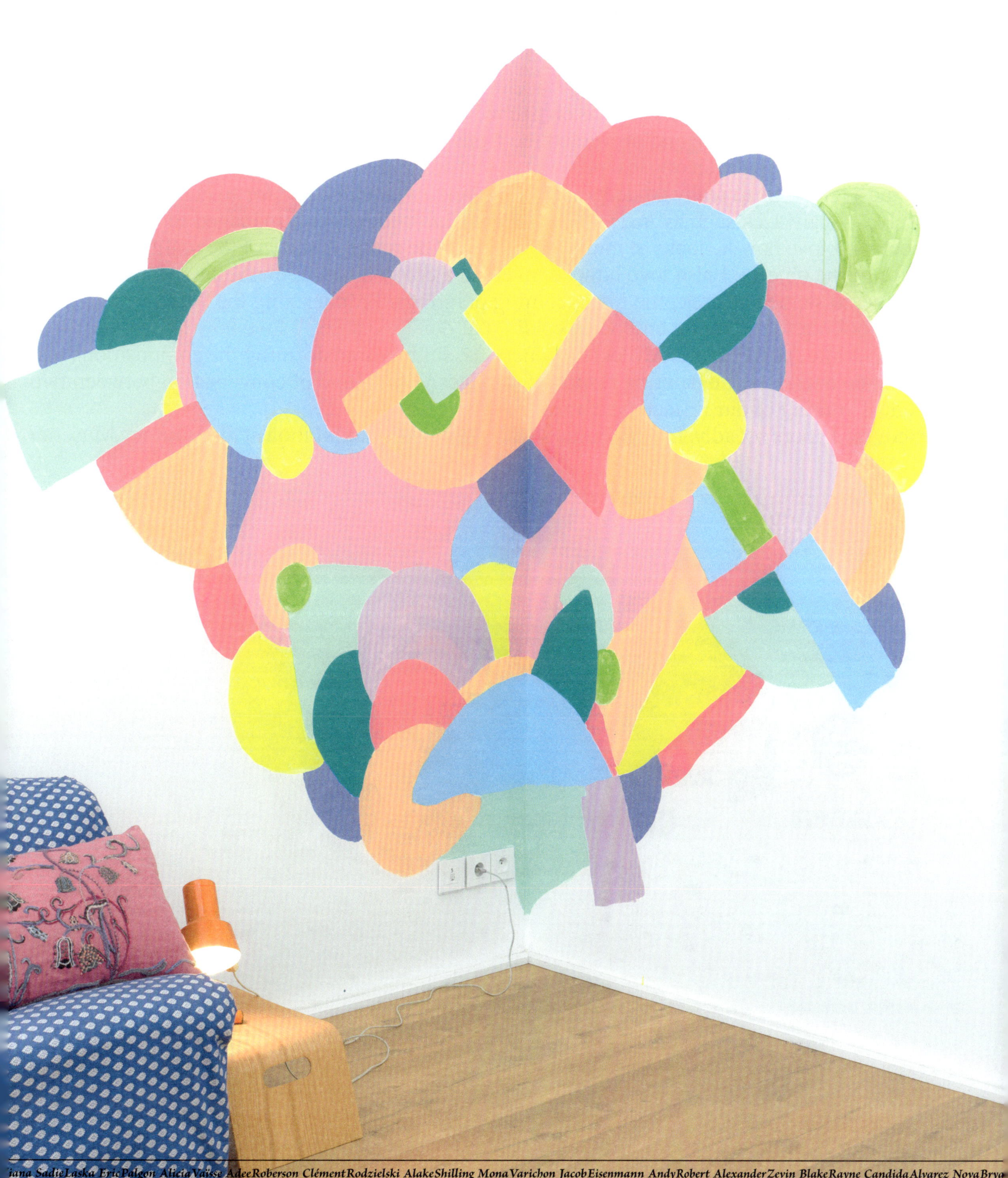

iana Sadie Laska Eric Palgon Alicia Vaïsse Adee Roberson Clément Rodzielski Alake Shilling Mona Varichon Jacob Eisenmann Andy Robert Alexander Zevin Blake Rayne Candida Alvarez Nova Brya

NOVEMBER 2022
Clément Rodzielski

For a long time, from my point of view, Vincent van Gogh has been almost more of a character than a real painter. Cultural industry has consumed the possibility to think about him as someone other than a touristic fiction and prevented me from really appreciating the work. Drama dominating the art. Looking at an original painting, it seemed that I was still looking at a reproduction. It took me a long time to really go deeper into the work. Eventually, and fortunately, the paintings themselves—canvases such as *Rain* or *The Night Café* and others—managed to overturn this perspective. I love how he looks at mundane objects. The rough quality of the reality, the strong presence of the objects. I also love how he invented a colored space, the Yellow House, 2 place Lamartine, to shape and welcome his upcoming paintings. Prophesizing the "high yellow note" that he's looking for. Painting embodies colors that don't exist yet. I love how he worked from black-and-white Jean François Millet reproductions, slightly transforming the compositions and inventing colors. How can painting respond to images? It is a kind of conversation between two painters. Thinking of our residency, it's resonating.

I discovered, more broadly, Laura Owens's work through her exhibition at the Whitney Museum

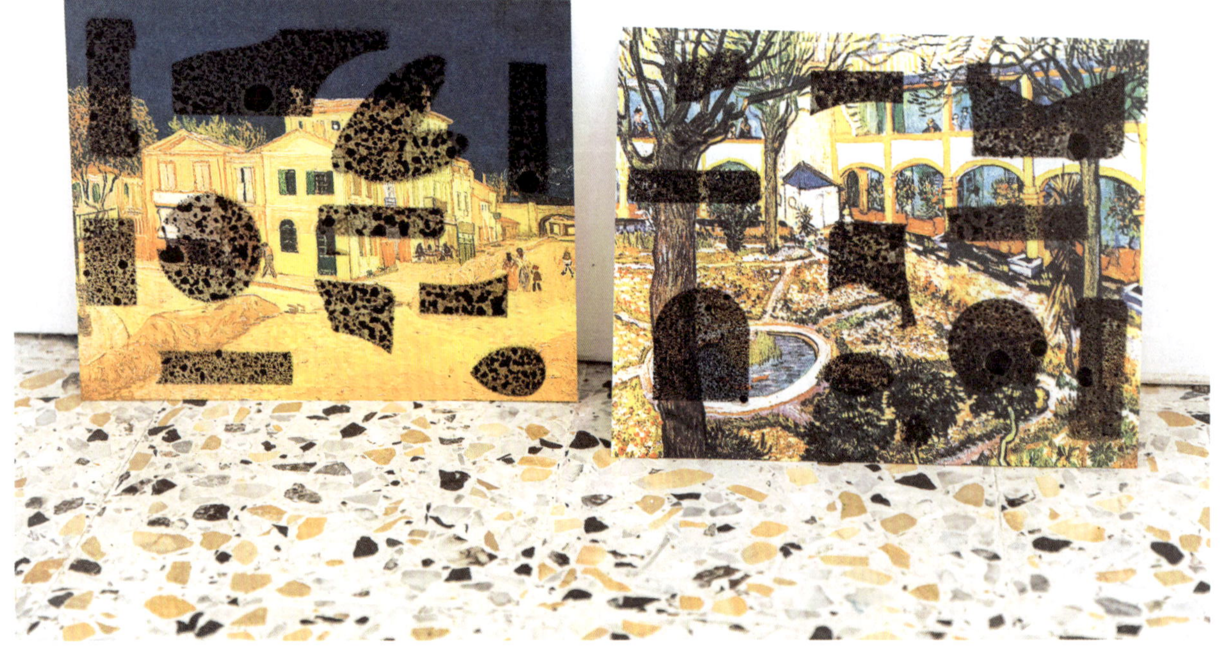

Clément Rodzielski, *Untitled (La maison jaune)*, *Untitled (Le jardin de la maison de santé à Arles)*, ink on postcards

of American Art. I very much like how she manages to respond with fantasy and with cleverness to specific problems. Redistributing figures, colors, canvas, skills, pictures…The catalogue is unique: it's not often that you get the opportunity to have a closer look into the several layers of what an artist's life is.

I met Laura thanks to Charlotte Houette. I spent one month in Arles—November 2022. Windy time, empty streets, arctic desert. A great time, though! It was my first time there. It was nice to be there, in that house, surrounded by works of art. It helps in having better nights. I moved from the second floor to the top floor to enjoy Laura's painting and to be close to the starry night.

I really wanted to make something specific for the house. I was interested by the question of decorative art. What happens if a shape occupies and spreads all over a space? How can a painting fit with architecture? What would a domestic shape be? First, I wanted to make some bed headboard paintings. At that time, I used to make long, horizontal paintings. Ultimately I didn't. I had also been wishing to paint a ceiling for a long time. At the very beginning, I was not sure it would work, because the studio—which was the perfect spot to make it—was not supposed to be a place for a permanent artwork. Finally, because I was one of the last residents, it was OK to paint this ceiling. So I got the opportunity to reenact an old idea that started with a special edition I had created for a publication named *Octopus Notes* ten years ago. It was a kind of goody: a stencil drawn from a pattern borrowed from fig packaging, a tool you can use. Sometimes, one can find

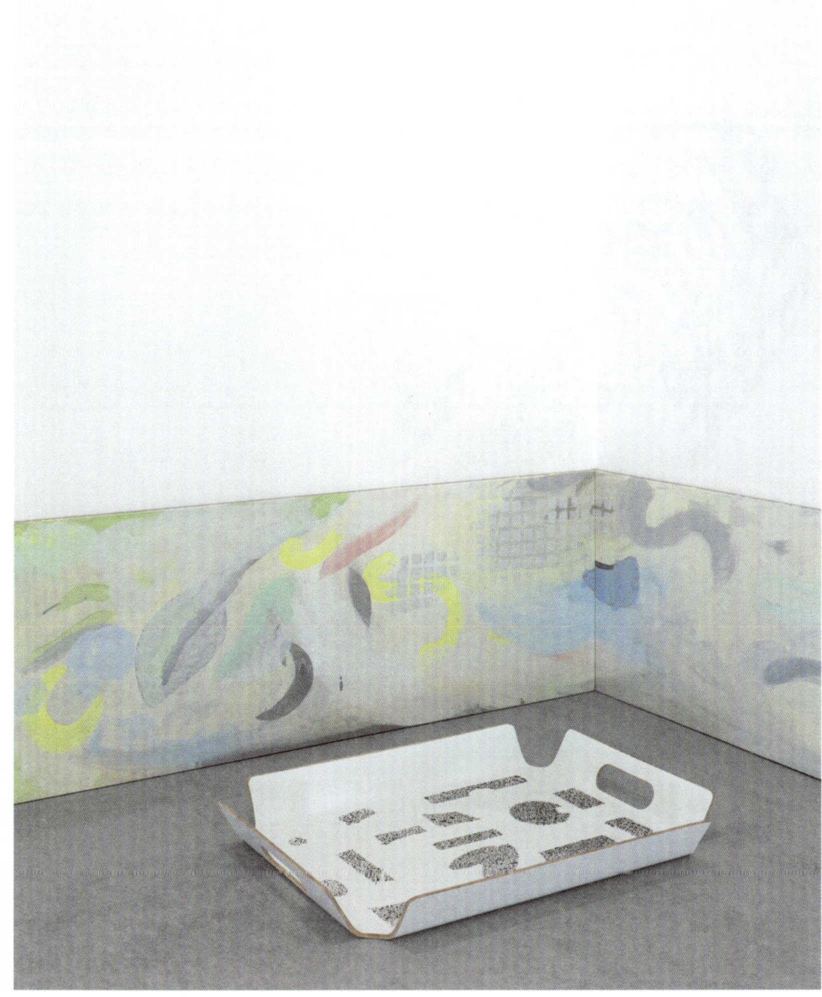

Clément Rodzielski, *Untitled*, ink on tray

shaped holes on cardboard packaging for products like pasta or pastries…I thought it could be interesting to think about them like tools in order to produce pictures, to use them as ready-made stencils. Thus, the shapes for the ceiling come from several products collected over the years and from some bought at the supermarket specifically for the project. Thus, my diet, what I ate in Arles, was the consequence of the packages I needed to get to paint the ceiling. I had never made such a huge work before. In the middle of my stay, I was afraid I would not have enough time to finish the work. In the end, it was a rush, and there was no time left for tourism anymore.

Besides this, I have also made kind of goody by covering Van Gogh posters and prints with the same patterns. I like the result. A tray too. And because Christmas was getting close, I covered some gift packages with it. My departure day, I quickly left the house and decided, at the last moment, to make one wink to Van Gogh: I hung up my old shoes on Naoki Sutter-Shudo's rope sculpture. Something else: during my stay, I made sketches with the motif of the house's number 3, edited stickers from one of the drawings, and, coming back later, stuck some on the entrance door as a hello/goodbye.

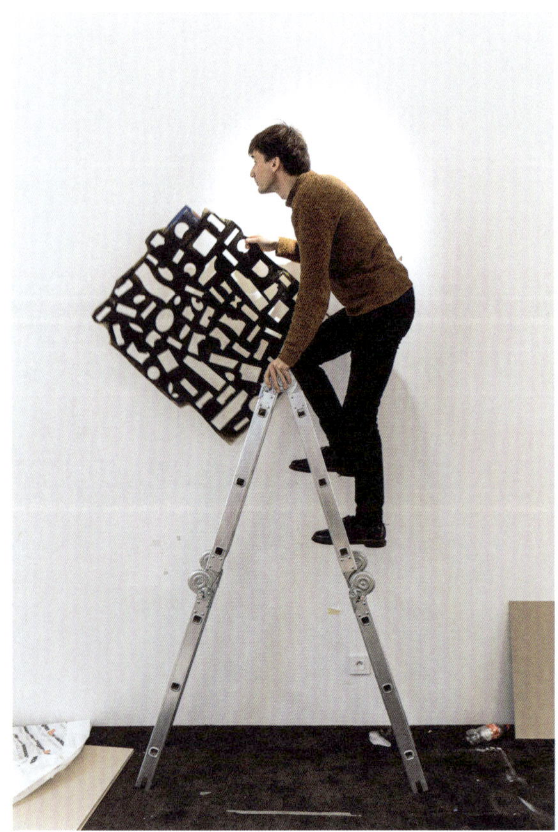
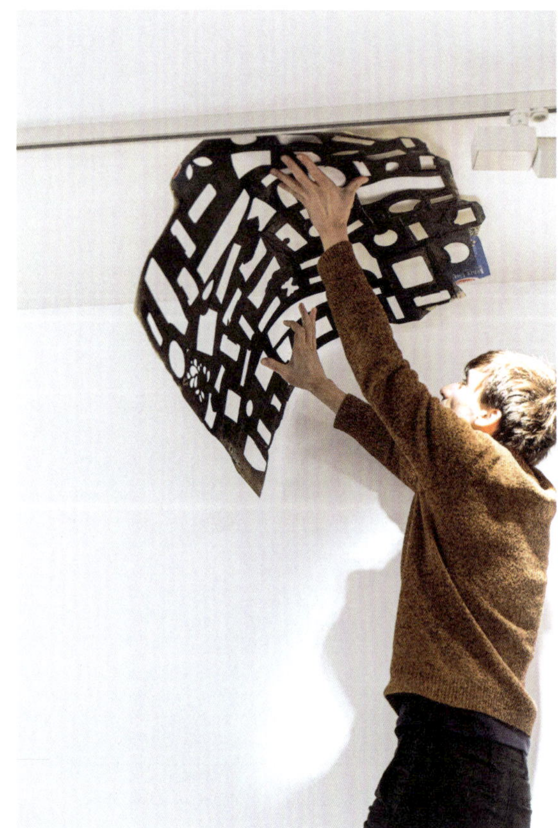

Clément working on *Untitled*

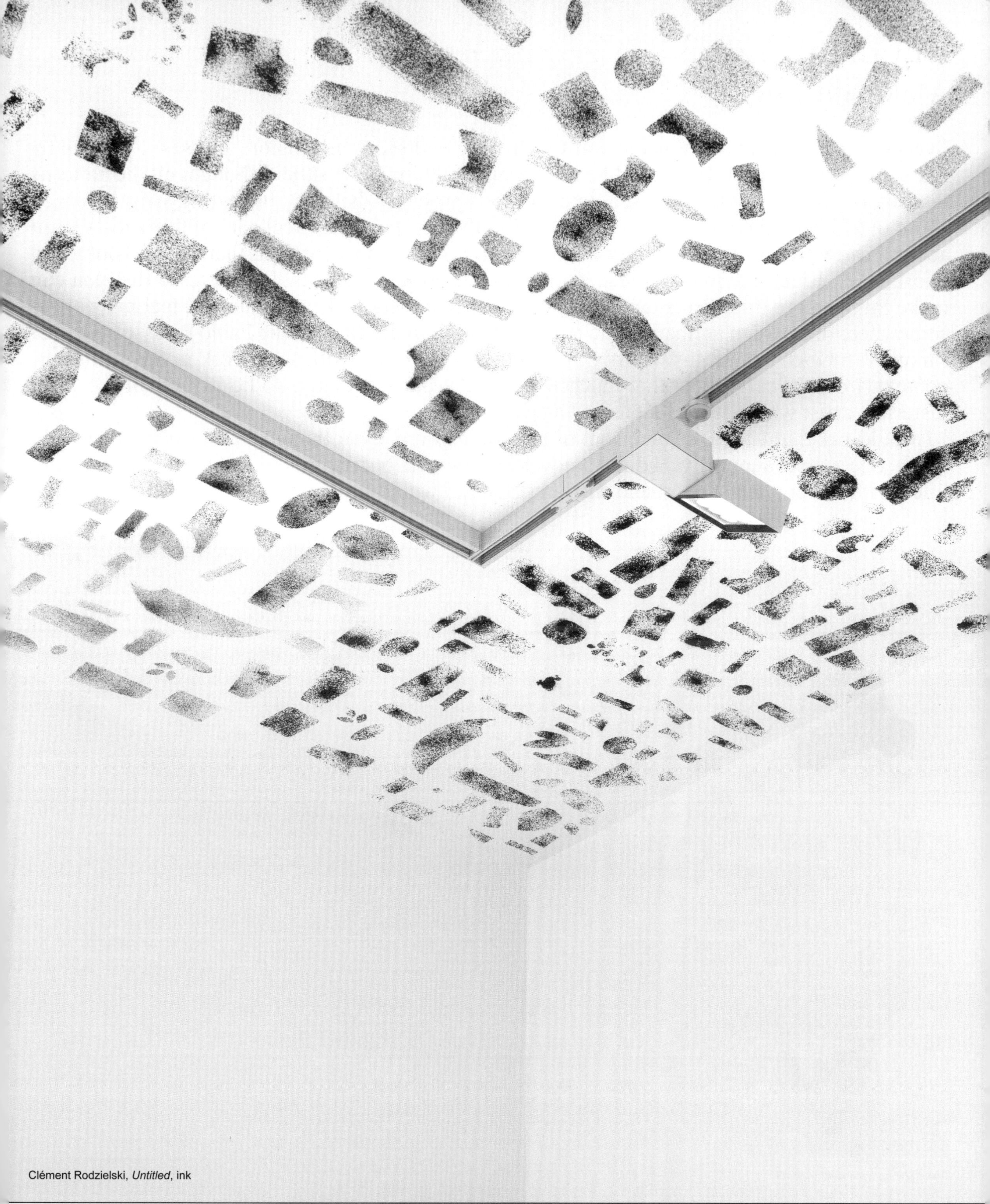

Clément Rodzielski, *Untitled*, ink

DECEMBER 2022
Alake Shilling

Everything I knew about Vincent van Gogh I learned in my art history classes. I personally liked his unorthodox style—I felt like it resonated with my own style. I thought all the patterns and colors resonated with my visual interest. He's probably the most interesting artist I learned about in a historical context. *The Starry Night* is the first painting I feel a lot of fine artists learn about. I can't say I had a particular relationship to his work. I really liked that he was kooky and unorthodox. I feel like maybe I leaned on his patterns and textures. I discovered that you can make things more ornamental and it's OK, even celebrated. I like animation; I feel his work is somewhere in between animation and realism. I didn't really care for the Pablo Picasso style, but I liked Van Gogh's style, his whimsy. I wish there was more whimsical work in the art history context. I didn't learn about that much whimsical work until later, so he is probably the first historical artist whose work I identified as whimsical.

I would say that Laura is somewhat of a mentor to me, even though I don't talk to her very much. She's super supportive. I didn't know her very well, but my first interactions with her were filled with nothing but support and encouragement. I would say she has done a lot to help me go

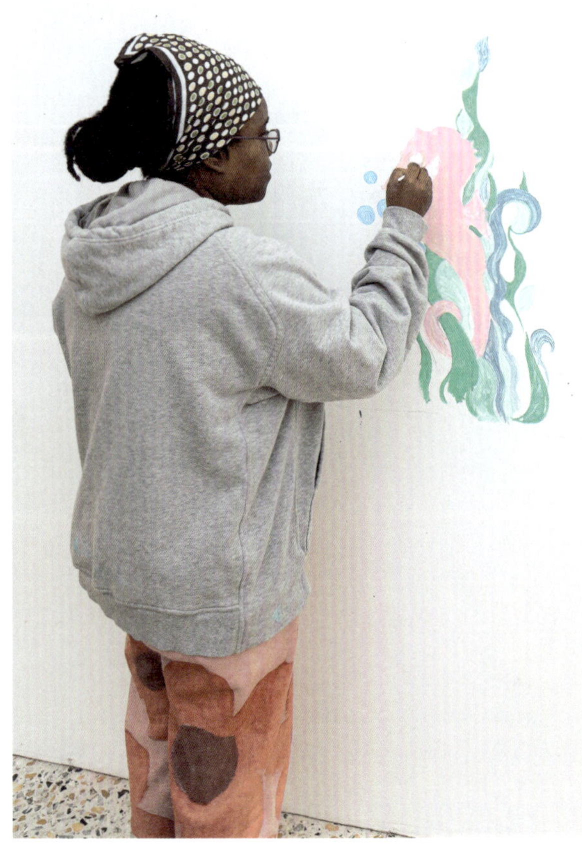

Alake Shilling working on *Untitled*

to other levels in my fine art journey. I met Laura at 356 Mission, Los Angeles, where I interned for a whole year, which is very lucky because it wasn't common to intern there for that long of a period. I made so many friends there, and I had my first show there. She created an incubator, a community where artists can grow and have resources, and I got to be a part of that community. I helped with setting up for openings, and I eventually was given the opportunity to participate in Clay Day, which she had once a week—a clay workshop—and eventually somebody let me run it, for some reason. I was there so often—that's how, I think, I got to do that. Because I didn't have an actual job, I went there every day like it was my real job, and it was just so magical. I mean, without Clay Day and 356 Mission, I don't know where I'd be now. I got to see other professional artists working, workshopping ideas, and I got to talk to them, pick their brains, and also use the space as my own studio. I got to experiment with new a material that I had never worked with before, got to take my time and think about things.

I got an email from someone who invited me to the residency on Laura's behalf. At first I thought it was going to be very difficult to do—a rigorous application process or something. I hate applications. I never do them; it holds me back. I asked a few questions about the residency, and she said, "Oh, no, you're invited. You just have to pick a time." Easy peasy. I actually never talked to Laura specifically until I got there, to Arles. She gave me the gist of how everything works in the town and some restaurants to visit. It was actually very casual. I prefer it that way.

My first impression of Arles was that it's really cold. I went in December and it was extremely cold. I was surprised how small-town vibes it was; it was old-timey, and I didn't know that there were Romans in France. I learned a lot about that. It was perfect for me, actually, because I was like, Great, I can explore the town by myself and not get scared. I felt like, This is just my speed, I can handle this. I went by myself initially, and my mother came on the second half of the trip. I was there for one month, and she came two weeks after me. In the beginning, I was sleeping a lot, because I got really sick the first two weeks I was there. But when I got better, I was exploring the town because I couldn't figure out the schedules. Things closed very early. Since I went in the winter, a lot of places were closed. Figuring out the times took a while. There was a Japanese restaurant I liked a lot that was very close, so I ate ramen almost every day. Right before you go up to the house, there was a big Italian restaurant. That one was pretty good. I had great pizza. I did a pretty bad job at finding all the cool things to do, though I felt like a lot of good stuff was probably closed as well. That was my biggest problem: finding the right lunch. Some places were closed totally for the winter. People told me the summer is the best time to go because there's tourists and lots of people, but I find I do better with less tourists. So I'm happy with the time I went. They have a big Christmas culture, so I saw Santa going through the town on the black horses and people in black cloaks walking around the fountain. I had never seen anything like that before. I enjoyed the Christmas culture. The Monoprix department store was probably my favorite experience. I loved that.

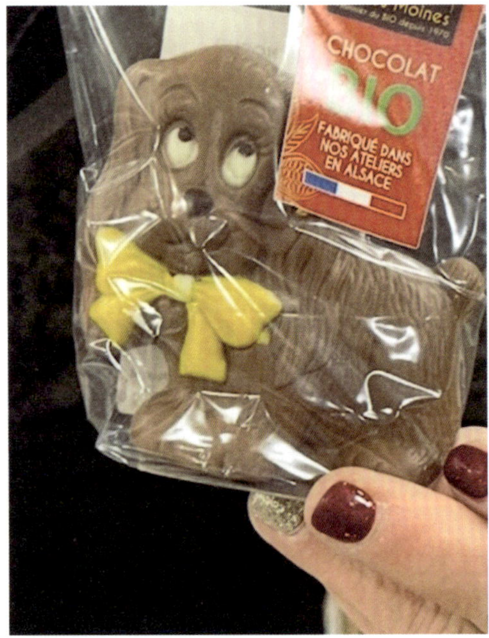

A chocolate dog

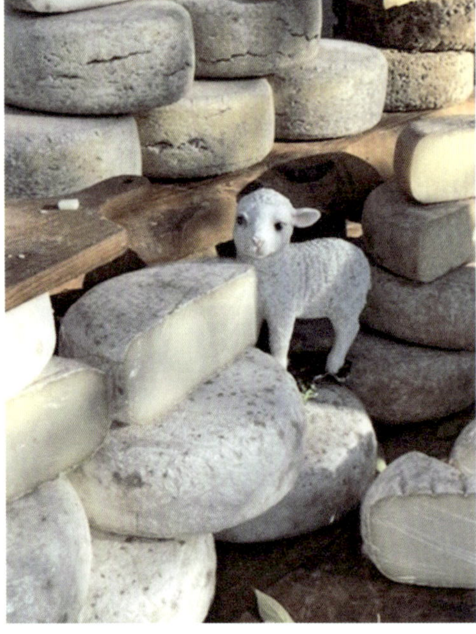

A toy sheep at the cheese shop

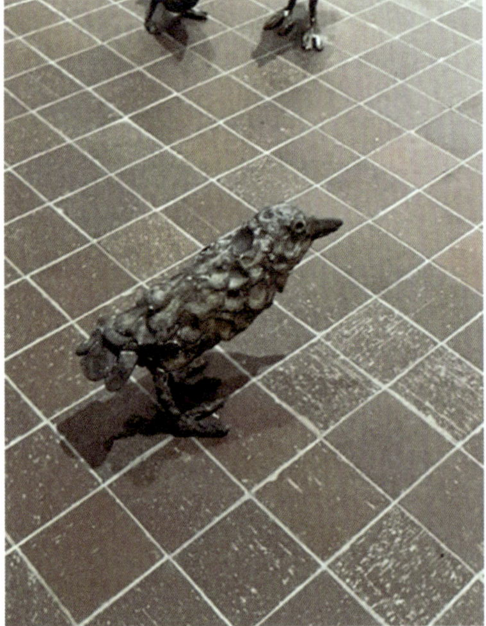

Ugo Rondinone, *Primitive*, at LUMA

My first impression of the house was like, This is so beautiful, I can't believe I get to stay here. I felt so inspired and felt like, Wow, look, everyone made something so beautiful. I also felt a lot of pressure to make something good. I'm not very good at making work on the spot. I wish I had planned something and then taken it there, or had a plan at all. The art supply store wasn't very good, I didn't know how to ship supplies, and I didn't bring any with me. I just wasn't that prepared. But I was super inspired, and I felt so lucky to stay there. I loved the kitchen, I loved the stairs. I felt like I could live there forever. You know, I was thinking, if I had to be sick anywhere, I'd love to be sick there, because I felt so cozy and comfortable. I noticed Asha Schechter's work right away. I noticed Julien Ceccaldi—I'm a big fan. Alicia Vaïsse's paintings going up the stairs depicting dogs were so good. I thought all of the work was so strong. I was like, I feel unworthy to be here. It's such good work. I didn't know it was going to be so overwhelming. I didn't know people were going to do such big works and incorporate it into the house. I was picturing maybe a wall with different paintings. I didn't know it was going to be so immersive. And, oh, Laura's work! I loved her mosaics. And, I mean, all the work fit together so well. I wouldn't imagine that so many different artists would make work that looks so good together—similar color palette, similar themes. But I guess she curated the artists, so that makes sense. Maybe she thought, Oh, these artists might look good together. Maybe. I don't know. But I was surprised at the scale of everything. I wasn't expecting that. No, I hadn't made a work on-site before, and I felt very

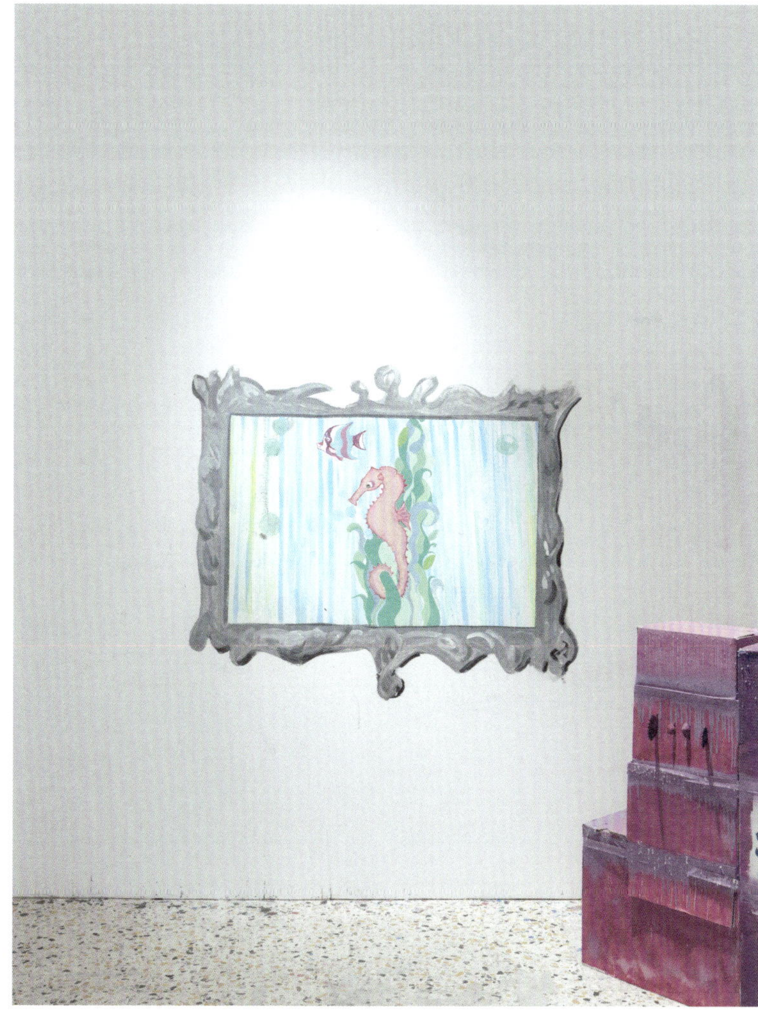

Alake Shilling, *Untitled*, wall painting

overwhelmed with making such a big, permanent work a part of the house without doing any planning. I decided to just do something tiny, because I didn't know what I wanted it to be. It was inspiring, but I didn't feel prepared. I wanted to make a painting, so I was thinking of doing it on canvas, but I just didn't have a good canvas or the right canvases. I did a small painting of a seahorse underwater, but it feels to me more like an underpainting. I did it in two weeks, which, for me, is not a lot of time. Even my small paintings take a long time. I'm just not a fast painter, so I didn't feel like two weeks was enough. I wish I could have had more time to work on it, but I just did something small in the studio because I didn't feel like I wanted to mess up the vibe that was so perfect. So that's why I did a small painting of a seahorse.

I didn't want to cover up anyone else's art, and I couldn't figure out a good way to interact with another person's work. I guess I just felt like I needed more time to think. But the themes were very nature oriented. I felt like almost everyone did a piece that had to do with nature in some aspect. I liked that because I only do nature, really. And so I felt like, OK, I'm in good company. That's why I decided to do a seahorse—because I saw the dogs and the leaves and flowers and beautiful things. I was like, OK, I'll do something natural too. And my color palette was based on a lot of the colors I saw around the house—pastels and neon. So I decided to stay within the same color range, which is natural to me anyway, so I felt like it was very easy to pick up on the vibe. I really liked the way everything was already, so I didn't feel like there was anything

I could contribute, kind of, because everything looked perfect already. But I know that's the point of it—to build. I just maybe got into my head about it a bit.

I felt like I would like to meet more of the artists that participated and get to know them. It's kind of hard to look at someone's work and not talk to them about it if you're looking at it every day. But I did meet people there. I met Alicia Vaïsse; she was very nice to me. She showed me around, and she was pregnant—pretty close to having a baby. So even though she could have stayed home and rested, she was there, and she had dinner with me, and she explained everything about her work to me. I love when artists talk about their work, especially when I admire it. I kind of felt like I was on the outside looking in, in some aspect, because I was one of the last people to go, so I kind of got to see the whole picture. Others didn't get to see the way everything came together. So I felt like, Wow, look at this beautiful community. And kind of like, I'm hanging on the outside—not in a negative way. I just felt like, maybe, I needed more time or to talk to more people. But I definitely felt really inspired by being a part of this project because it's really special. It's kind of like being in school together, but very strange, actually, 'cause you're alone. I know a lot of the artists' work, and I admire it. So that was like, Oh, wow! They're really good. I can't believe I'm here too. But I haven't actually met many of them.

I'd love to do a mural in a house. I would just need to prepare properly and think of a good idea. I thought the way Laura approached it was genius. She should do a collaboration with a company

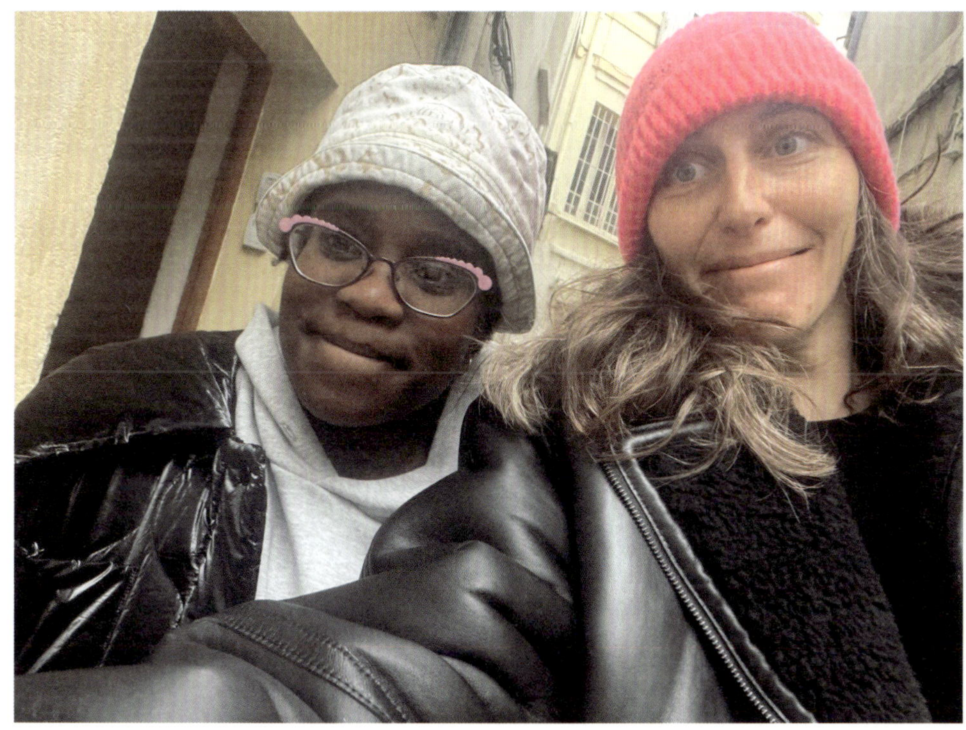

Alake and Alicia Vaïsse

for houses. That would be genius. But I love tiles and I love ornamental, personalized houses. So it was honestly a dream. I love *Architectural Digest*—that's, like, my second love: interior design. And I like the way it was approached. All the furniture and everything was really beautiful along with the paintings on the wall. So I feel inspired by beautiful interiors. I've always been scared to do a mural inside a house because I feel like it won't be perfect, you know? Because on the canvas, I feel like I paint over everything, I do lots of layers. My initial plan is never how it looks in the end. So doing a mural on a house—I feel like it would be very hard to do that. You have to have the plan and execute it. I think I could do a good job if I do my plan and stick to it.

When my mom came, we went to the Monoprix and she cooked. We were just fascinated by how the food didn't make us feel sick or anything. We were just blown away. You know, my gut problems, my acne cleared up. I just felt entirely better. That was really nice, her cooking. But that was the best part of the trip. I was like a new person. I felt amazing. I have terrible stomach problems in America, and to eat a meal and not be scared—I wasn't scared to eat anything—was absolutely so freeing. We went to a few restaurants together, and we looked at some of the knickknack shops. We didn't do anything crazy. We went to dinner with Alicia and one of her friends. That was really nice. We went to the big market, and my mom got some cool pants there. That was the biggest issue with not speaking French—because nobody at the farmers' market spoke English. I couldn't really get anything because I didn't speak French. I think I got a small roasted chicken. I had a lot of questions, like, "Oh, what's in this?" or "How much am I buying?" or, I don't know. I think I bought some cheese too. That was really good. I didn't buy clothes or anything. Oh, yeah, I think that almost everywhere I go: Maybe I will move to France one day.

Every day, there was a lady who always asked me for money, and we kind of came up with a good relationship. She was very funny, and I kind of think of her as a friend now, but I think she was kind of a gypsy lady. I almost made friends everywhere I went—the coffee shop, the bakery. I felt like everyone was really nice to me there. Let's see…What else happened? It wasn't a crazy, action-packed trip. I didn't do that much. My favorite part of it was going to l'Arlatan hotel, which had a beautiful tile floor and beautiful chandeliers. It's really beautiful. I walked around the city with Julie Boukobza a little bit, and I met her son. I thought he was really cool. I went to the museum, and I saw the group show they had up, which I thought was very inspiring. It's so weird for me to go somewhere and love all the work I see. But I really loved everything in the house. I loved everything in the museum. I liked how everything was so small. It kind of reminded me of Iceland, like a very small town. That was probably the best part of the trip for me: being inspired by all the art. It's easier for me to make work and feel like I want to make work when I see work that I like. So it didn't really help me there because I didn't plan, but when I came back home, I felt inspired to work and to try new ideas. That helped me outside of the residency. It was the best time ever. It's truly a gift. Laura gave people a gift.

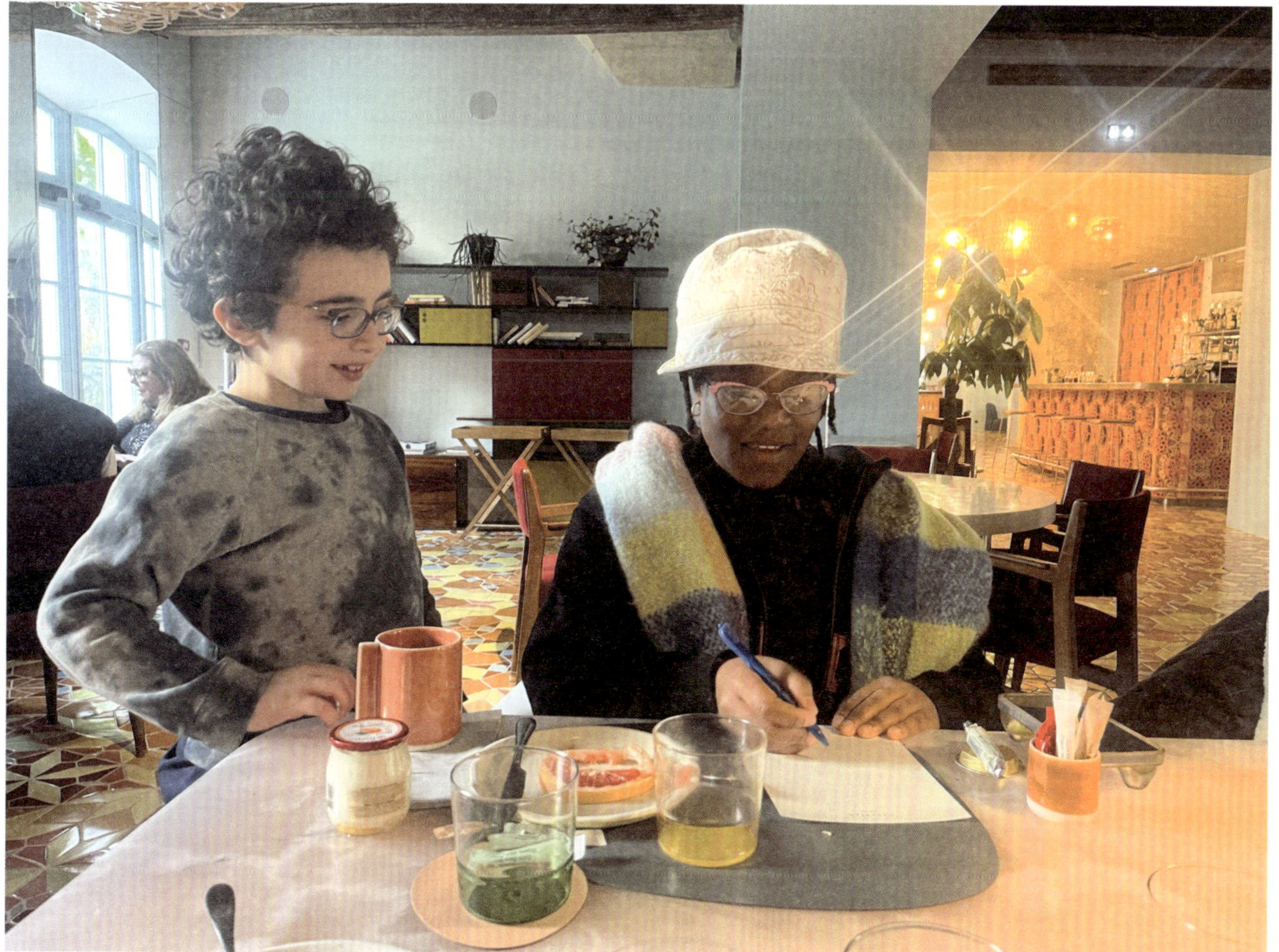

Albert (Julie Boukobza's son) and Alake

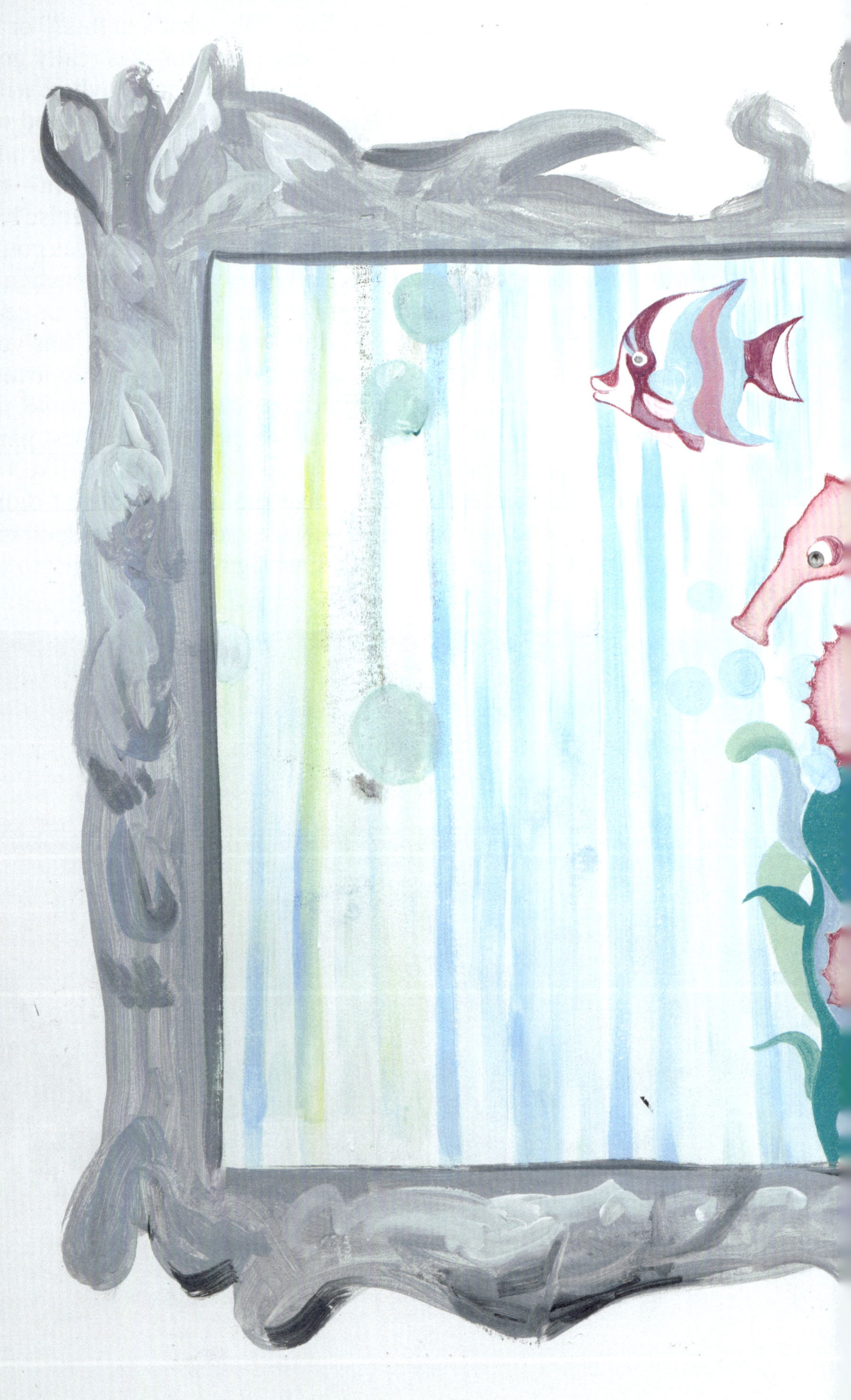

Alake Shilling, *Untitled*, wall painting

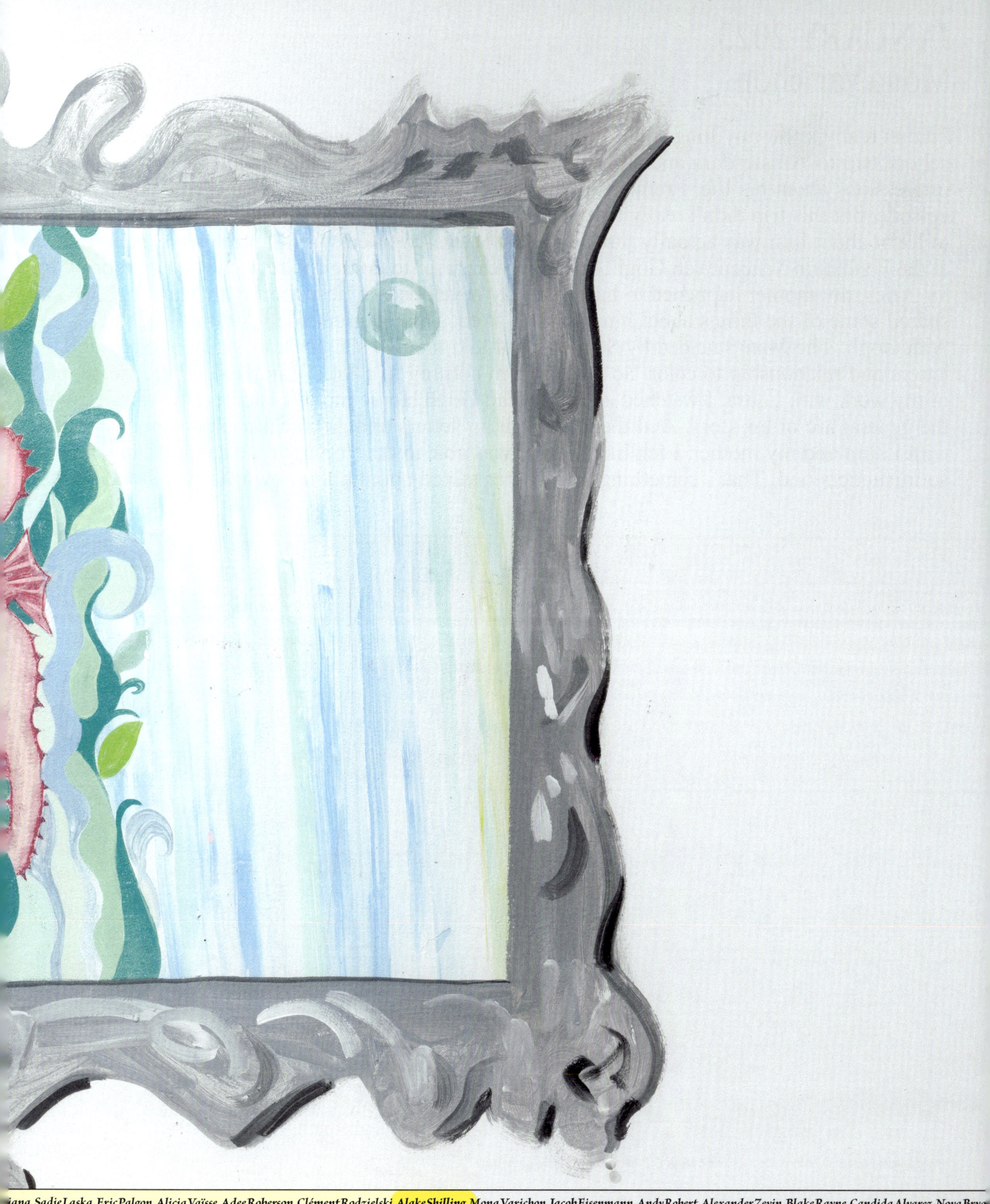

JANUARY 2023
Mona Varichon

I didn't really know anything about Vincent van Gogh before I went to Arles. I did take a middle-school trip to Amsterdam and visited the Van Gogh Museum, but it didn't leave any strong impressions about his life. I remember seeing some of the paintings and hearing about the ear episode, but this trip didn't really teach me much about him as a person. The way that I started to learn about him was actually through my mother. I worked with Laura Owens on her show at the Fondation Vincent van Gogh Arles the year prior to doing the residency, and before I left for Arles, my mother happened to have recently developed an obsession with Van Gogh, so she shared some of the things about him that she liked. She recommended Antonin Artaud's essay "Van Gogh: The Man Suicided by Society" and told me that she got into Van Gogh through his letters and relationship to color. So I went from nothing to a lot of knowledge because, as part of my work with Laura, I watched all of the Van Gogh biopic movies and became familiar with the general arc of his story. And then, through his letters and Artaud's book and conversations with Laura and my mother, I felt like I really was able to develop my own sense of how he was so misunderstood. That's something my mother talked about a lot: how misunderstood he was

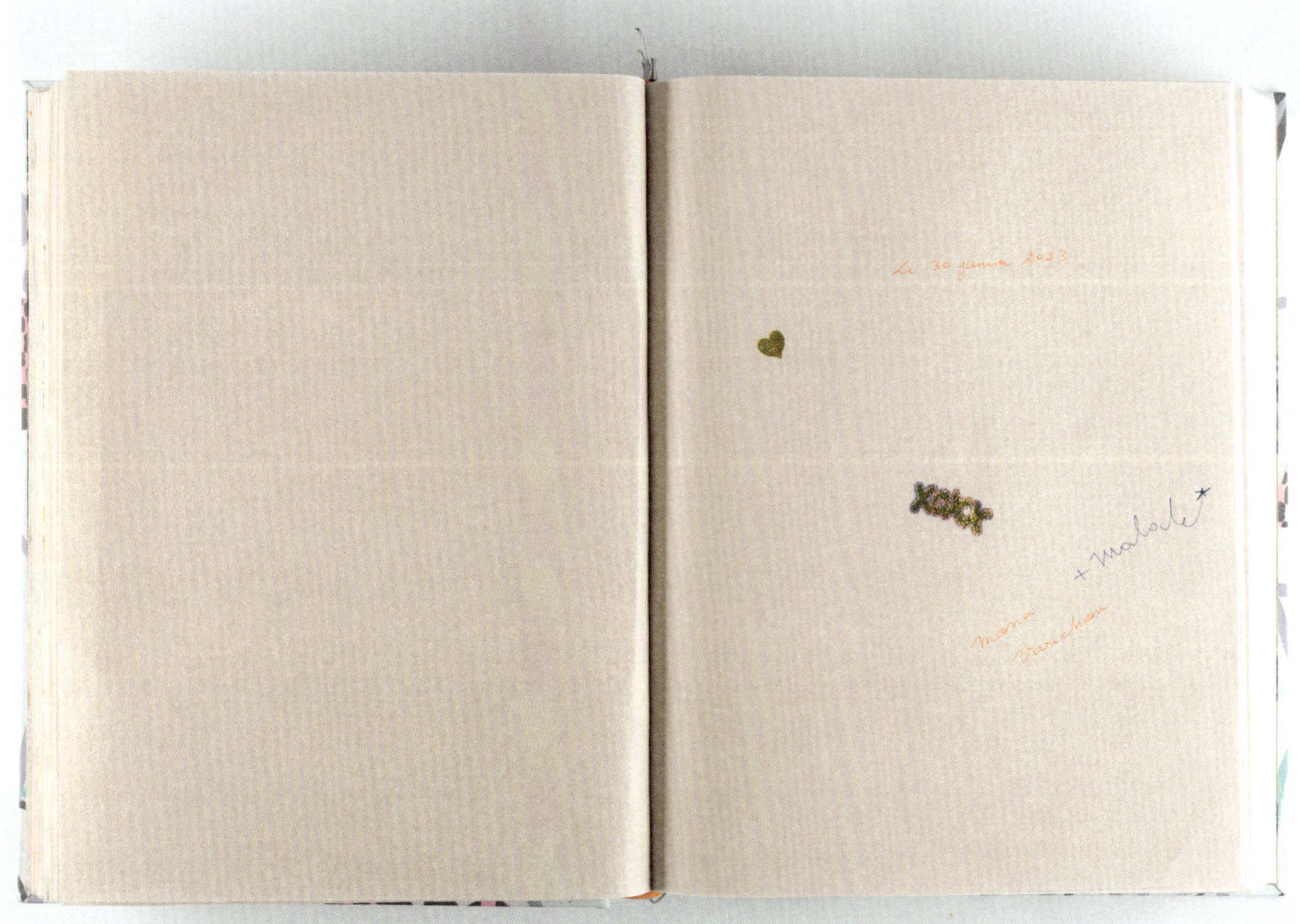

The signatures of Mona Varichon and her mother, Malak El Zanaty Varichon, in the guest book

and how he loved a lot and wasn't really loved back. It was interesting to discover that the artists of his time didn't like his work, but he kept doing it anyway. Through his letters, you get a sense of his commitment despite people not believing in him, how his brother also made it financially possible for him to keep doing his work, and the fact that his sister-in-law played a big role in preserving his work. So by the time I did the residency, I was quite familiar with him, whereas if you had asked me a year and a half before, I would have just seen him as an image that didn't really evoke anything other than some of his paintings. It did bring me to a new understanding of his paintings, spending time in Arles prior to the residency, knowing how deeply he felt about colors, what he was trying to do with painting, and how new it was at the time. I also was really able to actually *see* his paintings for the first time instead of seeing them as these overly reproduced images. I saw them for the documents they were of that time and what he was trying to convey. I also got very interested in his portraits as documents of the people that he was meeting and ways he experimented with color. So I got to appreciate the art through getting to know him as a person.

I first met Laura in 2015, during my first year in graduate school at ArtCenter College of Design in Pasadena. She was visiting faculty, so we did a studio visit and got along well. I was a little bit impressed because I'd heard so much about her and had read the book about *12 Paintings* at 356 Mission, Los Angeles. So I had an image of her from reading that book, how it talked about the way she created community through the making of that show and space. I remember reading

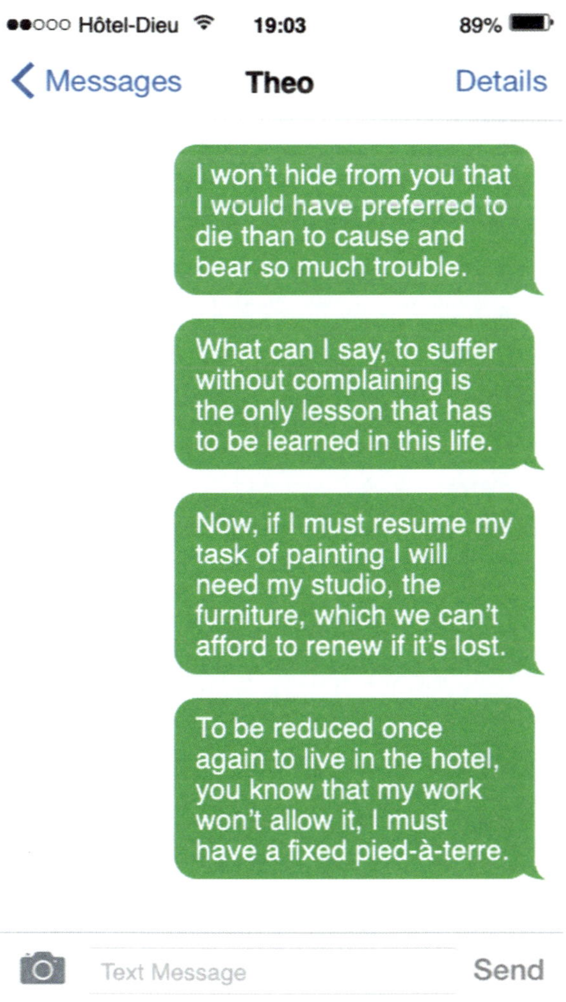

Mona Varichon, *Vincent to Theo, March 19, 1889, Arles [page 5 of 7]*, digital file

about how they did karaoke and would paint at all these different times together, so she seemed like an interesting and intimidating and exciting figure that I didn't know much about, but she was very nice and personable. So I got to know her as my teacher and would sometimes see her at 356 Mission before it closed. After I graduated, she hired me to be the nanny for her two children and as an assistant archivist in her studio. So my first year after graduating in 2019, I spent a lot of time in her home and her studio. And that's how she offered me the job in Arles. She was moving there for six months to prepare this show of her and Van Gogh's works at the Fondation Vincent van Gogh Arles, which was meant to happen in the spring of 2020. We moved there together in February 2020, and then the first COVID-19 confinement happened, so the show was postponed by a year. But we still spent six months there, living together with my partner, Jacob Eisenmann, and Laura's child Nova.

The main way I had heard about Arles was through the photo festival, the Rencontres d'Arles, but I really didn't have much of an image of the city. My first impression is tainted by COVID-19 because the outbreak happened a week or two after I moved there. It quickly became a ghost town, but it was beautiful, this simple little village that also had some very impressive architecture. I'm always impressed by the staircases there in most apartment buildings—they seem really extra. It's a very beautiful place.

I got to the residency in early January 2023. By then, there was quite a lot of art, and it was

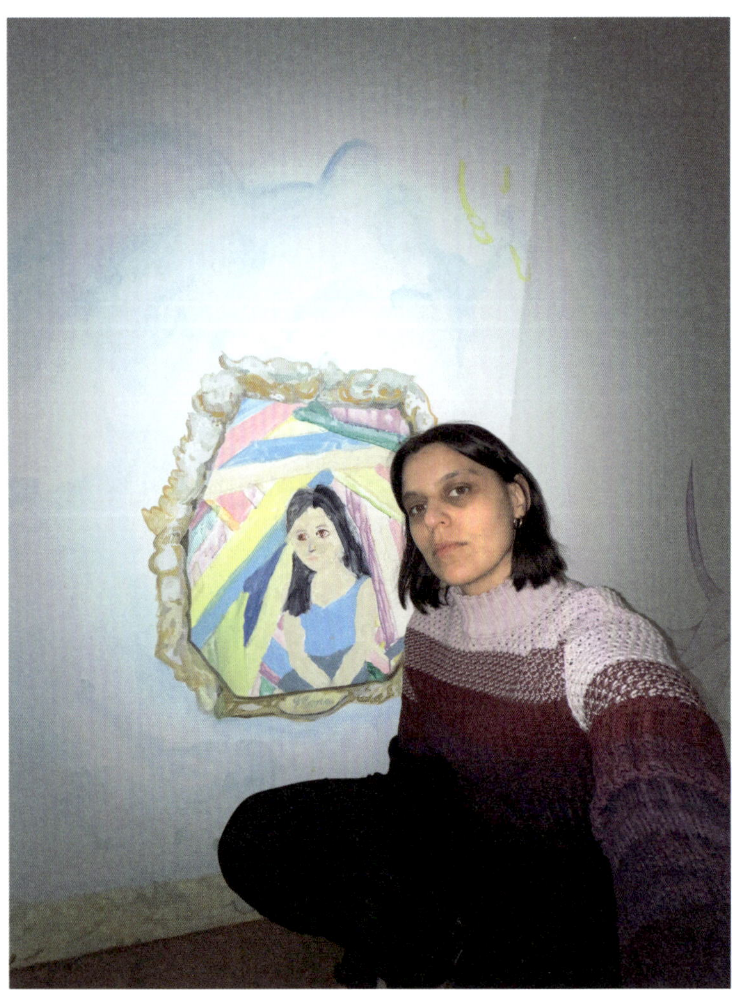

Mona with a painting by Nova Bryan

starting to be art that I couldn't identify. At first, I could tell who had made what, especially my friends, but there started to be works by artists I didn't know and works that were harder to decipher and know who had made them. It was both kind of exciting to discover all the new art and also a little confusing. I wouldn't say that it felt very coherent. It felt like artists were playing by different rules in how they were thinking of their contributions, which was OK, but it was something that I definitely noticed. And I didn't necessarily feel everyone's involvement with Van Gogh, which was also something that was up to each person.

There was, first of all, the question of space: like, where can I still fit works? Because by then, it was quite full. What got me excited was that it was a house. I was thinking a lot about Van Gogh, and one thing I love about his time at the Yellow House is that a lot of his most famous paintings started out as decoration. Once you realize that, it really helps you see them not as these iconic images but as objects that have a reason for being in a space and creating a certain atmosphere. Or works made for certain people, rooms, or contexts. In Van Gogh's case, it was for the guest room. From what I've read about the Yellow House, he wanted Paul Gauguin, or whoever would stay there, to feel comfortable and inspired, so he put up a lot of sunflower paintings. I like thinking about how having a place to put something up will give you ideas, and maybe he wouldn't have been so inventive with the sunflowers if he hadn't had the space to hang them. At the time, nobody was excited to see his paintings. So I was thinking a lot about that, and during the time I spent with Laura prior to the residency, I had accumulated an archive of photographs I was hoping to do something with. It quickly occurred to me that they kind of functioned as family photographs—in the sense of an extended family—because there were a lot of people coming through when we were staying in Arles. People connected to Laura through galleries and museums, but also friends of mine as well as family. So it was this interesting combination of all kinds of people with different proximity to the art world. I wanted to hang the photographs in a way that would be reminiscent of how family photographs are hung in a house, so they would immediately function in a straightforward way, whether or not you knew the people in the photographs. The second work that I put up is also something that had been in the works, but I had never installed it in a space, and this felt like the perfect place to try it. This was a mind map that I remade after a Jeremy Deller work. He had first drawn this mind map on an envelope while talking to a friend and describing the social and artistic meshing he saw in these different musical movements. After having drawn it, he was like, "Well, this is actually interesting and brings up a lot of new connections." So he's been reproducing this drawing into murals, and it's called *The History of the World*. I had made a similar drawing on a piece of paper, inspired by what he did, which I called *A Chapter in History*. It connects the yellow vest movement to the French rap band PNL. I had always known that one day I wanted to put it up on the wall somewhere like Deller did, but I was waiting for the right place to do it. And so, it being a house, and because there were already several murals on the walls, I felt like it would be a fun place to try it. And also, this made me think about ways that I could connect Van Gogh to these histories. One of the main things that links the yellow vests and PNL is their exclusion from central public space. The fact that Van Gogh had been excluded from the city of Arles when he lived there was on my mind, so this was a way to address it. So I made the mural and I added a few references to Van Gogh that made it a special version. I did it in the bathroom, first of all because there was space, but it was also a wink at the fact that, sometimes, you can find graffiti that is slightly subversive in a bathroom. I added the Yellow House to it as one of the little Van Gogh details and put it near the yellow vests' communities that they built at roundabouts, but other than that, it didn't address Arles directly, other than through ideas of inclusion and exclusion.

I was in Arles during the winter, which means that it was quite calm. Sadly, when I went, there were a lot of things on my plate. I only had a month, and I was also trying to go through the footage that I had filmed when I lived in Arles prior. I was anxious about getting all my projects done, so from the very beginning I was always working, and the fantasies that I had of revisiting hikes or having more leisure time quickly dissipated into trying to finish everything before the end of the month. The few things I would do in town were grocery shopping, buying bread near the place du Forum, or having coffee at Bar le Tambourin. I would often Shazam the music that they played there because it was always such a funny, nostalgic playlist. I like it there because

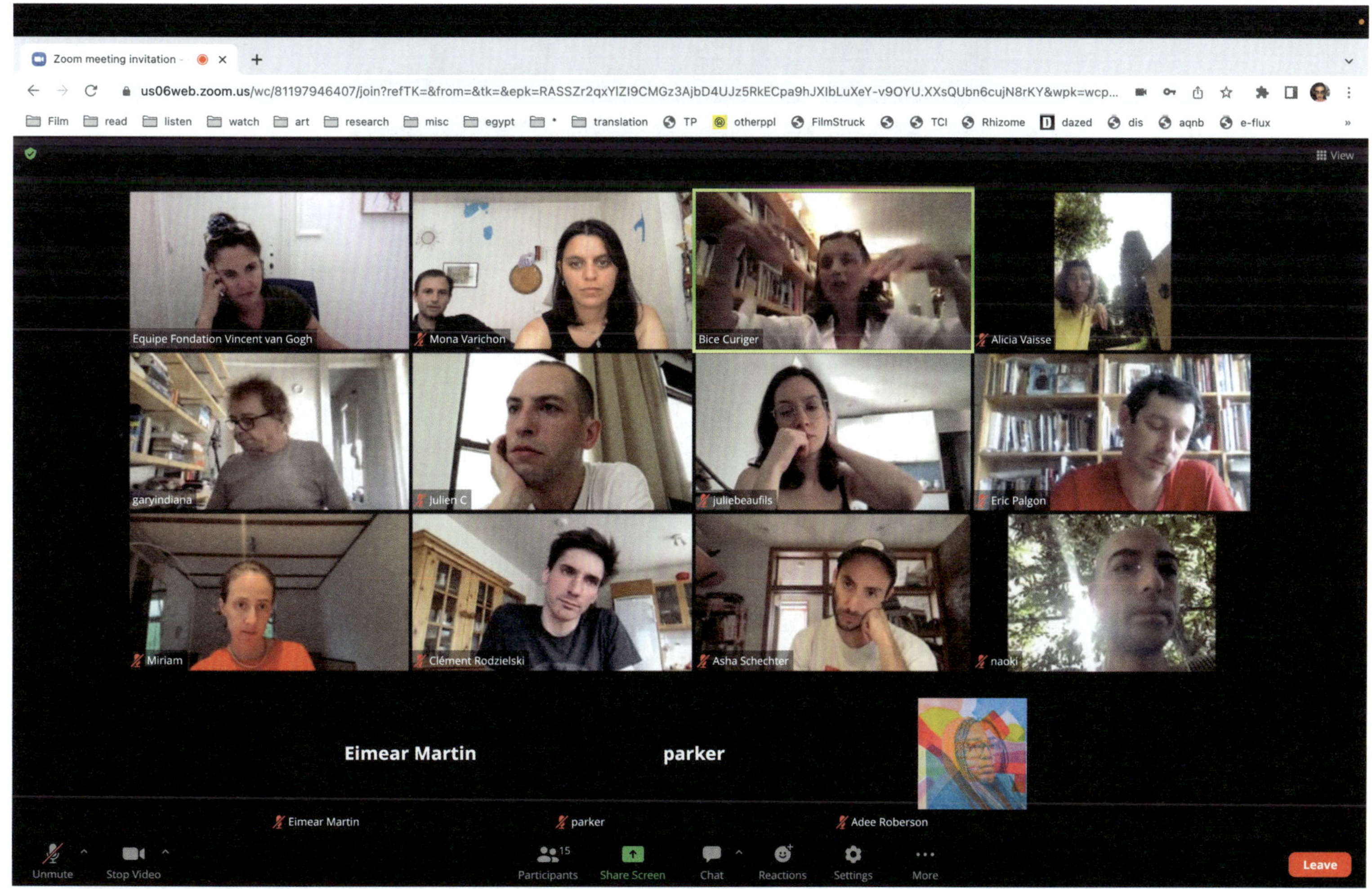

A Zoom meeting to discuss the residency artists' exhibition at the Fondation Vincent van Gogh Arles

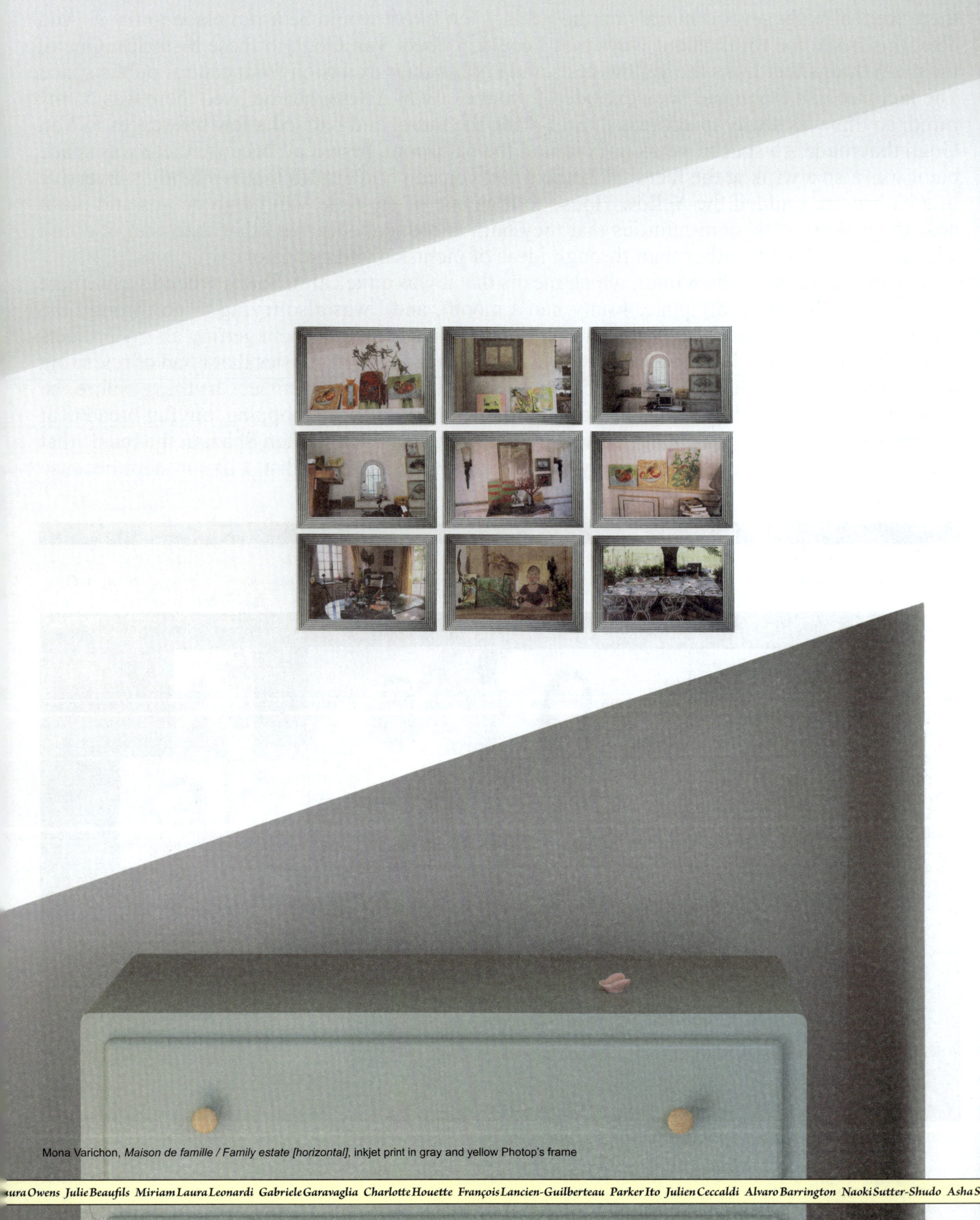

Mona Varichon, *Maison de famille / Family estate [horizontal]*, inkjet print in gray and yellow Photop's frame

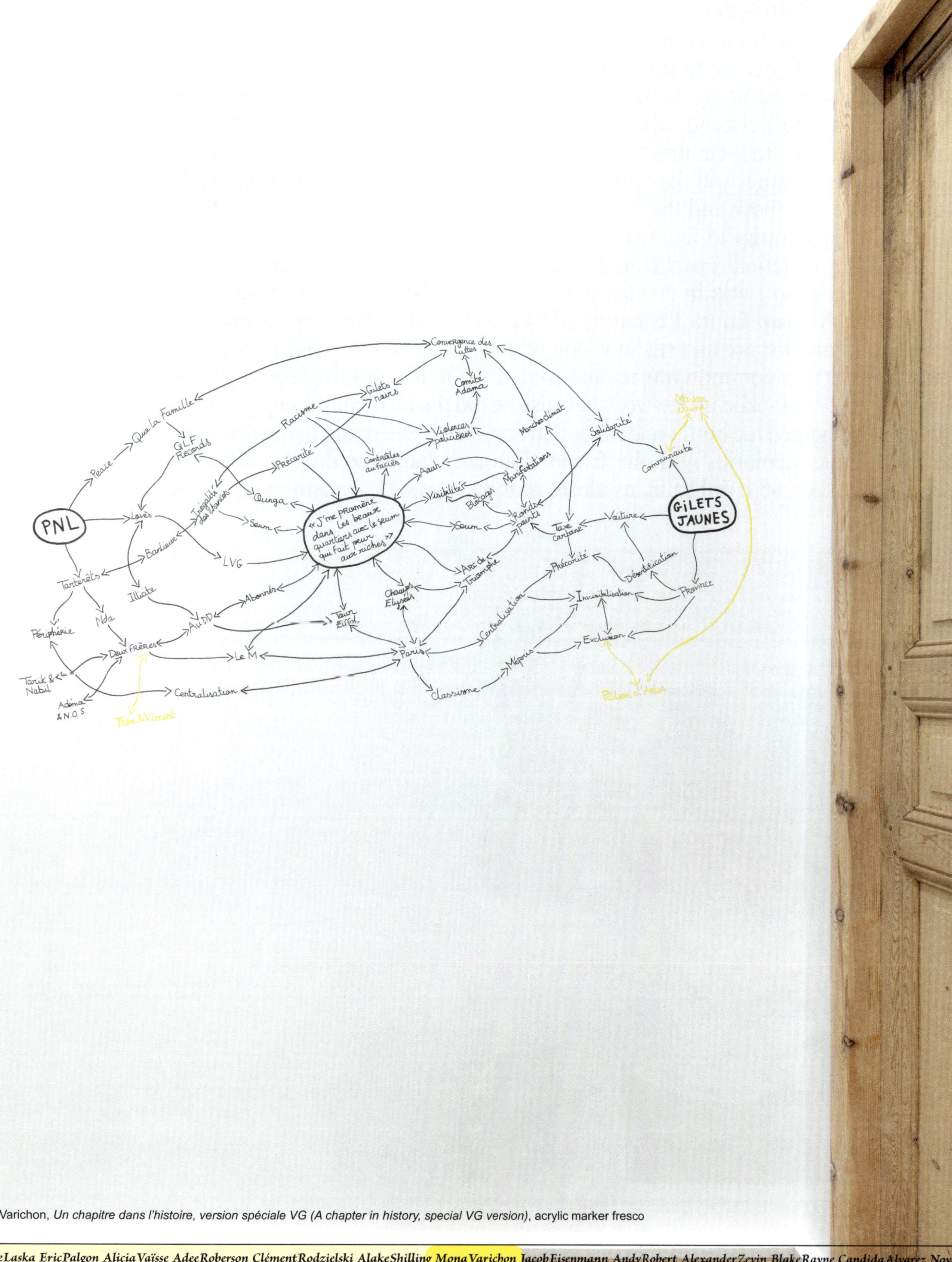

Mona Varichon, *Un chapitre dans l'histoire, version spéciale VG (A chapter in history, special VG version)*, acrylic marker fresco

it has a mix of different generations and social classes—lots of people from the town gossiping and hanging out. So it has a nice vibe that makes you feel like a local when you go there, which I like. My mother came to stay with me for ten days, and we had fun being together and working. She was also painting. Julie Beaufils also came to visit when my mother was there, and the three of us had a cute weekend. My aunt and my cousin came to stay in the guest room. It was really sweet to be able to welcome family. I'd never had the occasion to invite my aunt over and host her in a nice setting, and they both really loved it and had a great time. And then they came back and visited the show and the residency on their own, and I think they'll always cherish having had this opportunity to feel really special in this special town.

I think my situation is particular because of knowing Laura and maybe half of the artists who did the residency. So I was in contact with people like Naoki Sutter-Shudo, Charlotte Houette, Asha Schechter, Miriam Laura Leonardi, and Julie Beaufils. Those are people that I speak to semiregularly and that I share an artistic vision with, so the residency didn't necessarily play a role, other than it gave us a common project and something to discuss. But someone like Alvaro Barrington, for example—I looked up his work because he did the residency. I enjoyed getting to know his work, which also helped me better understand the mural that he made in the residency. I definitely created some unique memories with the friends I already had who did the residency, because we got to visit each other, so it did bring us closer in some ways, but mostly with the people I already knew.

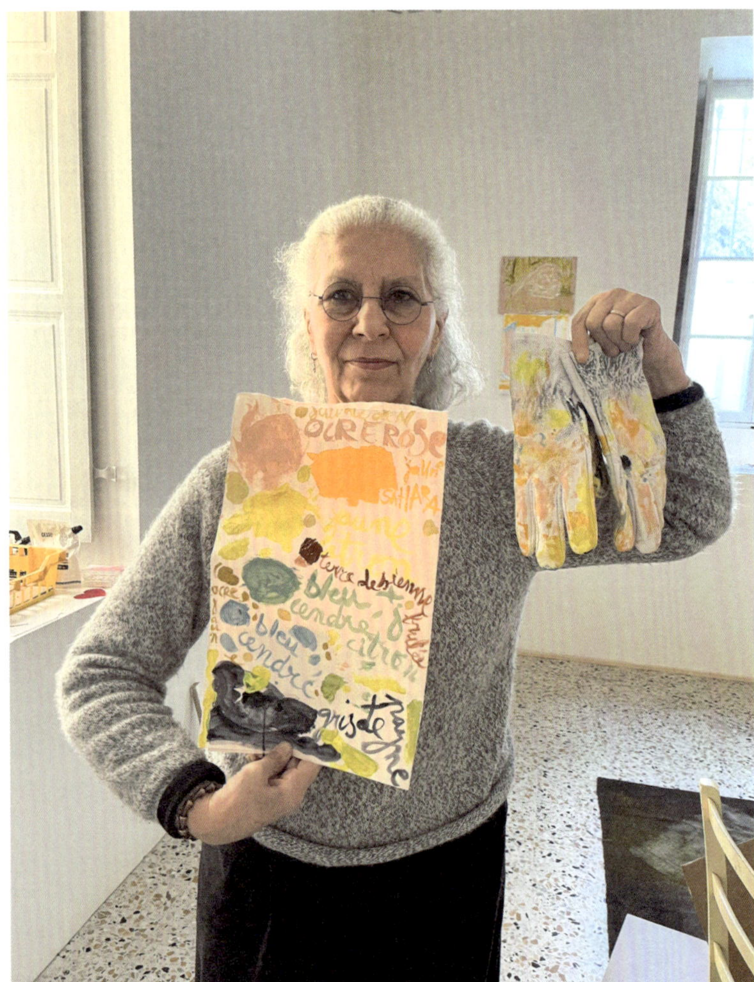

Malak holding *Second Hand Vince* (a collaboration with Jacob Eisenmann) in her left hand and her palette in her right

Around the opening of the exhibition, we had a little reception in the house, and it was a strange feeling because, all of a sudden, this space that has meaning to you and that you feel ownership over has become this public domain. It was funny because it's quite a big house, but at the party we all crowded in the living room and dining room. I think because there had never been so many people in there, it felt a little awkward; we didn't really know how to get ourselves comfortable in the space. Maybe because there was no longer a host, so it became this kind of unspoken space that we didn't know how to occupy anymore.

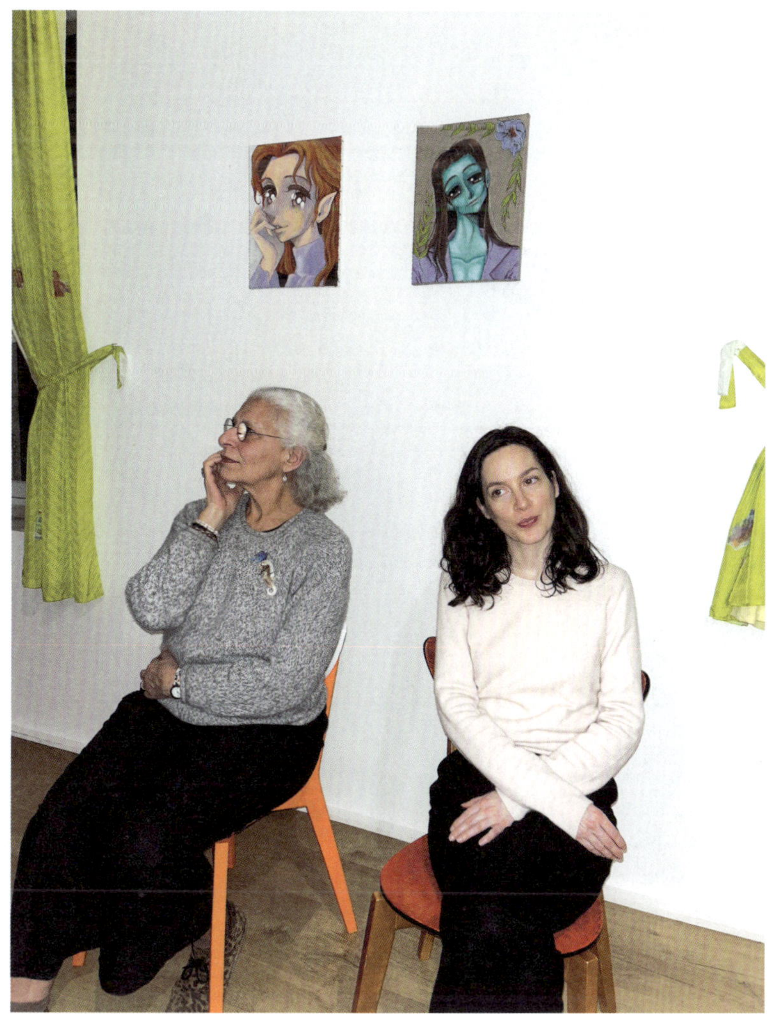

Malak and Julie Beaufils in front of paintings by Julien Ceccaldi

Jacob Eisenmann

I'm having trouble thinking in pre–Vincent van Gogh, post–Van Gogh; I'm not sure if I'm making up memories. I had been exposed to some of his letters, his obsession with the price of paint, and how he was constantly begging his brother Theo for money to buy paint, trying to describe the paint to his brother in order to get cash. People do go on about the letters, exclaiming, "He loves color." He did love the color, of course, but a quantity of those inspired descriptions were composed because artists beg.

I quit my job in January 2020 because I was preparing for the pandemic; I had heard from a source in Wuhan about a possible leak at a lab. And I said, "OK, I don't want to be in the United States anymore." So I came to France, and we were staying in Paris. Laura Owens was planning to come to Arles for a show scheduled to open in June at the Fondation Vincent van Gogh Arles, and Mona Varichon was going to go to help. There were logistical things: pallets of paint arriving from across France, brushes. Then my source turned out to be credible and accurate.

Because we were stuck there with many pots of paint, we painted. Laura asked, "Have you made more or less than a hundred paintings?" I said, "Less than a hundred." It was factual. She

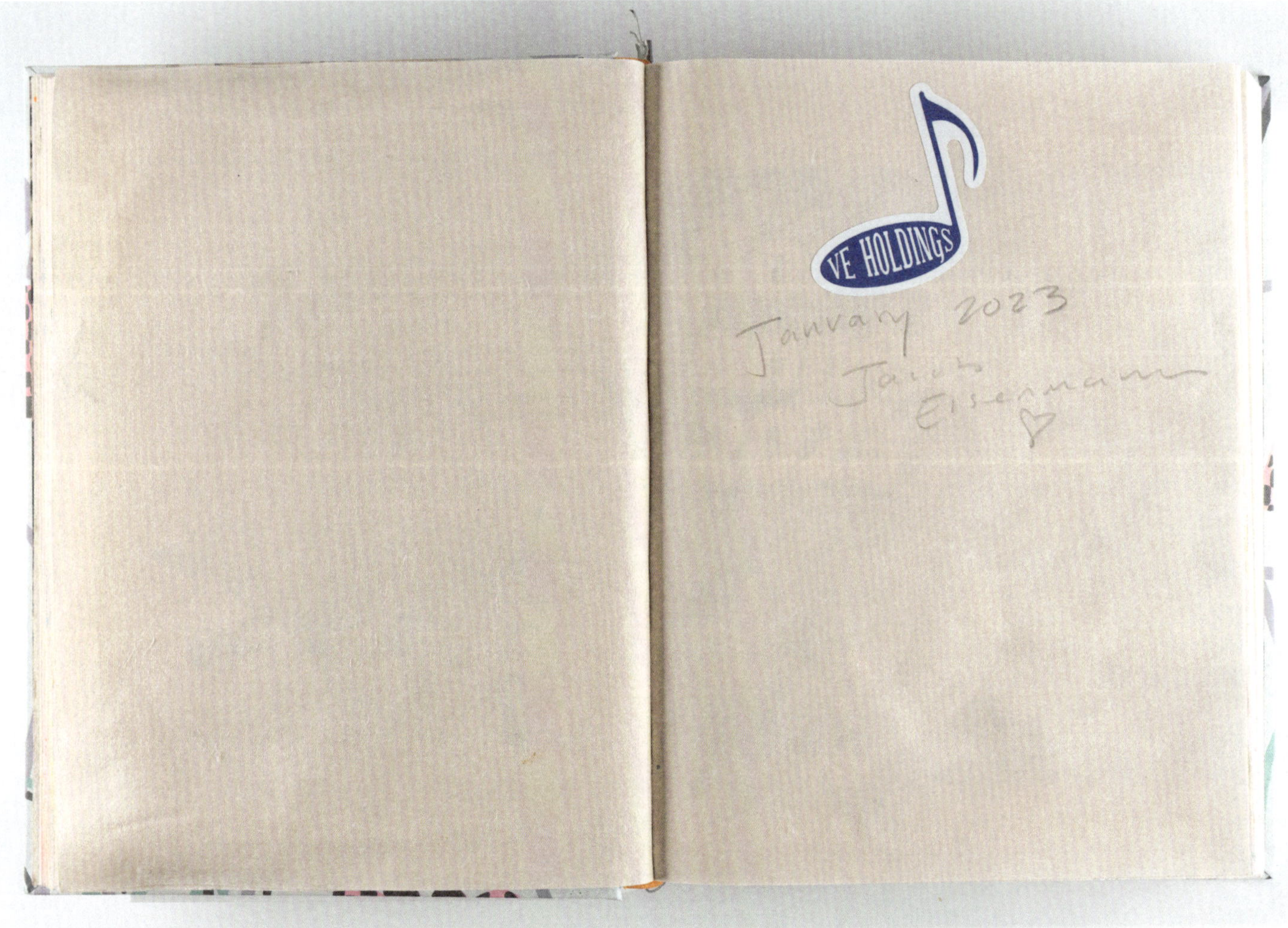

A sticker and Jacob Eisenmann's signature in the guest book

taught me how to make a surface with a piece of cardboard and an X in gesso on the back so it doesn't curl. We were in the countryside, and we'd go painting in the tall, yellow fields. Or the bleak, blank streets and stone and archways and ghosts, old figures, old memories. And the cemetery across the river, with the stone statue of the lion at the foot of the bridge destroyed in the bombings of World War II, when the Yellow House was also fatally damaged.

For the Studio of the South, Mona, Nova Bryan, Laura, and I helped set up the house a bit, painting a big yellow stripe down the winding staircase. Nova painted a portrait of Mona; I painted a gray mirror, which I'd later fill in; Laura painted wonderful and vivid ornamentation, flora, trills. Before Paul Gauguin came to Arles, Van Gogh spent a lot of time setting up the Yellow House, putting sunflowers in every room, putting an easel in Gauguin's room, making his bed.

In January 2023, Mona and I came back for a short residency. I made an instrumental track with a Sun Ra sample, "I dared to knock at the door of the cosmos," alongside a mural of a Sun Ra concert that happened in 1976 at the forum in Arles, right next to the house. A large crowd couldn't get in, and there was a riot outside the forum. I thought this was a special scene: Sun Ra, Arles, a riot outside the forum. I stacked the Frank Gehry LUMA Tower on top of the forum's wall, history collapsing a bit. European Union ministers came at the outbreak of the war in Ukraine to meet on the top floors. It's a way to have people who are in political and economic

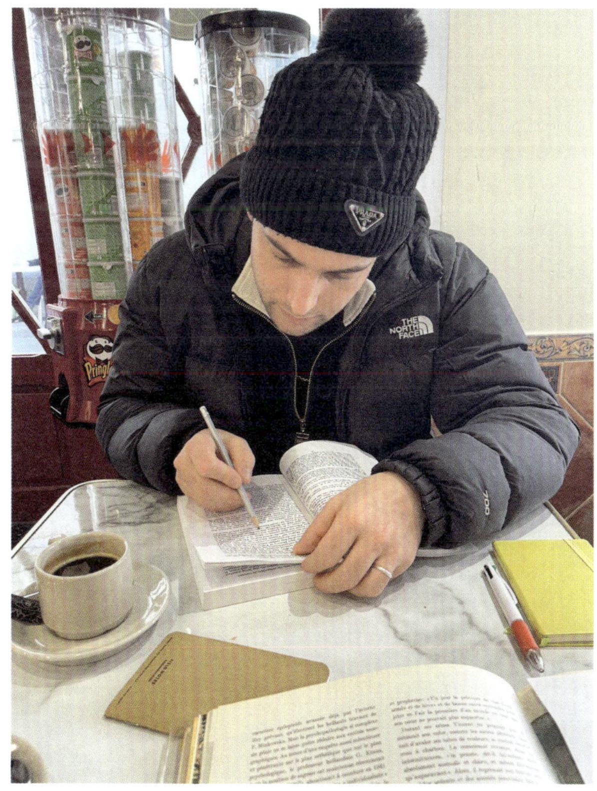

Jacob in Bar le Tambourin, Arles

iana Sadie Laska Eric Palgon Alicia Vaïsse Adee Roberson Clément Rodzielski Alake Shilling Mona Varichon Jacob Eisenmann Andy Robert Alexander Zevin Blake Rayne Candida Alvarez Nova Brya

control come together to determine the outer edge of acceptability, red teaming a political project to assess and control volatility. Then I sent the instrumental track to Le Jetski, and he made a legendary song with it.

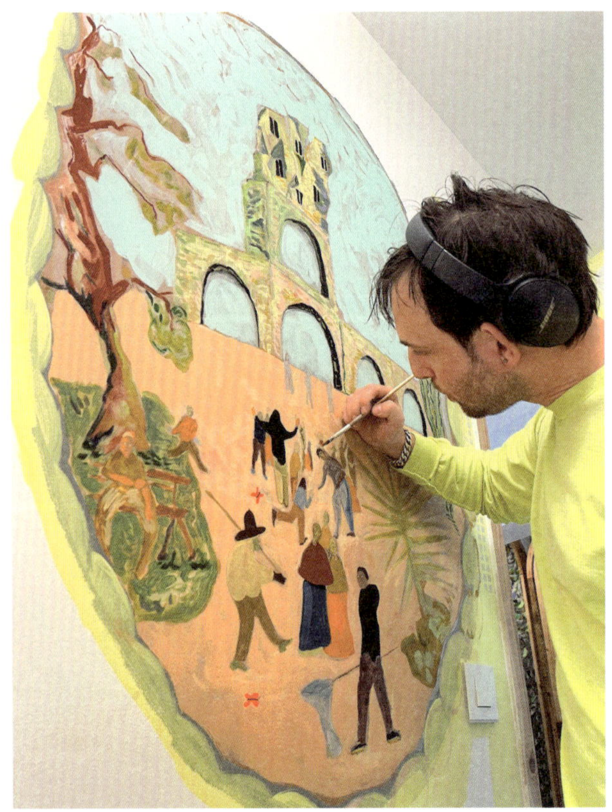

Jacob painting *1976*

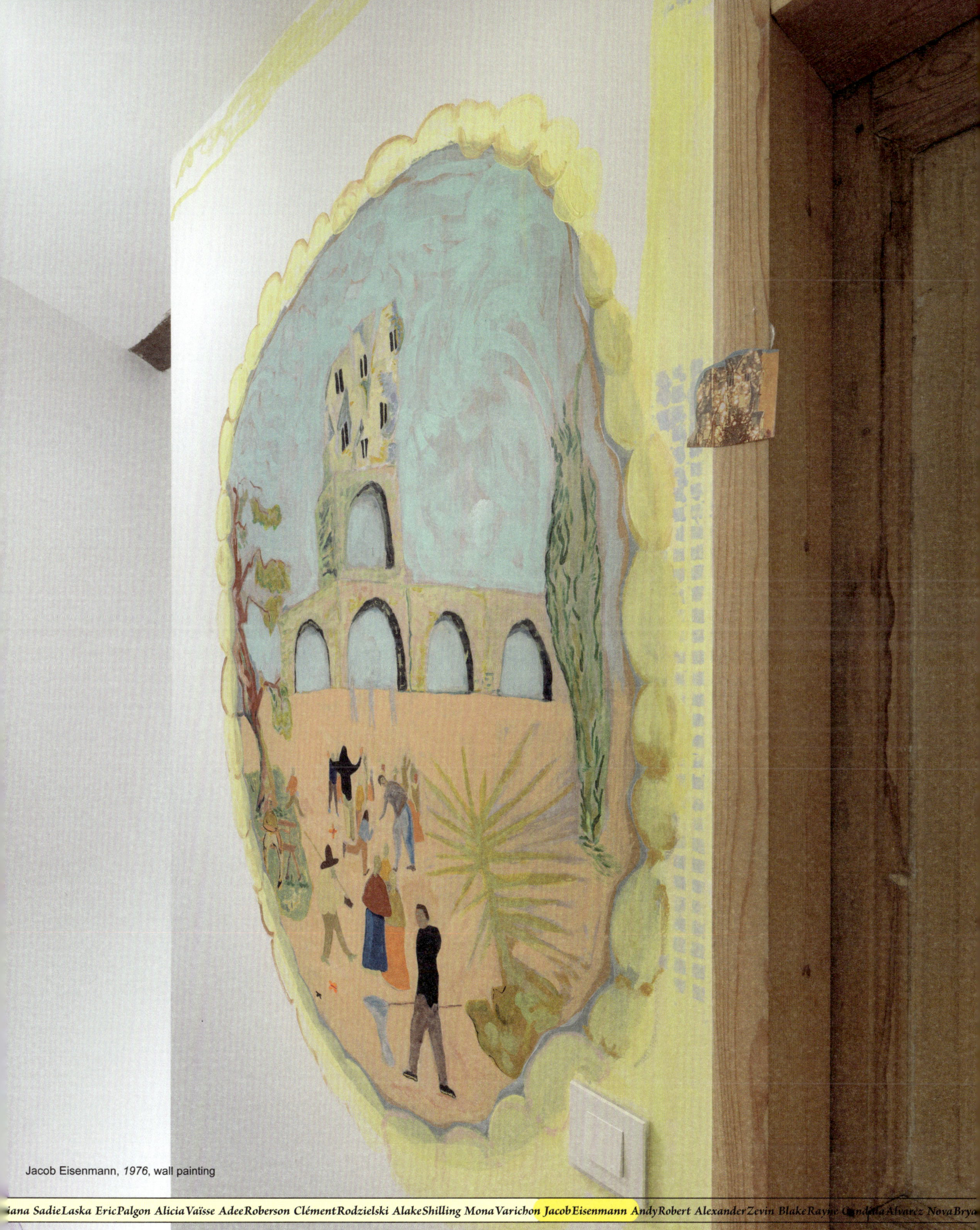

Jacob Eisenmann, *1976*, wall painting

December 4

"walking"

"Where?"

"To"

"the spot around the corner"

"at the corner"

"the lotto"

"—the deli"

When suddenly,
"they circle the
sky."

"Bodega"
"by the bodega"

"the laundrymate"
"the vultures circled

the people."

"I was just thinking"

"—who?!"

"The pigeons"
"the city"

"Just look!"

"winter air"
"O boy!"

"This city!"

"like that!"
"Dear momma,"

"that motherfucker!"
"—I know"
"been a while
been distant"

"Sometime
now"

"they"
"—the pigeons"

"still"
"—still here."

"Mornings"
"pigeons"
"circle."

"Almost"
"the only thing recognizable"

"here."
"We huddle too!"
"trying"

"Haven't spoken
since"

"since I left"
"for the city"

"Since school"
"really"

"Since you left"
"—distant"
"but things have been"
"for a while"
"for sometime now"
"trying"
"—to hold it together."

"still here!"
"On this day"

"making do"

iana Sadie Laska Eric Palgon Alicia Vaïsse Adee Roberson Clément Rodzielski Alake Shilling Mona Varichon Jacob Eisenmann Andy Robert Alexander Zevin Blake Rayne Candida Alvarez Nova Brya

Survivors guilt
"—how about you?"

"to know what human beings"
"…are capable of"

"They circle"
"—look!"
"the crisp air"
"the sky!"

"The air"
"the brutality
and compassion"

both
within.

"Vultures"

"since we left"

"the blue sky"

"that air"
"—miss it!"

"Some circle"
"some snake"
"some"
"scavenger"

"the city"
"huddles"

"Huddling
beneath
the
sun!"

"the violence"
"rages"

falcon
steel
and
metal

"boils."
"Beer cans"

"Huddled"
"—some drop
in mid-flight."

"Rent"
"stocks"

"circles the city"

"within"

"preys"
"the people"

"—drop dead;"
"some lie there like resting centipedes"

"—lining the top apartment buildings and streetlights;

fire escapes, billboards
among trees and sidewalks too."
"a people"

"among"

"—and upon;"

"Pulled over"

"pulled over!"
"—for walking"

"For what?!"
"—at a bus stop?!"

"for nothing!"

"hands up"

"Bullshit!"

"it's bullshit!"
a shelter
"a bus stop"

iana Sadie Laska Eric Palgon Alicia Vaïsse Adee Roberson Clément Rodzielski Alake Shilling Mona Varichon Jacob Eisenmann Andy Robert Alexander Zevin Blake Rayne Candida Alvarez Nova Brya

a murder
"crows"

"ravens"
"rooks"

"birds of"
"of all"

"perched"

"from a distance"
"—types"

"Of all types"

—watching
"Screeching" a city

 "—a crow"

"Atop telephone poles"
electrical lines

"stakes"

"atop buildings"
the city

"take it in"
"the cold air"

"—take it all
in"

—exhale
"congestion"
"the"
"exhaust"

"carbon"
"smog"

"—the carbon"
all a smoke

filled
all

"all the smoke"

and into
the
air

"a happy birthday"
wind

—blows.

The chill

the rubbing of
hands;
in an exhale
of breath;
—condensed and
then evaporate.

"A thick fog,
out here"
"a toxic
exhaust."

"Wintcr"

"it's all too
visible"
"the season"
"—it's all too
it's all too apparent."

"winter"
"boot."

"Just check it"

"Winter"

"—it's in the occasional "'stomping"

"of feet"
"—of their feet."

FEBRUARY 2023
Alexander Zevin

I had thought about Vincent van Gogh prior to coming to Arles or being familiar with Laura Owens's project. As a kid, I went to the Metropolitan Museum of Art and did drawing classes there. When I was about twenty, I took a trip to Amsterdam and went to the Van Gogh Museum. I remember being interested in the relationship between Van Gogh and Japanese prints, and the general relationship between modernism in Europe and in other places. But I don't think I had ever thought, in a systematic way, about Van Gogh, and maybe even had a tendency to think less about him than other Impressionists, simply because of the Van Gogh industry that is so prevalent at museums. So it was interesting to think about him as a figure with a relationship to a particular place that wasn't a museum in a capital city—this place where he suffered breakdowns but also experienced bouts of happiness. When I was in Arles, I learned more about it because I wanted to consider him in relation to figures in nineteenth-century France I was writing about—how and if there was any overlap. So I read his letters, some in French, some translated from Dutch. Laura pointed me toward his politics and the political arguments in those letters, and this made me have a deeper, more interesting view of him. That happened in Arles itself.

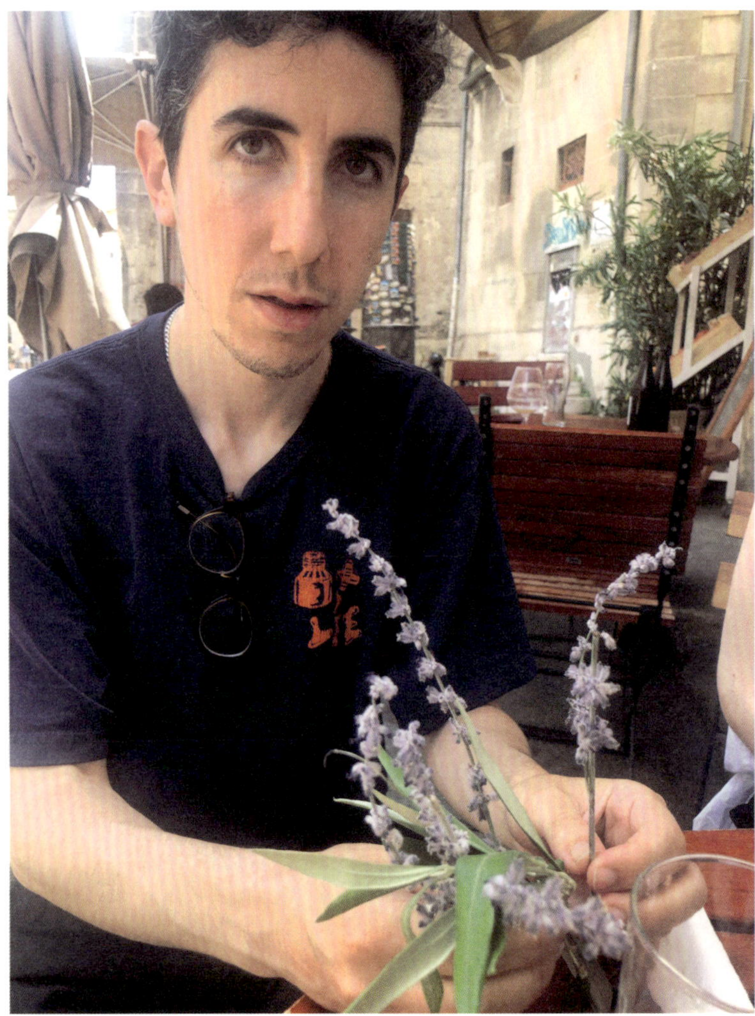

Alexander Zevin with lavender

I met Laura when I was studying for my PhD in Los Angeles at UCLA. I believe we met through a mutual friend, Rachel Kushner, who was quickly becoming a writer to be reckoned with. She had already written her first novel and was in the process of writing her second. I also met her husband, Jason Smith, at a protest at UCLA against tuition hikes and state cutbacks. So it was through left-wing politics and intellectual work at UCLA that I met Laura. I think there was a dinner. We quickly became frenemies and then friends. Laura and I always talk about what we're working on, and Laura is someone who has big dreams and visions and yet is also almost uniquely capable of pulling them off. Giant mosaics, huge murals, tapestries and wallpapers, and these collaborations with institutions that are born in her head or someone else's. The invitation to the residency came out of discussions about ways in which we could collaborate, and also, I was jealous of our mutual friends—painters, printmakers, photographers, and other writers— getting to collaborate with Laura, whereas I was doing academic stuff in a way that seemed totally disconnected. So I think there was a discussion, and then also, I was maybe like, "Hey, you are doing this project in France, Van Gogh is this nineteenth-century figure, I study French history—there's something there." And so I may have strong-armed her, slightly. I had got to know some of the people at the Fondation Vincent van Gogh Arles and at LUMA on different trips to the South to see Laura, so I already had a good sense of what was going on there. So it felt more obvious than at previous points to try to do the residency.

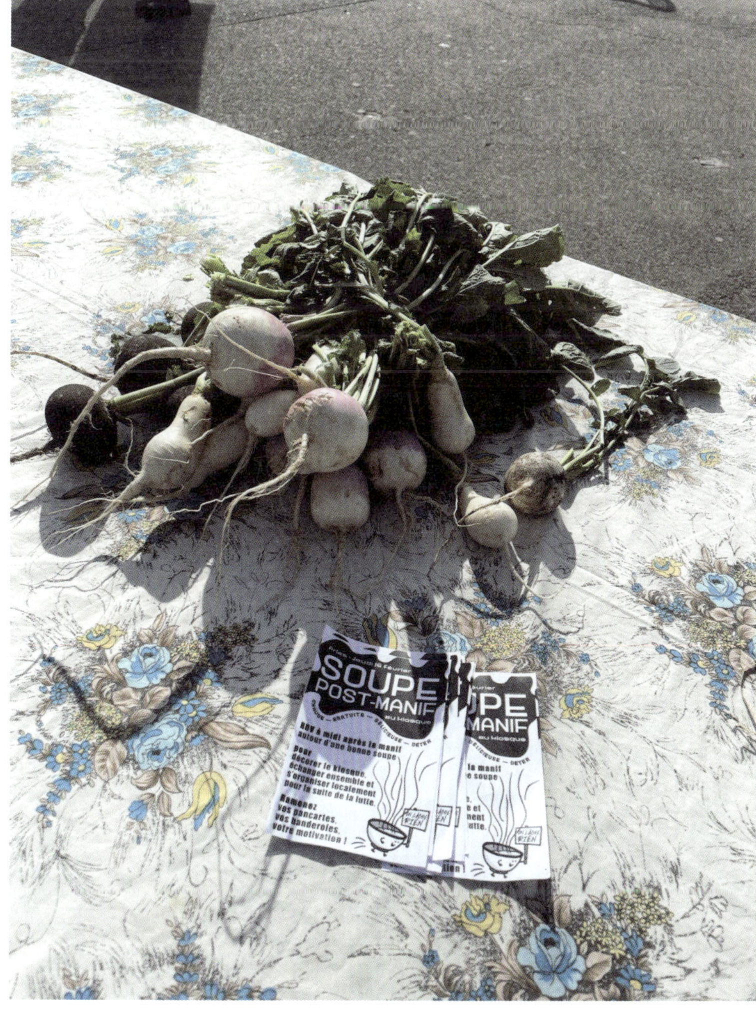

Root vegetables and flyers for the soup kitchen

I had come to Arles before for Laura's show. She was intensely in that phase of trying to finish a show because of the enormous nature of that work and the fact that it was the first thing that she'd done since the pandemic. It represented all of the effort and emotions and the camaraderie that she had developed with people during that period. It was exciting, as someone who knows Laura well, to be there for the show. I would normally go to an opening of Laura's. But to also be behind the scenes—helping finish books or do drawings or paint brush strokes or be asked to weigh in on the hanging of paintings or the order of the exhibit—was different. Maybe from the perspective of the curators, this was no way to do things, but it was fun, from the perspective of a friend of Laura's, to be conscripted into this orgy of last-minute work.

Arles is a picturesque, pretty town. I liked walking along the banks of the river, going to the place de la Roquette. I liked the Roman ruins, the amphitheater, of course. It's a small city, but it has a lot of history. I loved going to the market and getting a coffee from that little place that does espresso and fruit juices. And sitting by the merry-go-round as people's kids wailed and cried. I liked going to the squares where you kind of sit and watch, or *m'as-tu-vu* scenarios, as the French say. I liked the Spanish bullfighters café, where you can also get a really cheap *demi*—a half pint of beer—and sit and read the newspapers that you get at one of the kiosks in town.

I had seen all of these different buildings that had been created through LUMA or through the efforts of Maja Hoffmann. But this space was sort of a collaboration between Laura and

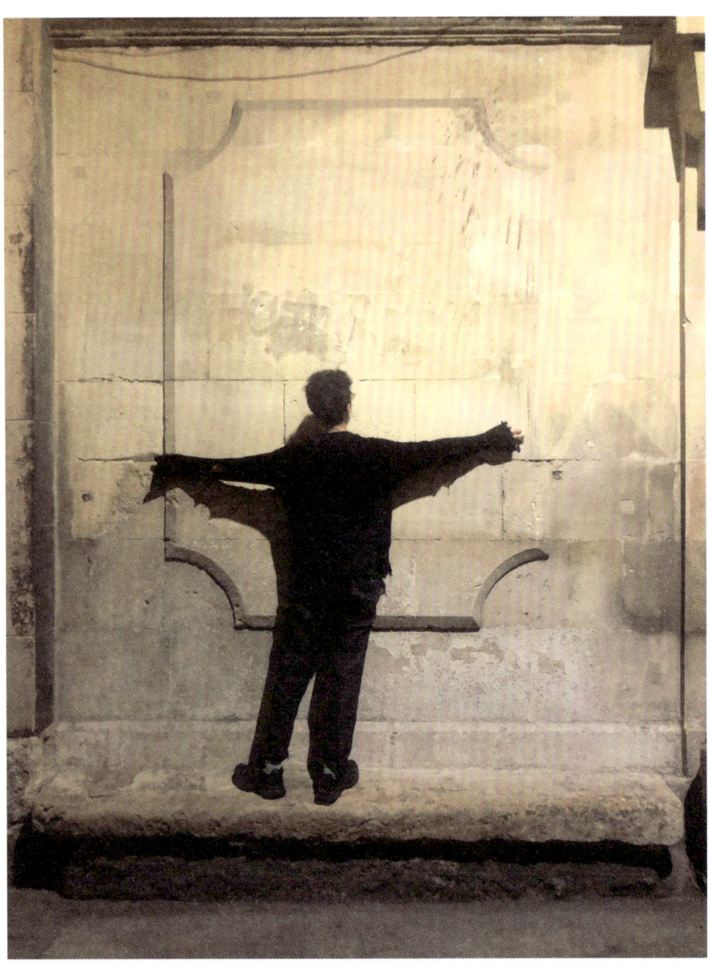

Alexander in front of Laura Owens's studio in Arles

Maja, so it had elements of both in it. It's a very vertical space. I liked working overlooking the ruins of the amphitheater, and the kitchen was far more spacious than someone from New York City is used to. But I liked taking the stuff from the market that I bought and whipping up stuff. I thought of my friend, Asha Schechter, who's a real gourmand, and what he might do in that space.

I felt that my prompt while I was there was to work on my writing. I had decided that I would work on one of my history projects, which is about French liberals in the nineteenth century who simultaneously erected the basis of the domestic institutions of the Third Republic, including the secular school system, as well as an independent judiciary, so to speak. And, at the same time, expanded the French Empire by leaps and bounds. Thinking about the connection between those two things.

At the same time, I had thought that I would make a visual diary of my experiences that connected some of what I was working on that was historical to what was going on in the present day, in order to make a contribution to the house. In other words, to think about my writing as connected to aesthetics as well as politics. And so that was my understanding of the prompt: to do my historical work, but also to step a little bit outside of what I normally do to meet the spirit of the house, the spirit of the other residents. As it happened, my stay coincided with a nationwide wave of protests against the raising of the retirement age in France—very unpopular—but that order was passed, basically by executive fiat, over the heads of what the majority of French people want. So that was also part of the experience of what was going on—these demonstrations

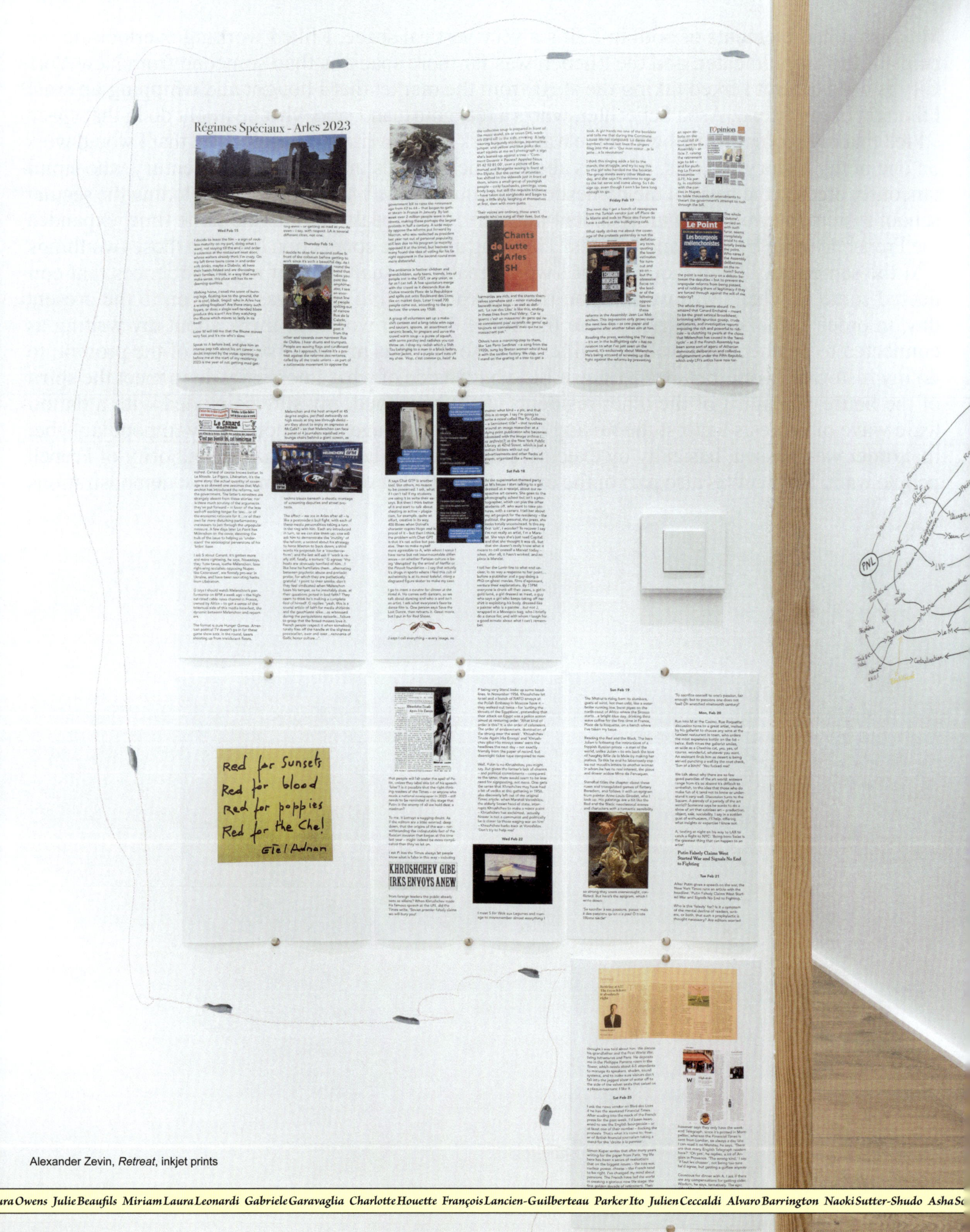

Alexander Zevin, *Retreat*, inkjet prints

aura Owens   Julie Beaufils   Miriam Laura Leonardi   Gabriele Garavaglia   Charlotte Houette   François Lancien-Guilberteau   Parker Ito   Julien Ceccaldi   Alvaro Barrington   Naoki Sutter-Shudo   Asha Sc

throughout Arles, which were interesting, because it was a different view of Arles. It wasn't the view of Arles as a place for the consumption or creation of culture that's disconnected from the city and who lives there, but actually meeting postal workers or train workers or school teachers or just young people who were in school without good employment prospects. And so seeing the city that way was actually really exciting for me. After one demonstration, a group put on a collective soup kitchen so everyone could have soup, whoever they were. It was really delicious. And then everyone sang songs. I met people who were part of a group who sing left-wing, revolutionary songs. And so I got to sing those songs, learn those songs with them. And that was a highlight of my stay. They had a little songbook that they had created: *Chants de Luttes d'Arles*. Some famous, like by Louise Michel, the exiled Communard leader. But others, I had never heard of—anarchist Spanish songs or revolutionary songs from Brittany, all kinds of songs that are inspired by workers' struggles or struggles for justice and equality. So I took that little booklet and some of the songs in there, and the cover of the booklet, and pictures of the march and the collective soup and the dirty beets that were sitting on the table, which reminded me of the painting of Van Gogh's boots—all of that went into the work that I made.

One of the things I struggled with was figuring out the right relationship between the text and images. There's the old adage about pictures, obviously, with respect to words, and I tend to be very wordy, so it was interesting to negotiate saying a lot less and letting an image speak for itself,

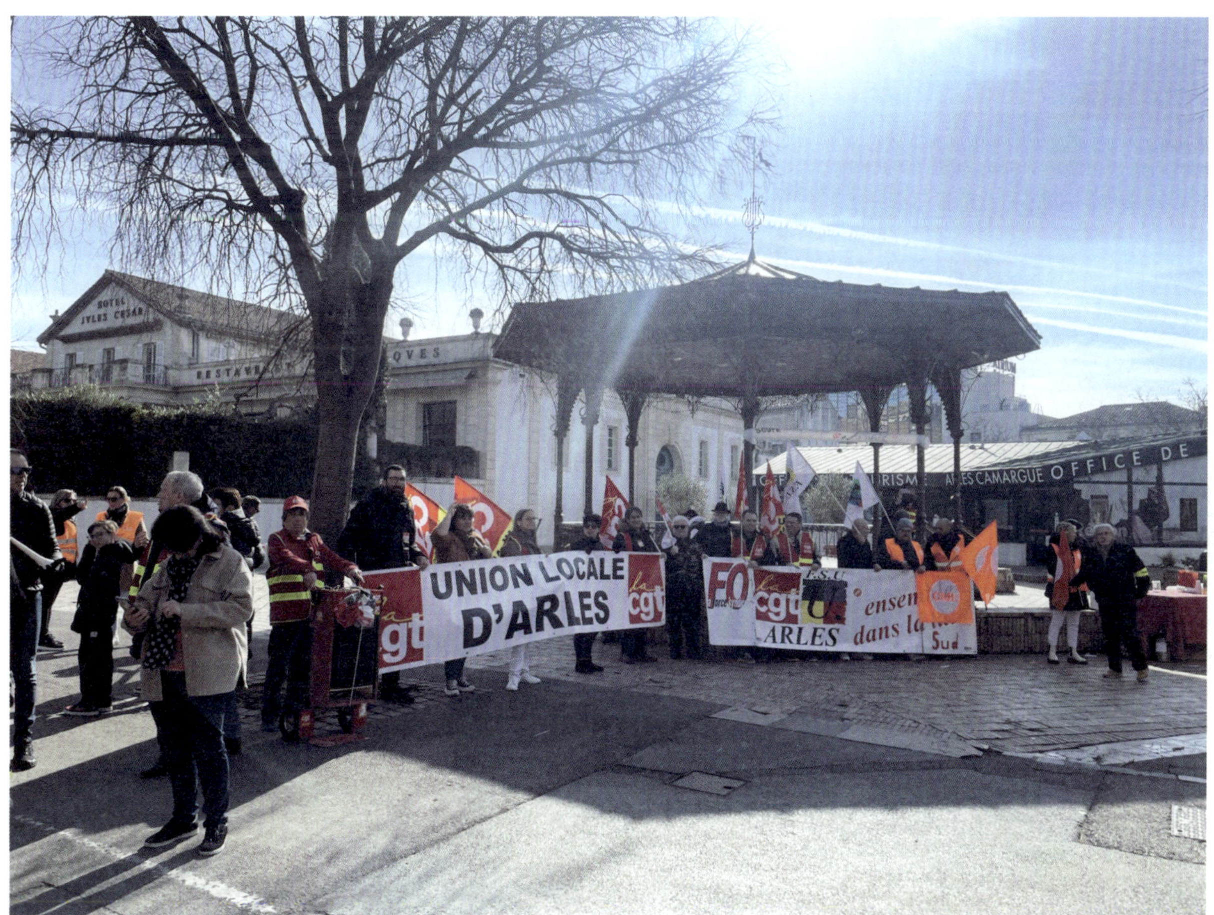

A trade union demonstration against the raising of the retirement age in France

liana Sadie Laska Eric Palgon Alicia Vaïsse Adee Roberson Clément Rodzielski Alake Shilling Mona Varichon Jacob Eisenmann Andy Robert Alexander Zevin Blake Rayne Candida Alvarez Nova Bry

or finding the fewest words that could make that image relate to another image. I don't think I got that quite right. In a way, I just needed more time, I think, to actually do both the historical project and the contemporary, visual part of it. I didn't have enough time to trial-and-error and figure out, you know—this was my first residency, so there was a lot to learn in a short time. I was only there for two weeks. I viewed myself somewhat as an interloper who was not about to take up a huge amount of wall space. I wasn't clear on the rules at all. It seemed to me that you could put anything anywhere. And it was clear also that some people had gone further than others in plastering stuff all over the place, and that that had not always been to the taste or delight of other people who came along afterward. So I could see that there was some tension in terms of placement, or things that might have been partly covered. People were creative about where they put their art. Some emplacements worked better than others, like incorporating work into the layout of the kitchen or its cupboards. Or things that were subtle that became part of the furniture of the house. I decided to put my work in the bathroom. That partly reflected my sense of myself as a discrete contributor, but also its writerly quality, and people like to read in the bathroom. So I guess this was a bit of a ludic touch.

To a certain extent, I felt a sense of community, although in my case, that reflected the fact that I'd been to Arles several times with Laura, so I knew curators at LUMA and the Fondation. So there were people for me to hang out with. I think if I had been just on my own, it would have

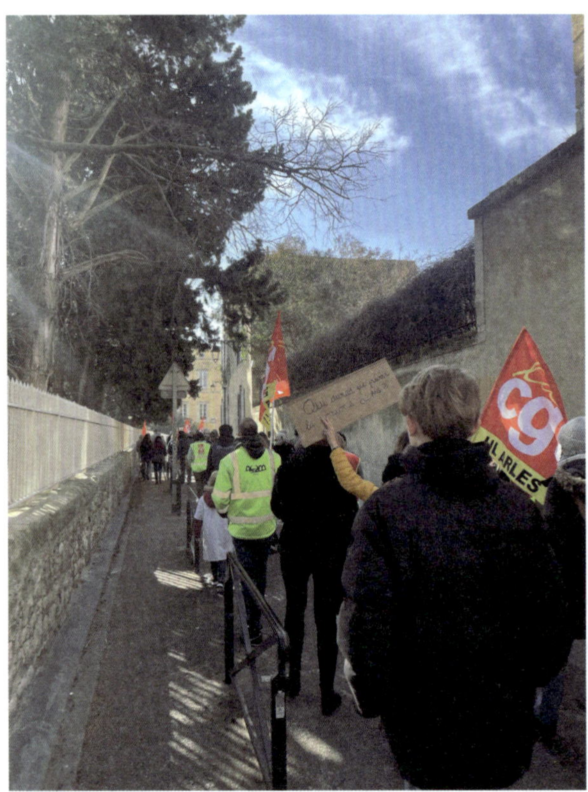
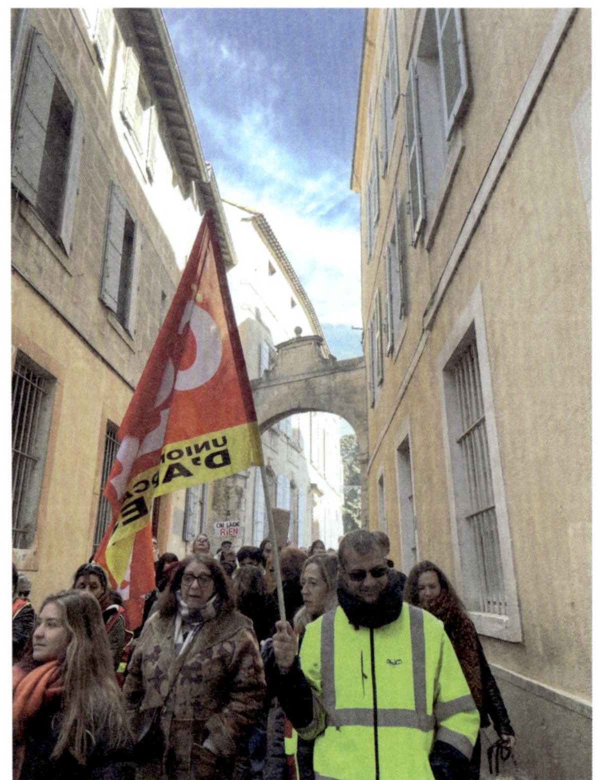

A trade union demonstration against the raising of the retirement age in France

been a more cloistered existence. It was also in a kind of down season, in February, a little bit cold. And I did feel that sense of community from the other residents who were not present. I know a lot of them and saw their art there, which made me feel inspired. People like Charlotte Houette and François Lancien-Guilberteau, who did the ciné-club that I went to when the residency was starting, which was a great collaborative experience. And seeing the artwork of Gary Indiana, who had done little photos overlaid with words much more elegantly and simply than me. So I felt many of the other artists that I met at one point or another through Laura. I felt their presence there, and I knew what the space could be in terms of that community. But when I was there, it was more of a dormant volcano than one gushing magma.

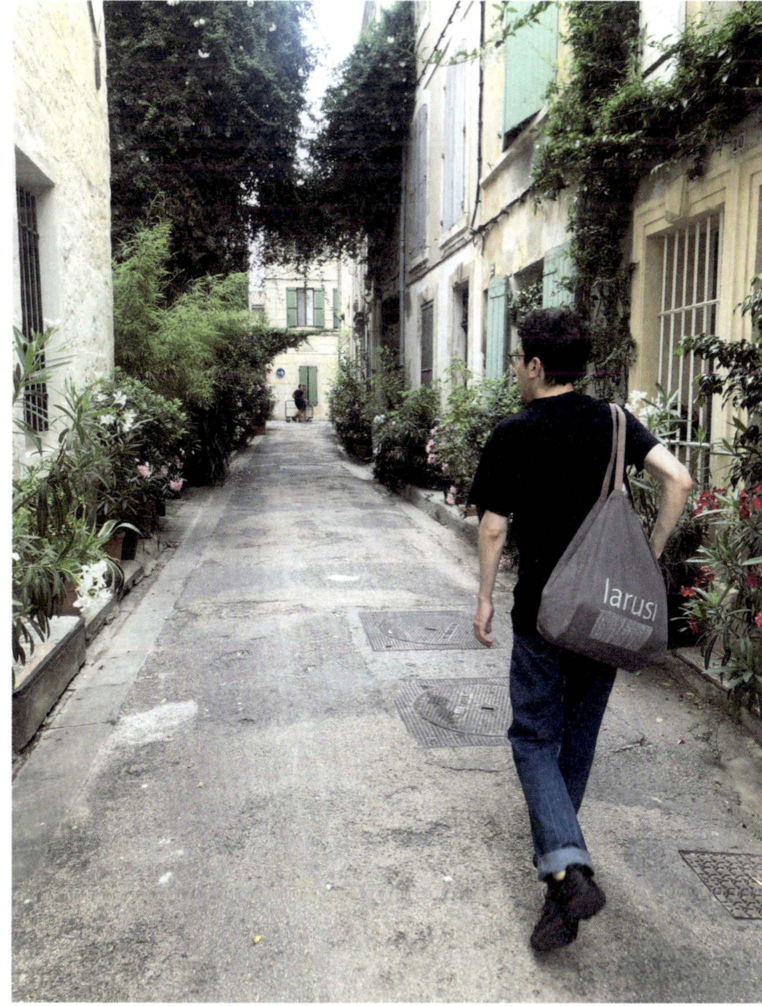

Alexander in Arles

MARCH 2023
Blake Rayne

It was fun to participate in Laura Owens's Studio of the South project. Coming out of the COVID-19 lockdown after spending way too much time at the computer over the previous year and a half, the setup in Arles was really nice. My experience in Arles was enjoyable yet a bit strange. It was the perfect place to regain my walking legs, pause, reflect, and engage with certain aspects of daily practice that had become a bit distant during lockdown.

Laura and I have known each other for some time now; we first met in the early to mid-nineties. Although we missed each other by a year or two, we both attended the California Institute of the Arts before we met. At that time, CalArts was one of the places where it was often said that we were at the end of the return to painting. I didn't entirely disagree with that assessment, but it was the total certainty with which that characterization was frequently presented that made me curious. I imagine that, when encountering that kind of statement, it didn't sit quite right with Laura either.

Anyway, in addition to my appreciation of the objects she produces, I've always admired Laura's approach to tackling big-picture issues—things that can feel pretty overdetermined, like

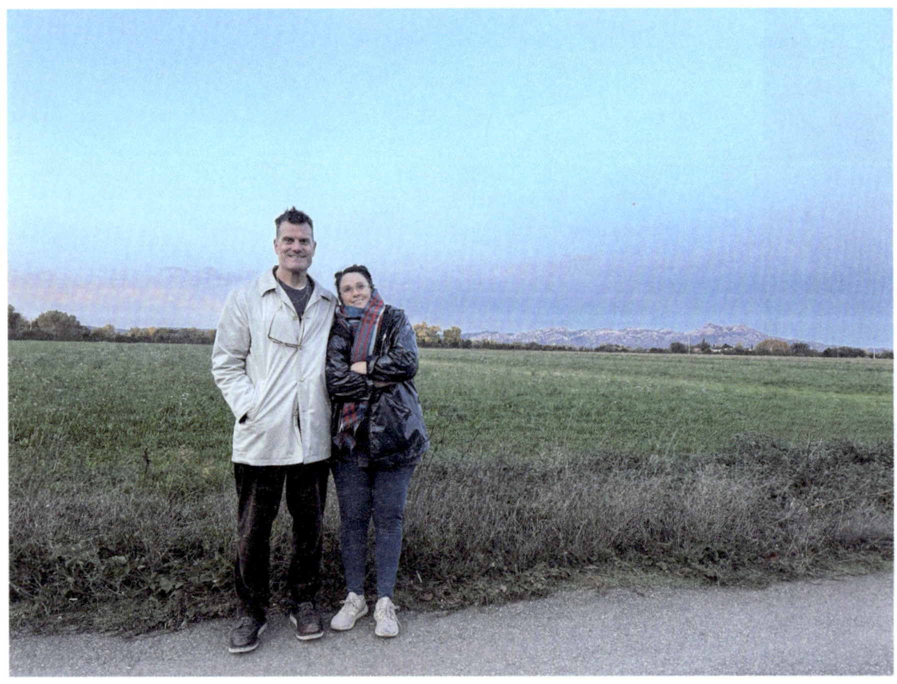

Blake Rayne and Laura Owens

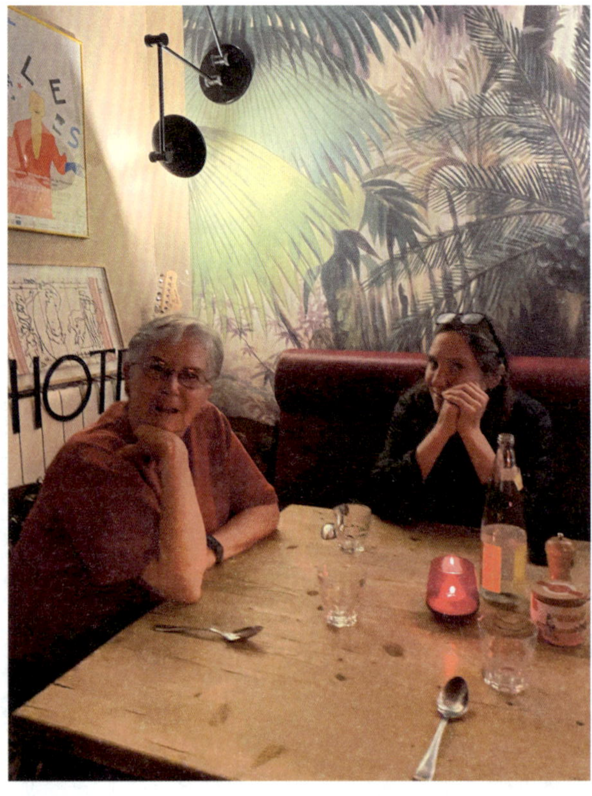

Blake's friend Maureen Murray and his wife, artist Gaia Schermerhorn

the function of the studio-museum relationship or Vincent van Gogh, let alone the "Van Gogh Experience" situation. Somehow she manages to engage with these sites, which can feel pretty locked down, and create space.

Laura's practice reminds me, although it often feels like quite the opposite, that artists create space and do this by unwriting space through their activities.

When I was in residence at the Studio of the South, I produced a work titled *Just Because You Can Doesn't Mean You Have To*. The title references a phrase I heard from the artist Gareth James sometime in the early 2000s, which I appreciated as a reminder. The work turned out to have four components, although it was originally conceived to have only one.

Firstly, the salon-style hanging of material in the entryway between the stairwell and the open-plan common space of the kitchen and seating area includes, except for the two portraits in the middle of the second row, found materials. These materials were collected from various places: a pile near the door at the entry to the house, under and in front of the sink in the downstairs bathroom, and lying around on the floor. My impulse to tidy up and pick up the gleaned materials from the house was an effort to make space.

Secondly, I shared an interest in formalizing Laura and Van Gogh's intentions to facilitate a site for collective production and communal discourse. Not being familiar with the other participants in the residency, nor knowing if the materials I had placed on the wall were already in

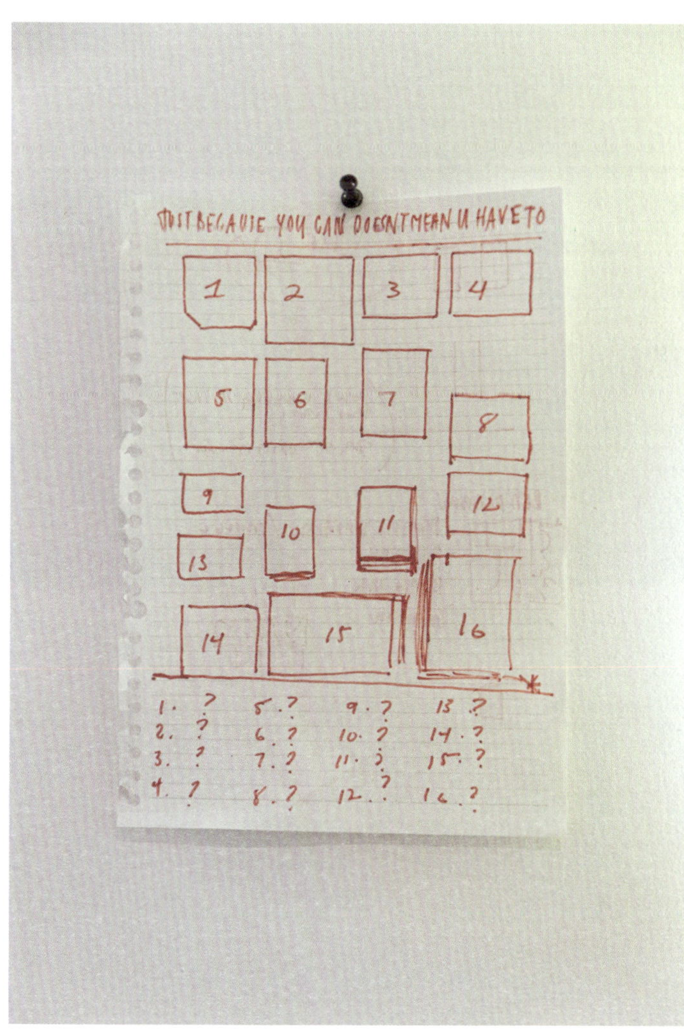

Diagram of *Just Because You Can Doesn't Mean You Have To*

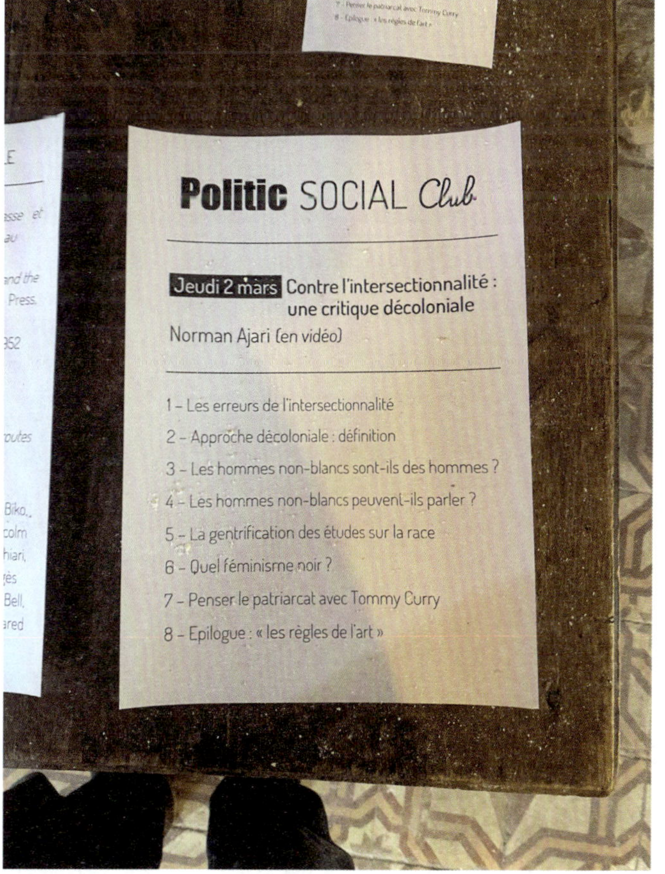

A program from the community space L'Angerie, Arles

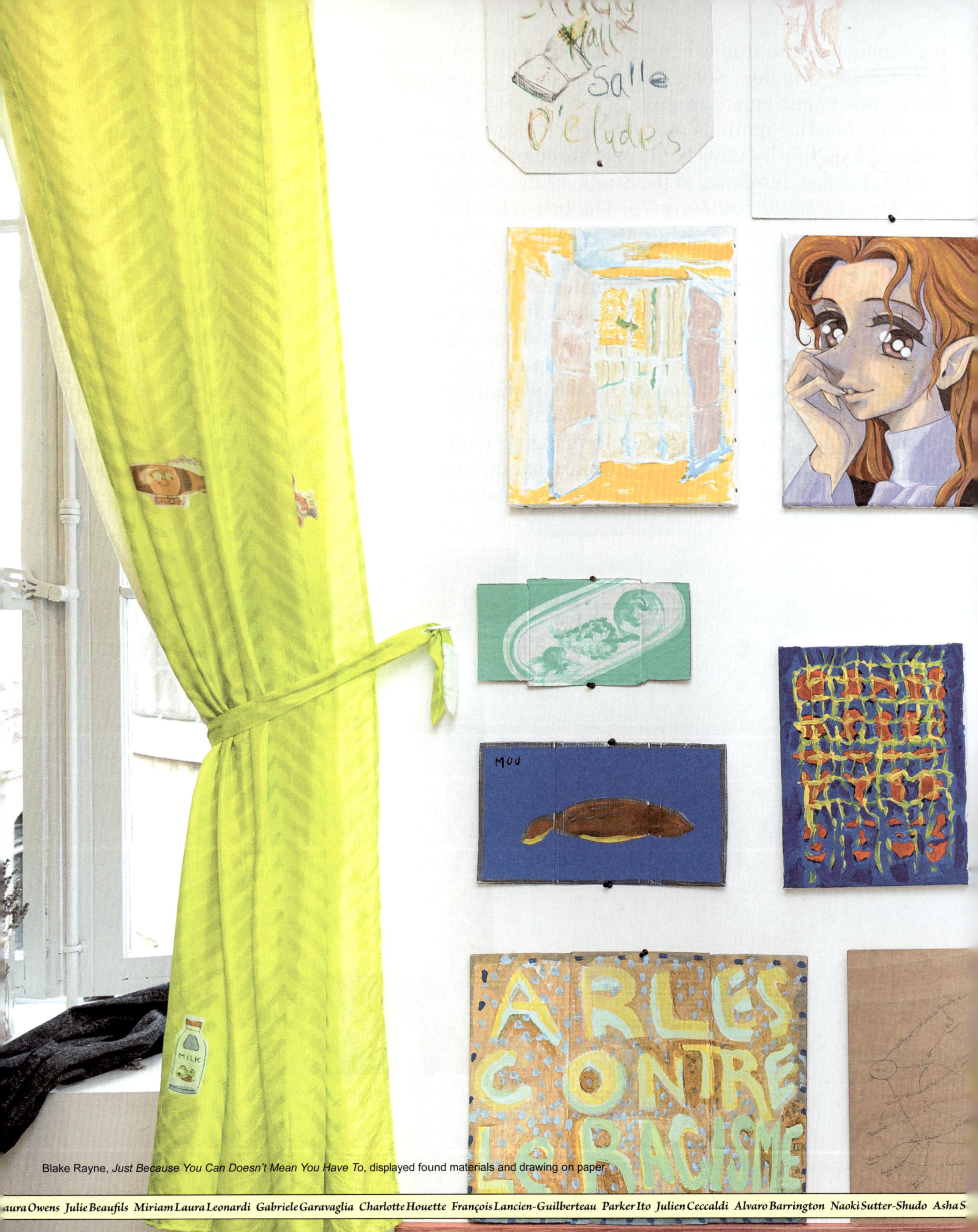

Blake Rayne, *Just Because You Can Doesn't Mean You Have To*, displayed found materials and drawing on paper

aura Owens Julie Beaufils Miriam Laura Leonardi Gabriele Garavaglia Charlotte Houette François Lancien-Guilberteau Parker Ito Julien Ceccaldi Alvaro Barrington Naoki Sutter-Shudo Asha S

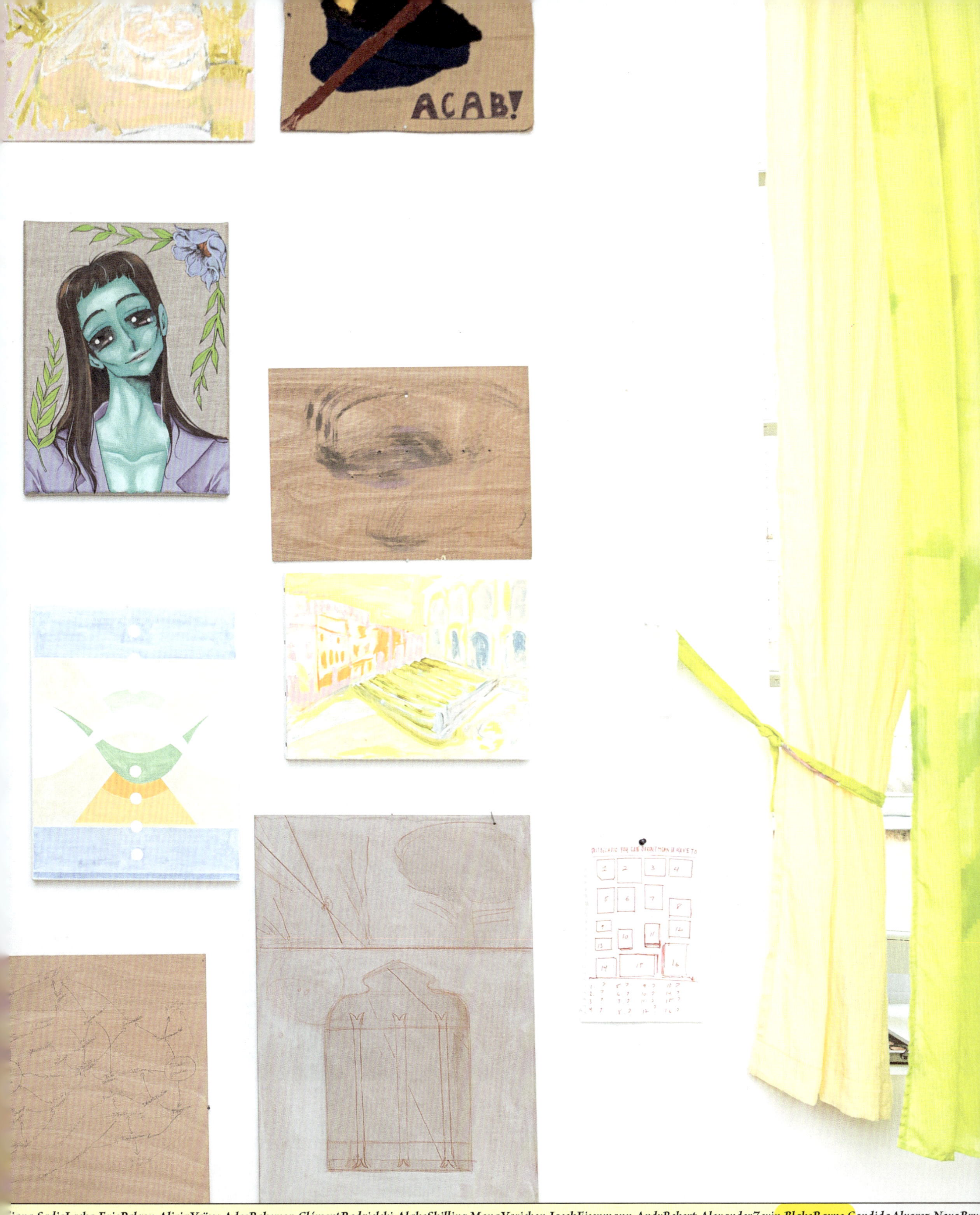

iana Sadie Laska Eric Palgon Alicia Vaïsse Adee Roberson Clément Rodzielski Alake Shilling Mona Varichon Jacob Eisenmann Andy Robert Alexander Zevin Blake Rayne Candida Alvarez Nova Brya

use as paintings on the floor, I produced a sketch of the installed work as a kind of institutional didactic, a legend, to organize my questions.

Thirdly, it needs to be said that, while at the Studio of the South, I was preoccupied with the types of human organization occurring in the streets of Arles at that time in the spring of 2023. Prior to my arrival at the residency, I had intended to produce a work titled *Southern Light* as an acknowledgment of both the commission aspect of the residency and a feature of the local ambiance: the southern light that continues to draw visitors from far and wide. This aspect of the work was created by extracting a one-inch circular piece of glass from the window in the stairwell, dipping it in gold paint, and reinstalling it back into the pane of glass. I consider this to be a permanent installation.

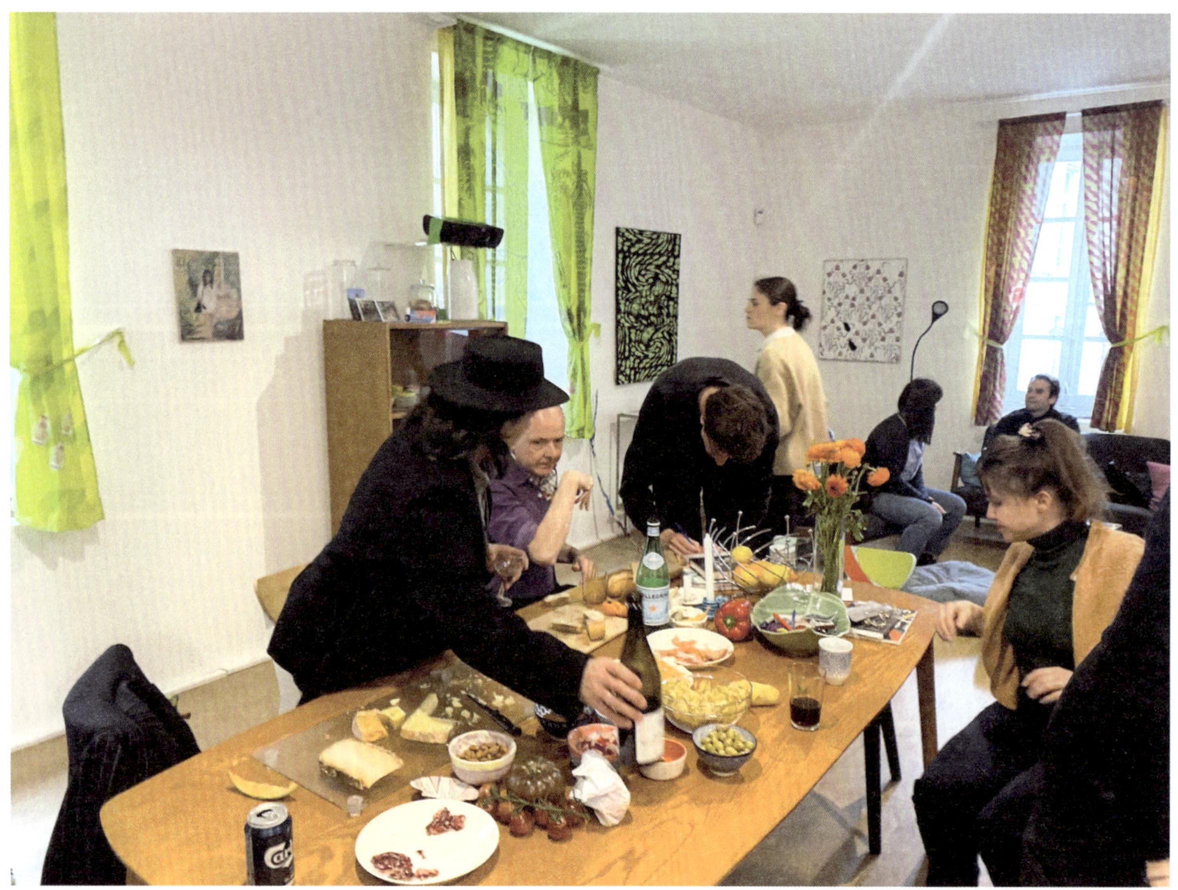

A dinner party at the residence for a screening of Blake's video *Mingo*

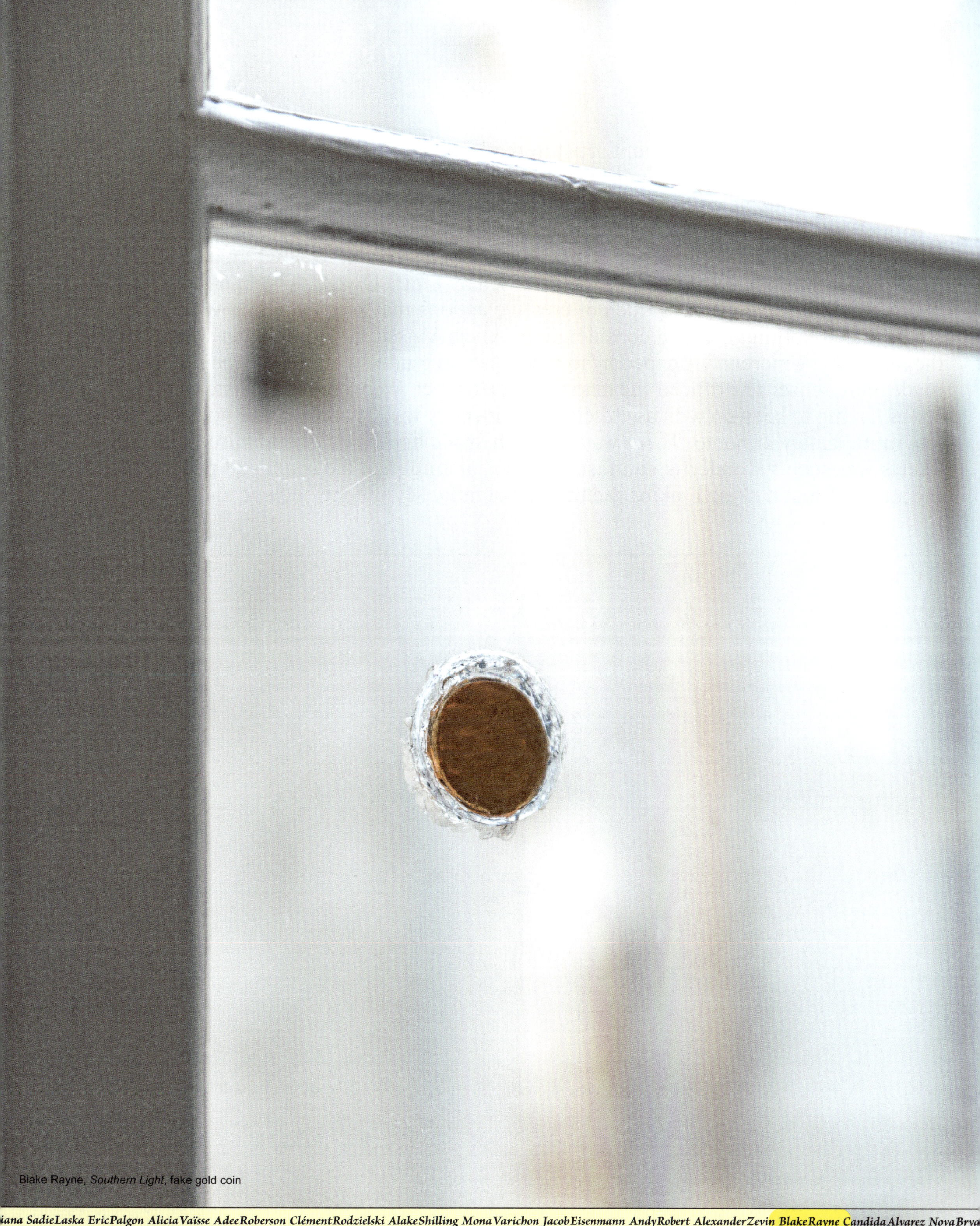

Blake Rayne, *Southern Light*, fake gold coin

APRIL 2023
Candida Alvarez

Vincent van Gogh is an important artist in the history of painting, a true visionary. His letters revealed his daily life, his thoughts and anxieties. They were poignant and revealing, defining a personality that was empathetic, generous, and lonely. It seems like he came to Arles with a dream of building a community with other artists, a dream ultimately deferred.

Throughout this artist residency, Vincent van Gogh's dream to build an artist community in Arles was so present. I was honored to be invited by Laura Owens. The four-story building slowly became a fertile, vertical garden of creative actions that kept evolving with every artist that contributed. Nothing escaped consideration. Alicia Vaïsse, a "local" artist who participated in the residency, generously stopped by to meet me and guided me through the space in a way that made more sense. The official site map did not exist yet. We were living history in real time, and it was having to keep up with us. Alicia could identify the artworks in the house and it made me feel immediately at home. There was so much space and light. The texture of the cobblestone streets was such a wonderful contrast. At times, it amplified the sounds of people walking past the studio. I found myself taking pictures constantly. My iPhone became another studio tool.

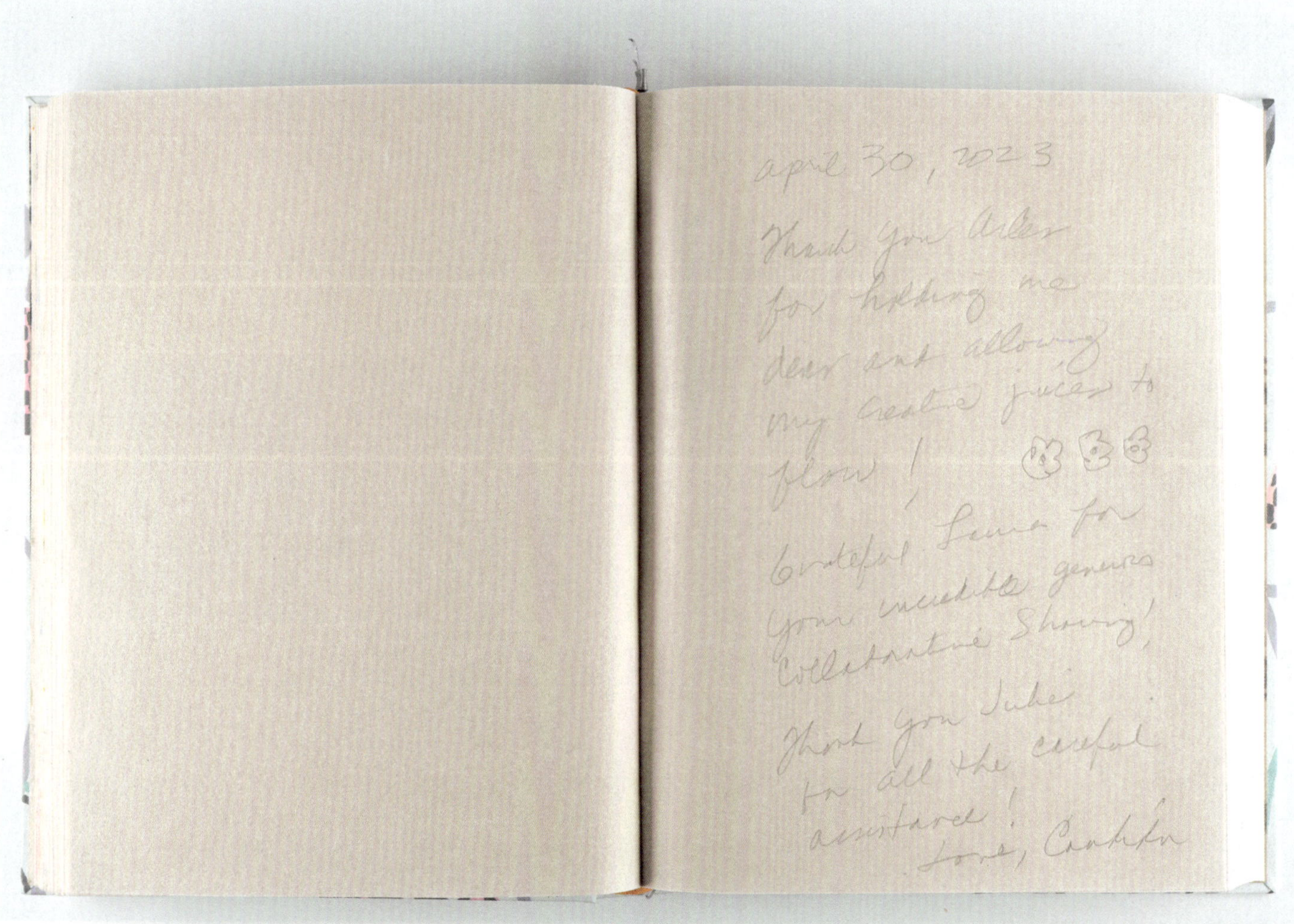

A note from Candida Alvarez in the guest book

My first destination in Arles was the museum at LUMA. It looked like a big, gold drum in the sky. I got lost a couple of times trying to find it because of the circular streets. It was not like the city grids I am used to. At first, I could not identify any markers to guide me. But it also occurred to me, as I walked around the city in wonder, that I was manifesting this idea of a living palimpsest. My mind continued to race through layers of my life and how I got to this town called Arles. Laura Owens's guiding hand was everywhere. What a brilliant idea—to dream and to share space with others. It's one of the most beautiful things, this generosity of Laura's. I could almost imagine Van Gogh wanting something close to that but, sadly, never attaining it. This residency is a manifestation of the generosity of spirit.

I met Laura through my colleague Terry R. Myers in Los Angeles several years ago. I had always connected with her work and her surprising paintings. I love the way she thinks outside the box, always having the courage to be herself. She always has multiple balls in the air, keeping things exciting. I really enjoyed her exhibition with Van Gogh at the Fondation Vincent van Gogh Arles in 2021. The exhibition she designed "with" Van Gogh. She has a wonderful way of saturating an environment with a minimum of gestures. She brought in Van Gogh to saturate the environment and, at the same time, she was able to push through it and carve out her own sensibility. That's magical, and it takes courage to tackle. Not everybody can do that. She's someone I deeply respect. When I arrived in Arles, I had one small suitcase and a carry-on bag. I was

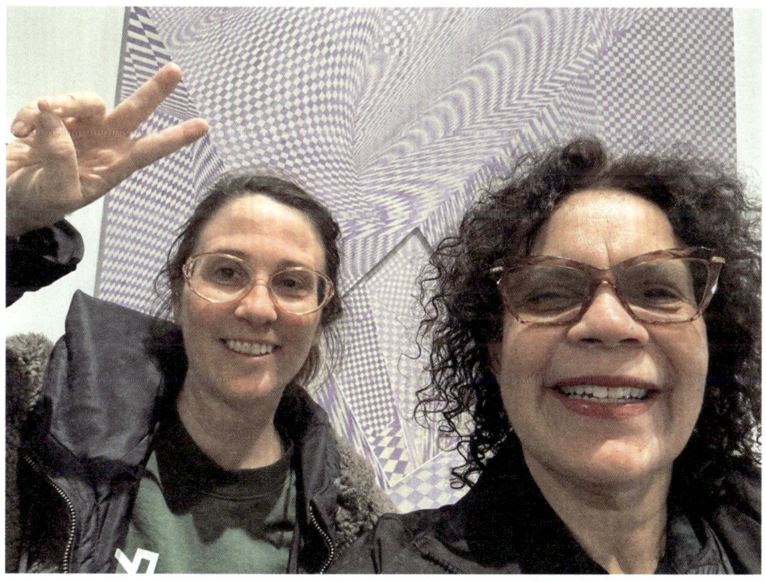

Laura Owens and Candida

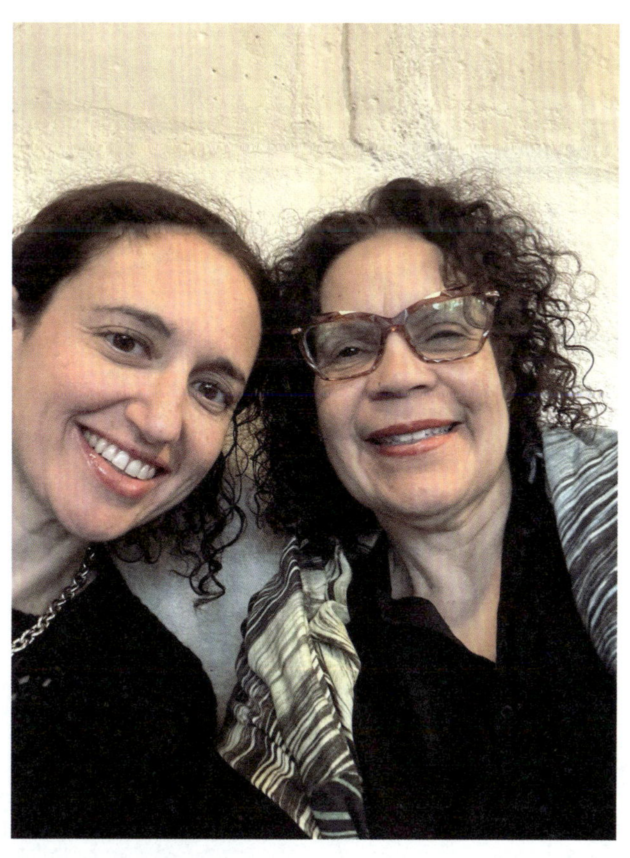

Candida and Julie Boukobza

able to fit four colors of paint: red, blue, yellow, and white. When Laura arrived at the studio to visit, she said, gesturing to my studio table, "Candida, you don't have any colors. I am going to take you to my studio." When we got there, she found a large, red shopping bag, opened up her paint cabinets, and said, "Take whatever colors you want." She loaded me up with colors. It was such a beautiful gesture, one that I will never forget. That was the beginning of my residency. When artists share their colors, you know they like you. When they share their paints, you're in for good. That was such a beautiful turning point. I used all the colors and more.

Toward the third week, I took the train to Paris to visit some friends and see some art. On the way back, I was reading *The New York Times*, and I learned that Harry Belafonte had passed. In his honor, I painted a tiny mural directly on the wall under one of the bedroom windows on the third floor. There was a potential spot over the bed, but I saw nails, so I felt like that was somebody else's designated area. It was kind of weird, going around the house, trying to figure out where I felt like I could "place myself." In that same section of *The New York Times* was a photography review including my dear friend Carrie Mae Weems. I rolled up that review and added it to another artwork that was hanging from the stairwell ceiling, made of rope with lassos hanging from the sides.

By the fourth week, I had completed several drawings on Yupo paper that I later would exhibit in Chicago at Monique Meloche Gallery. I also completed two dinner-napkin paintings that

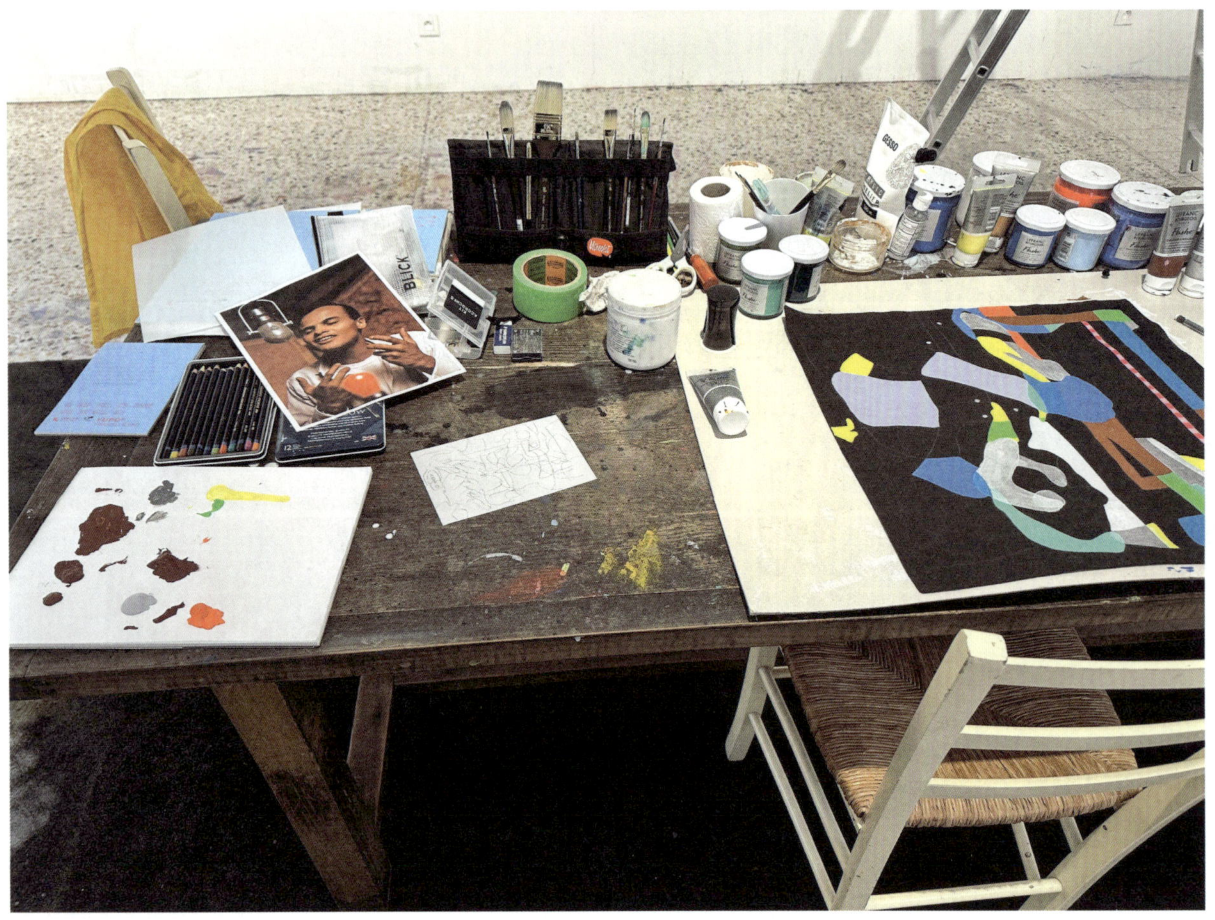

Work in progress in the studio

I would eventually hang in select places in the residence during the open house. Most of the time, I was working alone, but there were wonderful artists to meet, openings to attend, and sights to see. I was excited to hear that my dear friend Theaster Gates was going to do a show at LUMA a few months after I left. I felt like I was destined to be there at that moment.

It was a very special experience—not long, but enough time to open up your thinking about why you do what you do. The residency gave me a focus in the studio and an opportunity to renew myself in a city that was totally unfamiliar. I worked hard and enjoyed the peace that awaited me at the end of the day. Going to the farmers' market was so special. A fusion of languages and cultures all coming together, looking for local freshness. The anthropology museum was terrific. There was so much to learn. The Lee Ufan museum was one of the highlights. I became such a huge fan. Bumping into the world of Jorge Prado at a recently designed hotel was magical. I was surrounded by a nourishing environment where I could measure my capacity to live alone with the unfamiliarity that surrounded me. Getting lost and then finding my way was a wonderful affirmation of self-intentionality. I'm so happy I was invited and that I could accept the invitation. It changed my life, for sure. The light, the people, the market, the museums—it was all part of this incredible journey. At the end of it all, it was a gift, an honor, and I'm grateful for the experience.

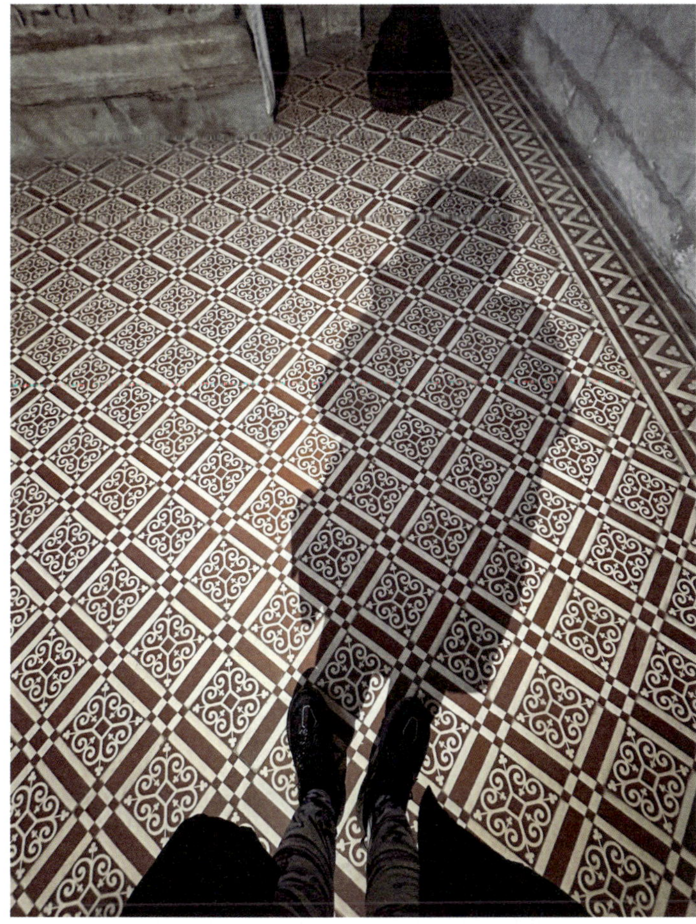

Candida's shadow

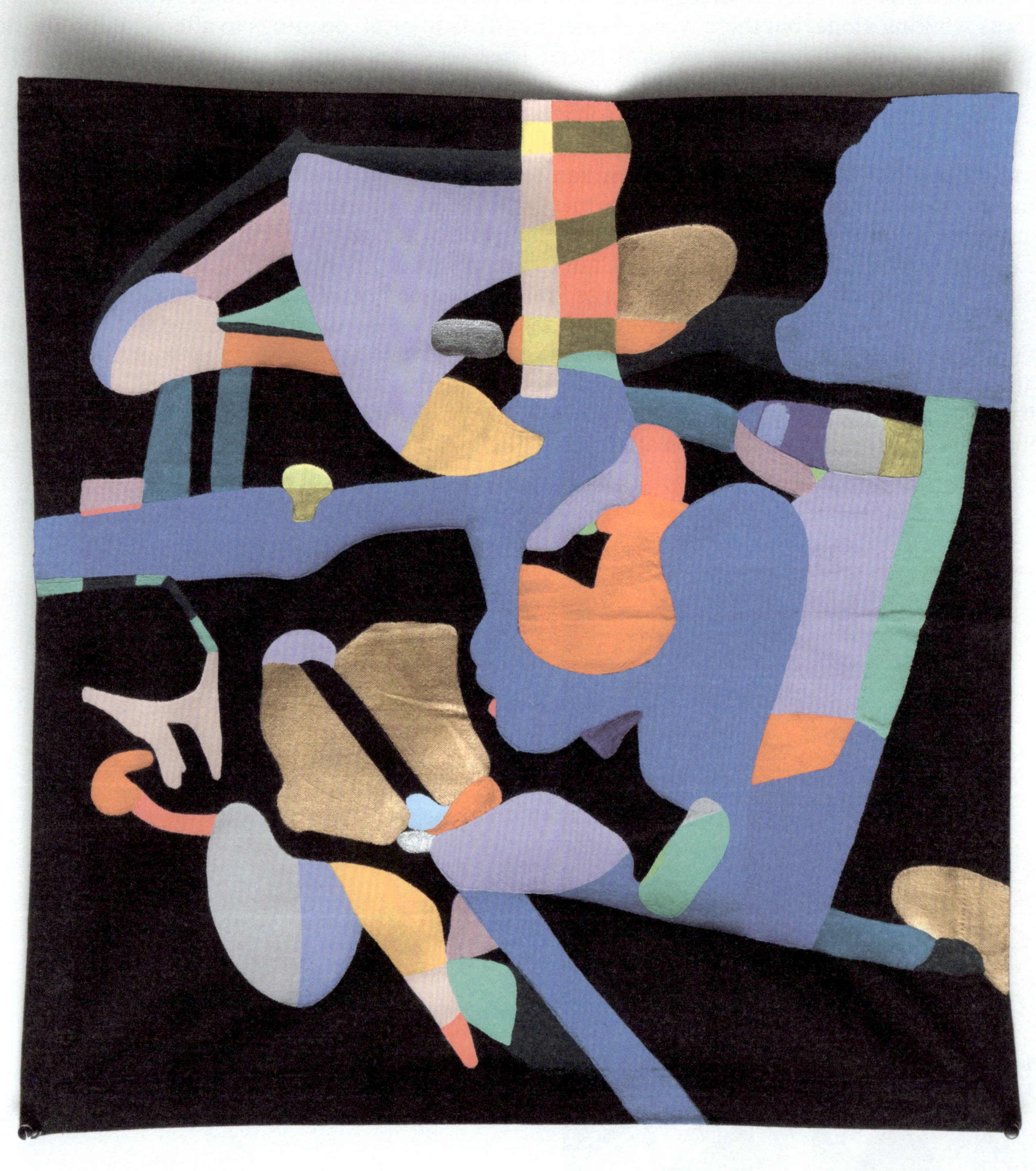

Candida Alvarez, *Arles #1*, fabric

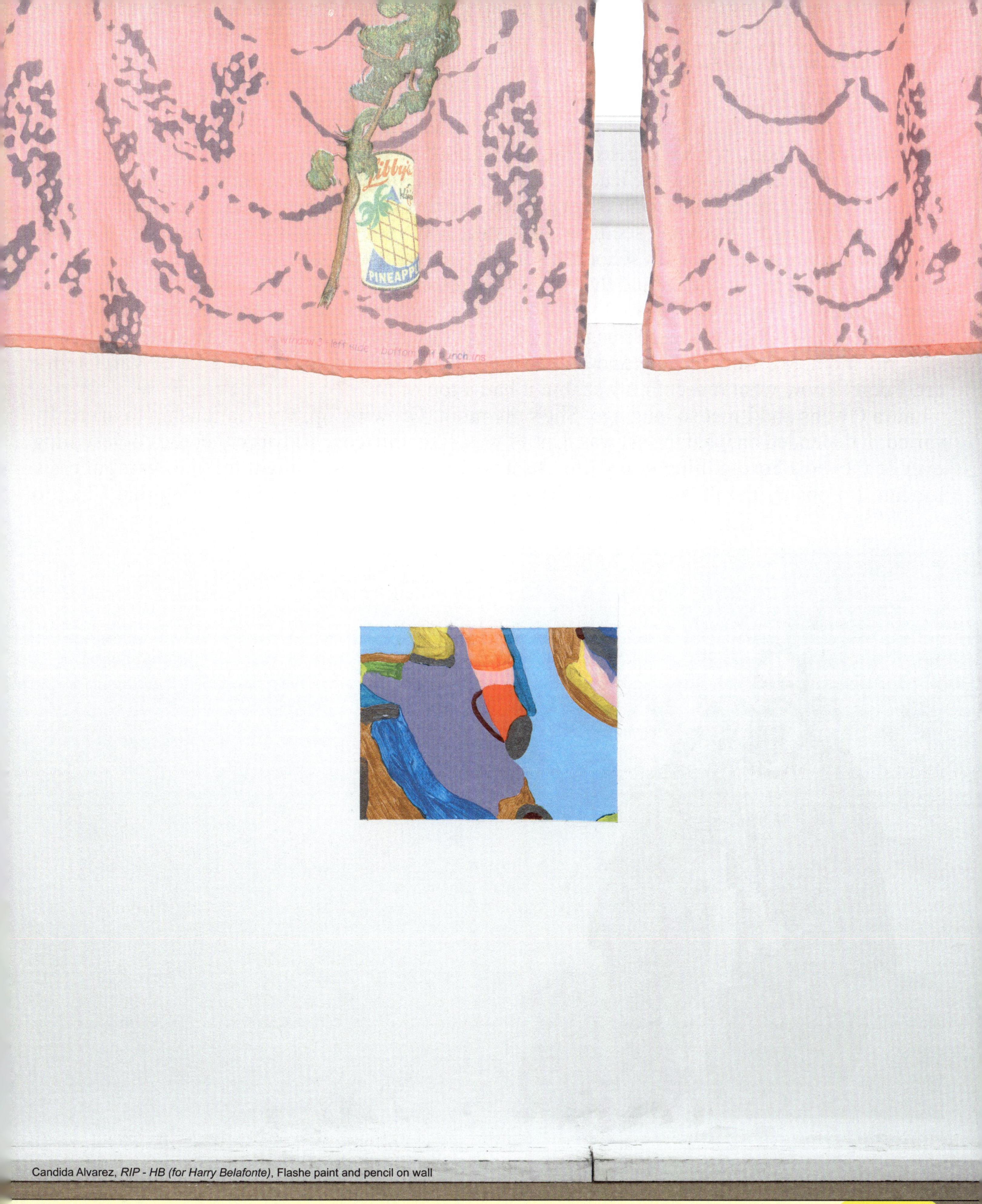

Candida Alvarez, *RIP - HB (for Harry Belafonte)*, Flashe paint and pencil on wall

Nova Bryan

In elementary school in Los Angeles, you learn about famous artists. There are about five you learn about: Vincent van Gogh, Claude Monet, Édouard Manet, Paul Cézanne, and Edgar Degas, I think. So in my mind, Van Gogh is very much like this idolized hero of art, like a really fancy person, and going to Arles and seeing all this stuff was very weird, it was a mind trip, because it's someone you learn about in school. It's like if you went and saw Napoleon's work. I was so small, I couldn't really understand that he was a real person. In my mind, it was like a thing you read in a book. I was tiny. I mean, I was, like, ten when I learned about him. I had a Van Gogh book, and it was all these pop-up images. I went and saw *The Starry Night* when I was, like, eight, with my mom. We went to Italy and France on a two-week trip, and I saw a lot of Van Gogh's art. I don't know what museum it was, but it had a ton of it.

Laura Owens and I met so long ago: She's my mom. Growing up, my relationship to art really varied; it depended on what the art was. Until I was, like, thirteen, art was either the coolest thing ever or the most boring thing in my life. Because I would go every night to, like, four galleries. I mean, I probably didn't, actually. But in my mind, it was this treacherous thing that I had to

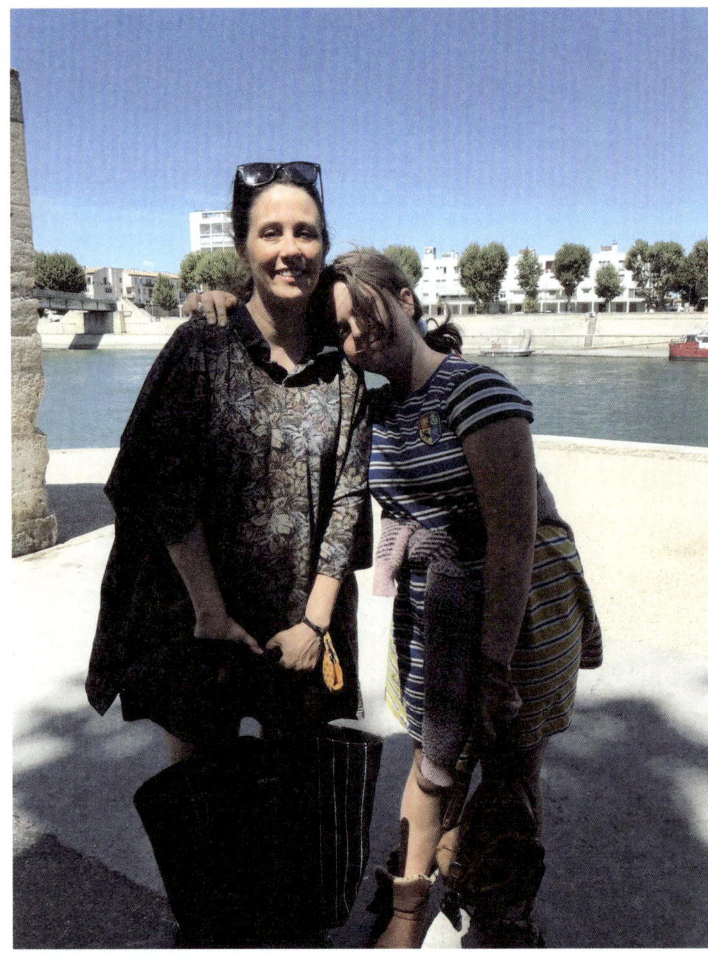

Laura Owens and Nova Bryan

do. Because galleries are all about the artists talking to each other, and I couldn't talk because I didn't know anything because I was five, and artists tend to take, like, ten minutes staring at each painting, and when you're five, you do not have the attention span to do that. So it was a lot of complaining and trying to drag my mom and dad out of art shows quickly. The idea being, I've seen it, I need to go now. I was processing so much art, but didn't really understand what art was. It was, like, pictures on the wall, but I didn't really get it. There were some shows that really were, like, Oh my God, this is crazy. There was one at 356 Mission, Los Angeles, of all the teddy bears. I don't know who that was [Charlemagne Palestine]. I thought that was the coolest thing ever. I remember that being a really big turning point for me and being like, "Oh my God. Art can be cool." But it's a weird situation, growing up with art. Now it's a really important part of my life, but back then, it was terrible.

I hadn't been to Arles before. I'd heard about it and seen a lot of pictures, but I'd never been. When I got there, the plan was that I would stay with my mom and with Mona Varichon and Jacob Eisenmann for six months, and I would go to this really weird, funny horse school where there were no grades. The day I got there was two weeks before everything shut down for COVID-19. I stayed inside for, like, five months. I didn't speak any French, and it was such a weird school. They didn't give me a schedule when I got there, which was the weirdest thing. So I was going to random classes every day. I went to English and art only. I was in sixth grade, but all the grades at the school

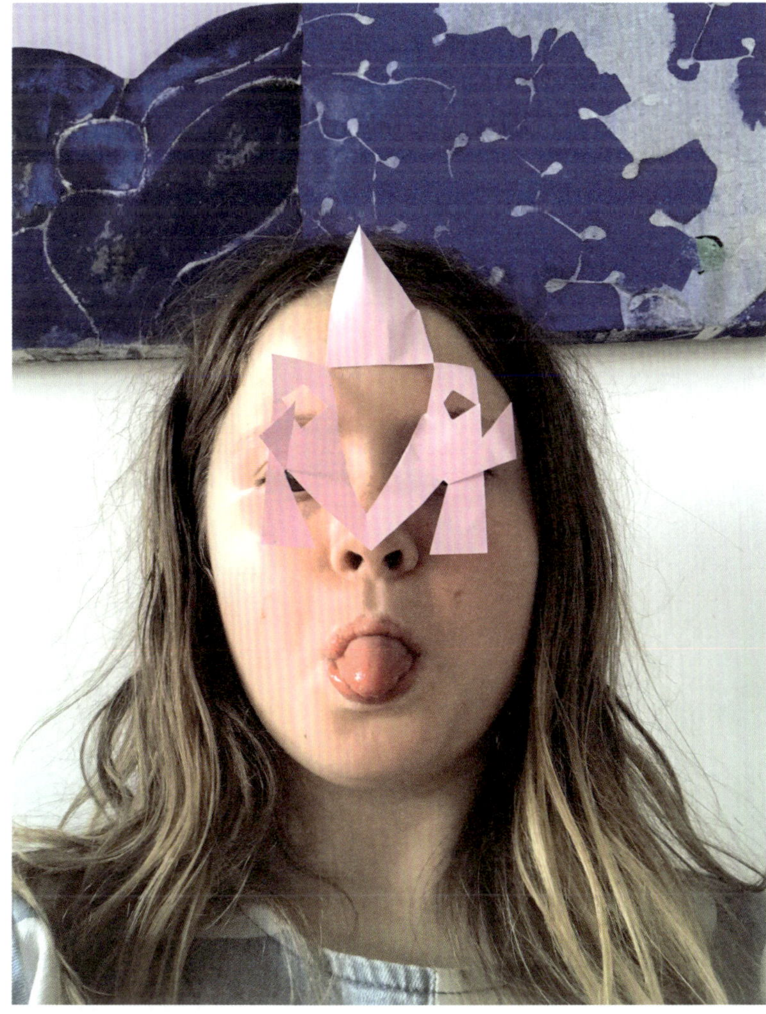

Nova

were melded together, and I was taking five language classes while I was there for some reason. When lockdown started, most schools went onto Zoom, but because the school was "interesting" and because I didn't speak any French, I didn't go on Zoom. I stayed home and didn't do anything, all day. I remember they gave me two assignments. One was an art assignment, painting a map of France and writing down all the major cities and the rivers and the bordering countries. And then one was trying to find the diameter of the moon solely with the diameter of a penny, which was super sadistic because it is physically impossible. I did so much math and I worked on that for, like, five hours before Mona looked it up and we realized it was not physically possible to find out. It was a much harsher lockdown there. When we were in Arles, I couldn't leave the house without getting fined because I was a kid and I didn't have any necessary reason to leave.

Arles is very beautiful. I remember loving the obelisks and it being a bit scary because everyone was speaking French. I had a lot of time when my mom would be working in the studio and I wouldn't be allowed to be in the house because she didn't want me to eat a ton of candy and watch TV, which is what I was going to do if she left me there. I was twelve, but because it's such a small town, I would walk around and explore. I would go sit in the place that used to be Van Gogh's hospital, with all the flowers, and I would read my one English book, *I Will Always Write Back*. I read it over and over again. I don't remember who it's by [Caitlin Alifirenka and Martin Ganda], but it's crazy—to this day, I can start reading a line of the book and I'll know

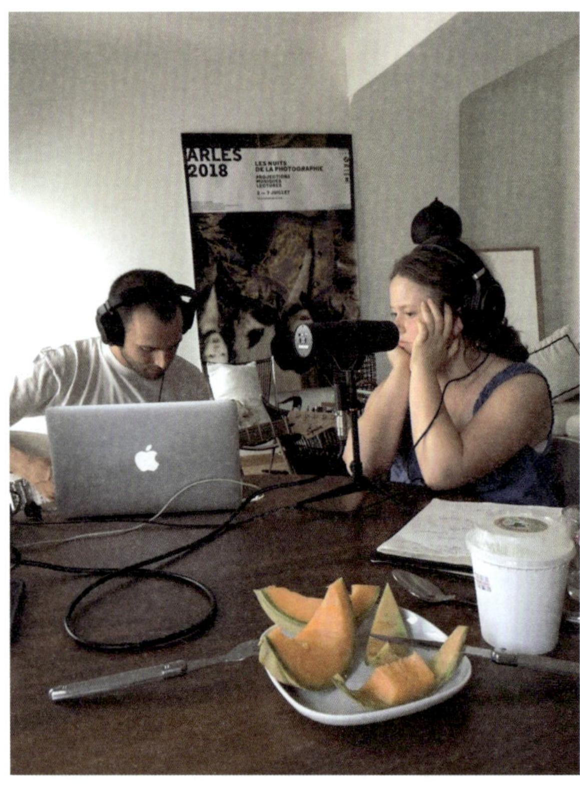

Jacob Eisenmann and Nova recording a song by Nova in Mouriès

the end of the line because I read it a solid eighty times. There's this one store that has all these comic books and all this Harry Potter merch. So I bought probably eight hundred Harry Potter merchandise things, because my mom would give me money to buy food, and I would buy Harry Potter merch instead. It's very cheap to get a sandwich at Carrefour, and I'd use the rest of the money to buy the time-turner device from *Harry Potter*.

I saw the residency house when my mom first saw it. We went in and there was nothing there. I remember we went with Mona and my mom, and then went and did all the ceramic plates and cups. They had the soft clay of the plates and the cups, and we would make designs, and then they fired it, and then we would paint it, and it was very fun. I made a lot of really dysfunctional plates. I remember being told that it was going to be a place where artists would come and live and hang out in Arles for a couple of weeks at a time, and then they would leave, and it would just go over and over again. While my mom was putting in the counters, I was explaining that the top room was the kid's room, and it was really funny because now there's Parker Ito's giant woman in there. And the giant main bedroom is for the artists, and there's the studio at the bottom, and I remember thinking it was really cool.

We got there and my mom told us that we would be painting the residency house. They were painting the walls and the trim while I was sitting and painting Mona—my funny twelve-year-old's picture of Mona, where she looks like a kid. I was painting it from a photo. It was definitely the first

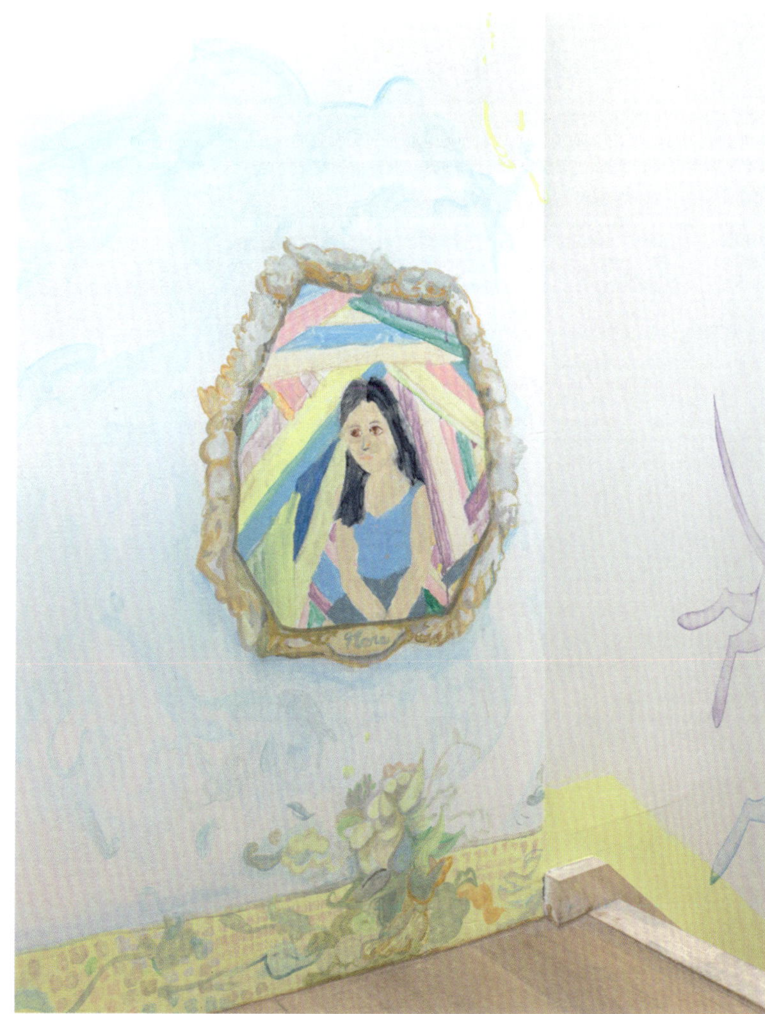

Nova Bryan, *Untitled*, wall painting

205

painting I ever did where I was actually trying to do something, where I thought, "I want to make this there." I had to ask Laura first, like, "Can I paint this?" And she would be like, "Yeah, good idea." I was originally going to paint all of us and started with Mona. I wanted to paint faces because I was twelve and had my little sketchpad, and I did nothing all day except draw people's faces, and I got really good. I was going to do a series of family portraits of everybody on the staircase, because everyone was working in the residency and I didn't have anything to do. I wasn't allowed to watch TV. What I would have done was watch TV all day, but I had to either watch it in French, which was torture, or do something else. So I ended up painting and reading a lot in the residency. I read *Fahrenheit 451* by Ray Bradbury a bunch of times, and I read this horror book about a school shooting, like, eighty times. It was a terrifying selection of books because I didn't want to read in French, and I couldn't. I was on Zoom every morning, learning how to speak French, and I was not good at it, not a cooperative student. But yeah, it was, like, four books.

I came back every summer and sometimes in the winter. My mom had rented the house in Mouriès for a long time because she loved being in the middle of nowhere. So we'd go back periodically. And when we did go back, there was a lot more focus on the residency rather than her show, which was the main focus the first time we were there—when she was making this giant show at the Fondation Vincent van Gogh Arles. I was helping with that, mainly, but then when we'd gone back after that first summer, I did a lot of wall paintings in the residency. I painted

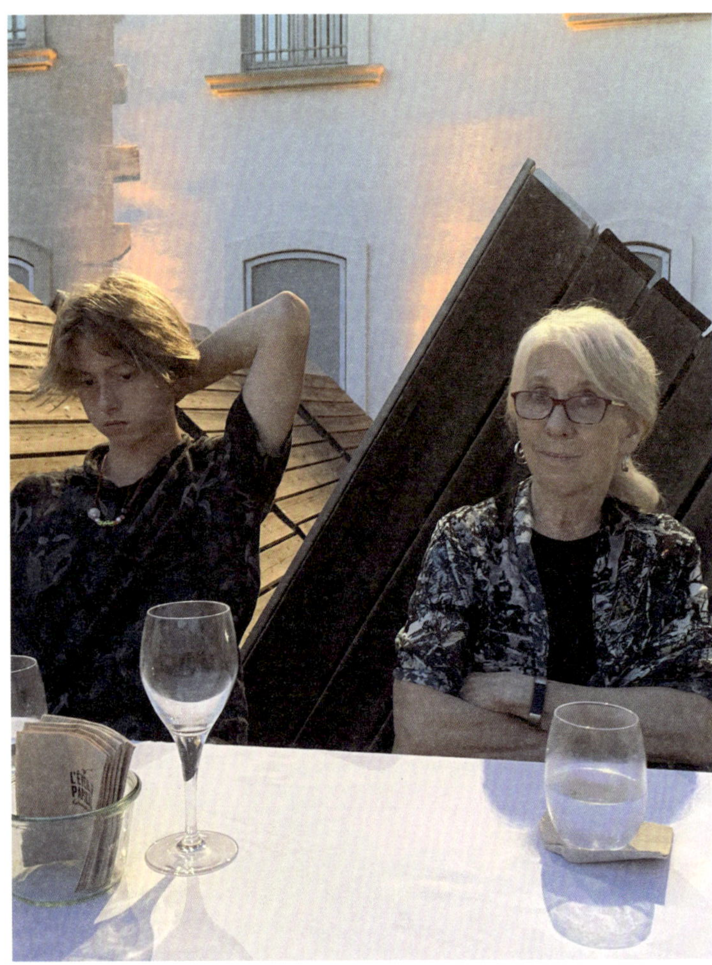

Nova's brother Henry and grandmother Carol

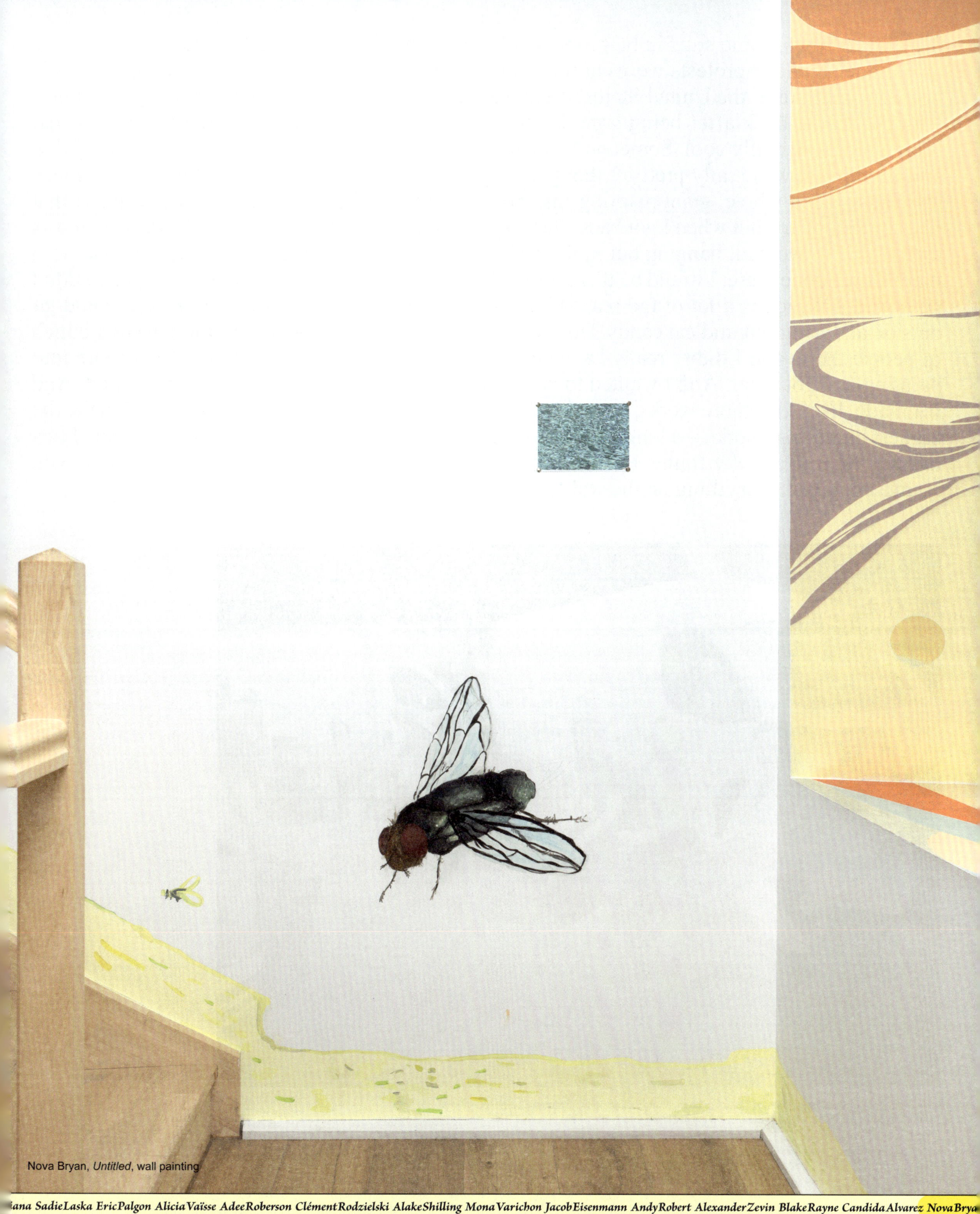

Nova Bryan, *Untitled*, wall painting

flies, water lilies, some stuff in bathrooms, a lot of stuff; but I can't really remember it all. We also made signs for protests we went to. There were Black Lives Matter protests in Marseille because, just like in the United States, there were people dying from police brutality in France.

When I came back after being gone for that summer in 2021, my first impression was that I thought it was really cool. Someone had painted the windowsills, and I remember loving that and thinking it was really pretty. I thought Parker's work was fun. I really liked it. The house was more like a whole, giant painting instead of a house. When I had left, it was a house that had some cool art, but when I got back, there was a bunch of different types of work, which was awesome. We were all hanging out in the residency at the very end, and I did the most painting that I'd ever done there. I would be there for twelve hours a day, and it was super hot, so I couldn't go outside. Which is a lot of the reason I hadn't done that much before—because I would go outside and hang out and eat candy. But then I was sitting in his house, and there were a bunch of people there, and I didn't really have anything to do. I wanted to paint, and I got more into painting as I got older. And I wanted to beat Parker Ito. We were really close, almost tied. And if I made, like, four more works, I would win the residency. The game was who could make the highest number of works—a long, running joke. Not between me and Parker, just with me. I just like saying it, it's really funny. I counted and I have thirty-something. It depends on what you count. I counted everything on the walls. If you count the plates, I have a lot more.

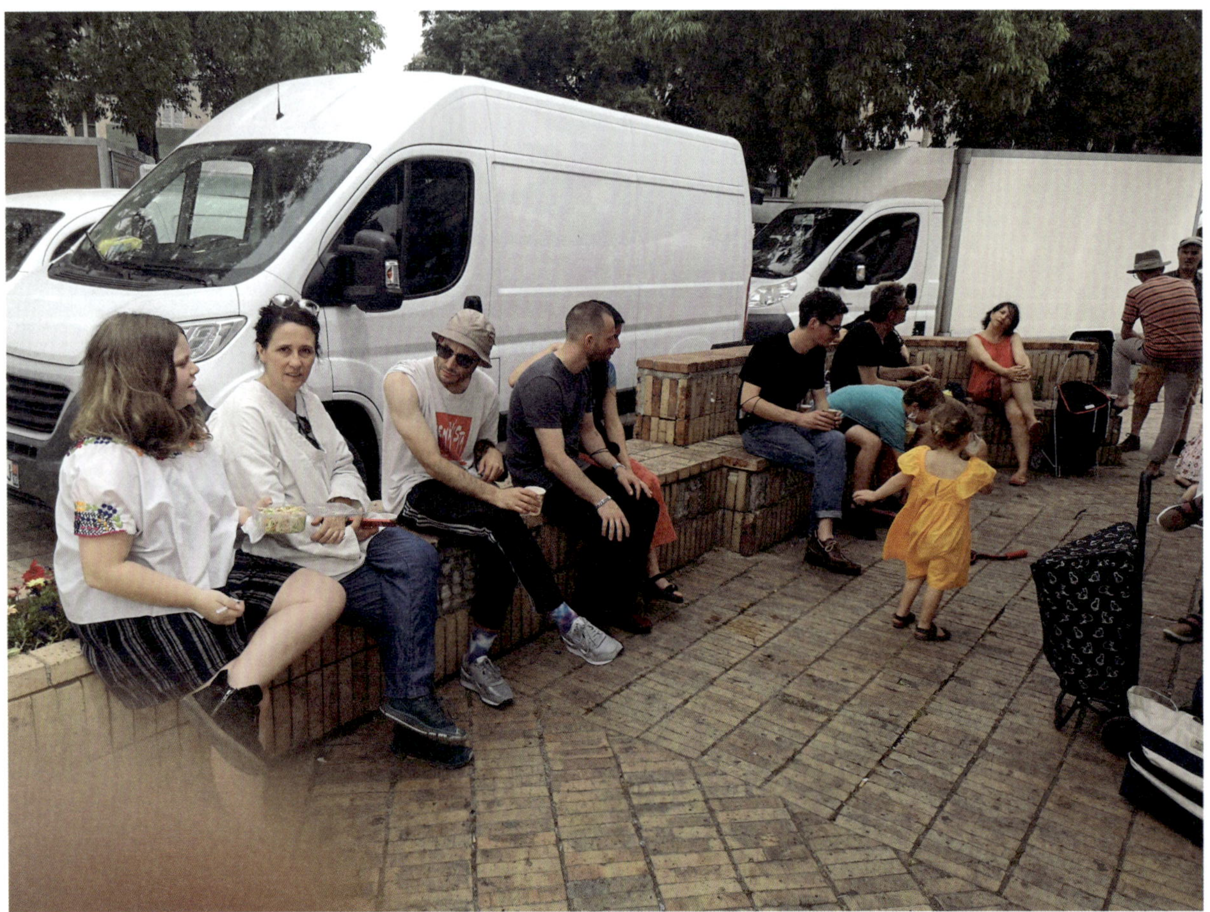

Nova, Laura, Asha Schechter, Jacob, Mona Varichon, François Lancien-Guilberteau, and François's daughter Hilma at the Saturday market in Arles

Final Form: The Residence as of July 2024

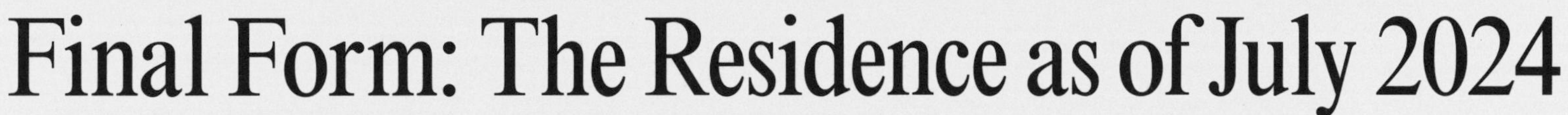

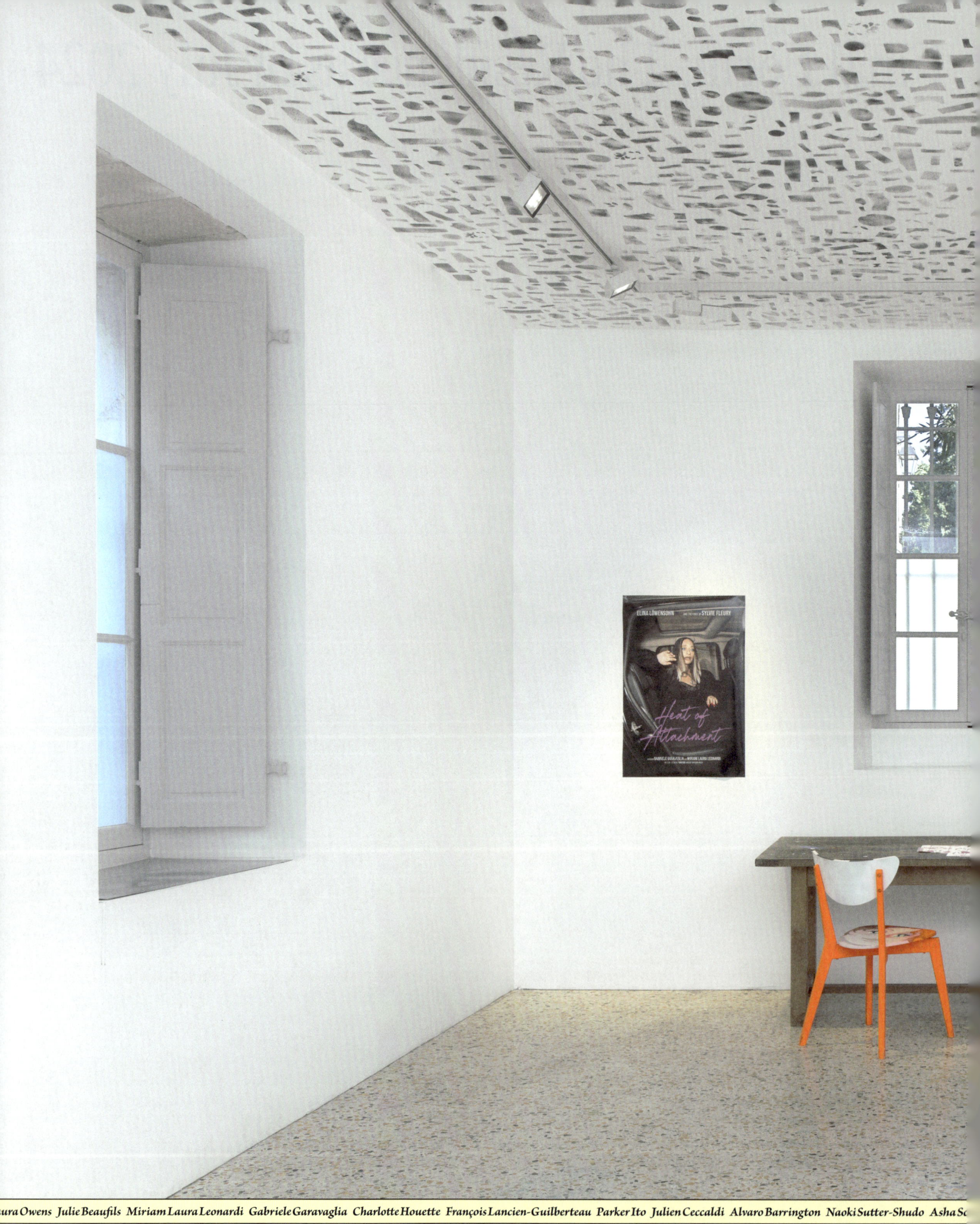

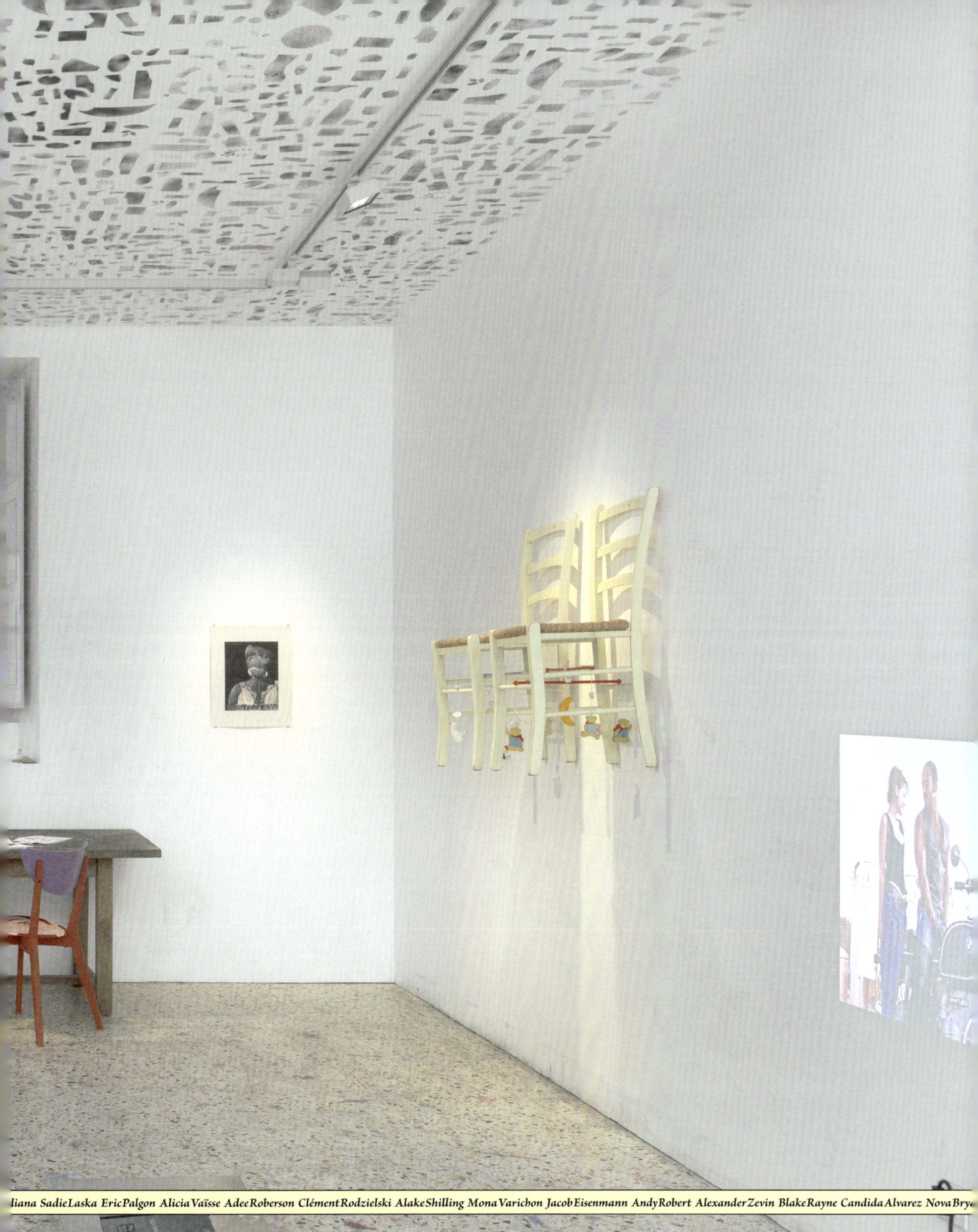

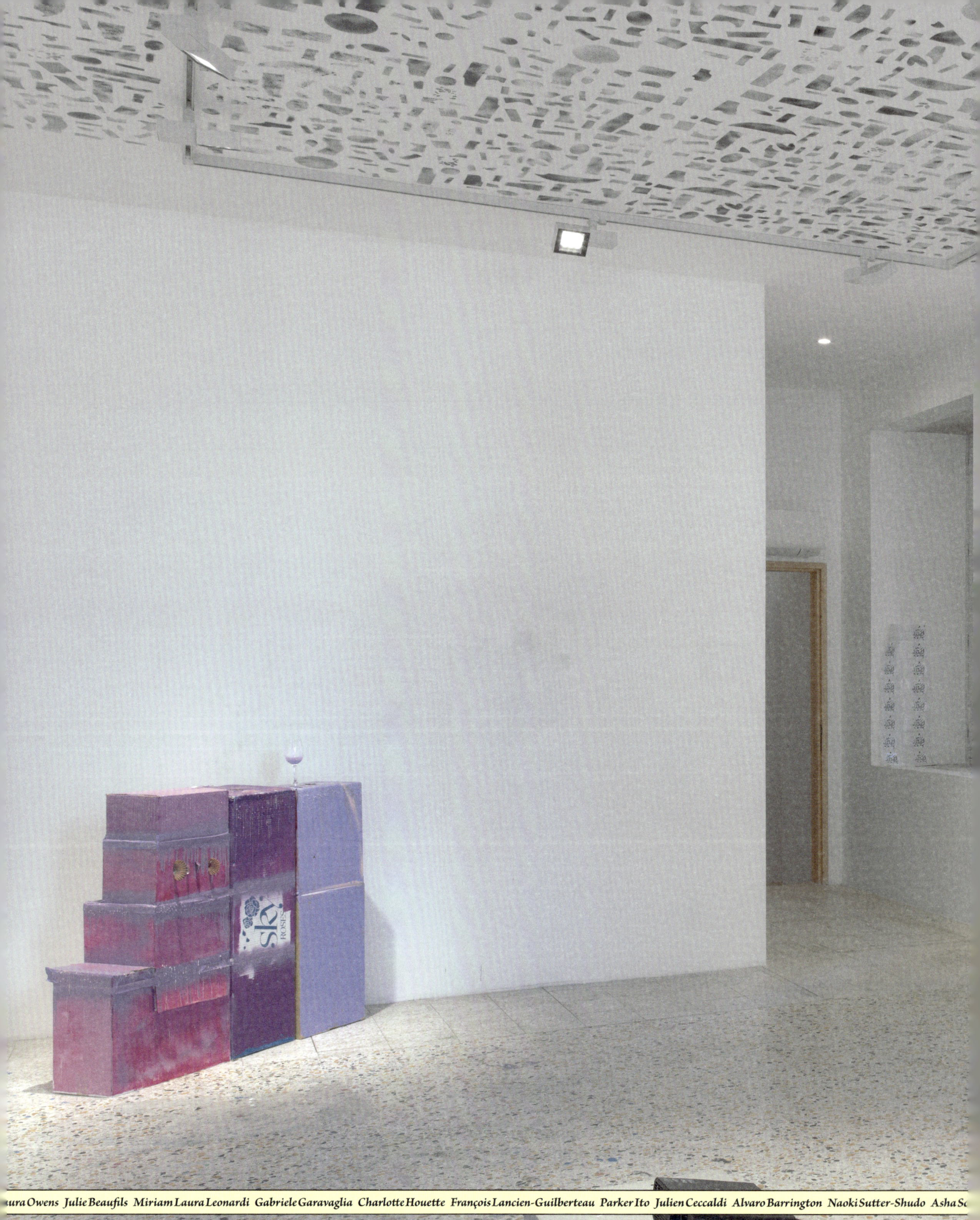

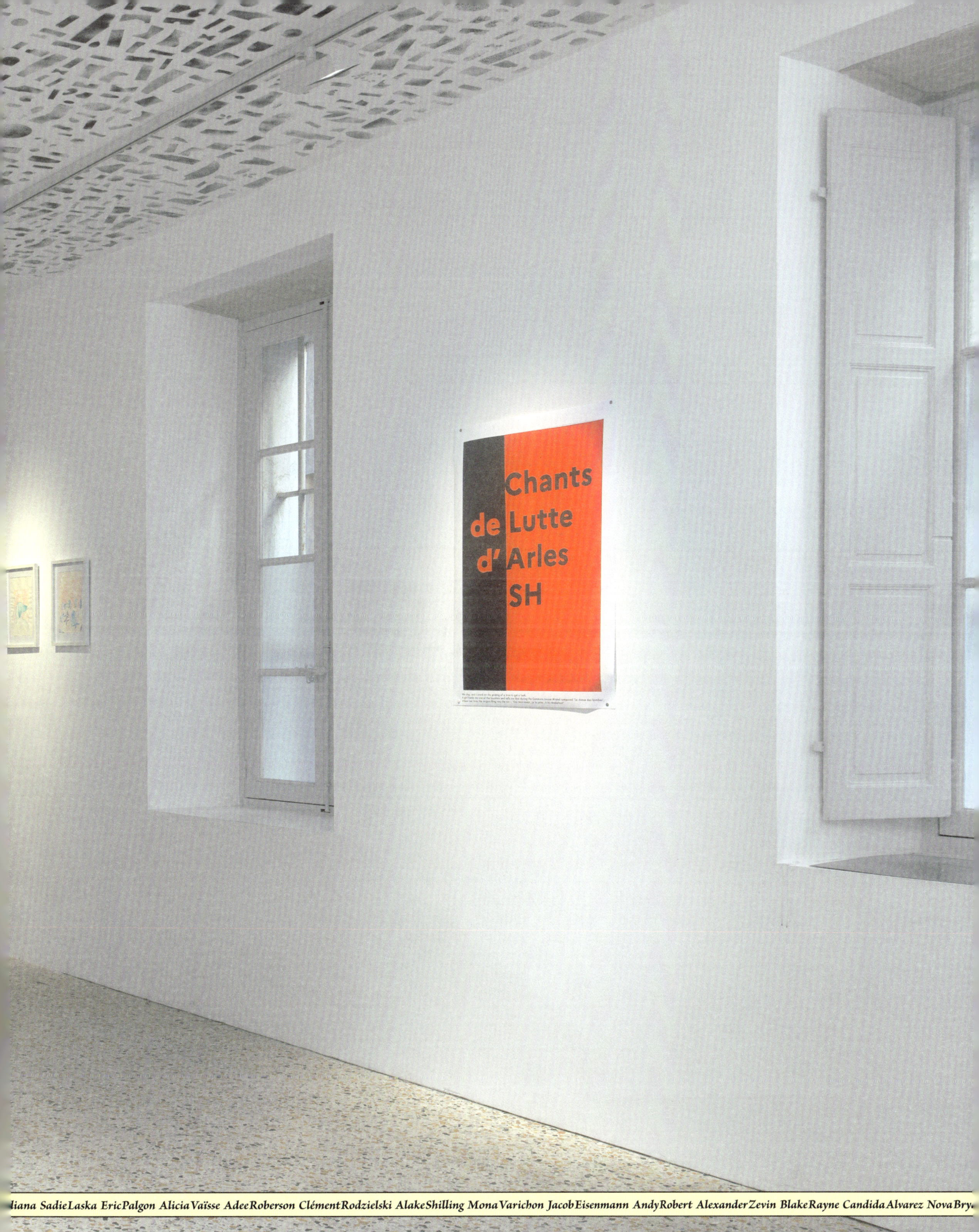

Chants
de Lutte
d'Arles
SH

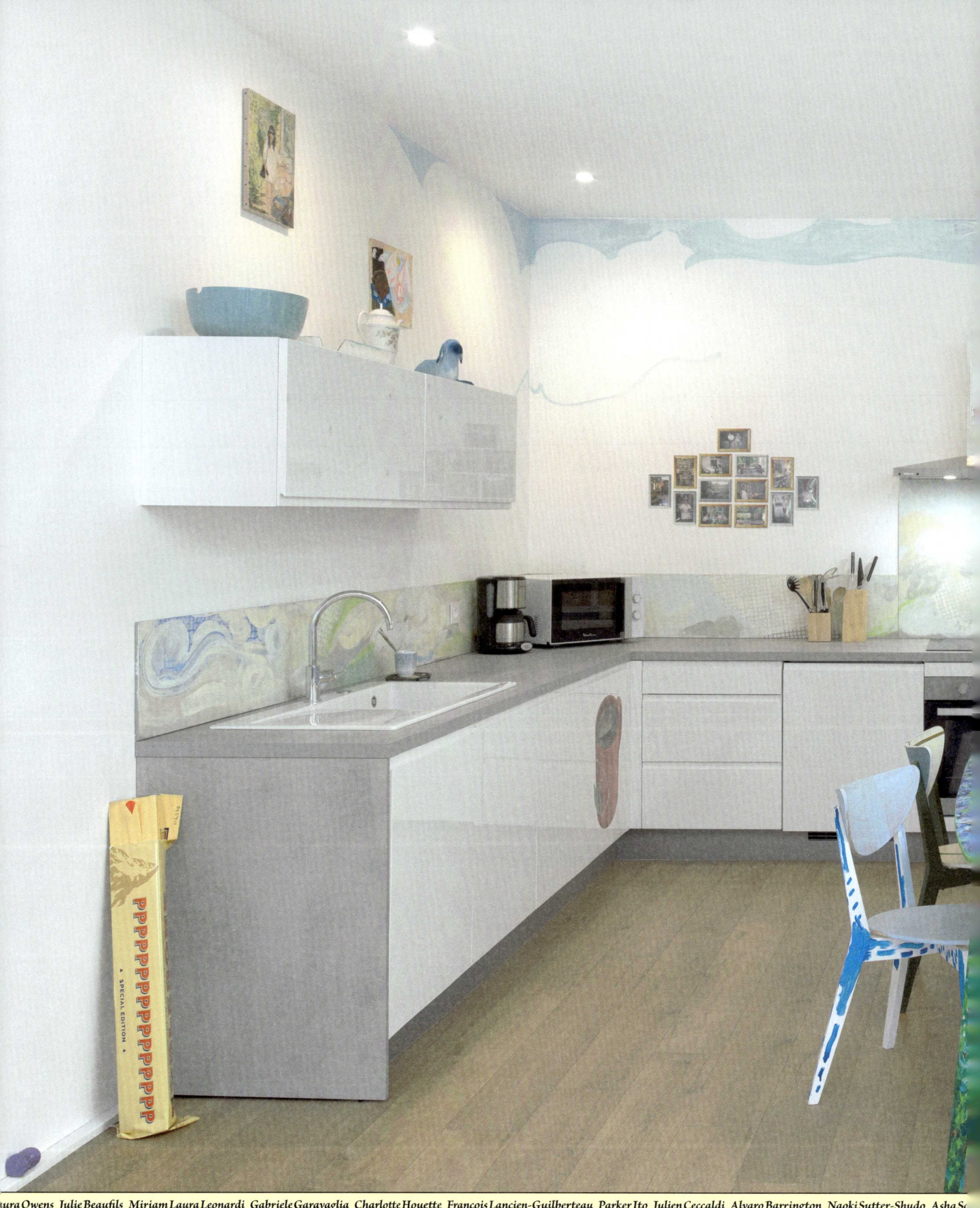

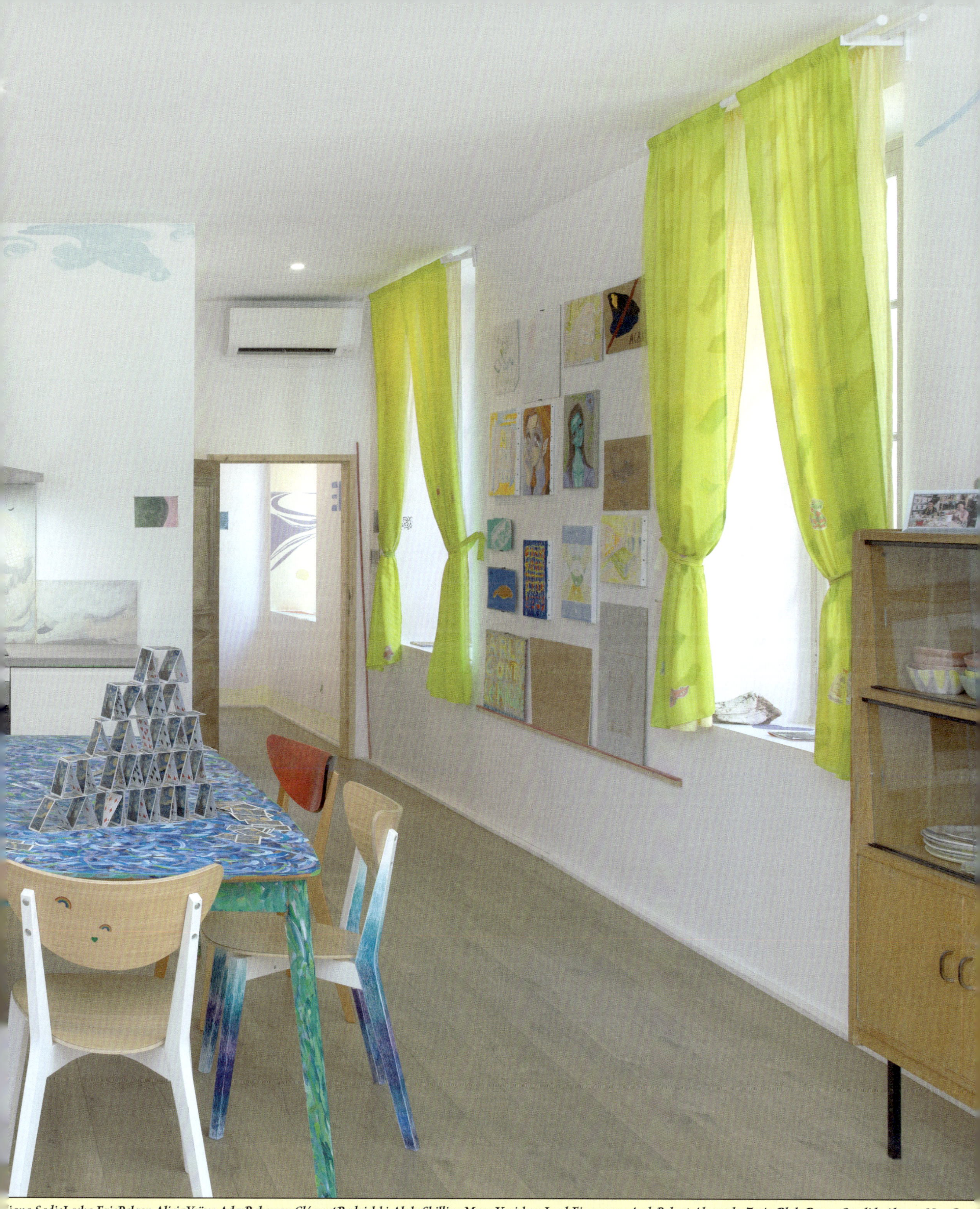

iana Sadie Laska Eric Palgon Alicia Vaïsse Adee Roberson Clément Rodzielski Alake Shilling Mona Varichon Jacob Eisenmann Andy Robert Alexander Zevin Blake Rayne Candida Alvarez Nova Brya

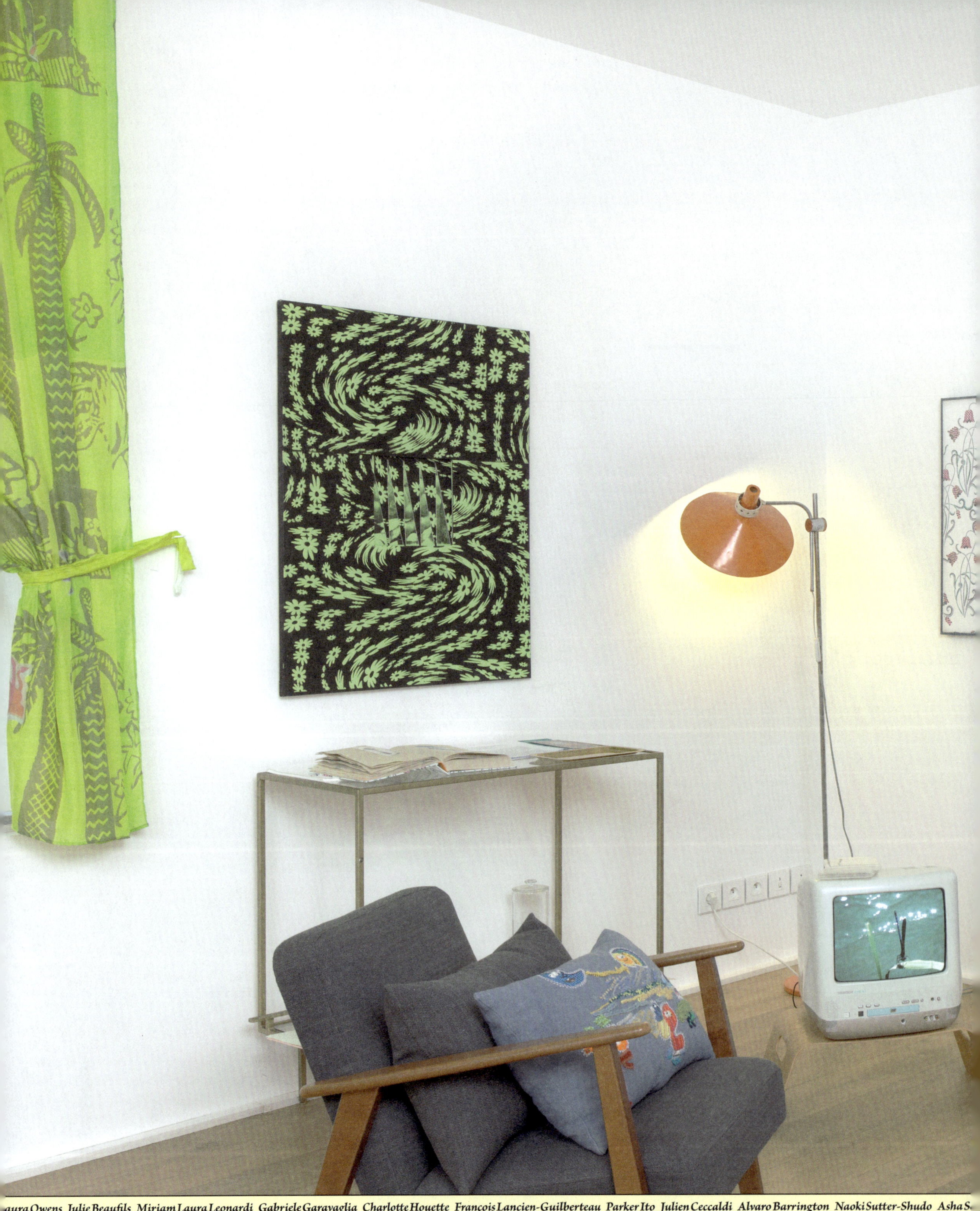

aura Owens Julie Beaufils Miriam Laura Leonardi Gabriele Garavaglia Charlotte Houette François Lancien-Guilberteau Parker Ito Julien Ceccaldi Alvaro Barrington Naoki Sutter-Shudo Asha S

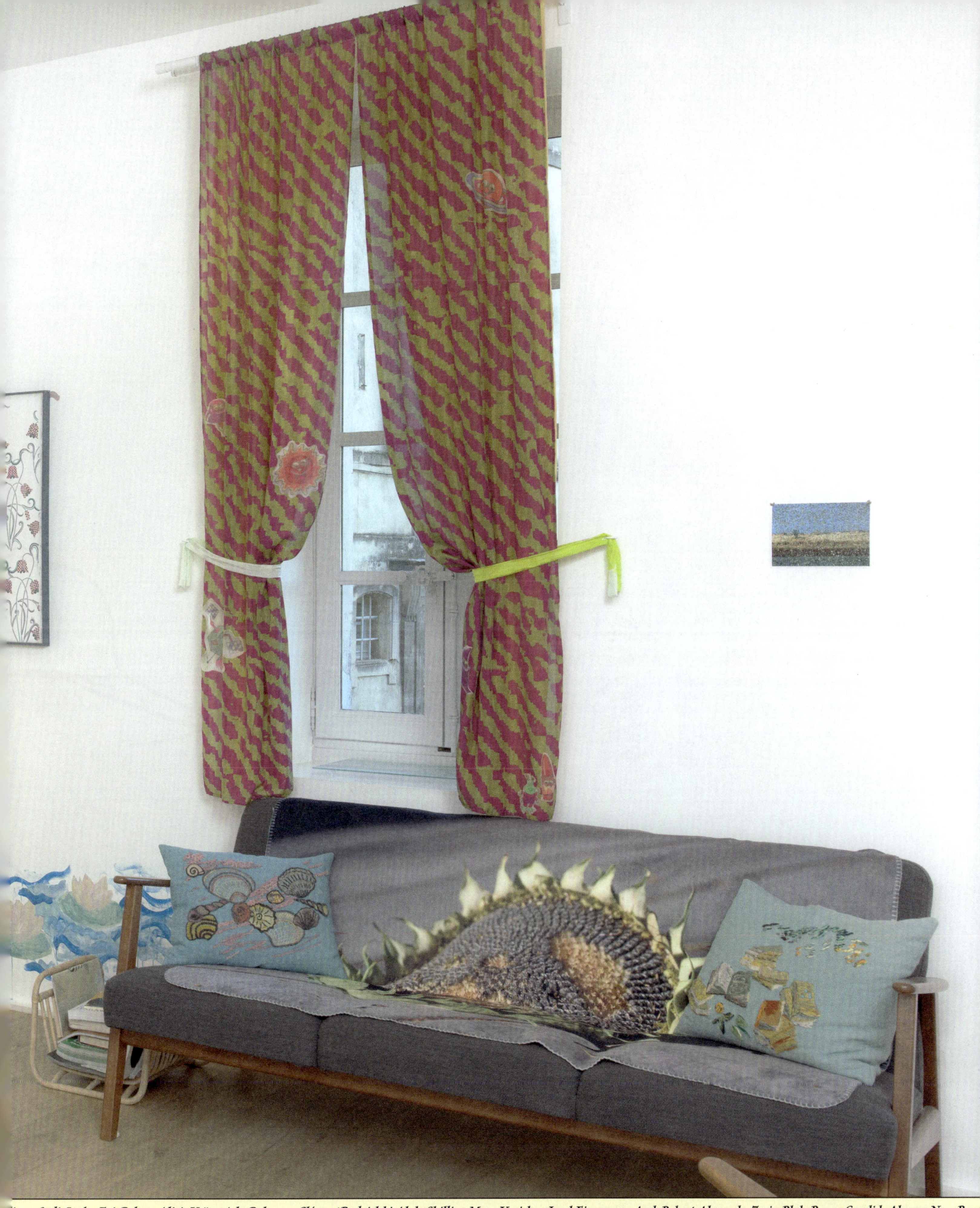

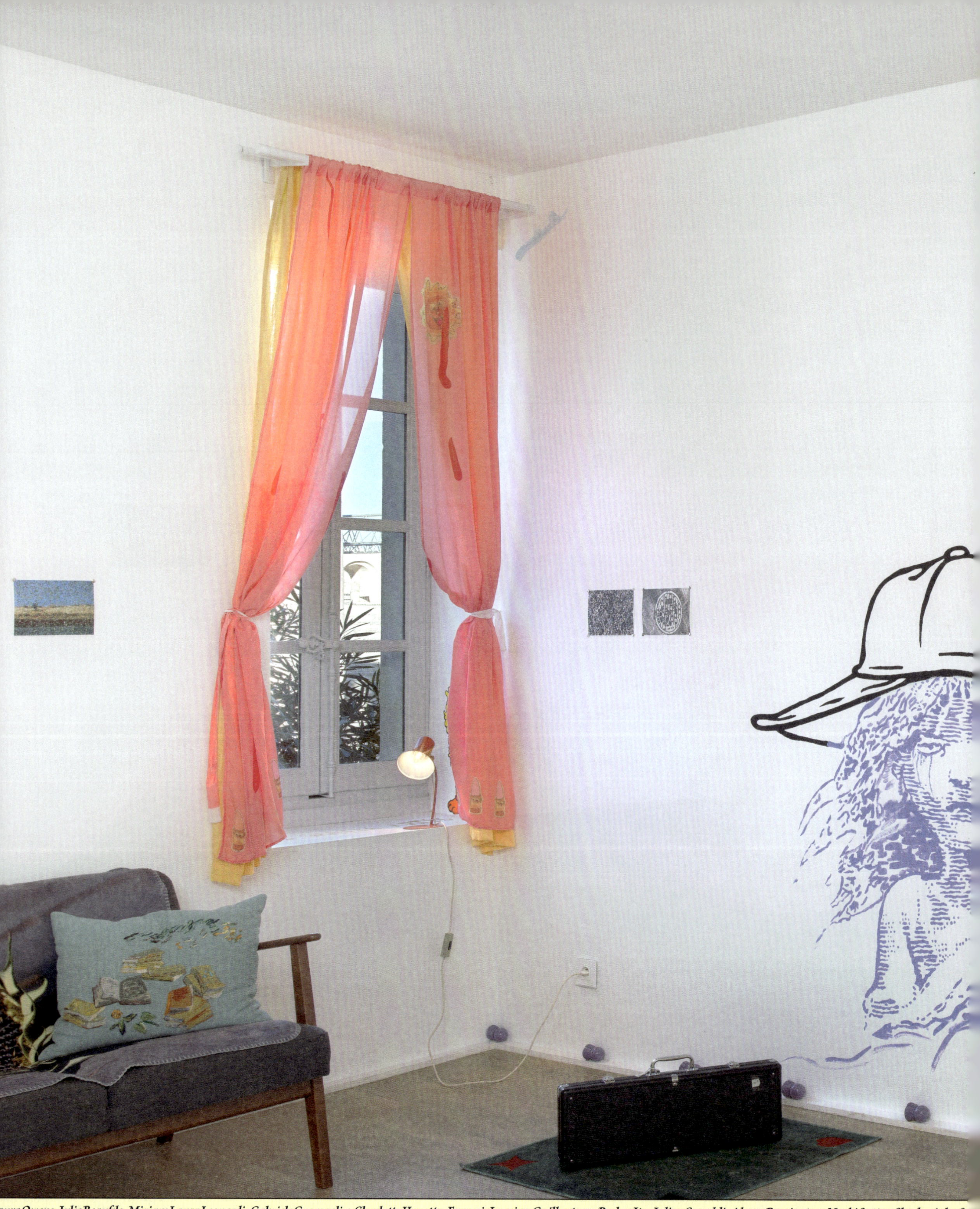

ura Owens Julie Beaufils Miriam Laura Leonardi Gabriele Garavaglia Charlotte Houette François Lancien-Guilberteau Parker Ito Julien Ceccaldi Alvaro Barrington Naoki Sutter-Shudo Asha Se

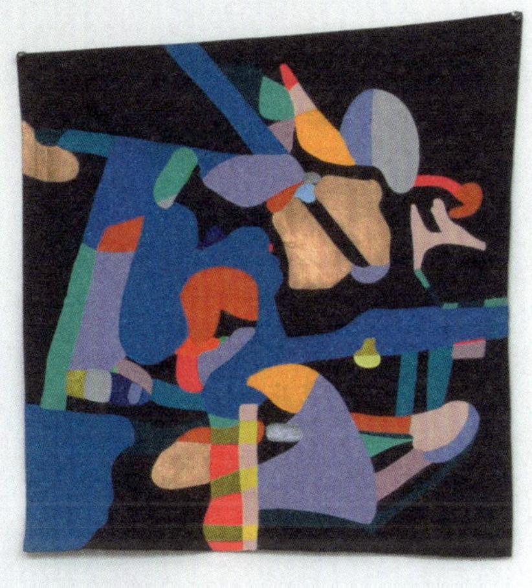

MOI
NON PLUS

iana Sadie Laska Eric Palgon Alicia Vaïsse Adee Roberson Clément Rodzielski Alake Shilling Mona Varichon Jacob Eisenmann Andy Robert Alexander Zevin Blake Rayne Candida Alvarez Nova Bry

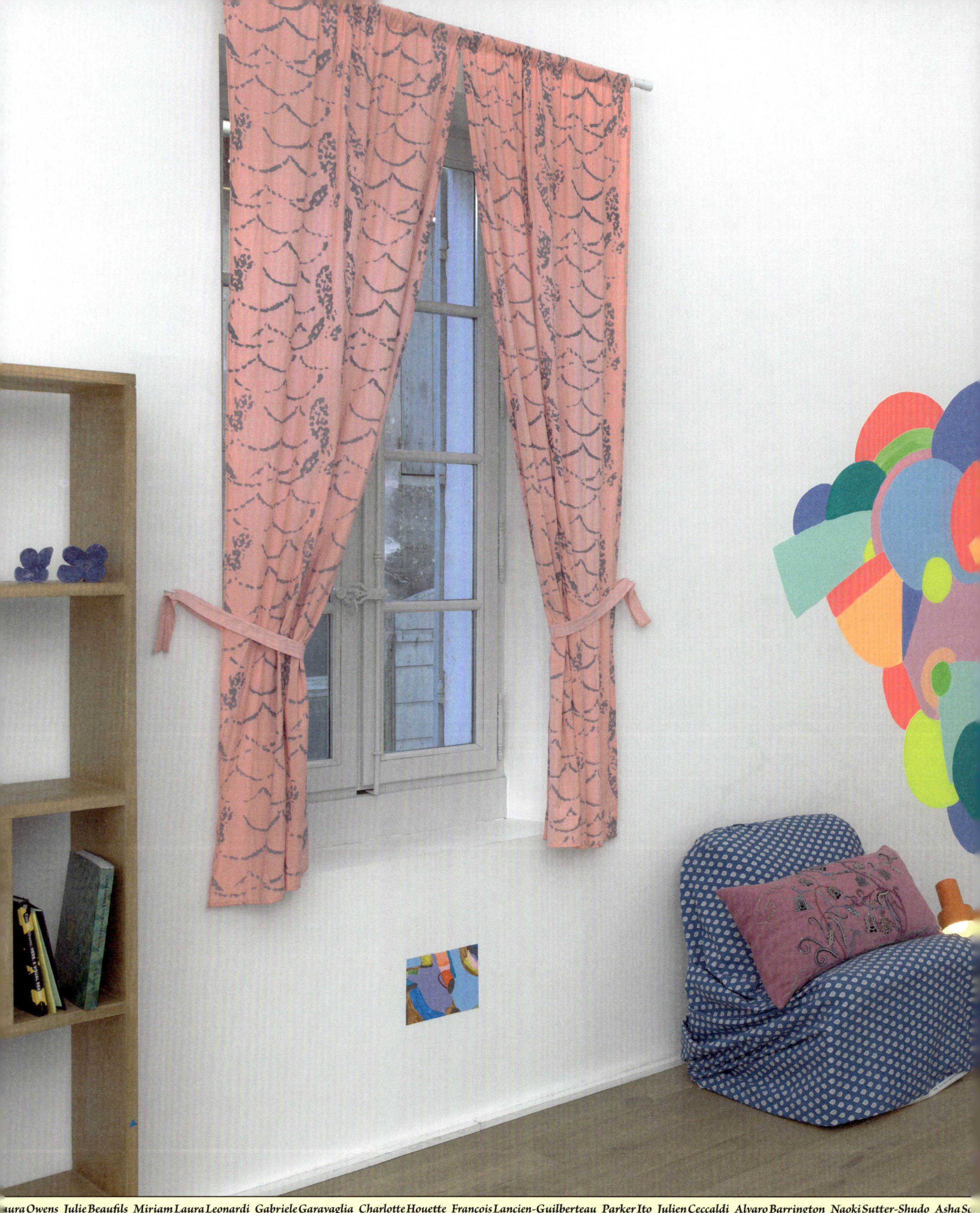

aura Owens Julie Beaufils Miriam Laura Leonardi Gabriele Garavaglia Charlotte Houette François Lancien-Guilberteau Parker Ito Julien Ceccaldi Alvaro Barrington Naoki Sutter-Shudo Asha S

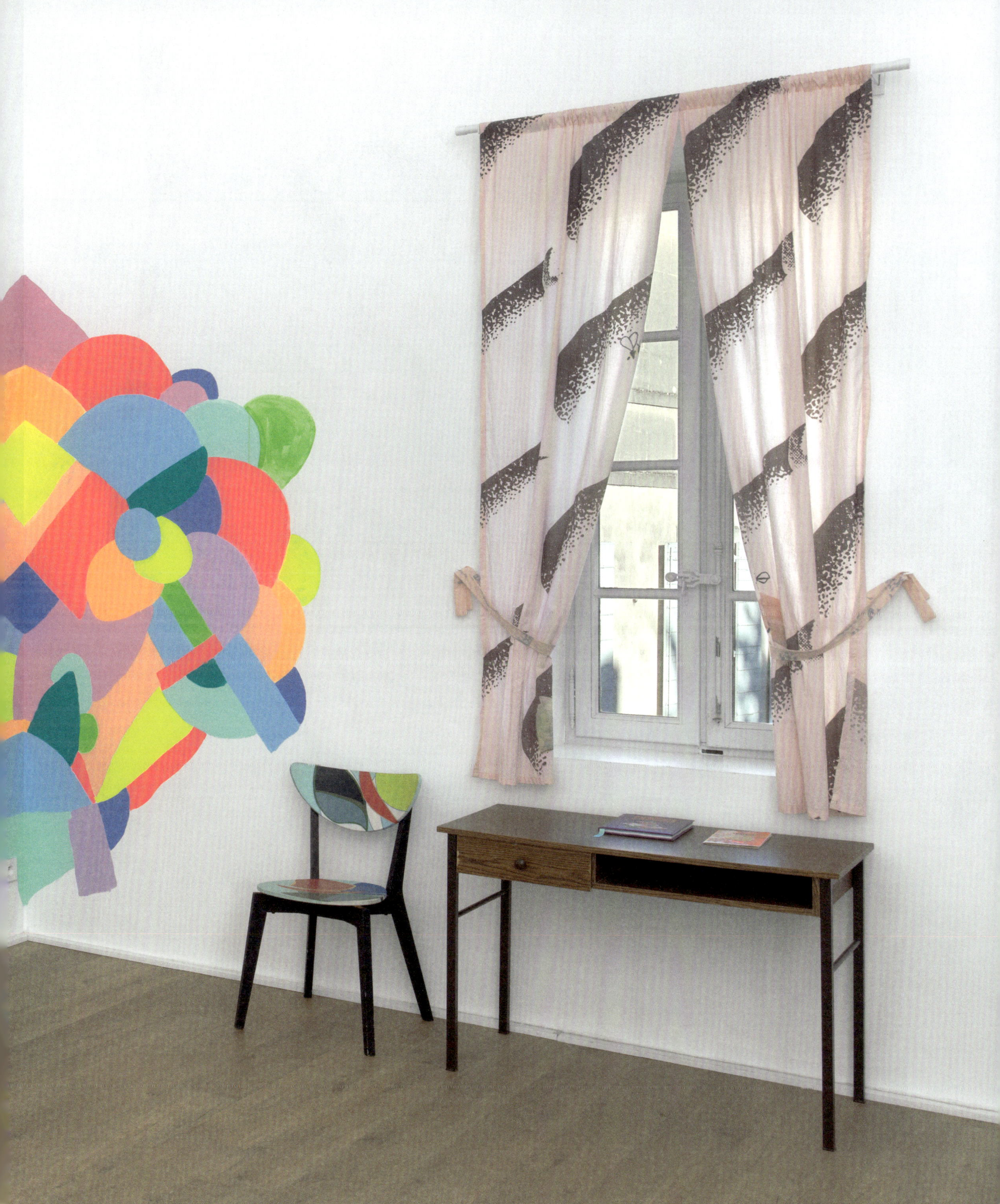

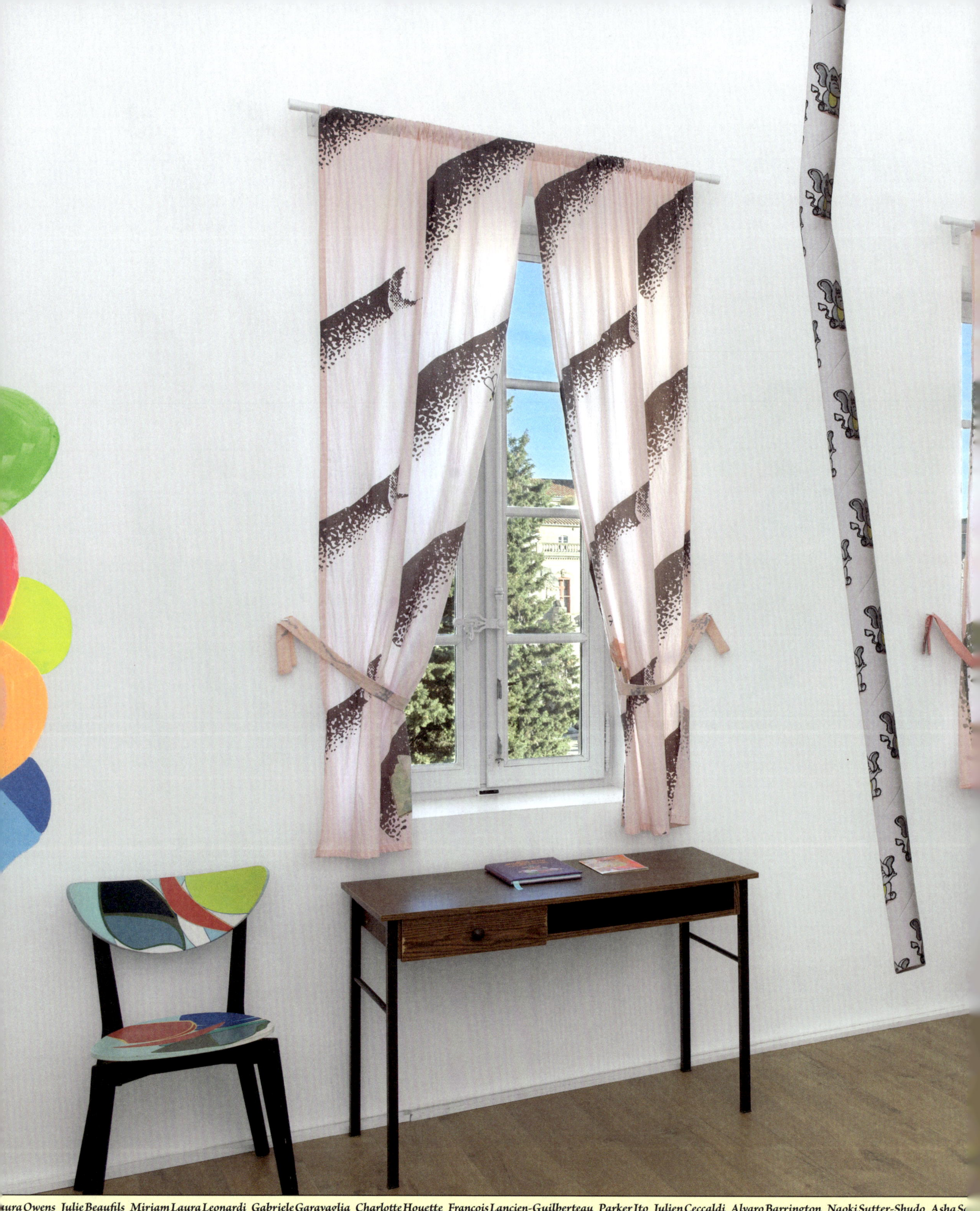

ura Owens Julie Beaufils Miriam Laura Leonardi Gabriele Garavaglia Charlotte Houette François Lancien-Guilberteau Parker Ito Julien Ceccaldi Alvaro Barrington Naoki Sutter-Shudo Asha S

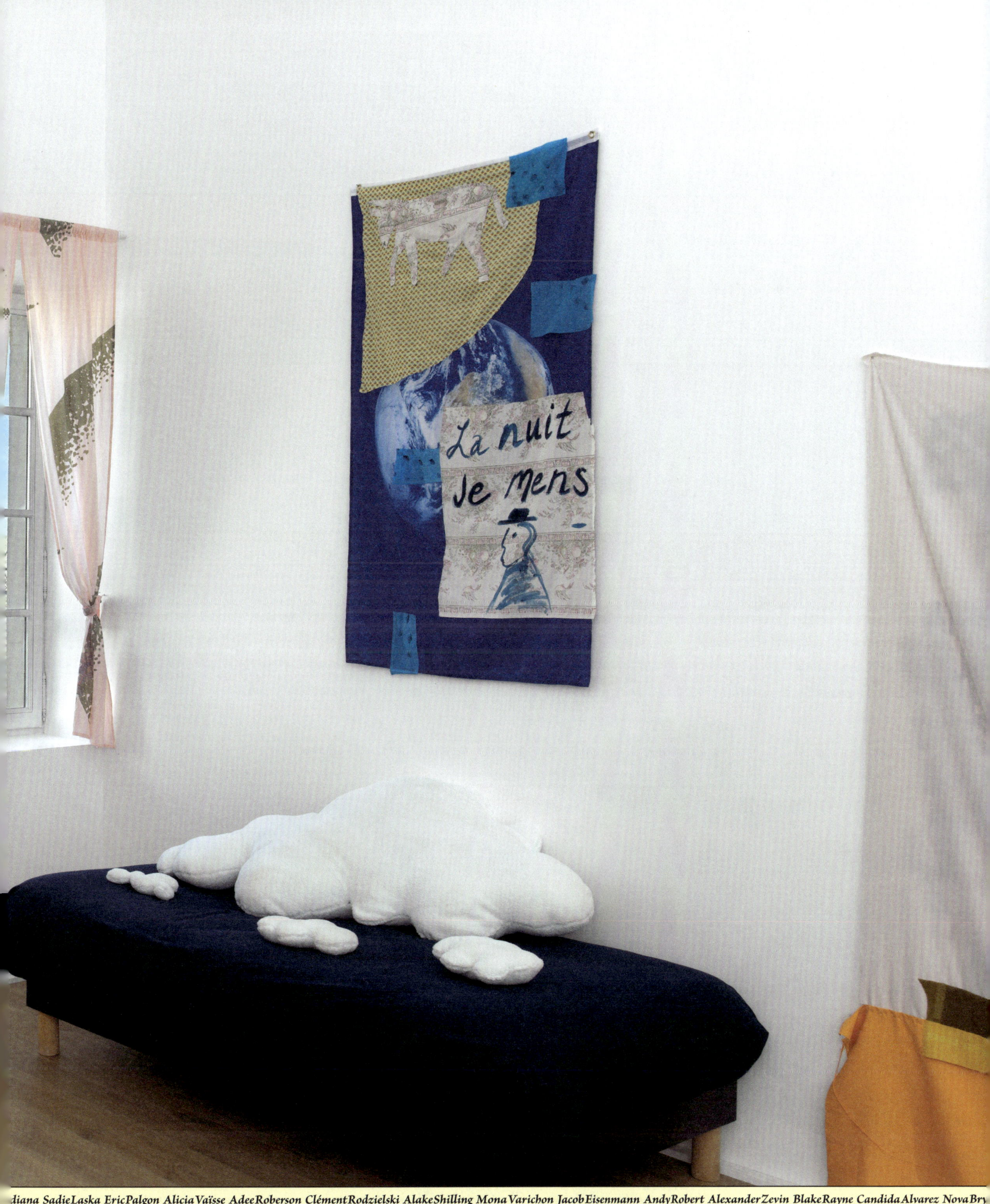

diana Sadie Laska Eric Palgon Alicia Vaïsse Adee Roberson Clément Rodzielski Alake Shilling Mona Varichon Jacob Eisenmann Andy Robert Alexander Zevin Blake Rayne Candida Alvarez Nova Bry

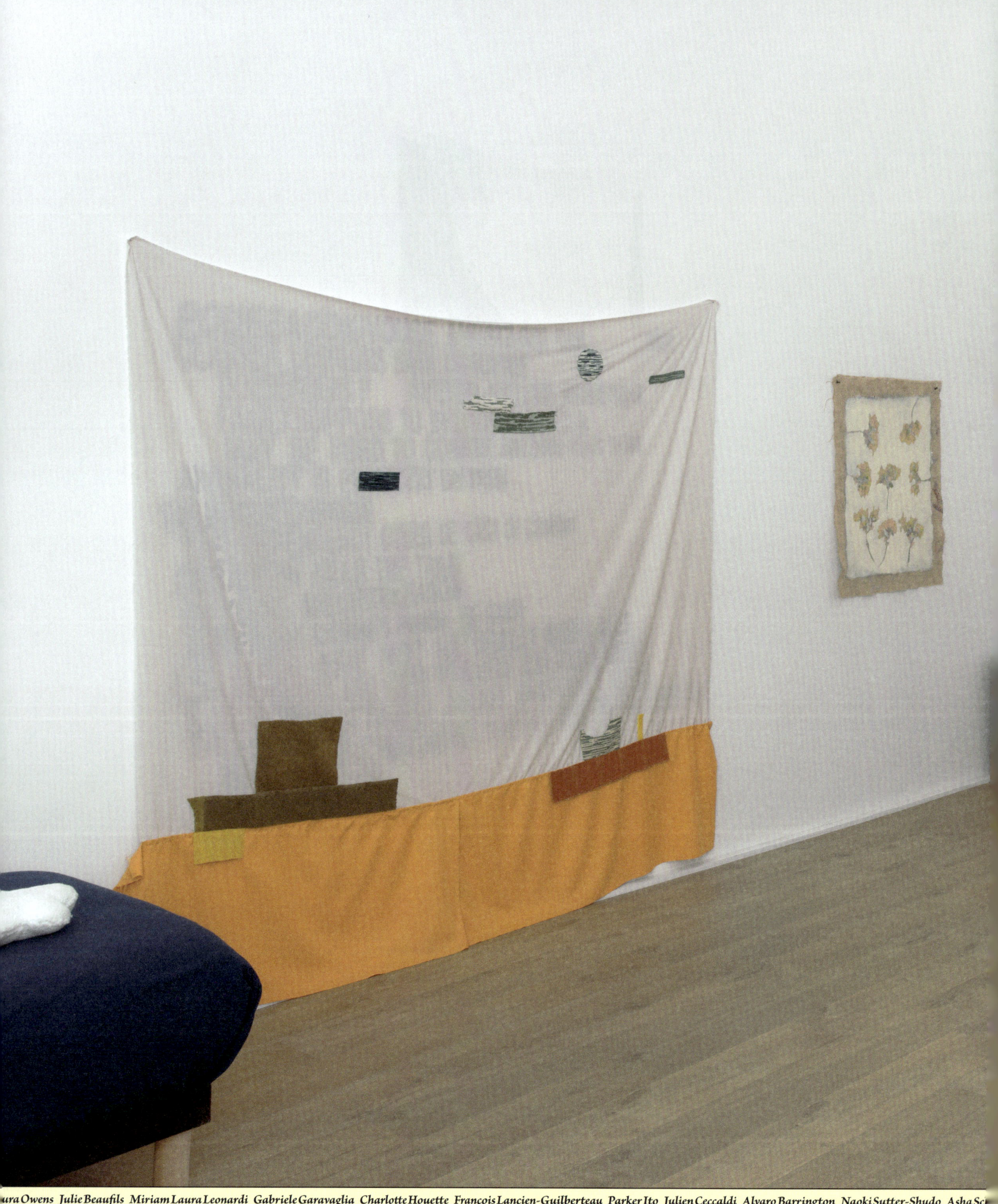

ura Owens Julie Beaufils Miriam Laura Leonardi Gabriele Garavaglia Charlotte Houette François Lancien-Guilberteau Parker Ito Julien Ceccaldi Alvaro Barrington Naoki Sutter-Shudo Asha Sc

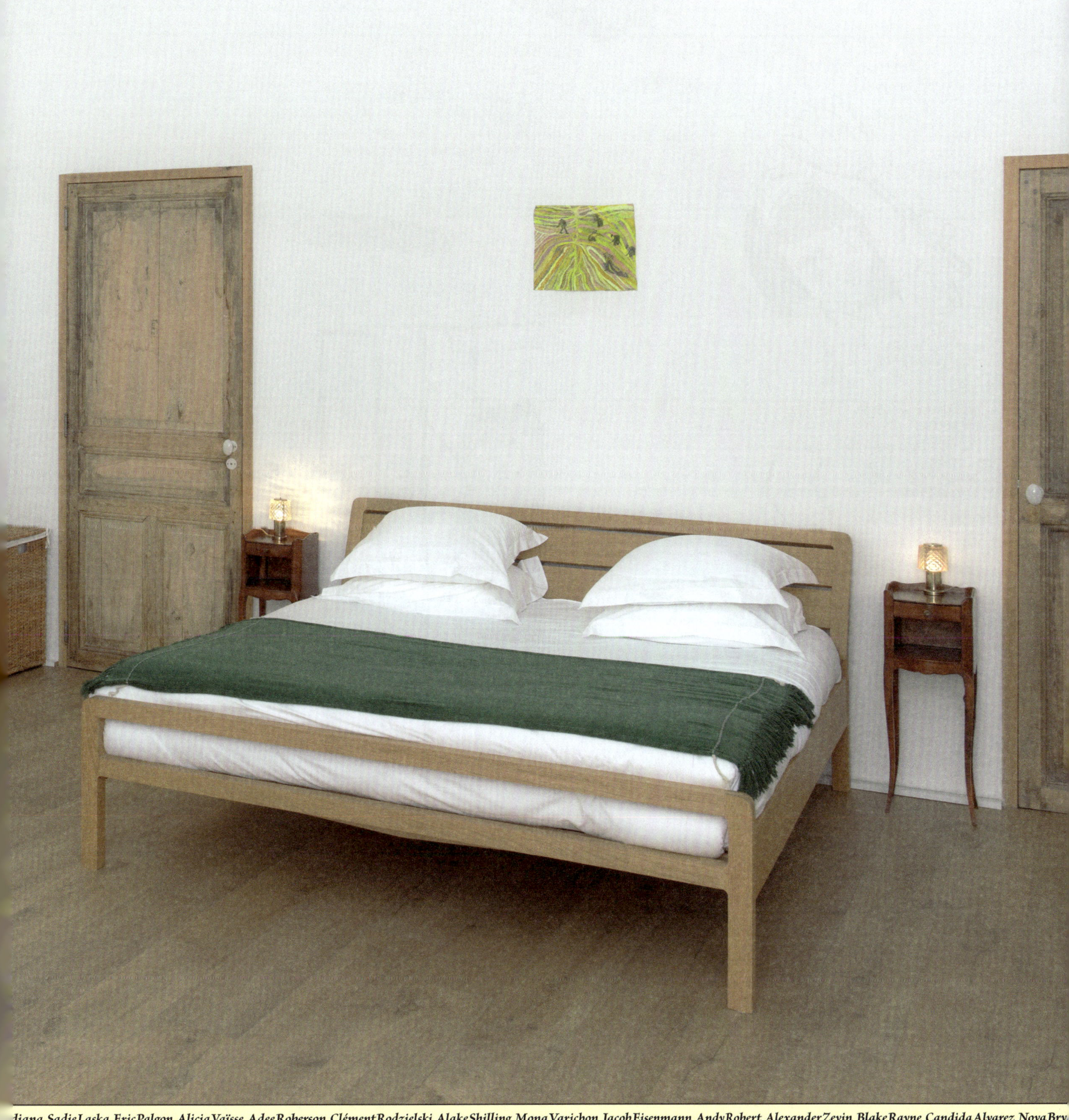

diana SadieLaska EricPalgon AliciaVaïsse AdeeRoberson ClémentRodzielski AlakeShilling MonaVarichon JacobEisenmann AndyRobert AlexanderZevin BlakeRayne CandidaAlvarez NovaBry

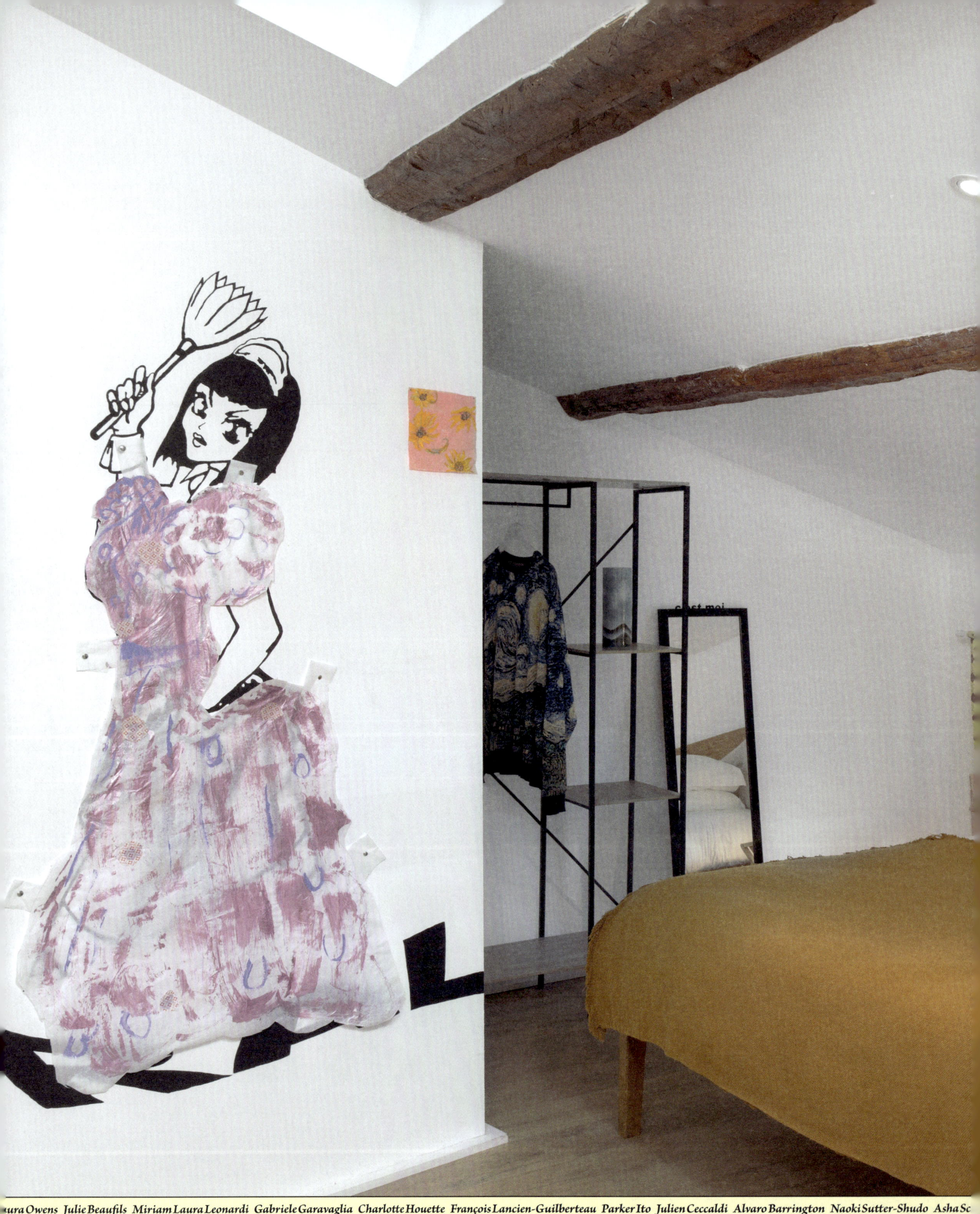

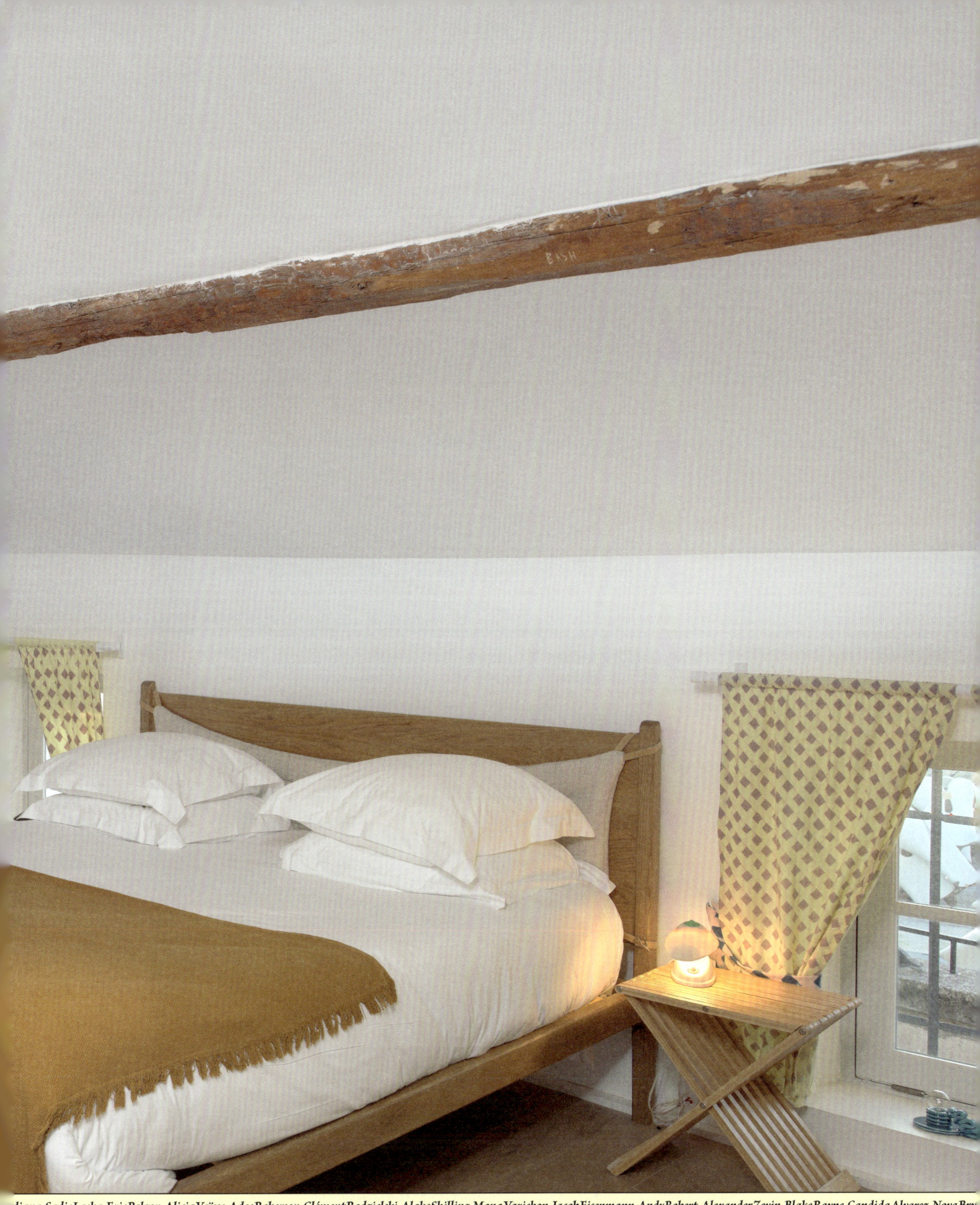

diana Sadie Laska Eric Palgon Alicia Vaïsse Adee Roberson Clément Rodzielski Alake Shilling Mona Varichon Jacob Eisenmann Andy Robert Alexander Zevin Blake Rayne Candida Alvarez Nova Bry

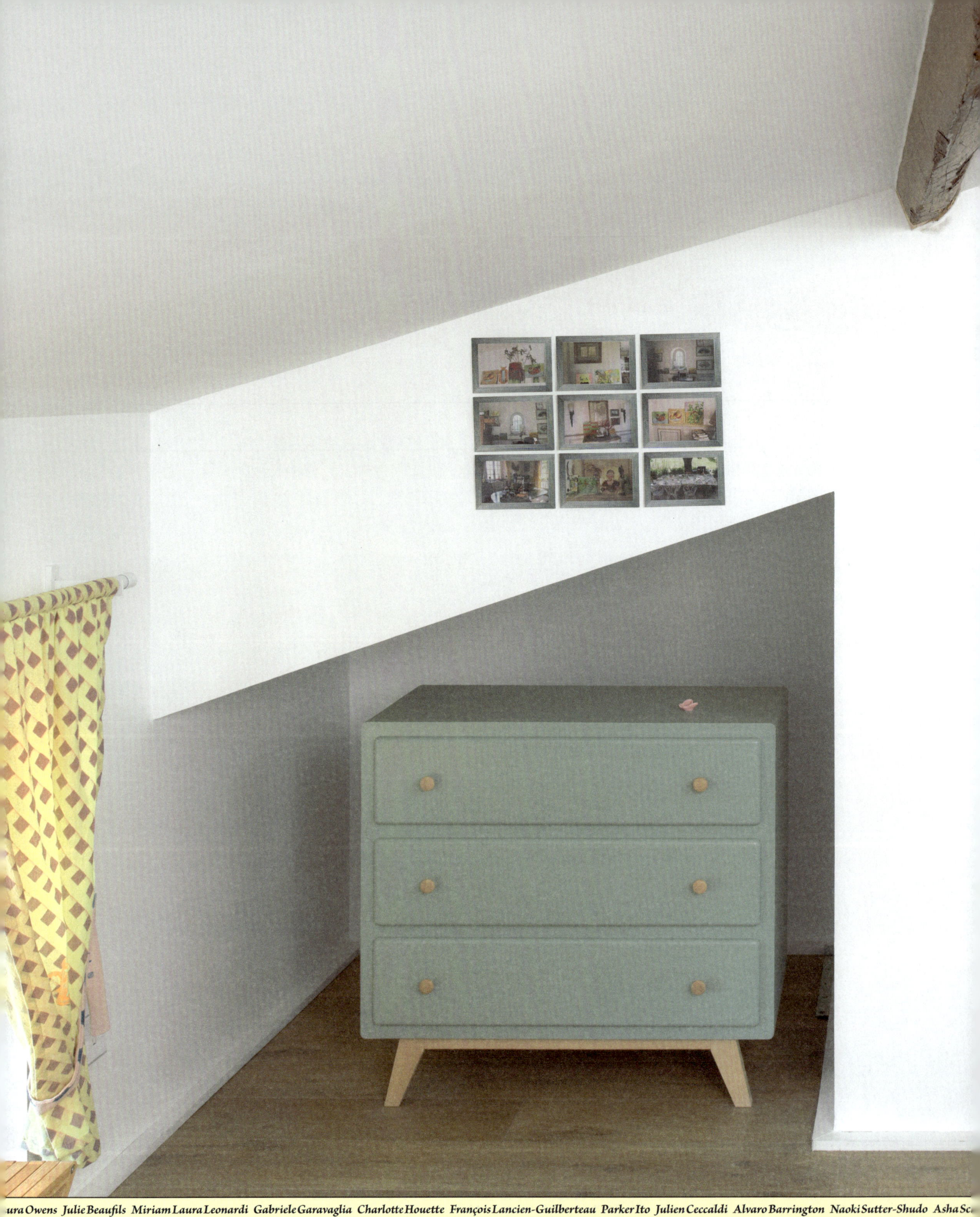

ura Owens Julie Beaufils Miriam Laura Leonardi Gabriele Garavaglia Charlotte Houette François Lancien-Guilberteau Parker Ito Julien Ceccaldi Alvaro Barrington Naoki Sutter-Shudo Asha Sc

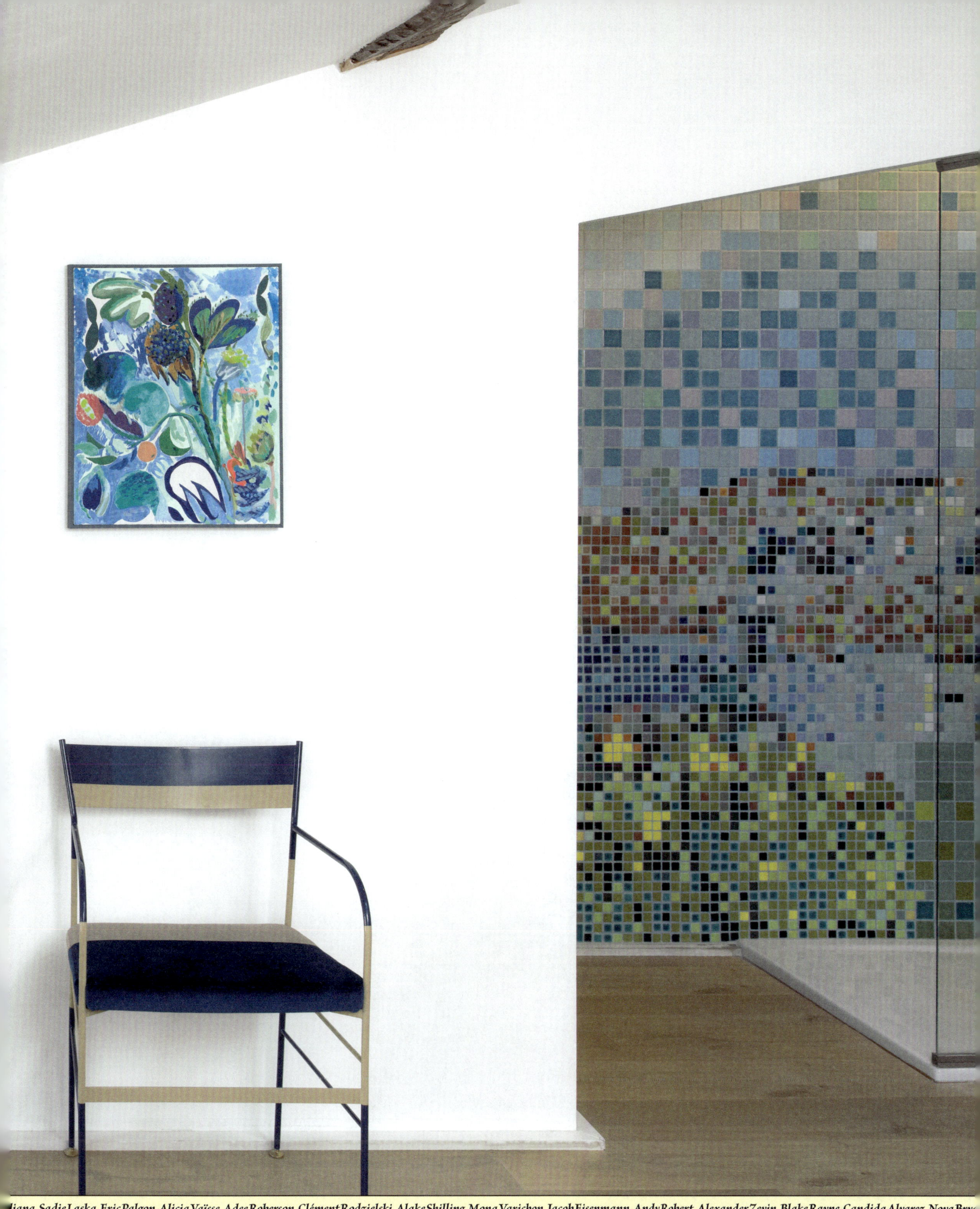

diana SadieLaska EricPalgon AliciaVaïsse AdeeRoberson ClémentRodzielski AlakeShilling MonaVarichon JacobEisenmann AndyRobert AlexanderZevin BlakeRayne CandidaAlvarez NovaBry

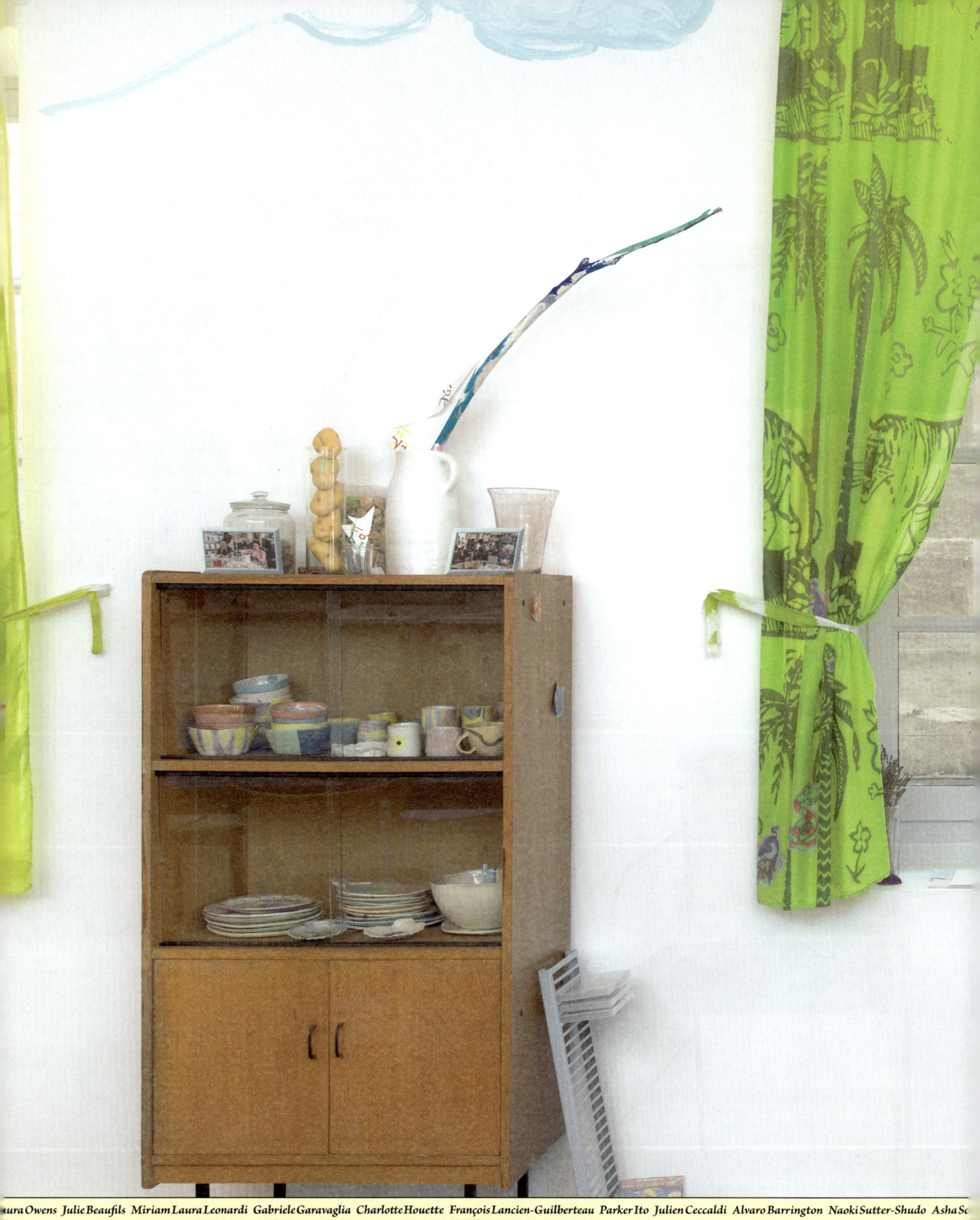

RQAL

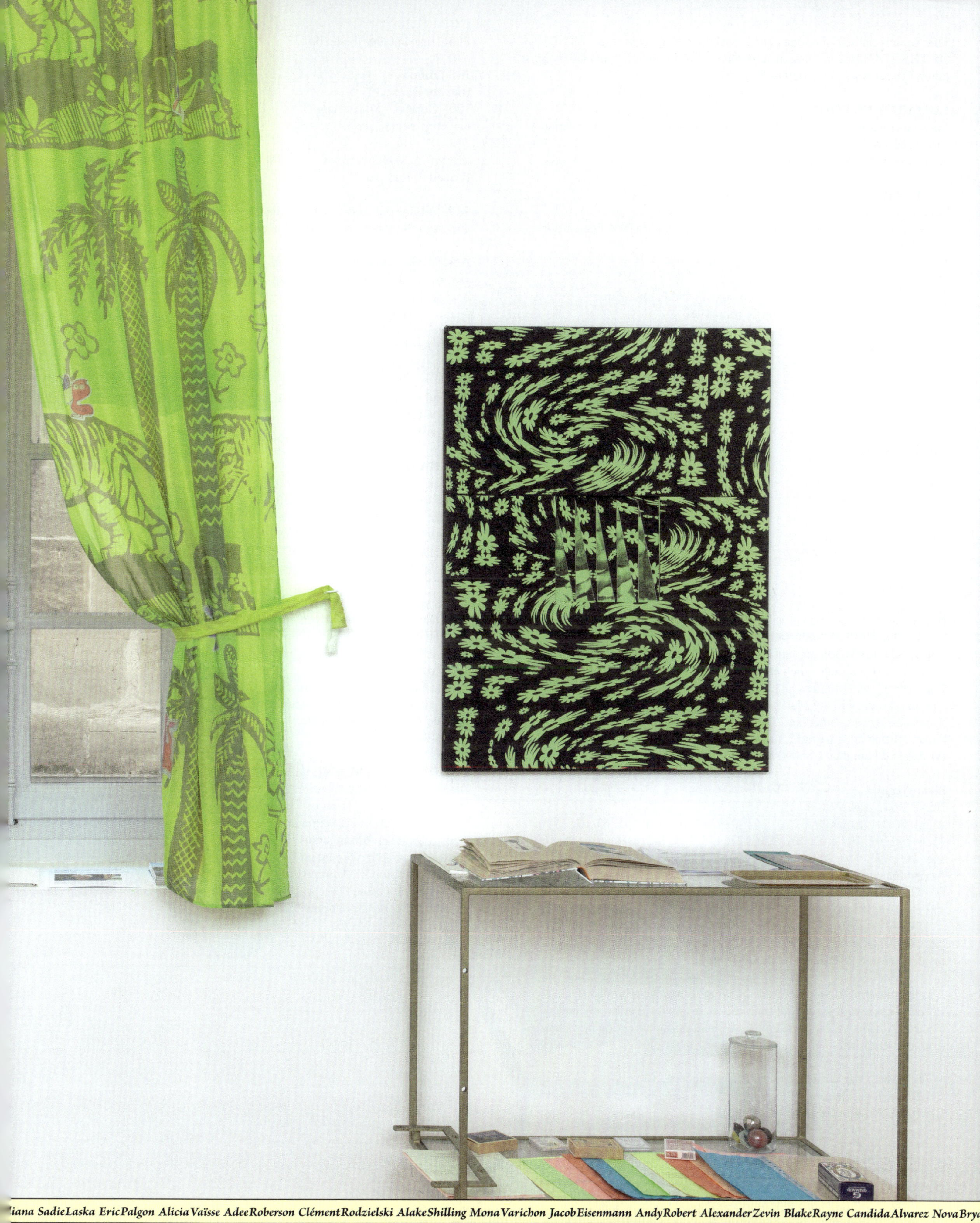

iana Sadie Laska Eric Palgon Alicia Vaïsse Adee Roberson Clément Rodzielski Alake Shilling Mona Varichon Jacob Eisenmann Andy Robert Alexander Zevin Blake Rayne Candida Alvarez Nova Brya

This book is published on the occasion of the residency program STUDIO OF THE SOUTH, commissioned by the LUMA Foundation and led by artist Laura Owens from July 2020 to July 2023.

LUMA FOUNDATION
Maja Hoffmann, Founder and Executive President of LUMA Foundation and LUMA Arles
Anna von Brühl, Managing Director

LUMA ARLES
Executive Committee
Maja Hoffmann, Founder and Executive President of LUMA Foundation and LUMA Arles
Mustapha Bouhayati, Chief Executive Officer
Vassilis Oikonomopoulos, Artistic Director
Christophe Danzin, Director of Development and Partnerships
Simon Castets, Director of Strategic Initiatives

Residency Program
Julie Boukobza, Head of Residency Programs

Conservation
Barbara Blanc

PUBLICATION
Editorial Direction
Vassilis Oikonomopoulos

Editor
Asha Schechter

Editor
Julie Boukobza

Production
Luz Gyalui, Head of Production, LUMA Arles
Juliette Kernin, Exhibitions and Publications Projects Manager, LUMA Arles
Translation: Catherine Schelbert
Copy editing and proofreading: Kate Woolf
Graphic design: Tiffany Malakooti
Typefaces: Brioso, Times New Roman, Times New Roman Condensed, Arial
Papers: Sirio Color Denim Limone, Munken Kristall Rough
Printed and bound by Conti Tipocolor, Italy

Photography
Hervé Hôte: page 23
Annik Wetter: pages 29, 32 (l), 34 (r), 39, 44 (l), 46, 47, 55, 63, 67, 73 (l), 75, 81, 91, 93, 101, 102, 107, 120, 121, 127, 138, 147, 149, 151, 155, 160, 168, 169, 175, 186, 200, 201, 205, 207, 210–231
Adrian Deweerdt: pages 24, 25, 30 (l), 33 (l), 37 (r), 53, 56, 58–59, 61, 76, 80, 92, 94, 96, 104, 108–111, 118, 128, 130–131, 137, 139, 148, 150, 152, 191 (l), 192–193, 195

All other photographs reproduced are by the artists and date from their residencies at STUDIO OF THE SOUTH.

All rights reserved. No part of this publication may be reproduced, stored in a retrieval system, or transmitted, in any form or by any means electronic, mechanical, or otherwise, without prior permission in writing from the publisher.

© The Artists, the Writers, and the Photographers, 2025
© JRP|Editions, Geneva, 2025
© LUMA Foundation, Zurich & Arles, 2025

Published and distributed by

JRP|Editions
Rue des Bains, 39
1205 Geneva – Switzerland
www.jrp-editions.com

ISBN 978-3-03764-632-8
Printed in Europe

JRP|Editions publications are available internationally at selected bookstores and from the following distribution partners:

Austria, Germany, and Switzerland
JRP|Editions (with AVA Verlagsauslieferung AG)
books@jrp-editions.com

France
Les presses du réel
www.lespressesdureel.com

UK and European countries, USA, Canada, Asia, and Australia
ARTBOOK|D.A.P.
www.artbook.com

LAURA OWENS STUDIO
Filework: Dave Berezin and Laura Owens
Installation oversight: Elliot Kaufman
Curtain screenprinting: Oliver Sweet, Chris Estrada, Ann Leese
Wordpress website: Henry Van Dusen
Tile manufacturer: Fireclay Tile
Contractor for tile installation: Fabrice Auffret, Les Maisons d'Arles

Thank you to Maja Hoffmann, Mustapha Bouhayati, Vassilis Oikonomopoulos, Julie Boukobza, Bice Curiger, Margaux Bonopera, Eimear Martin, and Julia Marchand for their support of the project and exhibition.

LES MAISONS D'ARLES
Karine Cassagne, Head of Hospitality
Carole Lyonsleroy, Housekeeper Manager
Fabrice Auffret, Technical Head
Violet Pienne, Driver

FONDATION VINCENT VAN GOGH ARLES
Bice Curiger, Artistic Director
Margaux Bonopera, Head of Exhibitions
Christine Joblet-Taris, Administrative Director
Nacéra Ouache, Administrative Assistant
Béatrice Lavigne, Accountant
Kaoutar El Khoudri, Administrative and Account Assistant
Anne-Sophie Foron, Director of Communications and Visitors Department
Laurent Éginard, Development Director